WORKFORCE EDUCATION:

THE BASICS

Kenneth C. Gray
The Pennsylvania State University

Edwin L. Herr
The Pennsylvania State University

Allyn and Bacon
Boston • London • Toronto • Sydney • Tokyo • Singapore

To Kenneth and Mary Gray
and Pat, Alicia, Amber, and Christopher Herr
for the support and love
that makes writing possible.

Senior Editor: Virginia Lanigan
Editorial Assistant: Kris Lamarre
Senior Marketing Manager: Kathy Hunter
Editorial Production Service: Ruttle, Shaw & Wetherill, Inc.
Manufacturing Buyer: Suzanne Lareau
Cover Administrator: Jenny Hart
Electronic Composition: Omegatype Typography, Inc.

Library of Congress Cataloging-in-Publication Data

Gray, Kenneth C.
    Workforce education : the basics / Kenneth C. Gray, Edwin Herr.
      p. cm.
    Includes bibliographical references (p.) and index.
    ISBN 0-205-19834-1
    1. Career education—United States. 2. Vocational education—
United States. 3. Technical education—United States. 4. Labor
supply—Effect of education on—United States. I. Herr, Edwin L.
II. Title.
LC1037.5.G737 1998
370.11'3—dc21   97-14993
                                                        CIP

Printed in the United States of America
10 9 8 7 6 5 4 3 2   RRD 04 03 02 01 00 99

Contents

Preface

One need only note the magnitude of investments by industrialized nations in educating their workforce to appreciate the degree to which policymakers and the general public alike perceive its importance to domestic and international commerce, national wealth, and social justice. In the mid-1990s the U.S. federal government alone spent over $16 billion for 125 different workforce education programs. Added to this is the reported expenditures by business and industry—estimated at anywhere from $30 to $180 billion—plus the $13 billion spent by states just for high school vocational education. These totals begin to suggest the enormity of the workforce education effort and suggest the large numbers of professionals who are involved. We wrote this book to assist with the preparation of the next generation of these professionals.

The book begins with the premise that workforce education is a profession. Although the clients and settings may vary dramatically, the "product" of the endeavor is always the same, namely, instruction; the goal is to promote learning that leads to an individual labor market advantage or solves human performance problems. It is this common product and goal that joins all workforce educators into a common professional bond.

A second premise of this book is that there is a common body of knowledge that, when mastered, will improve the professional effectiveness of all workforce educators, regardless of whether they are employed in the nation's high schools and community colleges, in state and federal employment and training programs, or in private sector business and industry. The purpose of this book is to provide, in a single volume, the knowledge base common to all workforce education settings and clients. Thus, the book was designed to be as relevant to those preparing for Human Resource and Development (HRD) careers in corporate America as it is for prospective secondary and postsecondary workforce education faculty, as well as professionals working in employment and training centers and other employment-related social programs.

The book consists of fifteen chapters divided into four parts: I. The Mission of Workforce Education; II. The Knowledge Base of Workforce Education; III. Designing Workforce Education; and IV. The National Workforce Education System: Policy, Trends, and Issues. The material was selected with the practitioner in mind; only material that we felt was central to improving the professional success of workforce educators was included in the book. The book stresses issues and trends in the field and the possible implications for the future. Even though the book lends itself to formal classroom settings, our intent was to make it attractive to anyone who may wish to become familiar with workforce education when practiced as a professional undertaking.

When appropriate, citations are included in the text, and a complete reference list is available at the end of the book. It should be noted, however, that the book is not intended to be an exhaustive review of the workforce education literature but an introduction to this literature. Each chapter ends with a summary and a discussion of the implications of the material presented for practitioners. Finally, we intend the book to be scholarly, yet readable; hopefully, we have succeeded.

ACKNOWLEDGMENTS

We would like to recognize and thank Tammy Fetterolf, Beverly King, and Kris Sefchick who helped with the multitude of details involved in this endeavor. Also deserving recognition are our colleagues in the field who encouraged the writing of a new foundations book for the workforce education profession. We would like to thank reviewers Barbara E. Hinton, University of Kansas; Rich Feller, Colorado State University; and Michael K. Swan, North Dakota State University for their helpful comments.

THE MISSION
OF WORKFORCE EDUCATION

One universal characteristic of a professional endeavor, such as workforce education, is that its members have a sense of the antecedents of the profession—how the profession evolved to where it is presently. Another characteristic is that its practitioners have a clear idea of the mission of the profession. The ethical obligations of the field flow from the mission. The purpose of Part I is to present these foundations. Aspiring practitioners are alerted to the fact that one of the most important characteristics of true professionals in the field is the degree to which these foundations become a guiding part of their professional behavior.

1

HISTORICAL, PHILOSOPHICAL, AND ETHICAL FOUNDATIONS

Workforce education is a professional occupation. Three characteristics or benchmarks of a professional endeavor are (1) a historical prelude that guides practice, (2) a philosophical basis for practice, and (3) a set of related ethical standards to evaluate the professionalism of practice.

Beginning practitioners may be inclined to dismiss the historical, philosophical, and ethical foundations of their profession as irrelevant to practice. The experienced practitioner knows better. Veteran workforce educators have learned from experience that an understanding of the historical development of the field, the philosophical points of view it embraces, and its ethical imperatives makes them more effective professionals. These foundations provide them with the insights and guidance for making the hundreds of daily professional decisions they are called on to make.

Thus, this book begins with a discussion of the historical development of workforce education. It continues with a discussion of the philosophical debate between social efficiency and democratic humanism and the two missions this debate suggests for workforce education. The chapter concludes with the most important topic—ethical obligations. Before beginning this discussion, however, we need a working definition of workforce education. Exactly what is workforce education?

WORKFORCE EDUCATION DEFINED

Arguably, all formal education beyond that necessary to achieve literacy and exercise responsible citizenship is workforce education. Most people participate based on the expectation that doing so will result in a better job later in life. Less than a hundred years ago in the United States, formal education for most young people ended at the eighth grade; in 1907, for example, only 57 percent of youth age fifteen or older were enrolled in school (U.S. Bureau of Education, 1908). Parents did not keep their children in school beyond this point for economic reasons; namely, it was not seen as resulting in more dollars in the pay envelope. It was not until this perception began to change that high school enrollments grew. Since then, the promise of better-paying jobs has been the prime motivator for individuals to seek formal education at all levels. The Annual College Freshman Survey (American Council on Education, 1994) reports, for example, that the number-one reason students give for going to college is to get a better job.

Yet, this book is not about all types of formal education. Its focus is a subset of pedagogy we term *workforce education*. For the purpose of this book, workforce education is defined as follows:

> *Workforce education is that form of pedagogy that is provided at the prebaccalaureate level by educational institutions, by private business and industry, or by government-sponsored, community-based organizations where the objective is to increase individual opportunity in the labor market or to solve human performance problems in the workplace.*

Workforce education differs from general education in that the outcome goals of the latter are independent of employment. Learning to read, for example, is general education; learning to read unique technical report manuals is workforce education. Learning how to solve a simple algebraic equation is general education; learning how to use Ohm's law in electrical work is workforce education.

The definition suggests that workforce education has two missions. One is to promote individual opportunity by making students more competitive in the labor force, thus allowing them to pursue personal career goals. The other mission is to make a nation economically strong and firms internationally competitive by solving human performance problems of incumbent—already employed—workers. These two missions are discussed in depth in Chapters 2 and 3, and the economic concepts are presented in Part II of the book.

Also, by definition, workforce education is offered at the prebaccalaureate level. Although medical schools, law schools, MBA business schools, and others are most definitely involved in workforce education (note, for example, that an individual is said to be "training" to be a doctor), this is generally considered to be higher or graduate education, not workforce education. Generally, workforce education is associated with the preparation of students or clients for occupations that do not require a four-year or graduate degree. Thus, workforce education is not found in higher education but at the two-year postsecondary certificate and associate degree level.

Finally, by definition, workforce education also includes human resource development (HRD) efforts for all types of incumbent workers including professionals. Thus, a trainer who is working with a group of engineers to help them improve their supervisory skills is conducting workforce education, the intent in this case being to make them more effective and their firm and the national economy more competitive.

HISTORICAL FOUNDATIONS

Why study history? For the purpose of this book, the advice of policy analyst Henry David is appropriate. David (1976) argued that the usefulness of history lies in its potential to explain why things are the way they are. Thus, knowing the history of workforce education gives the practitioner useful "feed-forward" signals about the present condition of the field. Understanding the history of workforce education, for example, explains why parents, particularly African American parents, are suspicious of high school vocational education and why, at the same time, they and the public as a whole hold the field in such high regard. Understanding the history of workforce education also explains why HRD has only recently become a credentialed profession separate from the overall personnel function. Here we present a brief review of the history of workforce education, focusing on those aspects that have relevance or provide "feed-forward" signals for practitioners. The discussion is divided into three parts: preindustrialization, industrialization, and workforce education in the United States.

The Preindustrial History of Workforce Education

Although it is impossible to know exactly when in human evolution workforce education developed, it can be speculated that, as soon as there was a division of labor between food gatherers and those who provided other goods and services, skills had to be passed down to the next generation and that required some level of formal training.

The historical record suggests that crafts such as stone masonry were highly developed in relatively early periods in history. What is interesting, however, is how few sources have survived regarding the preparation of skilled craftsmen (Barlow, 1990). Apparently, the crafts and how craftspersons were prepared were not considered important enough to be chronicled. For workforce educators this fact is an important historical clue from ancient times regarding the origins of present attitudes toward nonprofessional work even when highly skilled.

The modern influences of ancient Greece, for example, are many and varied in Western culture, including the status given to various types of occupational endeavors and thus workforce education. Plato, in his *Republic,* lectured that the ideal society was composed of three groups. In order of importance they were the philosopher kings, the military, and, finally, slaves, the implication being that having to work with one's hands assigned one to the lowest class. In ancient Sparta, for example, citizens were expressly forbidden to perform any mechanical tasks. A similar class system developed later in ancient Rome where the artisan work was performed by slaves and some freemen, both of whom formed the bottom of the social ladder; interestingly, engineers were typically soldiers and thus of a higher social status. The sign of one's status in both of these ancient societies, which are considered to be pillars of human development, was the degree to which individuals did not have to do manual labor. This prejudice survived over the ages; it is deep seated and not easily countered.

Medieval Influences

During the Middle Ages the nobility were still viewed as descendants of God and soldiering was the preferred second choice, but the status of artisans also improved. The skilled crafts became an important social and economic step between the upper strata of nobility, priests, and warriors on the one hand and the lowly serf on the other. Owning a set of tools, which were scarce and therefore valuable, and knowing how to use them became an important alternative to agriculture or domestic service. It was during these times that the term "journeyman" evolved, indicating that an individual owned a set of tools, possessed the skill to use them, and was free to "journey" to various jobs.

More important, artisans' skills came to be recognized as a source of social status or at least a source of economic security. It was during these times that "learning a trade" became viewed as the key to gaining a "position" or occupational niche that would ensure economic security of a sort. Indicative of this development, craft skills became a closely guarded secret. Craftspersons formed guilds to protect their livelihood by controlling the number who could learn these skills and own the appropriate tools.

The development of these guilds provides an important clue to the term "labor market advantage," which will be used often in this book. During the Middle Ages it became obvious that having specialized artisan skills might not lead to the same status as a knight or the independence of the clergy, but it did result in substantial income and some status beyond that enjoyed by those who did not have skills and who worked as laborers in the fields. The saying, attributed to Benjamin Franklin, that "he who has a trade has an estate" describes the reality artisans recognized during the Middle Ages. However, the value of these skills resulted from the fact that only a relative few had them. Thus, the lesson of the Middle Ages to the craftsperson was to limit the number who would be trained. This provides insight not only into the economic concept of labor market advantage and supply and demand in the labor market, but also into why at the turn of the twentieth century and even now in some cases, craft employee unions attempted to control entry. It also explains why certain employee groups and employers are sometimes suspicious of, if not downright hostile to, workforce education if they perceive it as leading to big increases in the numbers who can perform the work they do and thus threaten their livelihood.

The Colonial Apprenticeship

Perhaps the best documented and romanticized of preindustrialization workforce education systems is the apprenticeship system. In the apprenticeship system, individuals who wanted to learn a craft sought a master craftsperson who would take them on as apprentices. Typically, an apprenticeship was defined in terms of years of service, or indenture. Once the apprenticeship was completed, individuals would become journeymen and could work independently, though in some cases only under the overall supervision of a master.

Although not exactly a government-sponsored system, in colonial times the apprenticeship was a written, formalized agreement, regulated by the government and enforced by the legal system. It was also perhaps the first time that the importance or relationship between academic skills (reading, math) and occupational skills were institutionalized. By the seventeenth century, an apprenticeship or "indentured" agreement typically required the master craftsperson to teach the apprentice basic literacy skills; thus, to a certain extent, the system was a forerunner of more formalized public schools.

In the United States the apprenticeship system has enjoyed a unique place in the overall arguments about what is wrong with today and right with the past. In the nation's nostalgia for the past, the apprenticeship holds a special place, conjuring up thoughts of a close, fatherly relationship between master and apprentice. This idealistic image of the apprenticeship has led to the belief by some in the overall superiority of work-based or on-the-job training. Indicative is the opening section of the federal School-to-Work Opportunity Act of 1994 where the glorified image of the apprenticeship is used to rationalize the emphasis the Act places on work-based learning. Thus, it is prudent to take a quick, critical look at the apprenticeship system of old.

A little-known fact concerning one of the prominent founding fathers of the American nation, Benjamin Franklin, is that he was a runaway apprentice. Another rarely mentioned fact is that abuses of apprentices by masters became such a problem in the Massachusetts Bay Colony that it became necessary for colonial leaders to pass laws that required masters to actually teach apprentices skills instead of using them only for cheap labor. In short, the true history of the apprenticeship system is that in all too many cases the apprentices were exploited and taught little. In many cases the masters were illiterate themselves and, more important, less than excited about training future competitors.

There is a historical lesson to be learned from this "other side of the news" view of the apprenticeship system, namely, that except in the best of circumstances, teaching apprentices skills is secondary to the daily business of staying in business. This is particularly true in the United States, where, unlike in Germany, the apprenticeship tradition did not survive industrialization. At the turn of the century, an apprenticeship system—such as exists in Germany—was never seriously considered in the United States because both educators and parents were suspicious of industrialists; they feared that a work-based system of workforce education would result in little education and much exploitation (Gray, 1988).

INDUSTRIALIZATION AND WORKFORCE EDUCATION

Workforce education as it exists today is a function of industrialization. The centralization and reorganization of production, particularly manufacturing, into the mass production format transformed the status of the majority of workers from independent entrepreneurs working in small shops to that of employees. In this new status of employees, skilled craftspersons were no longer in a position to hire apprentices and the colonial apprenticeship withered.

With industrialization, the capital investment needed to buy the technology (machinery) necessary to produce competitively priced goods made all but the factory mass production techniques obsolete. The mass production technique was predicated on dividing the production process into as many little steps as possible. Learning any of these steps required little skill. This widespread deskilling of many trades broke the monopoly that guilds had on entry. Although the apprenticeship system survived in a few occupations, most notably precision metal and construction trades, with industrialization, it would train only a small percentage of the workforce. Thus, as industrialization grew, the traditional social structure for workforce education, the apprenticeship, declined, and there was nothing to take its place. This occurred at the same time that the newly emerging industrial cities were spawning a host of social problems, seeming to suggest the need for more job training.

Influences of the Industrial City

The transformation from an agrarian society to an industrialized society brought with it dramatic social changes and social problems. For the purpose of this analysis, the most notable of these was the rise of the industrial city and with it unemployment, poverty, and the fear of widespread social unrest.

Industrialization, virtually everywhere in the world, transforms cities from places where goods are bought and sold to places where goods are also produced. As industrial cities developed, individuals gave up—or, as was the case in seventeenth-century England, were forced to give up—the land and migrate to the cities in search of better employment. As the populations in these urban centers swelled, cities became centers not only of production but also of poverty.

In an agrarian society there can be much poverty, but there is little unemployment; typically, the tasks to be performed always outnumber the laborers to do them. Except in cases of famine, people generally do not starve. In industrialized cities, however, the work available is often either insufficient to employ the population, or work exists but wages are below subsistence level. The net result is a subclass of poor. As their numbers grow and the slums where they live worsen, social problems become acute. At the turn of the twentieth century in one slum area of New York City, 986 people lived per acre, and the infant mortality rate was 204 per 1,000. Particularly troublesome to the public conscience was that large numbers of indigent youth roamed the streets. Among the more fortunate, fear grew that widespread riots or even revolution was possible, and they looked for ways to bring stability. Historically, one solution was workforce education.

THE "SKILLS-EMPLOYABILITY" PARADIGM

Historical records suggest that as industrialization grows, so do concentrations of extreme poverty. Among the more well-to-do, the reaction is fear of riots and crime. Thus, solutions are sought. Historically, the answer was job training. The rationale that supports this conclusion can be called the "skills-employability" paradigm. The rationale was that individuals would be less a threat to society and more law abiding and self-sufficient if they had jobs. These individuals lacked jobs, it was rationalized, because they lacked job skills; therefore, if provided job training, they would find employment and no longer be impoverished or threatening. For example, as early as the seventeenth century, English poor laws required that job training be provided to orphans and delinquents, giving rise to the workhouse for youth and the plight of Oliver in Charles Dickens's novel *Oliver Twist*.

By the twentieth century, all industrialized nations had come to accept the "skills-employability" paradigm that equated job training with individual self-sufficiency and social peace. There is some ex post facto evidence to substantiate at least the social effects of unemployment. In a study of effects of diminishing economic opportunities, Merva and Fowles (1992) found that in the United States an increase in unemployment of 1 percent was associated with a 7 percent increase in homicides and a 2 percent increase in property crimes.

The power of this paradigm cannot be overstated. The belief in the "skills-employability" paradigm is a major reason why workforce education—in this case, employment and training programs—figures prominently in almost every social program worldwide. Worldwide workforce education is found in the public schools, in prisons, in programs for welfare recipients and displaced workers, as well as for the physically and mentally handicapped. The "skills-employability" paradigm does have some scientific validity, namely, the economic "human capital development" theory (see Part II). But data-driven proof is not necessary because the "skills-employability" paradigm is generally believed; it has become a part of worldwide conventional wisdom.

THE DEVELOPMENT OF WORKFORCE EDUCATION IN THE UNITED STATES

The first formalized workforce education system in America can be traced to apprenticeship agreements of colonial times. Attesting to the importance of the apprenticeship system in colonial times, the first education law passed in America, The Olde Satan Deluder Act of the Massachusetts Bay Colony, set specific requirements for masters to teach apprentices academic as well as occupational skills.

Perhaps a more important preindustrialization development in America was adopting the "skills-employability" paradigm. During the colonial period the colonies frequently cared for orphans, poor children, and delinquents by indenturing them to serve an apprenticeship. As apprenticeship declined, other institutions developed to care for these youngsters. By the mid-1880s, workforce education in the form of industrial education was synonymous with institutional programs for these youth. In the 1883 report of the U.S. Commissioner of Education, cited together in one table were statistics regarding the number of orphanages, asylums, and industrial education programs. The children of defeated Native American leaders, for example, were sent to the Carlisle Pennsylvania Indian School, and the curriculum was job training.

Following the Civil War, workforce education also became synonymous with education for African Americans in the South. Promoted by Booker T. Washington and supported by northern philanthropist organizations as well as the white southern establishment, high schools for blacks were separate from those of whites and were called training schools (Anderson, 1978).

The importance of these preindustrialization developments is that the only youth who participated in formal workforce education at public expense were those from the lowest of social classes. This reality no doubt partially explains why even today high school vocational education is stigmatized, why middle-class families want no part of it, and why African Americans, in particular, are suspicious of it.

The American Industrial Revolution

As suggested by historian Melvin Barlow (1990), the crucible of workforce education was the period between 1870 and 1906, which roughly marks the transition of the nation from agrarian to industrialized. Both the public and private segments of the present workforce education system developed at this time. The mood of the country at the turn of the century was captured by Elwood Cubberly (1909), who commented that the "wars of the future would be economic and to the victors, jobs and prosperity." By the turn of the century, a consensus developed that a workforce education system of some sort was needed if the nation's economic growth was to continue. The nation's principal international competitor, Germany, had such a system. For many, this was proof enough that such a system was an essential element of economic prosperity.

By 1900, the issue was no longer whether there would be a publicly supported workforce education program of study for school-age youth but what form it should take, whether it should be within the existing public education system, and at what grade level it should start. These issues were hotly debated and still are today. To understand the system that ultimately developed, it is helpful to first take into account several prevalent ideologies and the social climate that influenced the results.

TURN-OF-THE-CENTURY IDEOLOGIES

The workforce education system that currently exists in the United States developed at the turn of the twentieth century. Like all social systems, its development was influenced by the social climate and ideologies of the times. Just as it is impossible to truly understand the welfare debates of the 1990s without considering the changing mores regarding mothers working outside the home, it is likewise impossible to understand the history of workforce education in America, particularly some of the still unresolved issues, without knowledge of some of the key ideologies of the times, beginning with social Darwinism.

Social Darwinism.   At the turn of the century, Darwinism came to be accepted as a matter of scientific fact, and social Darwinism came to be accepted by many, though not all, as an unavoidable law of nature. Darwinism taught that survival of the fittest was a matter of evolutionary scientific fact. Social Darwinism applies this paradigm to society with two important implications. First, as taught by nineteenth-century economist Herbert Spencer, who invented the term "survival of the fittest capitalism," Darwinism justified the existing social class as inevitable: those who are rich are the fittest; those who are poor are the weakest. Second, given that this social or occupational hierarchy is inevitable, the more equitable educational solution is to determine where a students fits into the occupational hierarchy and tailor that student's education for success at this level. Thus the rationale that developed from social Darwinism was an important justification for the addition of workforce education (in the form of vocational education) to the curriculum of the American high school.

Dualist Nature of Intelligence. Darwinism was complemented by another widely held belief regarding individual differences called dualism. Intelligence was generally believed to be of two mutually exclusive types: some people were believed to be blessed with manual dexterity or "hand mindedness," and others were blessed with more conventional intellect or talent in acquiring "book knowledge." This belief also became a powerful rationale for the differentiation of the curriculum of the American high school; vocational education was for the "hand minded," and academic or general education, for the academically minded students. This view was not, however, universally accepted. The influential philosopher, John Dewey, for one, rejected the dualism argument.

Taylorism. Although many-faceted, Taylorism—named after its founding father, Frederick Taylor—is an industrial management design philosophy, which teaches that manufacturing efficiency, meaning low unit price and high quality, is obtained by subdividing as much as possible the various steps needed to produce a product and assigning an individual to each unique step in an assembly-line fashion. Furthermore, efficiency is achieved by concentrating all decision making at the managerial level and ensuring that workers have to make few if any decisions. Perhaps the earliest and best examples of the use of this management philosophy were the automotive assembly plants of Henry Ford, who claimed jobs had been so simplified that any worker in his plant could be trained in less than a day.

The Taylorist philosophy influenced development of workforce education in the United States in several ways. One effect of Taylorism was a national preoccupation with efficiency. All institutions, including government and the schools, were constantly accused of being inefficient. A single, classic high school curriculum was inefficient because it was relevant only to those few who would pursue professional occupations. Efficiency required the addition of a new curriculum, namely vocational education, for those who were not destined for the professions.

A second effect of the Taylorist management philosophy was that it resulted in little formal employer-provided training for hourly employees, a trend that would persist, except in time of war, until the 1990s. On a percentage of sales, American industry spends less on employee training than firms in competing companies. In the United States, most employer-provided training goes to upper management. Carnevale's (1990a) study of training in America, found that only one in five hourly workers ever received formal employer-sponsored training in their entire career. As suggested by Thurow (1997), American industrialists decided early on to embrace the Taylorist production system that required little of workers beyond basic literacy at the production level, but required highly trained individuals at the management level to compensate. As a result, the United States has the world's best higher education system and the worst educational system for workforce education skills. Germany, on the other hand, opted for a different system, investing heavily in production worker skills using the dual-system apprenticeship model but employing relatively few engineers or managers. Today U.S. industry and HRD professionals are finding themselves having to reverse this tradition.

Progressivism.   Much of workforce education in the United States not provided by employers is supported at least partially by public funds. This public support began with what is termed the progressive philosophy of the early 1890s. Before 1890, the idea that government had a role in providing workforce education to the general public was considered radical, if not unconstitutional. This attitude change came largely due to the work of what are labeled progressive reformers. Progressives argued that government had a responsibility to address social problems including equal access to skilled jobs. They rejected the Darwinian view that poverty was inevitable. One way government could fulfill this role was to create a public workforce education system. By doing so, it would ensure public access to occupational education that leads to high-paying jobs. No longer would such training be accessible only to the rich or the otherwise well-connected but to everyone. Progressive reformers, such as Jane Addams for example, lobbied for vocational education and vocational guidance in the public schools out of a belief that it would free urban youth from poverty by providing access to learning a trade. Others lobbied for agricultural education in the hope that it would improve the skills of young farmers, make farming more profitable, and thus stem the migration of youth from the farms into the cities.

Believing in the skills-employability paradigm and in the tradition of modernity, progressives came to promote workforce education as an intervention for many different social problems. Thus, today one finds job training an element in social programs ranging from welfare to substance abuse to displaced homemakers. The progressive point of view regarding government's role in helping those who cannot help themselves and providing equal opportunity to prepare for good-paying jobs is taken for granted today, and workforce education is one of the major beneficiaries.

Modernity.   Related to the progressive point of view regarding the role of government was the implied faith that many social problems could, in fact, be solved. At the turn of the twentieth century, rapid advancements in medicine, science, and manufacturing led to the belief that every problem was solvable, either by education, science, or human ingenuity. This belief has been labeled "modernity," and the belief in modern science has been termed "positivism."

One such area of extreme optimism that influenced the development of workforce education in both the public and private sector centered on the predictive powers of the newly developed psychological tests. Darwinism taught that it was natural that individuals were destined to work at different occupational levels. Taylorists argued that for the curriculum of the high school to be efficient, it needed to be differentiated by adding a new program of study called vocational education. Of course the thorny issue—and to this day still unresolved—was how to select in a fair and valid way which students would take which curriculum. The new psychometric tests provided the solution.

Psychological testing, particularly intelligence and aptitude testing, developed at the turn of the twentieth century. In the spirit of modernity, the public quickly believed in the predictive validity of these tests, particularly their ability to determine those occupations for which an individual was best suited. The new test appeared to be a fair and valid way to decide an individual's occupational destiny and, thus, what curriculum one should take in high school. The vocational guidance movement also began at this time. The role of this new breed of educator/ counselor was to help students interpret the new testing data in order to make an occupational choice.

It is worth digressing at this point to observe that the symbiotic development of the nation's public workforce education system, especially high school vocational education and the guidance counseling profession, is often forgotten by counselors and workforce educators alike. It is insightful for both to remember that the original role of guidance counselors was to "guide" students in making decisions about which curriculum—academic or vocational—they would select. Counselors were taught that vocational education was for those who were to enter the working class. Thus, when counselors advise students who aspire to attend college not to take vocational education, they do so based on their understanding of the historical mission of these programs and from this perspective they are correct.

In summary, the ideologies discussed earlier led to a mind-set that made the public supportive of the differentiation of the curriculum of the U.S. high school by the addition of vocational education as well as the use of state and federal tax revenues for this purpose. These same ideologies influenced the directions of human resource development in business and industry, particularly management attitudes regarding where training dollars should be spent. The chapter now returns to the development of the U.S. workforce education system, first in the public educational sector, then in private industry.

HIGH SCHOOL VOCATIONAL EDUCATION

By the turn of the twentieth century, many urban high schools had begun to develop quasi-occupational programs. The first was manual arts, which later developed into industrial arts and today is called technical education. Commercial education (today termed business education) was also widespread in larger city high schools. This curriculum was first designed to train businessmen, included a foreign language requirement, and was taken by mostly males. With the advent of the typewriter, the curriculum took on a secretarial emphasis and enrolled mostly females.

These two programs were not sufficient, however, to appease the increasingly vocal critics of the public schools. First they were not available outside of major metropolitan areas and second, they did not really prepare youth for jobs except as clerical workers, which was already viewed as women's work. Manufacturers in particular were disappointed that the manuals arts programs had turned out not to give occupational preparation and blamed this on general educators who controlled them. Other progressives had different concerns. Agricultural interests sought ways to keep youth on the farm, and in the progressive tradition looked to the schools to do the job through agricultural education. Others worried about the number of young women, who with the advent of industrialization and factory jobs, now worked outside the home. To some this threatened the social fabric of home, family, and the nation. They looked to the schools to ensure that young women learn the new science of home economics. These wide-ranging concerns led to a consensus that a vocational education system for school-age youth was needed and that it should include industrial education (now called trade and in-dustrial education [T&I]), vocational agriculture, and home economics.

By 1905, the only real major issue left was the question of whether these pro-grams should be added to existing high schools, and this led to the infamous "dual systems" debates. Although by early 1900 a consensus had been reached regarding the type of workforce education that needed to be provided, the appropriate model for providing it was undecided. Three models were under consideration. Industri-alists favored the German dual system model, in which the vocational schools were completely separate from the academic school system and controlled by busi-ness people, not professional educators. They wanted students involved by at least the eighth grade if not earlier. Educators, including the prominent education phi-losopher John Dewey, were suspicious of the motives of industrialists, and favored adding vocational education to the existing public high schools under the control of professional educators and local school boards. They preferred no specific train-ing at all, but if provided, wanted only high school juniors and seniors involved. A third model, one that was tried extensively in New Jersey, was the continuation model. Reminiscent of the 1990s school-to-work legislation and high school coop-erative education programs, this model relied on business to provide the training on the job. Students attended school part-time and worked part-time.

Manufacturers were, for good reason, suspicious of educators' motives, which they viewed as antibusiness and, therefore, believed that the workforce education system would be efficient only if it was separate from the general education sys-tem. They favored either the continuation school model or a completely separate or dual system, such as existed in Germany. The dual system in particular, was op-posed by most educators, including John Dewey, who rejected it as being decid-edly undemocratic, dismissing the plan as being a sign that "manufacturers are anxious to secure the aid of the state in providing them a somewhat better grade of laborers for them to exploit (Gray, 1988). These debates, particularly exchanges between Dewey and industrialists such as Herbert Miles of Racine, Wisconsin, were widely publicized.

Ultimately, educators won out, but the victory was less than complete. The federal Smith-Hughes Act of 1917 did place vocational education programs within the public school system and under the control of public educators and school boards. But the integration of vocational education into the regular education system was not total. States were required, for example, by federal funding regulations to have a separate state board for vocational education and a state vocational director to manage federal Smith-Hughes monies. This arrangement resulted in vocational education as being something separate from the regular school program even when housed in the same building. In some states, the teachers were actually paid directly by the state and therefore these educators often viewed themselves as different from other teachers. And they were. Unlike other teachers, most did not have college degrees. Industrialists had been successful in ensuring that particularly trade and industrial education teachers were required to have extensive work experience instead of formal college teacher preparation. This fact served to further separate vocational education and vocational educators from the mainstream of public education.

Although the public school–based workforce education development system that emerged at the turn of the twentieth century was not a dualist system, it was not integrated into the mainstream of American public education either. Nor did the programs have close ties to industry. Large corporations had decided from the beginning to do their own training. Small manufacturers would be more dependent on the public workforce education system but found they had little direct connection to it. Lacking close ties to industry, such as existed in Germany, the system that developed did not include a mechanism to systematically transition students from school into jobs. Thus, job placement became a problem from the beginning. Finally, each state was left to develop its own delivery system. The result was not a national system but a collection of different programs that varied by state, most of which had little real connection with industry or the general education community. This is the high school workforce education system that still persisted into the 1990s.

GOVERNMENT EMPLOYMENT AND TRAINING

Another common form of workforce education in the United States are programs that are funded and/or administered directly by federal, state, or local government or by community based organizations using public funds. An example is the Job Training Partnership Act (JTPA) program operated in the 1990s. By the mid-1990s, the U.S. federal government alone funded over 100 such programs. The roots of these efforts can be traced back to the colonial apprenticeship system and the belief in the skills-employability paradigm, progressivism, and modernity. Direct federal sponsorship in programs for unemployed but unincarcerated adults can be traced to programs for returning disabled World War I veterans. These programs eventually evolved into the present-day vocational rehabilitation system administered by the Department of Labor. The program for returning soldiers was the first of its kind in that it provided job training to a special group of citizens who were viewed as having special barriers to employment. Removing these barriers was agreed to be a responsibility of government. Although initially these programs were administered by the same federal bureau that administered Smith-Hughes funds, this arrangement proved unsatisfactory. Since then programs such as these have been separate and unique from those that fund educational institutions, being authorized by the Department of Labor and not the Department of Education.

Programs of this type expanded during the depression years and mushroomed in the 1970s. Unlike other types of workforce education efforts, the goal of these programs often was to provide both training and employment. Trainees were provided instruction and paid to attend as well. Originally called manpower development and now employment and training, such government efforts have evolved into four different categories of programs targeted to eight populations (see Table 14.1). A more detailed discussion of government-sponsored programs is provided in Chapter 14.

WORKFORCE EDUCATION IN BUSINESS AND INDUSTRY

After industrialization changed the basic relationship of most Americans from that of independent workers to that of employees (see earlier), the importance of the apprenticeship system ended as the major private sector workforce education system. With industrialization, private sector workforce education took three forms: that provided by large firms, that provided by smaller firms, and that provided by employee groups.

Large Firms

Training of workers presented different problems for large firms as compared with small firms. Large firms were much more likely to be in the mass-production business at the turn of the century, and although they employed highly skilled workers, the majority of their employees performed relatively low-skill work and thus needed little training. Indicative of this reality, labor contracts often provided access to various jobs based solely on seniority, implying that either additional skills were not necessary or, that if they were, these skills could be taught by on-the-job training (OJT).

This is not to say that large firms were not engaged in training. As early as 1913, the National Association of Corporation Schools (NACS) was formed, indicating that formal training was definitely a corporate function. From the beginning, however, large firms that were organized according to the Taylorist model of top-down management invested more often in training of managers or in executive training programs (EDP). Training in large firms became a corporate personnel function. For example, in 1920, NACS merged with the Industrial Relations Association of America to become the National Personnel Association. In 1923, this group changed its name to the American Management Association (Miller, 1996), a group whose focus is EDP.

It is important to note that although, in general, EDP was the focus of most large corporations, those that employed significant numbers of skilled craftspersons, such as precision machinists, adopted at the turn of the century the industrial apprenticeship model. In this model, corporations ran a somewhat traditional apprenticeship training program with the exception that the costs were borne by the corporation, who also controlled who was admitted and what was taught. While valid data are not available, these industrial apprenticeship programs were, until their decline in the economic restructuring of the 1980s, the main workforce education vehicle for training persons in the crafts related to manufacturing, such as toolmaking, precision welding, and specialized repair work.

Small Firms

The development of workforce education in midsize and small firms—firms of 500 or fewer employees—was quite different in the United States. Unlike large firms, smaller firms cannot as easily absorb the costs of training. Therefore, from the beginning, and still today, small firms did less training and were more dependent on training provided in the public sector at public expense. The training that was conducted in these firms was typically informal on-the-job training.

In some cases, smaller firms were forced to rely on training provided by labor unions such as the American Federation of Labor. This was particularly true in the building and metal trades. These relationships, however, were often stormy and totally unlike the apprenticeship system or apprenticeship tradition that had developed in Germany. In the United States, midsize and small employers were, at the turn of the century, undecided—and still are—as to what workforce education system is best. Although they preferred a system for which the public pays, they often were not happy with the results.

Growth of Private Sector Training: 1910–1980

The beginnings of private sector training, as it has evolved today, can be traced to the influences of the two World Wars. These wars resulted in unprecedented labor demands due both to the drafting of workers and increases in production. The shortage of skilled workers became a concern of crisis proportions and—as is the case in such situations—a consensus was reached that government should do something about it. In World War I the federal government established the U.S. Training Service to assist industry in starting training programs. Having a training room become as much a matter of national duty as sound business (Gray, 1990).

After World War I and when the GIs came home, training of nonsalaried employees again became a low priority; many training rooms closed. During this time, however, formal EDT in university settings grew dramatically. In 1928, Harvard Business School started its first summer session for experienced businessmen, and in

1931 M.I.T. followed. During this period, the training of sales personnel came to be viewed as important as EDT: production and management were nothing without sales. In 1940, the National Society of Sales Training Executives was formed.

The United States involvement in World War II again created a massive demand for training. As suggested by Miller (1996), a consensus grew among manufacturers at all levels that most training would have to be provided by employers and that first-line supervisors were totally unprepared for this role. As a result, many firms appointed training directors to supervise this essential function. Again government intervened via the national Defense Advisory Commission, and the "training within industry" service (TWI) became a part of the war effort. The emphasis of TWI was on the training of trainers or supervisors. Thus, for the first time, training, independent of the content, became a focus, and training methods became a topic of instruction along with the realization that training was a uniquely specialized field. These developments would lead to the 1942 formation of the American Society of Training Directors, which held its first national convention after the war in 1946.

After World War II, once again training of nonsalaried employees lost ground, and the training function again typically became submerged within the overall personnel function. Executive development and training of other professional ranks in business, such as engineers and salespersons, continued to grow, however. Instructional design became more of a professional focus among trainers. The National Society for Programmed Instruction, now the National Society for Performance and Instruction, was organized in 1962. This focus continued into the 1970s and 1980s with the growth of interest in formal needs assessment and competency based education or instructional system design methodology. The acceptance of organizational development (OD) as an outcome goal of training also grew at this time as well as an acceptance of training as working to solve human performance problems but also at the same time working with individuals to assist their career development, resulting in the growth in popularity of the term "human resource development" (HRD).

HRD Professionalization: 1980s to Present

In the 1980s the United States underwent a dramatic economic restructuring. Prior to this time the United States had the largest number of high-wage/low-skilled jobs in the world. In less than five years between 1980 and 1985 the term itself became obsolete: The realities of the new global economic competition became vividly apparent as most of these jobs went abroad where wages were consistent with the skill required. By the early 1990s, writers such Carnevale (1990a) and Thurow (1992) were arguing that the only comparative advantage a firm or a nation could hope to maintain stemmed not from technology but from the skill level of workers. To quote the American Society for Training and Development home page on the World Wide Web, "the most consistent advantage for firms and individuals is to learn faster than the competition." Equally important, a consensus grew that the most effective organization scheme to produce high-quality goods and services at competitive prices was to form work teams and drive decision making down to the lowest levels. The implication is that the nation would have to abandon its Taylorist model of training only executives and get serious about training all workers. This realization has literally brought the HRD profession out of the back office in the personnel department and into the boardroom.

By the mid-1990s even relatively small firms were hiring HRD directors. The reason is quite straightforward. Firms that cannot use the latest in technology quickly go out of business; being able to use the latest technology requires retraining of workers. Without training, firms do not survive. More specifically, firms require "just-in-time" training, meaning training that can be provided immediately when the need arises. Such a just-in-time capacity presumes either in-house training capabilities or access to quick delivery "outsourced" training. In either case, the implication is the need for greater numbers of HRD professionals. By the mid-1990s the world's largest group of HRD professionals, the American Society for Training and Development, reported a membership of more than 58,000.

Historical Summary

The development of the public sector United States workforce education system evolved from the directions established at the turn of the twentieth century. At that time, the nation developed two workforce education systems. One is in the public sector, which includes high school, prebaccalaureate, and government-sponsored employment and training efforts and is supported with public funds. The second is in the private sector and is supported directly by employers or employee groups. Perhaps the most important historical lesson is that traditionally, and unlike in other developed nations, there has been little interaction between the two systems in the United States. The two systems coexist independently of each other. To a certain extent, this reality is the result of historical tensions between democracy and capitalism, between educators and employers, and between the working class and the rich. Workforce education and its professionals find themselves in the middle of these tensions as evidenced by the classic philosophical debates of the profession.

PHILOSOPHICAL ISSUES

A key characteristic of a profession is a set of philosophical beliefs. The mission of the profession and its ethical code flow from these beliefs. Miller (1985) argues, for example, that philosophy provides a unifying theory for guiding education activity. Workforce education professionals will find it advantageous to have a philosophical position regarding the mission and objectives of the profession because these beliefs can serve as a basis for making ethically sound educational decisions.

Workforce education professionals have long labored, without much success, to develop a single unifying philosophical position for the profession. Law (1975) argued, for example, that vocational education, that segment of workforce education that takes place at the high school level, operates on what he termed a "pseudo philosophical base," that is, a "conglomerate of beliefs, indiscriminately interwoven and often contradicting." Miller (1985) felt that such an eclectic approach leads to discord, uncertainty, and inconsistency. On the other hand, this eclecticism may be due to the conflicting social values within which workforce educators must practice their profession.

It is argued here that the failure of the workforce education profession to reach a "unifying" philosophy reflects not some failure of the profession but, instead, flows from a basic disunity between two social systems: democracy and capitalism. Democracy values egalitarianism, equal access to opportunity, the common welfare, and, perhaps most important, relative equal distribution of wealth. Capitalism values efficiency, competition, and meritocracy, relying on the philosophy of Darwinism to rationalize the inevitable unequal distribution of wealth that results. As pointed out by economist Thurow (1996), the beliefs behind democracy and capitalism differ greatly in regard to the distribution of wealth. Capitalists generally adhere to the edict that what is good for business is ultimately good for the nation and for individual citizens. This "rising tide floats all boats" philosophy conflicts with the democratic ideal of valuing the individual ahead of industry and property owners.

The conflict between these two concepts has, in effect, prevented a unifying philosophy for workforce education. Some see the role of workforce education as promoting economic growth and thereby serving industry. Others view it as providing individual opportunity and thereby serving individuals. The most famous clash between these conflicting ideals occurred at the turn of the century between two prominent educationalists, Charles Prosser and John Dewey. The philosophical differences between these two individuals still are argued today, and being aware of the issue provides a useful background for workforce educators.

As Gregson (1995) argues, "To gain a greater insight into the problems, politics and possibilities of [workforce education], it is important to recognize two opposite perspectives that emerged in the late 1800s" (p. 8). Workforce education, in the form called vocational education, developed in America at the turn of the twentieth century. Educators looked for a new curriculum for the increasing numbers of youth who began to attend high school, and rural legislators sought to reverse the flow of youth from the farms by providing a relevant agricultural curriculum. The leading national figure promoting this development was Charles Prosser, acting as head of the National Society for the Promotion of Industrial Education (NSPIE).

Prosser promoted industrial education by using "social efficiency" or "instrumental" arguments. He drew from the popular ideologies of Darwinism, the new field of sociology, the efficiency movement fathered by Frederick Taylor, the faith in the new psychometric or psychological testing techniques, and the national importance of global economic trade reminiscent of the mid-1990s. Prosser argued that the most humane and socially efficient way to serve youth and ensure the prosperity of the nation was to differentiate the high school curriculum from a classic curriculum by providing a high school program that included a curriculum that prepared youth for employment.

The movement away from a common academic or classic curriculum to a diversified curriculum that included vocational education was lauded by many as an example of true democratic commitment to meet the needs of all children. Not everyone, however, shared this view. Opposing the idea of curriculum differentiation that included education for specific occupations, particularly the idea of a separate or "dual" educational system for the non–college bound, as is the case in Germany, was a large segment of the professional education community, the chief spokesperson being the American philosopher John Dewey. His view, sometimes labeled democratic humanism, or pedagogic instrumentalism, was that vocational education was an important topic of study for all students, not just for those who might end up in the workforce. Although Dewey (1916) believed that "education through occupation" combined within itself more factors conducive to learning than any other method, he opposed a curriculum that prepared students for narrow jobs, labeling it mean and illiberal. In Dewey's view, social efficiency meant giving all youth a broad education in the vocations so that they might better serve as agents of democratic change to make industrialization more responsive to all.

Most general educators and parents embrace Dewey's view. Embedded in Dewey's position is the idea that preparation for specific occupations is not appropriate for public schools because of its potential to both limit opportunity, not expand it, and to separate students, which is undemocratic. Since the development of high school vocational education, a persistent criticism has been that it requires students to make career decisions too early. This concern remains an important reason why many parents have been leery of the curriculum.

THE MISSION OF WORKFORCE EDUCATION

Imbedded in the Dewey-Prosser debates is the fundamental question of the mission of workforce education. Is the mission to promote economic efficiency or to serve the learner by providing opportunity? It would be reassuring to think one leads to the other, but in practice, the two ends sometimes conflict. The old adage that what was good for General Motors was good for the country was often rejected by members of the United Auto Workers. What is right for the individual may not be what is best for industry, thus the dilemma. For example, should a firm's HRD efforts exist exclusively to solve performance problems or to provide employees with career-enhancing skills? Similarly, should a building trades technology program offered in a rural area teach only those aspects of the industry that exist in that locality—which would serve these employers best—or all aspects, technologies, and materials that exist in all areas—which would serve the learner best? The answers to these questions depend on the practitioner's philosophy regarding the missions of workforce education.

This book takes the position that, in fact, there are two missions of workforce education. One is to promote individual opportunity; the other, though not necessarily the second in importance, is to promote economic growth by solving human performance problems and thereby increasing productivity. Of the two we suggest that a close examination of the public sector indicates that individual opportunity is the primary mission guiding these programs. Meanwhile in the private sector, the objective of most workforce education is to improve human performance in order to increase productivity. Even in the private sector, however, a goal of workforce education is often individual career development within the firm. In Chapters 2 and 3, each of these missions are discussed in detail. Before turning to these discussions, however, we must address the most important of all philosophical issues, namely, the ethics of the profession.

PROFESSIONALISM AND ETHICS

Workforce education is a professional endeavor. As argued by Thomas Green (1987), professions "are practices related to the central life-giving, life-sustaining, life-fulfilling events of human existence." Clearly, having an occupation either provides a life-sustaining and life-fulfilling event, or provides the freedom to pursue one's avocation. Although an individual's life calling or vocation may or may not be his or her occupation, having an occupation is often a necessary evil in order have the money to follow one's "calling."

Those involved in workforce education perform a practice that is essential to human existence and so engage in a professional activity. They, therefore, are viewed as professionals and should act accordingly. But what does "act as professionals" mean? Clearly, it means something more than dressing appropriately, joining professional organizations, and reading professional journals. Obviously, it includes preparing oneself and keeping current with the knowledge base and skills of the profession and using these skills to the best of one's ability. But something more is involved. We could envision, for example, an individual who is technically competent, dresses correctly, belongs to professional organizations, and reads professional journals but does not act professionally. Why? Because one important ingredient of professionalism may be missing—ethics. Only when individuals act ethically are we willing to embrace them with the highest of all accolades— namely, calling them professionals.

Implicit in a professional endeavor is the requirement that practitioners "do the right thing." As Green (1987) points out, professionalism implies "sacrifice." To do the right thing may require sacrifice, but to do so is to act ethically. The key question, therefore, is what are the standards for "doing the right thing," or acting ethically. Thomas Green calls these standards the "points of the profession." In medicine, for example, the point of the profession is to do whatever possible to improve health, short of doing harm. This simple point is a powerful guide to doctors and should be a hint as to the practical importance of knowing what is the point of the profession.

FOUR ETHICAL OBLIGATIONS

Simply being technically competent is insufficient to be called a professional workforce educator. What is required is using the skills and practices in accordance with professional ethical standards. Only when one practices the skill of workforce education and development in accordance with the ethical obligations of the profession, will one be acting both competently and ethically. Thus, a fundamental foundation of workforce education and development professionals is to know the ethical obligations of the profession.

To be considered a professional, an individual must conduct the practice of workforce education in accordance with four ethical obligations (see Table 1.1). Each is discussed below.

Promote Learning.   As implied by the title of the profession "workforce education," promoting learning among clients (students, employees, welfare recipients, and so forth) is clearly one point of the profession. More important, the reader is reminded that learning is not synonymous with time in training or even teaching; simply providing instruction in no way means that learning is taking place. Only effective instruction will lead to learning, when learning is defined as the act of acquiring knowledge or skill.

Ensure Health and Safety.   Conducting workforce education in a manner that promotes learning but also ensures the health and safety of the learner is another obvious point or obligation of the profession. One could imagine, for example, developing an instructional design that promoted a high degree of learning by making physical harm a consequence of failure. Clearly this is unethical behavior and is also called negligence in a court of law, a hint that professional ethics and legal liability are closely related.

Protect the Public or Private Trust.   Workforce education professionals are bound by a certain trust placed in them by their clients, their employers, and others, such as parents and the public. Some types of public trust are universal. For example, being a professional implies the need for sacrificing personal gain when it conflicts with a professional duty, such as promoting learning. It is a matter of public trust that individuals will not use their position for personal gain, be it outright stealing, or more covert methods such as kickbacks, conducting private for-profit business on employers' time, coercing subordinates for personal gain, and so forth.

Other public trusts are specific to the workforce education setting. In private industry, upper management supports training efforts based partly on a trust that the professionals involved will conduct training that is consistent with the mission of the organization, namely, to make a profit. Parents of teens, for example, allow their children to participate in high school occupational/technical education

TABLE 1.1   The Four Ethical Obligations of a Workforce Education Professional

- Promote learning
- Ensure health and safety
- Protect the public or private trust
- Promote the transfer of learning

because of a public trust that those in charge will not abuse them and will ensure their safety in potentially dangerous instructional labs. Violating these "trusts" is unethical and therefore unprofessional.

Promote the Transfer of Learning.   Unlike more general education, workforce education and development has a final more focused purpose, namely, that the learning that occurs effectively transfers to the workplace and thereby results in students or clients making the transition from one state of employment or occupational effectiveness to a more advanced state. This transition can take two forms. In the private sector, in HRD activities for example, an essential point of the profession is that the learning that takes place transfers back to the work site and results in improved performance of the learner on the job. In the military, this transfer to the real world can be a matter of life and death for the learner. In the public sector, workforce education clients typically are seeking knowledge that leads to labor market advantage in competing for limited high-skills/high-wage work. In other cases, the goal is simple employment in the primary job market. The ethical, thus professional, obligation for the workforce education practitioners is to do everything possible to ensure that this transition occurs. Conducting a postsecondary technical education program of study that has few ties with employers or the labor market and does not result in clear labor market advantage to the learner is unethical, and therefore unprofessional.

Ethics That Guides Practice

Beginning practitioners are likely to dismiss this discussion of professional obligation as having no practical use. They are wrong. As one indication, the courts consider these ethical standards as the benchmarks for deciding questions of negligence. Thus, professional codes of ethics, such as the American Society for Training and Development's (ASTD) codes of ethics for trainers and the American Vocational Association's (AVA) code of ethics for vocational educators have legal weight in a court of law, and civil suits alleging willful negligence are often centered on the accepted code of ethics of the profession.

A clear understanding of the points of the profession has, however, a much more important practical use than defending against legal challenges, namely, its usefulness in making the hundreds of professional decisions workforce education and development professionals are called on daily to make. Take a fairly common decision that faces secondary occupational/technical educators—deciding whether to conduct or approve a field trip. Is this a junket or something of value? How does one decide? By asking oneself how it relates to the points of the profession: Will it promote learning? Will it be safe? Will it violate the public trust? Will it promote transfer? A trip to a local manufacturing facility may not promote the learning of additional skills but probably is safe and will promote transfer by increasing student awareness of the workplace. On the other hand, a trip to the local amusement park may not.

Ethical Conflicts

Invariably, workforce education professionals will encounter ethical conflicts in their careers. These conflicts occur when they are faced with having to make decisions that conflict with the points or obligations of the profession. For example, in an administrative role, workforce educators may find themselves under pressure to reduce the budget, knowing that to do so will reduce learning. In this case the conflict results both from a public or an employer's directive to spend less and from the ethical obligation to promote learning. The best advice is to always try to make decisions that are consistent with professional obligations, recognizing that compromises may be inevitable. But one should never compromise on the issue of health and safety; to do so is career threatening.

SUMMARY AND IMPLICATIONS FOR PRACTITIONERS

This chapter began with making the case that workforce education is one of the nation's professional endeavors. A key aspect of a professional endeavor is that its practitioners have a sense of its historical roots, philosophical positions, and ethical standards. The practical usefulness of this knowledge lies in the insight it gives to practitioners as they debate policy and make the thousands of daily decisions professionals are required to make.

Tracing the historical development of workforce education in the United States leaves the practitioner with numerous useful insights. Several are worth reviewing. First, while the field benefits from widespread public support that stems from the belief in the "skills-employability" paradigm, it has acquired a negative image because historically those involved in early workforce education were the destitute, impaired, or incarcerated. It is useful to remember that there is also a prejudice against manual work that dates back to the Greeks and that workforce education outside of business and industry is associated with these types of occupations. These two factors combine to make workforce education at the prebaccalaureate level less attractive to some elements of society.

Second, the public sector workforce education system that has developed in the United States did so without any widespread involvement of employers. Also, because of unique federal funding, the system was never truly integrated into the public or higher education community either. Thus the system that developed was really never integrated into either the general education system or business and industry. The reality is that in the United States, there are two systems: one public, one private. And with no structured link between the two, it could be argued that the country really does not have a true system.

There are also historical lessons for private sector workforce education practitioners. One such lesson is that historically support for training in general and HRD in particular has been somewhat cyclical. To be specific, while support for executive development has remained relatively steady, the endeavor waxes and wanes, depending on the importance given to training, for front-line workers. Thus, in times of war, the profession grows. When the war ends, the profession shrinks. More recently, however, global competition has provided a new interest in the skill levels of hourly employees and again the profession is growing.

This chapter ended with a discussion of philosophical and ethical issues. The fact that workforce education lacks a unifying philosophy or mission is the result of serving two masters: democracy and capitalism. The first stresses individual opportunity and common welfare, the other places little emphasis on the individual, being concerned instead with efficiency that leads to profit. Thus, as will be discussed in the following two chapters, the profession has two, sometimes conflicting, missions. While lacking a unifying philosophical position or single mission, workforce education, like all professional endeavors, has a single set of professional standards that applies to all practitioners regardless of where they practice. To be a true professional requires that one's practice of the profession be consistent with the four ethical obligations of the profession: promoting learning, ensuring health and safety, protecting the public trust, and promoting successful transition.

2

THE MISSION: PROMOTING CAREER OPPORTUNITIES FOR INDIVIDUALS

The United States of America is known worldwide as the "land of opportunity." All can trace their heritage back to ancestors who emigrated to this country, seeking opportunity. For most, opportunity meant an improved standard of living. In fact "opportunity" in the United States is generally defined in terms of occupational opportunities. Providing the education necessary to compete for occupational opportunities is one mission of workforce education in the United States. In this chapter the role played by workforce education in promoting individual career opportunity will be explored.

WORK AND THE AMERICAN DREAM

The "American Dream" means a middle-class standard of living and economic security. For most, a prerequisite to achieving this dream is a career that will provide this standard of living. Even among today's teenagers a good-paying job and job security are among those things they value the most. Table 2.1 on page 28 compares the value placed on various life events for 1972 and 1992 high school graduates. In all cases work-related events such as job security and occupational success actually increased in importance among youth.

"To get a better job" is also the primary reason entering college freshman give for matriculating in college (American Council on Education, 1994). Likewise, researchers have found that 80 percent of all adult learners who enroll in any type of education beyond high school do so for occupationally related reasons (Zemke & Zemke, 1981).

Work, specifically one's occupation, also plays a central role in social identity in the United States. As argued by Lind (1995) in *The Next American Nation*, the defining characteristic of the class structure in the United States is occupation, and the entrance card is education. The entrance to the "over-class" in America is not

TABLE 2.1   Percentage of High School Seniors in 1972 and 1992 Who Believed Each Value to Be "Very Important," by Gender

Values	All Seniors		Males		Females	
	1972	1992	1972	1992	1972	1992
Being successful in work	84.5	89.3	86.2	89.0	82.8	89.6
Being able to find steady work	77.8	87.9	82.1	87.1	73.5	88.6
Having strong friendships	79.2	79.9	80.4	79.8	78.0	80.1
Marrying and having a happy family	81.7	79.0	78.5	75.7	84.9	82.3
Having lots of money	17.8	37.4	25.9	45.3	9.8	29.4
Working to correct social and economic inequalities	26.9	20.3	22.4	17.0	31.3	23.6

Source: U.S. Department of Education, National Center for Education Statistics, National Longitudinal Study, 1972 (Base Year); National Education Longitudinal Study of 1988 (NELS: 88), 1992 Second Follow-up.

birthright or inheritance but economic and social power associated with one's occupation. On a more mundane level Americans, more so than any other nationality, define each other not by race, ethnicity, or family but by occupation. In fact, the true American heroes are individuals who become occupationally successful without inherited wealth or higher education.

Workforce Education and Access to the American Dream

In light of the central role played by occupation in the United States, it is clear that a critical element in this democracy is equal access or opportunity to prepare and compete for all occupations, regardless of race, religion, socioeconomic status or other differences. Although the U.S. Constitution does not guarantee equal results, it does guarantee equal opportunity. Equal opportunity in American society is so central that it has become part of the nation's labor laws: All states have equal opportunity commissions that investigate employment discrimination complaints, and most employers advertise that they are an "equal opportunity employer."

Arguably, equal access or opportunity for employment results from two factors: first, equal opportunity to prepare for careers in order to be competitive in the labor market, and, second, an unbiased opportunity to compete in the labor market. But an unbiased labor market is meaningless if there is not also equal opportunity for career preparation. Virtually all publicly sponsored workforce education in the United States is funded at least partly in order to provide an equal opportunity to prepare for a career independent of family wealth.

Although developing the nation's workforce is an important mission of workforce education (see Chapter 3), close examination of endeavors outside business and industry suggests that promoting individual career opportunity best explains the collection of programs that exist. As a case in point, most higher education programs, including many workforce education programs, are supported directly or indirectly with public funds despite evidence that the labor market will not provide enough jobs for graduates. If these programs existed only to promote economic growth, labor market statistics suggest funding should be cut by at least a third. That such proposals are not being discussed implies that this and other types of education exist basically to provide individual opportunity first and develop the nation's workforce second.

Similarly, workforce education programs in the public sector also exist to assist those who, as adults, are out of the primary labor force completely and thus are impoverished. Lack of economic success in the United States is viewed as being related to the lack of workforce preparation. The conventional wisdom supports the "skills/employability" paradigm that unemployment and/or poverty is the result of a lack of occupational skills and, therefore, the solution is to provide such skills. A related role of workforce education is to provide remedial occupational preparation for those who are economically disadvantaged or displaced through layoffs, downsizing, or other circumstances.

In summary, it has been argued that of the two missions of workforce education, in the public sector at least, providing training opportunity programs is the primary mission of workforce education and the motivation for its clients to enroll. How effective is workforce education in achieving this mission?

Economic Returns to Workforce Education

Untold numbers of research studies have confirmed that workforce education is associated with higher earnings, less unemployment, and increased job satisfaction. John Bishop, writing in the *Economics of Education Review* (1989), reported an 8 percent increase in earnings for high school graduates who took a concentration of vocational education courses in high school provided they were employed in training-related occupations. Bishop (1989) concludes that the

> research implies that the benefits of occupationally specific education are primarily economic and that they are derived from using the skills and knowledge gained. When jobs requiring a great deal of on-the-job training are being filled, employers prefer recent high school graduates with vocational education in the field to high school graduates with no vocational training in the field. (p. 8)

Gray and Huang (1992), using a national data set, found that of the three high school programs of study—college prep, general, and vocational—only vocational education had positive labor market effects. The college prep program of study paid off only if (1) the student matriculated and then graduated with a baccalaureate degree, and (2) was able to find work in the professional/managerial ranks.

Similar results have been found for postsecondary technical education. Grubb (1992) found that technical education did result in increased earnings but only when students completed the program of study and when they were able to successfully find related employment.

Human Returns to Workforce Education

In a social organization that values opportunity, such as the United States, the essential glue of the social fabric is "hope," specifically, an individual's hope that he or she can successfully compete for economic prosperity and personal satisfaction. Perhaps the most important aspect of hope is the expectation that upward mobility is possible. From this hope stems motivation; without this hope there is little motivation.

Education in general, and workforce education in particular, provides the mechanism for upward mobility and thus hope. Workforce education is supported at public expense not only because it is viewed as essential to economic growth, but because the public views it as a way to ensure equal access to high-skills/high-wage work. In fact, vocational industrial education was supported by many at the turn of the twentieth century because it had the potential to break the lock on high-paying jobs in the skilled trades that were controlled by unions and nepotism. The central point to be made here is that the lack of access to workforce education and, therefore, lack of hope for social mobility have dramatic social consequences. It is said that hope is the best contraceptive; lack of hope among the nation's youth, particularly those in urban areas and rural America, leads many youth to all kinds of self-destructive behavior. Providing hope becomes an essential element of social stability, and access to workforce education is a central element.

Providing Career Opportunities for Individuals

There are three ways workforce education "provides" career opportunities for individuals. The remainder of this chapter discusses each of these tasks:

> ### *Mission: Providing Career Opportunity for Individuals*
>
> Task 1. Providing Opportunities for Career Preparation
> Task 2. Providing Career Preparation for the Disadvantaged
> Task 3. Providing Opportunities for Career Advancement and Retraining

TASK 1. PROVIDING OPPORTUNITIES FOR CAREER PREPARATION

It has been argued that in the United States, the definition of opportunity almost always includes equal access to high-paying and self-fulfilling employment and thus equal opportunity to gain the prerequisite skills to be competitive in the labor market.

The first role of workforce education related to providing career opportunity for individuals is to provide programs of study designed to prepare individuals to "enter" the labor market. The emphasis of this goal is preparing those who will be "new entrants" to a labor market for a particular occupation. Programs of this nature are typically offered at the high school level; at postsecondary two-year community, junior, and technical college levels; and at "for-profit" proprietary schools. The intent of such programs is to provide enrollees with specific occupational skills that will give them an advantage to compete for employment. The importance of this type of education has increased dramatically since the 1970s. One indicator is the worsening distribution of wealth in America.

The Worsening Distribution of Wealth in America

A distinguishing characteristic of the United States, and one of the principal reasons it is the envy of the world, is its large middle class. In fact, most Americans perceive themselves as members of the middle class, and opportunity is defined as the ability to obtain or retain this socioeconomic status. It is cause for concern that data indicate that the middle class is shrinking. Between 1973 and 1993, the real income of all but the top 20 percent of wage earners fell. Wages of young men, ages 25 to 34, fell 25 percent during this time. Thirty-two percent of all men in this age group in 1993 earned less than the amount needed to keep a family of four above the poverty level. The median wage for women also has fallen for all except the college educated (Cassidy, 1995).

This has all happened at the time when the real domestic product rose 20 percent and corporate profits were increasing. Between 1994 and 1995 alone, the economy grew by 3 percent but wages fell by 2 percent. Obviously, some must be benefiting, and in fact some are—namely, the top third of wage earners whose income rose 8 percent between 1979 and 1995. Some did even better. Those in the top 5 percent experienced earning gains of 29 percent, while those in the top 1 percent had a 78 percent gain. Twenty years ago the CEO of a large U.S. company earned 40 times as much as a typical worker; in 1995, a CEO earned 190 times as much (Cassidy, 1995).

The social implications of the worsening distribution of wealth are of serious concern. Lester Thurow, professor of economics at MIT, warns that survival of the fittest is capitalism on the march (Thurow, 1995). Falling middle-class wages have led increasingly to two-wage-earner families and parents spending 40 percent less time with their children. It has become economically advantageous for couples to divorce; the real income of divorced men increases, on the average, by 73 percent, while the family they leave behind falls by 42 percent. By the mid-1990s even those who benefited were realizing some concern. The president of the U.S. Federal Reserve Bank of New York warned in 1995 that the worsening distribution of wealth was threatening the equity and social cohesion of society (Cassidy, 1995).

The reasons for the worsening distribution of wealth are debated among economists and policy makers. Four top the list: foreign trade, displacement of workers by technology, decline of labor unions, and increased immigration. Of these, the effect of workers displaced by technology becomes of utmost importance in workforce education. Specifically, the rapid increase in computerized systems has led to a dramatic change in the amount of work that is termed "skilled" versus "unskilled." In

The End of Work, Rifkin (1995) observed that in the past, when technology led to workers' displacement, a new segment of economy developed to fill the gap. Manufacturing filled the gap left by the decline of agriculture, and the service sector filled the gap left by a decline in manufacturing. Now, however, computerization of many service functions is leading to a decline in this occupational sector with nothing to take its place. In 1950, 20 percent of all work was professional, 20 percent skilled, and 60 percent unskilled. Today 20 percent is still professional, but the relationship between skilled and unskilled has reversed. By the year 2000 it is predicted that only 15 percent of work will be unskilled and 65 percent skilled.

The essential point for workforce educators to grasp is that, if one major cause of the shrinking middle class is the decline of unskilled employment, the long-term solution is to increase the skill levels of the workforce. From an individual point of view, if one's goal is to be a member of the middle class, the way to do it is to become skilled. Unfortunately, this economic paradigm has led many to confuse skill with education and to purse a single plan—going to college.

The "One Way to Win" Mentality

Although the worsening distribution of wealth has led to an increased need for access to workforce education and thus availability, ironically, these same economic issues are working against the profession. Fewer and fewer youth aspire to anything but a four-year college degree (see Table 2.2).

When asked, 85 percent of high school graduates in the early 1990s indicated they planned to obtain at least a four-year college degree. The percentage who planned to pursue a two-year degree actually decreased. In the mid-1990s, less than 1 percent of all students who took the Scholastic Aptitude Test (SAT) indicated they planned to pursue a two-year technical education. As a result, while the

TABLE 2.2   Percentage of High School Seniors in 1972 and 1992 Who Expected to Attend Various Types of Postsecondary Institutions, by Gender

Highest Level Expected	All Seniors		Males		Females	
	1972	1992	1972	1992	1972	1992
None	18.9	5.3	15.5	6.7	22.2	3.9
Two-year technical community college	18.0	10.8	17.4	11.8	18.6	9.9
College	50.4	50.6	50.8	50.4	50.1	50.8
Graduate/professional	12.6	33.3	16.3	31.1	9.1	35.4
Total	100.0	100.0	100.0	100.0	100.0	100.0

Note: Percentages may not add to 100 due to rounding.
Source: U.S. Department of Education, National Center for Education Statistics, National Longitudinal Study, 1972 (Base year); National Education Longitudinal Study of 1988 (NELS:88), 1992 Second Follow-up.

percentage of high school seniors who pursued higher education climbed steadily in the 1980s and 1990s to where almost 70 percent continued their education, the majority pursued either a four-year college degree directly or enrolled in two-year general studies programs in order to transfer.

Almost 60 percent of these same young people also indicated that their hope was to be working in the professional ranks by the time they reached the age of 30. Adding these aspirations to the figures regarding postsecondary higher education attendance, the "one way to win" mentality is defined mainly by obtaining a four-year degree in the hope that it will lead to a job in the professions.

The impact of the "one way to win" mentality on high school and postsecondary technical education and, in particular, programs of study has been significant. As discussed in Chapter 13, enrollment of traditional students in both has declined as a larger percentage seek college degrees. The problem for many is that it is a bad postsecondary plan (Gray & Herr, 1995).

The "one way to win" plan is a good strategy for some youth, but not for 85 percent. To begin with, only about 30 percent graduate with sufficient academic skills to do college-level work. Therefore, when almost 70 percent of high school graduates continue their education, it is not surprising that at best only half graduate even six years later. According to a report from American College Testing (ACT), college dropouts hit an all-time high in 1995–1996 and the five year graduation rate stood at 53 percent ("College Dropout Rates," 1996). Even among those who do graduate with a four-year degree, many still face disappointment and end up underemployed in jobs that do not require a college degree. The nation's higher education system, for example, in the 1990s graduated 1.2 million students yearly with credentials in professions such as accounting, engineering, teaching and so on, while the economy was generating only half that many openings (see Table 5.1).

In the 1960s, four out of five college graduates obtained commensurate employment; today, it is only two out of three, and in the professional specialty areas, it is one out of two. Added to this dim outlook is the fact that of those who do graduate, more than half acquire student loan debt along the way. Clearly the "one way to win" mentality is leading many of the nation's youth to failure, and the costs to the nation are staggering. Fortunately, workforce education, defined as preparation for gainful employment that occurs below the baccalaureate level, can provide an important alternative.

Workforce Education: The Other Way to Win

One of the fastest growing groups of students in higher education in the United States in the 1990s is reverse transfers. These are individuals who have earned at least a four-year college degree but re-enrolled in workforce education programs in two-year postsecondary technical education programs in community, junior, and technical colleges. They have learned, although a little late, of the best alternative to professional employment, namely, nonprofessional high-skills/high-wage occupations in precision manufacturing, the crafts, specialized repair, the health fields, and in the service sector.

While the supply of applications dramatically exceeds opportunities in professional/managerial areas, in many cases the complete opposite is found in many nonprofessional high-skills/high-wage occupations. For example, the United States annually admits approximately 25,000 internationals to take jobs in precision manufacturing alone because the domestic labor market cannot supply them. This issue will be discussed further in the next part of this text. The point to be made here is that public sector workforce education and employer/employee-sponsored apprenticeship programs are the prime providers of training for these occupations. The argument to be made is that two-year postsecondary workforce education, not four-year baccalaureate programs, are a better investment for the majority of today's youth. Workforce education, not more baccalaureate education, has the greatest potential to reverse the worsening wage gap.

TASK 2. PROVIDING CAREER PREPARATION FOR THE DISADVANTAGED

Although competing for good employment is a great challenge for everyone, some individuals face obstacles; for this they are termed "disadvantaged." As a result of these obstacles, they are either underrepresented in the labor force or are underrepresented in certain segments of the labor force. These individuals share the same middle-class dream as everyone else but, in many cases, they face special circumstances that make this hope more difficult to achieve.

Providing career preparation to allow these individuals to realize this dream is a uniqual goal of workforce education. It is unique because often the curriculum content, settings, schedule, supportive services, and methods of instruction must be different from that designed to achieve Task 2. What follows is a discussion of the unique characteristics of these groups that relate to employment and therefore need to be considered in the development of a workforce education curriculum for them.

Women

The percentage of women entering the workforce began increasing in the 1960s and the trend will continue, though at a slower rate, through the year 2005. The department of labor predicts that by the year 2005, the number of white women entering the labor force will outnumber white men. Three fifths of all women older than the age of 16 are expected to be working by the year 2005.

Despite this gain, there is evidence that the true talents of women have yet to be fully utilized. Women still earn on the average 70 cents to every dollar earned by men. Women are not only facing a "glass ceiling" in gaining access to the corporate offices, but, more important, even larger numbers are finding it difficult to escape what Barbara Noble (1992) calls the "sticky floor" of low-skilled/low-wage assembly and clerical work. Women, for example, account for just 9 percent of all precision metal, craft, and specialized repair workers, a group whose average annual earnings is exceeded only by college graduates who are managers or specialized professionals.

Minorities

As reported repeatedly in the press, the percentage of minorities in the workforce continues to climb. Nonwhites are expected to constitute 27 percent of all "new entrants" to the labor market by the year 2005, compared with 23 percent in 1992. In total, this equates to an increase of 12.6 million minority workers, or roughly a million a year. As a result, by the year 2005, the labor force will be 74 percent white, 11 percent black, 11 percent Hispanic, and 4 percent Asian. Despite this growth, the unemployment rates of nonwhites continue to be significantly higher than that of whites. In 1993, for example, the unemployment rate for blacks was 12.8 percent, twice that of whites. Like women, minorities tend to be underrepresented in higher paying occupations. Yearly earnings for blacks and Hispanics continue to lag behind whites. Discrimination aside, one reason for this lag is the lack of occupational skills that would enable minorities to compete for high-skills/high-wage work. Gray, Huang, and Jie (1993) found, for example, that two-year technical education was particularly effective in increasing the earnings of African Americans. Industries, particularly large successful industries that pay high wages, are actively recruiting both minorities and women with skills in the crafts. There is a labor shortage of these workers and, therefore, great opportunity. An obvious role for workforce education is to assist women and people of color in qualifying for these jobs.

The Handicapped and Disadvantaged

Typically, the composition or demographics of the labor force is described in terms of total numbers, gender, and race. This broad brush, however, hides several other important labor force groups. Using the federal definition, the disadvantaged include the physically and mentally impaired, the economically disadvantaged or low-income groups, and those of limited English proficiency—all of whom face unique challenges in gaining employment.

Workplace educational efforts to increase labor force participation of the handicapped and otherwise disadvantaged are already many and varied. Suffice it to say, state and federal agencies have spent billions on such employment and training efforts since the 1960s, and the results have not been impressive. Improving this track record is a particularly important challenge for workforce education.

A relatively recent national effort to bring the physically impaired into the labor force resulted in the Aid to Disabled Americans Act (ADA). The intent of this legislation is to remove "unreasonable" barriers to disabled individuals participating in the workplace. These individuals will need highly specialized workplace education to take advantage of this opportunity. To a certain extent, workplace education sponsored by state vocational rehabilitation programs has been conducting these efforts for a number of years, but the scope of this form of workplace education will expand as does the legal definition of "reasonable modification."

Non–College Bound Youth

Undoubtedly, from a historical point of view, the most traditional population served by workforce education has been non–college bound youth. As pointed out in Chapter 1, high school vocational education was an outgrowth of high school curriculum differentiation designed to provide a relevant program of study to young people who at the turn of the twentieth century were entering high schools in large numbers but not to prepare for college. Although the percentage of students going on to higher education continues to climb, 63 percent of all 1991 high school graduates enrolled in higher education, compared with 47 percent in 1973. Still, about a fifth of all high school graduates do enter the labor force immediately after graduating from high school. It must be remembered that even in National Collegiate Athletic Association Division One colleges and universities, only 56 percent of all those who begin a baccalaureate program finish within six years. When one adds those who start programs but never finish, young people who do not obtain four-year college degrees will continue to make up the largest source of new labor market entrants and ultimately will be the largest consumers of workforce education. The job to be done is important. To a great extent, the workforce education of this group will determine the relative strength of the U.S. skilled craft or blue-collar technical workforce in the future.

There is reason for growing concern regarding the education received by non–college bound youth. As popularized in the publication *The Forgotten Half* (W. T. Grant Foundation, 1988), the unemployment rates of this group are typically six or seven times that of the total workforce. In 1991, for example, the overall unemployment rate was 7 percent, but it was 40 percent for recent high school graduates and 67 percent for African Americans (see Table 2.3). Between 1973 and 1990, the adjusted income of young workers 25 to 34 years of age declined by 31 percent (NAVE, 1994).

There is evidence that workforce education can significantly improve the economic outlook of non-college graduates. High school graduates who complete a high school vocational education program are less likely to be unemployed and more likely to outearn their peers (Bishop, 1989b). Ironically, although high school workforce education has been proved to be effective, enrollments in these programs across the nation are declining (NAVE, 1994). Revitalizing and legitimizing high school workforce education is an important challenge for the profession and the nation. This revitalization is especially important for an "at-risk" subgroup of non–college bound youth, namely, those who fail to graduate from high school.

Non–College Bound "At-Risk" Youth.   With the larger group of non–college bound youth there is a subgroup of youth often referred to as "at risk." At-risk

TABLE 2.3   Unemployment Rates for Recent High School Graduates and Dropouts Not Enrolled in College

Year	Recent High School Graduates				Recent High School Dropouts			
	Total	White	Black	Hispanic	Total	White	Black	Hispanic
1975	35%	31%	63%	*	60%	54%	78%	51%
1985	38	29	66	*	56	50	71	62
1991	40	33	67	*	63	62	75	*

Source: U.S. Department of Education, National Center for Education Statistics, Condition of Education, 1993. Washington DC: U.S. Department of Education.

youth include high school dropouts, the physically and mentally disabled, and those in poverty, particularly minorities from urban centers. Again, the economic outlook for these groups is rather grim. Although the unemployment rate for non–college bound youth is six or seven times that of the normal population, the unemployment rate for high school dropouts is double that. In 1991, 63 percent of high school dropouts were unemployed. Between 1973 and 1990, the income of this group dropped 42 percent (NAVE, 1994).

The plight of minority youth is desperate. Because they are concentrated in urban centers where economic conditions are the worst, the unemployment rate of African Americans and Hispanics is often double that of whites. In 1991, the unemployment rate of African American high school graduates was 67 percent, which is not much incentive to stay in school. In fact, there is only a 10 percent difference between unemployment rates of African American youth who graduate and those who do not.

Again, however, research suggests that high school workforce education (vocational education) decreases the likelihood of at-risk youth—be they urban or rural, minorities or majority students—to be unemployed and increases their earnings. Indicative is the research of Bishop (1989b). To begin with, he found that enrolling in high school vocational education raised the chances of at-risk youth graduating from high school by 6 percent. Meanwhile, if vocational education graduates obtain a job related to their training, on the average they earn 31 percent more than their peers who did not go on to college or who did not take vocational education in high school. These results highlight both the importance of workforce education, in this case high school vocational education, and related job placement services in improving the economic plight of at-risk youth.

Senior Citizens

Another group needing workforce education is citizens who re-enter the labor market. In the early 1990s, the average age of the workforce in the United States was 36, by the year 2000 it is projected to be 39, and by the year 2005, 41. Although the aging of the population has tremendous social significance, of importance here is the prediction that more and more seniors will return to the labor force. For some it will be meaningful activity, but for many it will be a necessity, since statistics suggest that very few of today's middle-age workers have made adequate plans for retirement. Also there is increasing evidence that seniors will eventually be needed in the labor market as the total number of workers under the age of 20—the traditional source of part-time employees in the service industry—declines. In some cases seniors will be entering the labor force for the first time. Although this group will, on the whole, be well educated, firms that plan to utilize this resource will need to design special workforce education programs to serve this unique group.

Immigrants

One source of greatness for the United States has been and will continue to be the skills and talents of those it attracts from other countries. In light of the slow future growth in the domestic labor force, immigration is expected to play a larger role in labor force expansion than at any other time since World War I. Predicting exactly the number of legal or illegal immigrants that will enter the country in the next twenty years is, to quote the labor department, "the most problematic component of the population projections" (Fullerton: 32). Because most people immigrate to obtain work, the Bureau of Labor Statistics predicts that immigration will add 1.4 million workers a year or 35 percent of the yearly new entrants to the labor force between 1992 and 2005. It is projected that among new entrants to the labor market, immigrants will in fact outnumber resident minorities (Hudson Institute, 1987). The United States is the most common destination of immigrants worldwide: In the 1980s, 7.9 million people moved legally to the United States while the total number of immigrants to the rest of the world was 7.9 million (Borjas, 1994).

Many immigrants to the United States, perhaps as many as 25 percent, are well-educated professionals. If the rest are to be utilized to their fullest potential, significant investments in workplace education will be necessary. Why? Because compared with the native born, immigrants (including the estimated 3.5 million here illegally), are 112 percent more likely *not* to be high school graduates (Borjas, 1994).

The task of training immigrants may well be one of the most strategic roles workforce education will be called on to play in the next century. HRD professionals will face a unique challenge. If, for example, one-third of all new labor market entrants will be immigrants, then the workforce of firms will become more and more *multicultural* and will, in turn, require retraining of managers and workers alike. It is not surprising, therefore, that workforce education is one profession that is leading the research and design efforts in multiculturalism in the workplace.

Welfare Recipients

During the mid-1990s, welfare—public assistance for the impoverished—became a political issue, and the reform of welfare became a major objective of elected officials. The goal was to change welfare into "workfare," meaning that employment or preparing for full-time employment was to be a condition of receiving benefits. In many cases, however, those on welfare are high school dropouts lacking both literacy and job skills. Preparation for full-time employment has become the major focus of welfare reform. In most states welfare reform includes considerable redirection of funds into mandatory job training. As of the mid-1990s, exactly how mandatory workforce education for welfare recipients was to be delivered was still unclear, although undoubtedly programs of the type run by the Job Training Partnership Act (JTPA) would serve as a model (see Chapter 13).

TASK 3. PROVIDING OPPORTUNITIES FOR CAREER ADVANCEMENT AND RETRAINING

A final goal associated with the mission of providing career opportunity for individuals is to provide programs for those seeking career advancement, either through promotions or job changes, or to update their skills in order to keep their jobs. Considering that the average age of individuals enrolled in community and technical colleges is typically late twenties to early thirties and that part-time evening enrollment often is larger than full-time enrollment, it is clear that many programs at these institutions are serving this population.

Many times, special programs will be offered in cooperation with business and industry in order to upgrade the skills of employees, which, in turn, results in individual career advancement within the firm. This is particularly true with small firms. An American Society for Training and Development (ASTD) study (Carnevale et al., 1990a) found that small firms were much less likely to provide formal on-the-job training and relied on local providers of workforce education, such as community and technical colleges, to provide opportunities for their employees to improve their skills and thus advance.

A related function of workforce education is providing retraining for those who become displaced because of plant closings, for example. As companies in the United States downsized in the 1990s, retraining became an increasingly important function of workforce education. Again, many of these individuals enrolled in existing workforce education programs offered at community, junior, and technical colleges, as well as proprietary schools. Not infrequently, however, particularly when a major employer lays off a large number of workers at the same time, special workforce education programs are developed either with public or industry support.

Retraining in situations of large scale permanent layoffs is one of the most challenging endeavors for workforce education. In these cases clients often have not had formal education for years and find that making the adjustment is difficult. Likewise, the employment opportunities that await those who are displaced quite often either require significantly higher levels of training skills or are lower paying. Finally, more often than not, when a major employer closes, the local primary job market is not able to accommodate all of the displaced workers and is hardly ever able to accommodate them in single occupations. Therefore although clients may have all been displaced from a single occupation and/or industry, typically no similar single employment opportunity exists to accommodate them all. The only realistic solution is a program that prepares individuals to make the transition to many different jobs. In such situations, occupationally specific training is unrealistic, and a work-based learning delivery system must be considered.

SUMMARY AND IMPLICATIONS FOR PRACTITIONERS

This chapter discussed one mission of workforce education, namely to provide individual career opportunity. The workforce education professional needs to have an understanding of the importance that opportunity has in the United States and the subsequent role played by workforce education in providing opportunity by providing access to occupational preparation. It also is important for practitioners to be aware that although economic development, the second mission of workforce education, receives significant emphasis, in the final analysis it is providing individual opportunity that carries the most weight in the public sector. This emphasis explains why workforce education is often funded by government, even when employment projections are poor. This chapter discussed in detail the three roles or functions of workforce education in promoting individual opportunity. Although these endeavors share a common objective, namely, providing increased labor market advantage to the learner, they differ in terms of the populations served. Although the ultimate objective for most clients will be to prepare them to compete for high-skills/high-wage employment, the practitioner must recognize that for some populations, even low-skills/low-wage employment is a step forward and is a legitimate program objective. Finally, it is important to realize that in the future those seeking workforce education—individuals over 22 years of age—will exceed the number of adolescents and that curriculum and instructional design for these adults calls for special considerations.

3

THE MISSION: DEVELOPING THE NATION'S WORKFORCE

Peace and prosperity are the basic goals of most democracies. As conceptualized by Greek philosophers long ago, nations are founded on an unwritten "social contract": individuals give up certain inalienable rights in return for being provided a stable environment conducive to a better life. Today we measure the "better life" by the metric called "standard of living." Citizens of economically successful nations enjoy a high standard of living. Nations that are economically successful grow rich and powerful, disproportionate to their territorial size or military might. Nations that are economically unsuccessful are labeled "third world" or "undeveloped." Thus, the pursuit of a high standard of living for its citizens is, arguably, the root motive of most national policy. Those endeavors that are perceived as related to this goal are valued, considered a public priority, and proliferate. Workforce education is one such human endeavor.

Among all the riches a nation may possess, its people—its human resources, its human capital—is the most important. The value of this human resource depends not on size, however, but on the occupational and intellectual skills its members possess. At least in this regard history is clear: A large "unskilled" population is a detriment to national economic growth and to a high standard of living. For this reason most developed industrialized nations have established systems of workforce education, and most underdeveloped nations seek to develop such a system as a prerequisite to improving their economy.

The nexus between workforce education, a skilled workforce, and economic development is one reason for federal and state support of programs such as high school vocational education, postsecondary technical education, and employment and training programs. Likewise, firms invest in training or human resource development (HRD) for similar reasons. Firms that have the highest skilled workforce, other factors held constant, will be the most productive and produce the best products or services at the lowest costs, earn the highest profits, and dominate the market. Therefore, workforce development or human capital development is a priority

41

of both government and business and is one of the missions of workforce education they sponsor. This chapter discusses this human capital development mission of workforce education. The chapter begins with a discussion of the sources of the wealth of nations and the part played by workforce education.

NATIONAL WEALTH AND WORKFORCE EDUCATION

Why are some nations rich, with their citizens enjoying a high standard of living, whereas others are poor? Over time the answer has changed as the world economic structure changed. In Roman times, for example, conquest was viewed as the principal policy leading to national wealth as conquering nations exacted tribute or taxes from the conquered. In the sixteenth and seventeenth centuries the "bullionist" belief was popular. Bullionists believed that national wealth came from treasure, particularly from rare metals and gems. Cortez, for example, was sent to the new world to search not for new markets but for gold; though, ultimately, new world markets would prove much more valuable than all the rare metals found. Since the eighteenth century and the growth of market economies, the wealth of a nation is now understood to be dependent, in the long run, not on treasure or conquest but on commerce: producing, selling, and buying goods and services. It is commerce that leads to jobs, individual wealth, and a high standard of living.

In the broadest sense there are two types of commerce: domestic and international. Domestic commerce is that which takes place within a nation's borders. Within a nation individuals and firms compete against each other to sell their products and services. Those who are the most successful enjoy the largest market share, enjoy the highest profits, and pay the best wages in the industry.

In international commerce a nation's firms compete against firms from other nations. Those countries that sell more to other countries than they buy are said to have a positive balance of payments. Selling more products abroad than purchasing from abroad leads to a net increase in jobs and wealth. The opposite is also true. A negative balance of trade means a country buys more foreign products than it sells resulting in a net loss of jobs and wealth. Considering that each billion dollars in foreign trade represents roughly 2,000 jobs and that the United States had a $116 billion trade deficit in 1993 and that it is projected to grow to $190 billion before improving (Crutsinger, 1994), one can get a hint at how important the competition for foreign markets has become and the importance of endeavors like workforce education that have a link to improving national competitiveness.

Within and between nations the key to success in commerce is to produce the best quality products or services at the lowest price. Thus, those factors that make a country's firms competitive, factors that give it a strategic advantage in commerce and that allow it to produce goods and services of the best quality at the best price, become, in fact, essential to a nation's economic wealth, its economic growth, and the standard of living its citizens enjoy. Workforce education is one of these factors and arguably the most important. Why? Because of the importance of a skilled workforce to the strategic market and the advantage of firms at the micro level and nations at the macro level.

Strategic Economic Advantage and Workforce Education

What are the factors that lead to one nation's having strategic advantage over the firms of another in commerce? There are three variables that account for differences in national wealth: natural resources, capital and technology, and the skills and ingenuity of its people—its human capital (see Figure 3.1). Economist Lester Thurow (1992) argues that in modern terms human capital is the most important of the three. Let us look briefly at each of these factors that promote economic growth in order to understand the importance of workforce education to a nation's economic competitiveness and wealth.

Natural Resources.   Natural resources, those raw materials such as iron ore or oil, that a country can extract from its soil, or flowing water that can be harnessed to produce electrical power, are one source of national wealth. In the past natural resources were considered to be an important, if not the most important, source of national wealth. To be sure, a country that possesses large reserves of critical resources, particularly oil, still can reap considerable wealth by selling these necessary raw materials to other nations that must have them.

Yet Thurow suggests that, outside of a few oil-rich Gulf nations, natural resources have ceased to be important sources of strategic advantage. Some of the world's most successful international competitors, countries such as Japan and Taiwan, have few natural resources; Singapore has none. The former Soviet Union had tremendous natural resources, but its people did not enjoy a high standard of living. In fact, having few natural resources can sometimes be an advantage to a country in that it is not required by political realities to use domestic raw materials that may be inferior to higher grade raw materials that can be purchased on the world market.

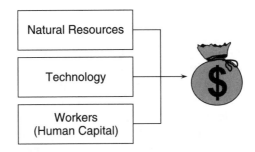

FIGURE 3.1   Sources of National Competitiveness

Capital and Technology.   Capital, in simple terms, means buying power. A firm can buy the latest in production equipment (technology) only if it has the capital or the money to buy it. Rich countries with firms that have large amounts of capital can buy the technology necessary to be the most competitive. Poor countries cannot, and this is one reason why they remain poor and constantly have to seek foreign investment (capital).

Closely related to capital is technology. Technologies range from machines, computers, and chemical processes to inventory and data management systems. Those who have the latest in technology will typically be more productive, build the better product, and be able to sell it at the best price. The United States enjoyed an unprecedented economic success following World War II because it was almost the only industrialized nation left with intact production technology and a monopoly on the world capital market to adopt newer technology as it became available.

In this era of high-technology production and information science, the availability of the latest in technology and/or the capital or money to buy such technology would seem logically to be the most important variable in determining a nation's international competitiveness. Yet this is only partially true. Thailand, a country with double-digit economic growth, had neither the latest in technology or the wealth to buy it. How did it get the technology it needed? It came from abroad. Technology, with the possible exception of trade secrets, is relatively mobile. The manufacturers of the latest in technology are willing to sell it to anyone, anywhere, if they can get their price. If, to be competitive, a product requires a combination of technology and low-skill wages, international companies will send the technology to countries like Mexico to take advantage of favorable labor costs. For these reasons both natural resources and technology/capital are less important than in the past. This leaves only one factor from which a county can gain strategic advantage: its people, its "human capital."

HUMAN CAPITAL

The most important elements in the quest for a competitive advantage in commerce, be it at the micro, or firm, level or at the macro, or national, level, are the skills and initiative of its workforce. Technology is only as good as the ingenuity of those who can both maintain and use it to its fullest potential. Most business software packages, for example, are available to any firm at a relatively low price. Few firms begin to use the potential of these packages because their workers lack the skill and/or initiative to learn. Those who have a workforce that can use the technology to the fullest will have the advantage over those who cannot. The same analogy holds for nations. Those with the highest skilled labor force will be able to adopt technology faster and use it to produce the best quality at the lowest price.

In a world economic climate where natural resources and man-made competitive advantages from machines and technology are more mobile and thus relatively less important, the importance of workers expands. As stated by Thurow

(1992: 52), "People will move, but more slowly. Skilled people become the only sustainable source of competitive advantage."

As will be explained later in this chapter, the skills of the workforce are particularly important in the development of a high-skills/high-wage workforce and to compete in these markets at the global level. Before turning to these topics, however, we need to understand one final point about the importance of a nation's workforce to economic wealth.

To a certain extent the relationship between a highly skilled workforce and prosperity has always existed. Today, however, there is a very important difference. Previously it was generally believed that a nation needed to be concerned only with the skills of the top third of its workforce, those who would be inventors, engineers, managers, entrepreneurs, and chief executive officers. This elite cadre of professionals was mostly trained at the baccalaureate level or higher; therefore, colleges and universities were the central focus of a nation seeking to improve their human capital. Workforce education systems existed and some industrial training took place, but it was not a priority. Times have changed. This Taylorist view is outdated.

The Growing Importance of the Total Workforce

In the past it was generally believed that the key ingredients of economic success were abundant natural resources, up-to-date production technology, and a small cadre of highly trained engineers, scientists, and managers. Other workers, of course, were needed, but in the Taylorist mass production model only a relatively low-skilled workforce was necessary because most workers would do routine repetitive tasks anyway, and they were definitely not allowed to make decisions. As Thurow (1992) points out, however, this management philosophy is no longer accurate.

If the route to success is inventing new products, the education of the smartest 25 percent of the labor force is critical. If the route to success is being the cheapest and best producer of products, new or old, the education of the bottom 50 percent of the population moves to center stage. This part of the population must staff those new processes. If the bottom 50 percent cannot learn what must be learned, new high-tech processes cannot be employed (Thurow, 1992).

If the education of the bottom half moves to center stage, so too must workforce education, which we have defined as education and training below the baccalaureate level. Business and industry are now beginning to recognize this reality and that the majority of their employees are hourly workers, not salaried professionals. Even in capital intensive industries, such as chemicals, 70 percent of all employees are hourly. Furthermore, it is predicted that, as firms continue to downsize or rightsize, the percentage of salaried workers to hourly workers will continue to decline as professionally trained middle level management is pruned back. If a firm or a nation is to compete, it is this majority of workers, the nonprofessional/hourly workforce, that will need significant training. There is evidence that there is much work to be done.

Lack of Workforce Education for Nonprofessional Workers

At first glance it would seem that the United States should have a clear advantage in the skills of its workers. Higher percentages of both men and women go on to higher education in the United States than in any other country in the world. Since the late 1980s the country's colleges and universities graduate more students each June with bachelors degrees than live in some small states such as New Hampshire. Whereas in 1970, 14 percent of the workforce held a B.A. degree, the percentage has increased to 27 percent (Eck, 1993). The country graduates higher percentages of women in both mathematics and science than any other nation. Roughly one-quarter of all college graduates worldwide live in the United States and Canada (Auberbach, 1991). In fact, there is a growing surplus of college graduates in the United States. In the early 1960s one in five college graduates failed to find a college-level job. Beginning in the late 1980s, the percentage has climbed to one in three and is projected to continue at this level at least through the year 2010 (Eck, 1993).

Arguably, the United States has the best educated professional or salaried workforce in the world. But still the country is not doing as well in global commercial competition as would be expected. What is the problem? The problem is that, unfortunately, the country also, by some indicators, has the worst educated and unskilled nonprofessional/hourly workforce among the major economic powers. One reason is the lack of investment in workers at this level.

Despite all the hype firms in the United States spend less on training at all levels of the workforce than any major competitor nations. Only 1.2 percent of all private sector worker compensation is spent on training (Fletcher & Robison, 1991). Only one in five workers ever receives any training from their employers during their entire career, and those who do are mostly middle and upper level managers (Carnevale et al., 1990a). A good example is that reported by Krafcik (1990) in his study of training in the automobile industry. Workers in Japanese automotive plants, even when they are in the United States, receive three times as much training each year as their counterparts who work for Ford, General Motors, or Chrysler (see Figure 3.2 on page 47).

This relative lack of training for nonprofessional workers is not because the need does not exist. On the contrary, many studies of hourly workers in the late 1980s and early 1990s suggest that the need for training is dramatic. In a 1993 study by the National Center for Educational Statistics (NCES), 48 percent of the population volunteered that they did not feel they had adequate basic literacy skills to perform their job (NCES, 1993). In a survey of 2,500 firms with over 100 employees, the National Association of Manufacturers (Eisen, 1993) found that the respondents rejected five of every six job applicants because they lacked adequate basic skills, appropriate occupational skills, or a conducive work ethic. The situation is no better in small firms that hire most young workers and employ 57 percent of the total workforce. A study conducted by the Southport Institute for Policy Analysis (Chisman, 1992) found that 40 percent of small firms were experiencing basic skills deficiencies with their workforce but, because of their size, only 5 percent were able to conduct training to correct the problem.

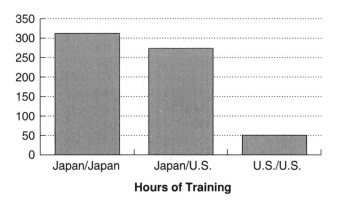

FIGURE 3.2   Hours of Training, Newly Hired Automobile Assembly Workers

Source: Krafcik, J. F. (1990). *Training and the Automobile Industry: International Comparisons* (pp. 8–9). Contractor report prepared for the Office of Technology Assessment (N3-1910), February 1990. Washington, DC: U.S. Government Printing Office.

Young workers, the key to future economic prosperity, are the least likely to get formal training. This is partly because the majority of young workers work in small firms that are the least likely to provide training. For example, 60 percent of all workers aged 25 work in firms of less than 50 employees, and 40 percent work in firms of less than 20 employees (Gray & Wang, 1989). Thus, those who think there is no need for occupational training at the high school level because firms will provide it are clearly uninformed. It is obvious that workforce education is needed at all levels, including our nation's high schools. In a study conducted by the Harris Pollsters (1991), only one-third of employers in a national sample reported that recent high school graduates had sufficient reading comprehension skills, and only one-fourth had sufficient arithmetic functions skills. The *Wall Street Journal* (1990) reports that, depending on the location, anywhere from 20 to 40 percent of job applicants flunk an entry level exam of fifth-grade reading and seventh-grade math. Clearly, the nation must turn its attention to the basic skills education received by students who make up the academic middle of the nation's schools. This includes renewed efforts in workforce education, such as vocational technical education, business education, and cooperative education, because for many youth, academic skills are best taught in an occupational context (see Figure 3.2).

THE WORKFORCE DEVELOPMENT MISSION

Within the workforce development mission of workforce education there are three tasks: preparing a "world class" workforce, preventing labor shortages, and making firms competitive. Obviously, these tasks are interdependent and overlapping. Preparing a high-skills/high-wage workforce is, for example, an important part of preparing a world-class workforce. Yet there is enough of a difference in each of these roles to address or consider them separately.

Workforce Development Mission

Task 1: Preparing a "World-Class" Workforce
Task 2: Preventing Labor Shortages
Task 3: Making Firms Competitive

TASK 1: PREPARING A "WORLD-CLASS" WORKFORCE

Not that long ago America had the highest paid low-skilled workers in the world, particularly in the steel, automotive, and apparel industries. No longer. Economic activity that relies solely on low wages for competitiveness has left the country for places where wages are really low. In the early 1990s, wages in China, for example, were about one-fifth of those in the United States. Meanwhile, as wages in the United States stagnated in the 1980s, those in other industrialized nations, particularly Germany and Japan, rose sharply, making it also difficult for them to compete in a low-skilled environment. Even small developing nations such as Taiwan no longer can compete internationally on the basis of low labor costs alone. Most economic powers in the 1980s, therefore, began seeking alternatives to low-wage/low-skill production, namely, the high-skills/high-wage alternative.

Industrialized nations with relatively high standards of living now realize that they cannot compete in low-skills/low-wage production environments. Thus, these nations seek instead to develop an economy based on producing goods and services that require a highly skilled workforce. The rationale for this goal is that a high-skilled workforce will be able to produce goods and services at high levels of efficiency or productivity which will, in turn, allow sufficient profit margins to pay high wages.

The assumption is made throughout this book that a majority of any industrialized nation's firms will pursue a high-skills/high-wage strategy. It should be pointed out, however, that this is by no means a certainty. For example, the Commission on Skills of the American Workforce (1990) reported that 95 percent of firms were still pursuing the old low-skills "dumping down" strategy, the goal being to increase productivity by decreasing skill levels and paying low wages. Ultimately, the low-skills/low-wage strategy, however, cannot be successful in a free global market. Production that relies on low wages for profitability and competitiveness will ultimately go to where wages are the lowest, namely, third world nations. Thus, although some firms will still try to pursue the old strategy, a majority will have to pursue the new high-skills strategy if the nation's prosperity is to be maintained.

International Competition

It should come as no surprise that a high-skills/high-wage economy is the goal of all industrialized nations, nor should it be surprising that the number of different types of industries that will support this goal is not infinite. In fact, the list is quite limited and includes industries such as semiconductors, commercial aircraft, consumer electronics, chemicals, textiles, motor vehicles, machine tools, and biotechnology. International competition is and will be fierce in the industries that hold promises of high wages for high skills. Thus, the goal of workforce education must be to develop not just a high-skills/high-wage workforce but a workforce that is "world class," meaning one that compares favorably with the workforce of our worldwide competitors, if the United States is to be competitive internationally.

Characteristics of a "World-Class" Workforce

The importance of international trade to the economic future of nations has been discussed. In 1981 the United States had a trade surplus of $6 billion, meaning that the value of exports exceeded imports by this amount. For six years the value of imports exceeded exports by $144 billion, and in the mid-1990s the trade deficit (explained in detail in Chapter 4) was still hovering around $145 million. Considering that every $60 billion in imports results in the loss of one million domestic jobs, it is not surprising that unemployment rose, the standard of living stagnated, and some industries that were not competitive internationally, such as steel, became a commercial version of an endangered species. If the country is to maintain a world-class standard of living, it must hold its own in world competition and improve its trade deficit.

Cutting the trade deficit can be accomplished in two ways: cutting imports and expanding exports. Because cutting imports will result in a declining standard of living (goods from other countries would become scarce and expensive) the preferred strategy is to increase exports. This requires a high-skills/high-wage world-class workforce that can produce high quality goods at a level of productivity that can support high wages (see Chapter 4).

One popular definition of a "world-class worker" is an individual who is highly educated, technologically skilled, and, as a result, highly productive, and by so being achieves a low per-unit cost of production and thus earns high wages (see Chapter 4). In the most general terms the implications for workforce educators is that the standard for skilled workers is no longer set within our borders but by the skill levels of workforces of other nations. To a very great extent world competition has dictated, and will continue to dictate, the instructional content of workforce education and the standard of skills that students must master.

The new skills required of a "world-class workforce" will be discussed in detail in Part III. What follows is a discussion of three broad characteristics of a world-class workforce that are increasing the need for, and molding the content of, workforce education, beginning with the importance of the new emphasis placed on quality.

The Quest for Quality

The importance of quality in international competition cannot be overstated. Although quality—defined as products and services that exceed customer expectations—has always been the key to commercial success, today the importance of quality has taken on new dimensions. The emphasis on quality by Japanese producers is generally believed to be the main reason they were so successful in the 1970s and 1980s. Although U.S. manufacturers still labor under the "planned obsolescence" paradigm—if it wears out, people will have to buy new ones—the Japanese were listening to Edward Deming (1986), the American who preached that a country making quality products at competitive prices would have buyers pounding on its doors. History proved him correct. Even in 1994, when Japan was suffering from its worst economic downturn since the end of World War II, it still had a $50 billion positive balance of trade with the United States alone.

Of course, quality along with price has always dictated the marketplace. What has changed is the standard of quality. This is best illustrated by the worldwide "continuous quality improvement" (CQI) movement and the zero defects goal, defined as when a "process produces no waste of material, capacity, or time, and typically measures in zero defects or parts per million" (American Society for Training and Development [ASTD], 1991b). New worldwide standards for quality control have developed, such as the American "6th sigma" standard, which is based on identification of defects that are introduced not from human error but from the process itself, or the European ISO 9000 manufacturing standards. To a growing extent only companies that can meet these criteria will be able to sell their products internationally. In the competition for market shares, given relatively equal wage cost and technology, quality is what will count. Thus, the quest for quality has become a focus of much economic activity, and quality depends on people and therefore on the role for workforce education.

There is no quick fix to ensuring quality. The bottom line is that quality is ensured by people, not just by the managers and engineers but by everyone in the organization. In fact, the quality movement has led to a dramatic rethinking of the role of management and the role of nonprofessional/hourly employees. Indicative of improving quality is one of Edward Deming's (1986) fourteen points, which is to break down barriers between managers and hourly workers. In the Deming model quality is achieved by empowering those who are the closest to the product and the customer. In the traditional Taylorist model of production, managers are the heroes who know all, can do all, and can solve everything. The quality movement, the teaching of Deming, and the success of the Japanese have led to a rethinking of this old paradigm. Gone is the concept of the heroic manager who makes all decisions. Ensuring quality calls for a new involvement of workers at all levels of the business enterprises. Only with significant increased investments in workforce education will the workforce be prepared for this expanded role. Specifically, the Total Quality Management (TQM) movement has led to a rethinking of how workers should interact at all levels. Work teams are "in"; top-down management is "out." Preparing nonprofessional workers for this role will take a revolutionary rethinking of all of education including workforce education—especially an emphasis on teams or cooperative learning.

Work Teams

The adoption of the TQM approach in the late 1980s and early 1990s, especially the organization of workers into work teams and the elimination of layers of middle management, has had a significant impact on workforce education. The new roles that workers are to play will require that vast numbers of both managers and hourly employees be retrained. Work teams require not just increased decision-making skills but also depend on every member having cross-occupational skills. Obtaining work on a high-skills/high-wage mechanical team, for example, may require basic knowledge in welding, sheet metal, mechanical repair, hydraulics, and even basic AC circuitry. In the past workforce education has typically treated each of these as separate unique occupations and programs of study. Workforce education has been designed to train individuals for these cross-skilled, high-paying occupations and thus will need to be redesigned. More about this follows in Chapter 10. Furthermore, the content of workforce education must be restructured to emphasize a new, expanded set of workplace literacy skills.

The New Workplace Literacy Skills

The quest for a strategic advantage in world trade in general, and the TQM quality movement in particular, led in the late 1980s to a large number of studies designed to determine the skills the nation's workforce would need to ensure that the nation was competitive. Among the more noted or influential was the American Society for Training and Development's study *America and the New Economy* (1991a) and the U.S. Department of Labor's *What Work Requires of Schools* (1991), or SCANS, as it is more typically referred to in the press. The purpose of both was to delineate across all industries a set of skills that workers would need in the future if a high-skills/high-wage economy was to develop. The exact nature of these skills is discussed in detail in Chapter 10 (see Figure 10.4).

The point to be made in this chapter is that these and other reports generally predict that workers in the future will need higher levels of academic skills, particularly in mathematics, science, and reading comprehension as well as new decision-making and group-processing skills. Perhaps the most important workplace literacy skill will be what is typically called "self-directed learning," or the ability to teach oneself new occupational tasks. Importantly, these are not the skills that were thought to be important for the hourly workforce ten years ago and are not the skills that the majority of the present workforce education program emphasizes. Changes are in order.

TASK 2: PREVENTING LABOR SHORTAGES

Related to the mission of providing a skilled workforce is the implied objective of preventing shortages in specific skilled occupations as well as ensuring that the size and skill level of the total labor force is adequate to sustain a high standard of living. Labor-force projections made in the 1990s, for example, predicted that shortages would exist in selected occupations such as precision metals, crafts, and repair. Labor shortages such as these drag down economic growth. In a study of the effect of labor shortages of precision tool workers Passmore (1997) found that 22 unfilled positions in one rural region resulted in the loss to the region of $2.4 million in personal income alone.

The total size of the domestic workforce may well also become an issue in the future as well. Projections regarding the size of the total labor force for the year 2005 are mixed. The labor force in the United States is estimated to grow only about 1 percent a year through the 1990s compared to almost 3 percent a year in the 1970s. Despite this slower growth the total number of new workers is expected to be larger between 1992 and 2005 than in the previous 13 years. At the same time this growth may not be enough. Thurow reports (1986), for example, that in the mid-1990s there were roughly four and one-half people working for each person retired, but by 2030 it could be only a ratio of one and one-half working to each retiree. It is important to realize that an economy reaches its maximum efficiency—and thus can support its retired population—only when all who can be economically productive are productive. Thus, increasing the involvement in the labor force of all groups will likely continue to be an important role for workforce education in the future.

TASK 3: MAKING EMPLOYERS COMPETITIVE

A nation cannot be competitive unless the businesses and firms, or at least a high percentage of them, are competitive, meaning that they can produce a product or service at the level of quality and price that meets national or international standards. Thus, perhaps the bottom line goal of the workforce development mission is to make firms competitive. Obviously creating a high-skills/high-wage "world-class" workforce that would prevent labor shortages and ensure full employment, roles already discussed, will result in firms being competitive. Why? Because their employees will ultimately be more productive, better able to make total use of the technology that is available, make the best daily business decision, respond to market changes quicker, and be the most responsive to customer needs.

In discussing the goal of making firms competitive, it is important to make a distinction between large and small firms. Although firms of both sizes benefit from workplace education, large firms are typically less reliant on public sector or private nonindustry supported workplace education than are small firms. This is because large firms with large numbers of employees are more able than small firms to absorb the cost of lost time to training. Therefore, industry-sponsored training is much more apt to take place in large rather than in small firms. For example, the U.S. Small Business Administration reports that, of all employees that had obtained training in firms of fewer than a hundred employees, 75 percent attended training off the job, mostly at their own expense (Carnevale, 1990a). Workplace education in both large and small firms serves to make employees more productive (see Chapter 4), but in small firms, nonemployer-sponsored workplace education serves to reduce training costs and shorten the time it takes new hires to reach acceptable levels of productivity. This and other important differences in firm size that affect workplace education will be discussed in detail in Chapters 4 and 5.

SUMMARY AND IMPLICATIONS FOR PRACTITIONERS

In this chapter we have explored one mission of workforce education, namely, preparing the nation's workforce, its human capital, in order to ensure that the nation's firms, its business and industry, will have strategic advantage and be successful in global economic competition. In fact, the recent emphasis placed on workforce education by both government and industry is largely the result of this mission and workforce education's perceived importance to global competition. Few have missed the fact that U.S. firms spend less on workforce education than most other industrialized nations and most have concluded that American competitiveness would be increased if the nation invested similar amounts in workforce education, particularly for the training of nonprofessional or hourly workers. Within this mission are three specific roles. Each of these roles has unique implications for the part to be played by workforce education and the content of its programs. The most important implication is that, although the importance of global economic competitiveness has increased public as well as private support for workforce education, the structure, goals, and content of its programs will need to change if it is to meet the challenge. The workforce education community must expect that, as expenditures increase, so too will the call for accountability; business as usual will not suffice.

PART II

THE KNOWLEDGE BASE
OF WORKFORCE EDUCATION

Every profession has a knowledge base that guides practice. In medicine it is physiology, pathology, and others. In workforce education this knowledge comes from the academic fields of economics, sociology, and psychology. Effective workforce education practice is enhanced by an understanding of this knowledge base. Workforce education programs designed and implemented by those who lack this knowledge have a high probability of failure. The purpose of Part II of the book is to provide this knowledge base.

4

ECONOMIC FOUNDATIONS
OF WORKFORCE EDUCATION

The outcomes of workforce education are ultimately economic in nature: employment, productivity, and economic growth. An understanding of economic concepts related to labor markets is as essential to workforce educators as understanding the interaction of wind and sail is to a mariner or the relationship of club loft to distance is to a golfer; one may practice the endeavor without this understanding but probably will never be very good at it. This chapter introduces the rudiments of economic analysis that relates to workforce education, beginning with supply-and-demand analysis. Chapter 5 then discusses labor markets in detail.

SUPPLY-AND-DEMAND ANALYSIS

An understanding of labor markets is essential to the creation of effective workforce education. Such an understanding requires, in turn, familiarity with supply-and-demand analysis techniques. This chapter begins with an introduction to the use of this analytical tool with issues relevant to workforce education.

From the viewpoint of an economist, a "market" exists when individuals who want something interact with individuals who have the same thing to offer. In such situations, the buyer establishes the demand and the seller the supply. An exchange between the two occurs when a mutually agreed on price is determined. This relationship is graphically demonstrated by the supply-and-demand curve analysis.

Figure 4.1 on page 58 demonstrates the hypothetical interaction of the supply and demand for technicians. The vertical axis measures wage rates, and the horizontal axis the quantity of technicians in the labor market. The demand curve slopes downward and to the right, based on the prediction that the demand for technicians would increase as the wages they would have to be paid decrease. Similarly, the

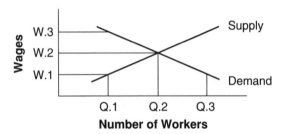

FIGURE 4.1   Supply and Demand for Technicians

supply curve slopes upward and to the right, predicting that as wages increase, more individuals will be attracted to these occupations.

Figure 4.1 illustrates the interaction of the demand for and supply of technicians and what happens when wages are too high or too low. At the lowest wages (W.1), few individuals would be willing to pursue this type of employment; considering the level of skill this training required, few would make the investment unless anticipated wages were higher. Thus, at this wage (W.1), a labor shortage exists. The demand is for quantity (Q.3) but the supply is only (Q.1). At the highest wage (W.3), more workers (Q.3) seek jobs as technicians than there is demand for their services (Q.1). At this wage, a surplus of technicians exists (Q.3–Q.1). At wage (W.2), however, the number who are attracted to the occupation equals the numbers of jobs available. Thus, wage (W.2) is called the equilibrium wage.

In theory when demand exceeds supply or supply exceeds demand, wages, over the long run, are predicted to move toward the "equilibrium" wage (W.2), thus either reducing or increasing the labor pool. In reality, however, the equilibrium wage is rarely reached because of constant economic change and because wages are "sticky," meaning that they do not move quickly up or down in the short run. Thus, at any point, in most occupations shortages or surpluses exist in the pool of labor, meaning that either employers are not able to fill vacancies or individuals are unemployed.

The national economy and individuals, of course, are best served when supply does equal demand. Importantly, public policy makers expect the workforce and higher education systems to be the prime mechanisms necessary to achieve this goal. As evidence of this expectation, funding agents typically require workforce education administrators in the public sector to supply labor market justification for the programs they offer. In reality they are being asked to demonstrate that in the occupations for which they are training individuals the demand for workers is, or will be, either equal to or greater than the supply.

Practical Applications of Supply-and-Demand Analysis

The value of understanding the interaction of the supply and demand for labor to practitioners lies in the potential to assist in understanding and thus explaining situations they face in practice. To illustrate this point, several scenarios are given below.

Scenario #1: Occupational Shortage and Sticky Wages.   There seems to be a constant shortage of individuals in certain occupations, ranging from clerical workers in metropolitan areas to injection-mold operators nationwide. Employers, policy makers, and the public typically view such shortages as a supply problem and therefore either a failure of the workforce education system or at least a situation it should correct.

But is this really a supply—that is, a training—issue, or is there another explanation? Supply-and-demand analysis suggests there is another explanation. The fact that these shortages are chronic would seem to suggest that a more plausible explanation is that wages are too low to attract individuals with the intellect and skills necessary to perform the work. Stated another way, if wages rose, the shortages would vanish. If low wages are the true cause of the shortages and wages do not increase, it is unlikely that any amount of workforce education will correct the problem.

Scenario #2: Labor Surpluses and Sticky Wages.   An equally familiar dilemma, especially for workforce educators at the postsecondary level, occurs when wages remain high despite a surplus of applicants. Take the case of accounting. Despite the fact that labor market projections suggest that as few as one in two who prepare will get jobs, student interest remains high. The reason is that the salaries for those who do find work are high and remain high despite the oversupply of credentialed individuals. Thus, as predicted by supply and demand theory, high wage creates an oversupply of workers, and unemployment results.

Shifts in Demand-and-Supply Curve

In the simple supply-and-demand analysis presented in Figure 4.1, increases and decreases in the number of available workers were attributed to changes in wages only. Obviously, in the real world, wages are very sticky, yet changes in supply and demand for an occupation occur all the time. Why? Because economic or social circumstances cause the whole demand-and-supply curve to shift inward or outward.

Figure 4.2 on page 60 illustrates the effect of a shift in the supply curve (S.1 to S.2). Such shifts in the supply curve can occur, for example, when there is a shift in occupational preferences among a certain segment of the population, thus causing the curve to shift out. Thus, at every wage, more individuals are available to work. In this case, the demand stays constant as do wages. Due to the shift in supply, the number of workers available at wage (W.1) is now quantity (Q.2). The difference (Q.2 minus Q.1) is the resultant unemployment. An example of such a shift occurs in every college town when students return for fall semester; suddenly the supply of college students available to work at any wage increases resulting in the supply curve shift to the left. In this particular case, the wages may already be at the legal

**FIGURE 4.2   Shift in Supply of
Workers**

minimum and therefore cannot decrease. The result is that many college students who want to work cannot find work.

Figure 4.3 illustrates the effect of a shift in the demand curve for workers (D.1 to D.2). Shifts of this type are common and sudden because they typically are caused by firms expanding, and therefore needing new workers, or contracting, and therefore reducing their labor force. In cases of expansions the demand curve shifts to the right; in cases of contractions the demand curve shifts to the left. Note that when the demand curve shifts and wages do not rise or fall, which typically they do not in the short run, either shortages or surpluses occur. In Figure 4.3, for example, if the demand for labor shifted from D.1 to D.2 and wages did not rise to attract more individuals, labor shortages would result (Q.2 minus Q.1).

Practical Significance of Shifts in Supply and Demand

Scenario #1: Shift in Supply.   Between the early 1980s and 1990s, the percentage of all high school graduates in the United States who went directly on to college increased by 20 percent. When polled as to why they were going to college, 50 percent of all males and 68 percent of all females indicated they hoped to be working

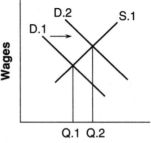

**FIGURE 4.3   Shift in Demand
for Workers**

in the professional ranks by the time they were aged 30. Therefore, the supply of individuals credentialed in the professions increased dramatically.

Figure 4.2 illustrates the results. In this case the demand curve represents the demand for professional workers and the supply curve the supply of individuals credentialed. As the numbers graduating from college with degrees in teaching, accounting, and engineering increase, the supply curve shifts out. Demand, however, does not shift. Professional work has consistently represented only 20 percent of all employment since the 1950s. It is clear that many college graduates with degrees in the professions will not find employment in these professional fields despite their qualifications. In fact, the Department of Labor predicts that one half of all graduates with degrees in the professions will not find professional jobs (Eck, 1993).

Scenario #2: Shift in Demand.   A traditional role of high school workforce education programs is to prepare individuals for careers in the building trades. This industry is very cyclical, especially when mortgage rates rise or fall. This situation is illustrated in Figure 4.3. In this case the demand curve is for skilled home-construction workers. With a decrease in mortgage rates home sales increase, and more construction workers are needed, thus the demand for construction workers shifts to the right (D.1 to D.2). Because these occupations are skilled, the supply curve is relatively fixed in the short run. Thus, in the absence of increases in wages the demand for construction workers (Q.2) exceeds the supply (Q.1), and labor shortages exist (Q.2 minus Q.1). The shortage will exist until the workforce education system can train new workers—thus shifting out the supply curve—or wages increase.

This scenario is a common dilemma for workforce educators. Although interest rates rise and fall rather quickly, they often are unable to increase or decrease programs as quickly, nor is it possible to train a reasonably skilled individual in a short time. Employers often view this slow response as a sign of ineffectiveness. The problem is that this type of worker cannot be trained as quickly as entrants into lesser skilled occupations: therefore we say the supply curve for construction workers is inelastic. A final aspect of supply and demand analysis that is useful to workforce educators is to understand the concept of elasticity.

Elasticity of Supply

Although the workforce education professional typically has little or no control over the demand side of the labor market, the workforce education system itself was partly created to equate supply and demand by affecting the supply of labor. This mission has led to some criticism of the profession for its inability to perform this task quickly. One reason for this failure is what economists refer to as the elasticity of supply (see Figure 4.4 on page 62).

Elasticity of supply for a particular occupation is the rate or degree to which an increase in wages will result in additional workers. Some occupations are highly skilled and have inelastic supply curves, meaning that even a great increase

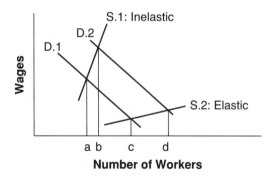

FIGURE 4.4   Elasticity of Supply for Labor

in wages will result in only a relatively few more workers available. The supply curve (S.1) is inelastic. Precision machining is a highly skilled occupation taking years to perfect; thus, the supply of this type of worker is relatively fixed. Even if wages rise significantly, the only hope for new workers in the short run is that some individuals with these skills who are employed in other occupations will change jobs or people will come from other countries. In occupations such as these, the supply is inelastic. As illustrated in Figure 4.4, a shift in the demand curve for an occupation with an inelastic supply curve will result in little additional supply (Qa to Qb), even if wages went up dramatically.

Other occupations, such as nurses' aides, have a very elastic supply curve, meaning that a small increase in wages will result in a large increase in the number of workers available. The supply curve (S.2) is elastic. The occupation of nurses' aides, although very important work, requires only a limited amount of training. Therefore, a small wage increase, will result in a large increase in supply (Qc to Qd). In occupations such as these, the supply curve is said to be elastic. As illustrated in Figure 4.4, a shift in the demand curve for an occupation with an elastic supply curve will result in a large increase in the number of workers available, with very little increase in wages.

Practical Significance of Elasticity of Occupational Supply

The two scenarios, one for precision machinist, the other for nurses' aide, serve as good examples of the significance to workforce educators of the concept of elasticity of labor supply. It will be very difficult to respond quickly to shifts in occupational demand if the supply curve for that occupation is inelastic. This inelasticity is partly caused by the rather steep and lengthy learning curve associated with these occupations. As the mix of skilled to unskilled occupations continues to increase, more occupations will have inelastic supply curves. In light of this reality, it can be anticipated that the workforce education system will be pressured to develop quicker response strategies in order to decrease the time it takes to prepare highly skilled individuals. Programs, for example, in community colleges that take two years may find themselves losing students to private sector proprietary schools that can prepare a person with the same skills in half the time.

HUMAN CAPITAL INVESTMENT THEORY

As discussed in Chapter 3, of the three traditional capital components of national wealth (natural resources, capital/technology, and labor), labor or human capital is considered the most important. The pivotal point is that the quality of the workforce will determine the degree to which technology can be used to its fullest potential and thus its international competitiveness. Countries seeking to compete for a share of the world's high-skills/high-wage production must, therefore, invest in the skills of its workers. The formal economic theory behind this strategy is called the human capital development theory. Typical human capital investments include higher education, technical training, and formal on-the-job training. As illustrated in Figure 4.5, it is theorized that as investments in human capital increase so too will productivity and, thus, earnings.

As illustrated in Figure 4.5, the human capital development theory predicts that investment in human capital will, in fact, lead to greater economic outputs. The human capital investment theory, for example, would predict that individuals with advanced skills—and therefore higher levels of human capital investment—earn on average higher salaries, and that is what the data show.

The importance of this theory to workforce educators is that education and training, as defined in Chapter 1, is the principal form of human capital investment. Though other types of human capital investment exist—such as money invested by firms to improve safety and health in the workplace, resulting in less lost time from work due to injury—workforce education is the primary mode of human capital investment. It is worth keeping in mind that the human capital investment theory is only a theory. Unfortunately for workforce educators, particularly for human resource development (HRD) professionals in business and industry, data supporting

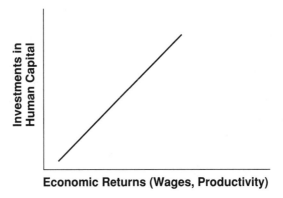

FIGURE 4.5   Human Capital Investment Theory

the validity of the theory are not always easily obtained and are sometimes contradictory (see Chapters 13 and 14). When trainers seek to provide cost/benefit proof of training effectiveness, or return on investment (ROI), they are, in fact, attempting to prove that the human capital investment theory applies to their setting.

Human capital investment theory relates to individuals as well as to employers. The theory predicts that individuals who invest in advanced training (human capital) will be less likely to be unemployed and more likely to earn above-average salaries. Conversely, the theory provides one explanation of poverty and unemployment, namely, that poor individuals lack sufficient amounts of human capital investment. This should remind the reader of the "skills-employability" paradigm described in Chapter 1. The human capital development theory is, in fact, a sophistication of the widely held conventional wisdom that education and training will solve a wide range of social problems that the public views as being caused by lack of education and training.

The question remains, Why does investing in human capital lead to economic growth and higher individual salaries? The answer lies in the concept of productivity. Workforce educators need to have a working knowledge of this concept.

WORKFORCE PRODUCTIVITY

Productivity, for the purpose of this discussion, is defined as the output of goods and services that results from an hour of labor. Given the same materials, technology, and machinery, different workers will produce different results; some will be more productive than others.

At the macro or national level, countries have differing overall levels of productivity. Given that natural resources and technology are relatively mobile, this productivity level ultimately will determine the wealth of each nation. Economist Lester Thurow (1992) points out that "productivity or output per hour of work is the central factor determining the ability of any society to generate a world-class standard of living; it is not possible to divide what is not produced" (p. 164). This echoes the observation of Adam Smith three centuries ago.

At the micro or firm level, productivity is the key to profits and business survival. Unless protected from competition a firm must compete in the marketplace, and competition is based on quality and price. Firms that produce the highest quality at the lowest price dominate the market; being able to do this requires that the firm be at or above the productivity average for the business it is in. A firm's decision to invest in human capital through training is based on the expectation that it will result in increased productivity and profits. This relationship is illustrated below in a very simple static case that assumes a fixed world price for a unit produced, with labor being the only cost necessary to produce it (see Table 4.1 on page 65).

In most domestic and international markets individual firms do not control enough shares of the market to control the price (in the United States, antitrust legislation is designed specifically to prevent this from happening). Thus firms must sell at the marked price. In the case illustrated, the world price of a unit is $1. The

TABLE 4.1   The Relationship between Productivity and Wages (World Market Price per unit = $1)

Firm	Output per Hour of Labor	Possible Hourly Wages
A	1 unit	$1
B	10 units	$10
C	20 units	$20

three firms have different levels of productivity: Firm A is the least productive, producing only one unit per hour of labor; Firm C is the most productive, producing 20 units per hour of labor. The market price is $1; thus, if it had no other costs, Firm C could pay a wage rate of $20 per hour, but Firm A could pay only $1 per hour. This simple example also provides an explanation of the concept of high-skills/high-wage strategy for economic development.

The High-Skills/High-Wage Strategy

In any commercial market, price and quality are the basis of competition and are the keys to a firm's success. In a global economy the standard of quality and price is set on an international market. Putting quality aside, price becomes the key point of economic competition, and given that a worldwide price exists for most materials and technology, the cost of labor becomes a key variable.

When labor costs alone become the key to competitiveness, industrial nations are at a significant disadvantage because they have higher wage rates than less developed nations. The average wages in the United States are six times greater than in Mexico and ten times greater than in China. Even domestic producers find it cheaper to have goods produced in Mexico or China and pay to have them shipped to the United States. For this reason, industrialized nations cannot compete on the basis of low wages but must, instead, seek to create a high-skills workforce that will enable firms to pay high wages and still be price competitive. The strategy is to make workers in the United States so productive that they produce much more per hour of labor than foreign workers and therefore can be paid a higher wage. This strategy is illustrated in Table 4.2.

Table 4.2 illustrates how a nation with high wages can compete with a nation with low wages if its workforce is more productive. The example includes only

TABLE 4.2   Comparison of Low-Skills/ Low-Wage (LS/LW) and High-Skills/High-Wage (HS/HW) Competitive Strategies (World Market Price per unit = $1)

Firm	Hourly Wage	Units per Hour	Price Per Unit
A (LS/LW)	$1	1	$1
B	$10	10	$1
C (HS/HW)	$20	20	$1

labor costs and assumes a fixed world price of $1. In this illustration, firms in each nation have different labor rates, ranging from $1 per hour in Country A to $20 per hour in Country C. Based solely on labor rates, Firm A would have the advantage if the output per worker in all firms were equal. But, as illustrated, if the workers in Firms B and C are better skilled and thus more productive, these firms can pay higher wages and still produce a product at $1 per unit. The workforce in Firm C would be termed high-skills/high-wage. It makes twenty times more than workers in Firm A and twice as much as Firm B, but still the firm is competitive.

The high-skills/high-wage rationale explains why union labor rates can sometimes be higher than nonunion rates. If unionized workers can produce more work in a day than nonunion workers, the employers or contractors are willing to pay the higher rate because they will need fewer workers and their costs are the same.

Implications of a High-Skills/High-Wage Strategy

There are several implications of the high-skills/high-wage strategy for workforce educators. First, workforce education is the vehicle for bringing the workforce to the level of skill necessary to support high wages. Firms that pursue the high-skills strategy will need to invest heavily in workforce education as will a nation that already has high wages and cannot compete using the low-skills strategy.

Second, the high-skills strategy holds the prospects of significant worker displacement and unemployment. Returning to Table 4.2, if each firm's production goal was 400 units a day, and assuming an 8-hour workday, Firm A would need 50 employees, Firm B, 5 employees and Firm A, only 2.5. In situations where firms move from production level B to C, they will need one-half of their current workforce. This reality partly explains why many firms downsized in the 1980s and 1990s. The implication for workforce educators is that, as firms seek to compete on a high-skills/high-wage basis, they will need fewer workers, and rather widespread displacement and unemployment will occur. When workers are laid off, the public workforce education system is asked to provide retraining to those displaced.

Value Added and Transfer of Training

The human capital development rationale suggests the goal of workforce education is to make individuals more productive. A term frequently used to describe worker productivity is *value added*. Value added refers to the increased value employees add to the product or service produced; the more value they add, the more they can be paid. Discussions regarding how to increase the value added by employees to a firm's product or service is another way to discuss the issues of human capital development, productivity, and the role of workforce education. Assuming that in the short run all firms have the same technology, then the only way to improve human performance and thus the value added by individual employees is via training. This assumes that knowledge gained in training is *transferred* to the work site.

Workforce education is only effective to the degree that skills and knowledge gain result in improved performance on the job. Increased productivity resulting from workforce education instruction occurs only when what is learned is transferred to the work site. As many experienced practitioners will attest, success in the classroom does not necessary translate into changed behavior back at the job. This explains the preference for formal/planned on-the-job training as a human capital development/workforce education strategy. The transfer of learning is more direct in on-the-job training because instruction occurs at the work site. Finally, when firms attempt to measure the effectiveness of HRD expenditures, they are not attempting to measure knowledge or skills gained—which is relatively easy—but instead the degree to which this increased aptitude transfers to increased performance and productivity on the job.

INTERNATIONAL TRADE AND LABOR MARKETS

Because of its effect on domestic labor markets, international trade and international labor markets are becoming of increasing importance to workforce education. No longer can workforce education planners rely only on domestic labor market data; for some occupations the labor market is already international. To understand the workings of this market, it is useful to be familiar with the basic concepts of international trade.

Balance of Payments

The importance of international trade to a nation is that it increases a nation's "consumption possibility curve," meaning that either its citizens can buy things that cannot be made domestically, such as coffee from Jamaica, or they can buy goods cheaper, such as cut flowers from Mexico. Meanwhile, international trade allows the French to buy bourbon whisky from the United States and the Mexicans to buy Hershey's chocolate. Of course, whenever a U.S. citizen buys something imported from another country, at least part of the money paid flows out of the country into the hands of foreign firms and foreign workers. Ideally, a country's exports should exceed, or at least equal, its imports, because, if imports exceed exports, the net result is a steady drain of wealth out of the country and, in the long run, a decline in the standard of living.

The accounting metric or score card for foreign trade is called the balance of payments. When a nation's balance of trade is positive, exports of goods exceed imports, and, conversely, when it is negative, imports exceed exports. The balance of payments figures include things other than merchandise. They include, for example, foreign aid and the cost to station the military abroad, both of which have a negative effect on the balance of payments. These variables, however, are small in comparison to goods and services. The balance of payments, therefore, is an excellent indicator of the state of a nation's exports versus its imports.

The implication of the balance of trade indicator for workforce education professionals is that it is a good indicator of national interest in workforce education. Whereas a country's workforce is the only strategic variable that is thought to provide lasting competitive advantage, a negative balance of payments is taken as an indicator that additional investment in training is necessary. In the early 1990s, for example, the U.S. Secretary of Labor called for firms to increase investment in training in order to pursue a high-skills/high-wage strategy as a way to improve the balance of trade.

Exchange Rates

A second fundamental of international trade is the role played by exchange rates. In the case of the exchange between France and the United States, the French want to be paid in francs for their wine, and Americans want to be paid in dollars for their bourbon. Meanwhile, the average American citizen has only dollars and one dollar does not equal one franc. Without some mechanism to reconcile this dilemma, foreign trade would be seriously curtailed. The mechanism that exists is called the exchange rate. Exchange rates exist between all major currencies. They establish the ratio of one currency to another and vary accordingly.

A practical example of international exchange rates occurs when individuals visit a foreign country and need foreign currency. Typically, one exchanges dollars for the currency of the traveler's destination. Individuals traveling to Thailand in the 1990s received 25 bat for every dollar; however, if they were traveling to England instead, they would have to pay about $1.30 to buy a one pound coin. How these exchange rates are determined is beyond the scope of this discussion, but from the example just mentioned it should be evident that American goods will be expensive in Thailand, where citizens must pay 25 bat for every U.S. dollar worth of goods, and cheaper in England, where it costs less than one pound to buy a dollar's worth of American products.

When a nation's currency becomes more expensive in terms of another currency, it is said to have appreciated; conversely, when it becomes cheaper, it is said to have depreciated. When a country's currency appreciates, its goods become more expensive abroad; thus, its exports fall because its goods now are more expensive, and its domestic employment ultimately falls. Conversely, when its currency depreciates, its goods become cheaper abroad, its exports grow, and domestic employment grows. When Mexico depreciated its currency in the early 1990s, the effect was that all Mexican goods became cheaper in the United States, and all U.S. goods more expensive in Mexico. Employment in Mexico increased, and employment in the United States decreased proportionally. Employment in U.S. retailing in border states suffered particularly, and employment in this sector fell.

At the same time, exchange rates can serve to create jobs. As the U.S. balance of trade worsened, for example, the U.S. government allowed the dollar to depreciate on the foreign exchange market—one often hears in news reports that the dollar has weakened against the Japanese yen. Although such news seems a negative commentary, it has a silver lining in that, as the dollar depreciates against the yen, Japanese goods become more expensive. Today, a comparable Japanese car costs more than a U.S. car, domestic production has increased, and imports decreased.

In some cases, these exchange rates alone can make the difference between the profitable and unprofitable operation of a firm and the fate of workforce educators who work there. A good example is the steel industry. The production costs of a ton of steel between U.S. steel makers and the Japanese is now so close that exchange rates alone determine which will be the cheapest in the United States. The fate of many jobs in both countries rests solely with exchange rates. Thus, exchange rates ultimately effect the demand for workforce education.

Free Trade and Workforce Education

One of the more hotly debated domestic issues in the United States is free trade agreements such as the North American Free Trade Agreement (NAFTA). Such agreements reduce trade and border restrictions between countries in order to stimulate greater commerce. Free trade debates are of relevance to workforce educators because the political aspects of the debates are largely about the effects on employment, and therefore the demand for workforce education.

The argument for free trade is attributed to David Ricardo, who argued in 1817 that every country would be better off economically if it produced only those goods it had a "comparative advantage" in producing over other countries. Likewise, it would be better off buying from other countries those products it was at a comparative disadvantage in producing. Thus, the United States, for example, should perhaps stop producing steel and concentrate on producing pharmaceuticals.

The dilemma with free trade is it can have dramatic impacts on labor markets. Theoretically it may make economic sense to close all inefficient steel mills in the United States and concentrate on pharmaceuticals unless of course you happen to be a steel worker who is put out of a job. Although such a policy might increase employment in the pharmaceutical industry and even total employment in the country, it provides little compensation to the steel worker who probably does not have the skills required to compete for commensurate employment. While arguable free trade may stimulate total economic growth, workers in industries that are at a comparative disadvantage often end up unemployed.

Free trade agreements affect the demand for workforce education in two ways. First, workers displaced because of free trade agreements will often need retraining in order to compete for commensurate employment. Typically this type of retraining is provided in the public workforce education settings such as community colleges. Often the government provides specific training funds for workers displaced by free trade agreements, as was the case with NAFTA. Second, free trade agreements result in increased demand for workers in industries that experience increased sales. This results in the need for more workforce education provided by firms.

The International Labor Market

The most important result of international economic competition for workforce education is the development of a worldwide labor market. Whereas one mission of workforce education is to provide individual opportunity—which for most clients means a successful transition to an appropriate occupation—the potential of the developing global economy has tremendous implications. Specifically, in the United States it has the potential to dramatically shift the supply curve outward for many occupations, causing domestic labor surpluses in the short run and lower domestic wage scales in the long run. A very real example of this development is the occupation of computer programming.

Experienced computer programmers in the United States are highly skilled and highly paid, earning on average $4,000 to $6,000 per month. Computer programmers in India with the same skills earn on average only $1,200 to $1,500 per month. They work, however, on a product, computer programs that can now be transported electronically anywhere in the world. Texas Instruments now designs some of its more sophisticated computer chips in India, and Motorola, Inc. has opened computer programming operations in China, Singapore, Hong Kong, Taiwan, and Australia (Brasher, 1995). The net result is that the labor market for certain types of computer programming has become worldwide.

Although the most obvious implication of this development for workforce education professionals is the need to consider worldwide labor supplies, not only domestic markets, other possibilities also exist. Workforce education and training itself may become worldwide in nature. Distance education has already enabled some training programs to be offered around the world, and the development of more international labor markets suggests that this trend could develop rapidly. Even the design of workforce education programs could be influenced. If, for example, the world labor market prefers German-trained electronic technicians, then U.S. workforce education professionals will be forced to consider their training methods if their clients are to be competitive. Regardless of whether these developments occur, it is already certain that in some fields the competition graduates of U.S. workforce education programs will be graduates from around the world. The importance of truly understanding the concept of labor market advantage is the central topic of Chapter 5.

SUMMARY AND IMPLICATIONS FOR PRACTITIONERS

Like any professional endeavor, workforce education has a knowledge base that serves to guide decisions about best practice. In this chapter, several basic economic concepts were introduced that have particular relevance to workforce educators. Supply and demand analysis, for example, is particularly useful in assisting workforce educators to understand and therefore plan for fluctuations in the labor market and promote the ability of workforce education to react to these fluctuations. Equally important is the formal version of the skills-employability paradigm called the human capital investment theory, which theorizes that investments in workforce education will result in benefits both to individuals and to employers. The concept of worker productivity is central to this theory and to the high-skills/high-wage rationale as well. Finally, it has been pointed out that, in the future, workforce education planning will need to take into consideration international labor markets and the effects of free trade and exchange rates.

Having discussed these general economic concepts, Chapter 5 discusses labor markets. It begins with perhaps the most important of all economic concepts for a workforce education professional to understand, namely, the concept of "labor market advantage."

5

LABOR MARKET BASICS

One primary mission of workforce education is to prepare individuals to be successful in competing for vacancies in the labor market. Thus it stands to reason that professional practitioners need an understanding of labor markets. The purpose of this chapter is to provide such a foundation, beginning with the concept of labor market advantage.

THE CONCEPT OF LABOR MARKET ADVANTAGE

The harsh reality of the labor market is that it generates too few jobs that pay wages commensurate with a middle-class standard of living. As discussed in detail in Chapter 2, evidence suggests that the percentage of these jobs relative to all employment may be shrinking. Between 1970 and 1990 four-fifths of all wage earners suffered a decline in real wages. Wages of young men ages 25 to 34 fell 25 percent during this time (Cassidy, 1995). In all professional occupations except doctors, job applicants exceed job openings by almost 50 percent, and this difficult labor market is predicted to continue at least through the year 2005 (Eck, 1993).

In the foreseeable future the competition for jobs that ensure a middle-class standard of living is predicted to be stiff. Individuals who are successful in getting these jobs will be those with what economists call labor market advantage, namely, credentials that give them an advantage over other applications. One role of the workforce education profession is to prepare clients for this competition; their role is analogous to that of a coach of an athletic team, preparing it for competition. In the case of workforce education the competition occurs in the labor market, and the winners are those who have labor market advantage. It is critical for workforce educators to have a crystal clear understanding of the sources of labor market advantage.

Essential Skills: The Source of Labor Market Advantage

The question of what skills are needed to enhance labor market advantage in vying for competitive employment or of simply obtaining a job of any kind seems deceivingly simplistic, deceiving because it is not simplistic at all. In fact, as the experienced workforce educator knows, opinions vary dramatically, depending on who is asked and how. Employers, particularly when they are removed from the hiring process, are often apt to indicate that all they need are workers who have work-conducive behaviors such as reliability, cooperativeness, and the ability to follow directions. Others argue that in today's increasingly technical and changing workforce, occupational skills become obsolete quickly and the emphasis should be placed on basic academic skills which are more transferable and useful in learning new work skills (see *The Economist,* March 12, 1994).

Causing further confusion is what one reads in any "want ads" section of the Sunday metropolitan paper. From such a review it is difficult not to conclude that at least some employers are looking for individuals with very specific occupational skills, not only individuals with good work habits and basic academic skills. Furthermore, it is important for workforce educators to remember that the issue is not what minimal qualifications employers will accept but what additional credentials will lead to labor market advantage for their students/clients.

This book argues for the rationale most recently presented by John Bishop of Cornell University (1995), who reminds us first of all that, if the goal is high wages, wages are determined by the interaction of supply and demand. Therefore, high wages are a return to skills that are scarce. In particular, skills that are new and in demand are the most highly compensated. The key to labor market advantage is to have a set of unique skills that are related to occupations that are high paying and in demand. As Bishop (1995) points out,

> It is unwise to devote one's entire education to learning things that everyone else already knows (such as basic academic skills). One must select a vocation for which there is market demand and for which one has talent, and then pursue expertise and excellence within this niche. Expertise and excellence are impossible without specialization. (p. 3)

Figure 5.1 on page 74 provides a model for understanding the relationship of basic work skills and labor market advantage and resolves the seemingly conflicting beliefs as to which is the most important.

The model recognizes three levels of essential basic occupational skills: Level I, work ethics; Level II, basic academic skills; and Level III, occupational specific and advanced workplace literacy skills, such as being able to teach oneself new technology. A full discussion of these skills and instructional strategies to teach them is included in Chapter 10.

Hierarchy of Skills. The labor market advantage model presented in Figure 5.1 suggests that there is a hierarchy of basic skills that leads to labor market advantage. The beginning levels are work habits and people skills. The models predict that such skills are a prerequisite for all employment; individuals with even advanced occupational specifics will not be employable if they lack fundamental workplace ethics. The models suggest that, as occupations become more skilled, fundamental

FIGURE 5.1   Sources of Individual Labor Market Advantage

academic skills become an essential prerequisite. Finally, as work becomes truly high-skills/high-wage, occupational skills specific to the job and advanced workplace literacy skills are prerequisites to compete for this scarce and much sought after commodity. Individuals who seek labor market advantage in competing for this type of employment will need all three levels of skills in order to be competitive.

This hierarchy of workplace basic skills explains the inconsistency that workforce educators encounter regarding what employers expect from employees. When an employer states that all that is required is an individual with good work ethics, the work in question is probably low-skills/low-wage employment.

Failure to fully comprehend the sources of labor market advantage is one of the major reasons workforce education programs fail. There are two points that are critical to remember.

The Importance of Work Ethics

The first essential point for workforce educators to remember is that an appropriate work ethic is fundamental to employability. Often this reality is either overlooked or avoided because workforce educators are reluctant to make suggestions or to confront clients regarding their behaviors, dress, speech, and values. An all too familiar scenario is workforce education and training programs that focus on Level III occupational skills and attempt to remediate Level II basic academic skills but avoid dealing with Level I work habits and people skills. When it comes time for placement, frequently few are successful in the interview process, and those who are all too often are either dismissed or quit in a matter of weeks despite having the Level II and Level III skills to do the tasks required on the job.

Not all practitioners are guilty of this omission. One coordinator of a program for at-risk youth seemed to have it right when he stated, "A lot of time our kids can get jobs easily enough. The malls are always crying for help. But the skill, motivation, and responsibility necessary to keep a job is difficult for these students." Thus one can see the importance of all levels of basic skills but especially interpersonal skills and work ethics.

The Importance of Occupational Skills

The second point to be made is not to underestimate the importance of occupational skills. Employers of technical workers require occupational skills as a prerequisite. Those who possess them will have the advantage in the hiring process, even if occupational specific skills are not required.

Also, it is important to keep in mind that, when dealing with special populations, especially slow learners, skills that can be easily learned on the job by the more academically blessed individuals may not be able to be learned by those less blessed, particularly in the time allowed by employers. Thus, these individuals need occupational-specific skills development, even when they are preparing for occupations in which prior skills are normally taught on the job.

LABOR MARKETS

Labor market advantage is exercised in the labor market. The application of supply-and-demand analysis to labor markets was discussed in Chapter 4. In this chapter we take a more detailed look at labor markets. The first important distinction is the difference between internal versus external labor markets.

Internal versus External Labor Markets

An internal labor market exists in which jobs are filled solely by employees from within, or internal to, the firm. Often jobs are filled internally because of collective bargaining, seniority provisions, or a simple preference by employers to promote or rotate incumbent workers. In an internal job market, training those who successfully bid for jobs often becomes a major function of workforce education human resource development (HRD) professionals.

Conversely, an external labor market is one that is open to individuals who are currently not employees of the firm. When a firm seeks new additional employees, it seeks them in the external labor market. It is not uncommon for an internal labor market to become external when a firm adopts new technology. Although firms may have a preference to train existing and therefore trusted employees, they often are faced with the reality that too few have the Level II skills and/or the motivation to learn the new technology, and thus they must turn to the external labor market.

Formal versus Informal Labor Markets

A second labor market distinction is between formal and informal labor markets. A firm that needs additional employees and has to go to the external labor market has the choice to do it either formally or informally.

A formal labor market is one that is characterized by firms that have an organized "formal" procedure for selecting employees. In a formal labor market, jobs are posted or advertised, applications are evaluated formally, resumes and letters of application may be required, and formal interviews and often formal technical skill assessment (testing) is common. Formal labor markets exist in which either the firms are mostly large or the work is mostly technical or professional.

An informal labor market is characterized by firms that have an informal, unsophisticated, or "word of mouth" recruitment and hiring procedure. Firms that operate in the informal job market seldom advertise or do so only as a last resort. Typically they rely on word of mouth or nepotism to fill vacancies. Resumes are usually not required, and employers rely on previous work experience as an indicator of skill. Informal job markets are typical of small firms in all industries. The entry point for occupations in industries dominated by small firms, such as in the construction industry, is almost always the informal job market. Importantly, it is generally believed that 70 percent of all employment is filled through the informal job market.

Primary versus Secondary Labor Markets

The primary labor market includes those occupations that offer full-time employment with benefits, opportunity for advancement, and some degree of security. The secondary labor market is characterized by occupations that are typically low skills/low wage that offer little opportunity for advancement and provide less than 40 hours a week of employment, with few or no benefits. The secondary labor market is also characterized by frequent turnover as workers quit for better opportunities and/or because of frequent and sudden layoffs.

Part-Time versus Full-Time Employment

Full-time employment is typically defined as working 35 hours a week or more. One of the most dramatic and perhaps troubling changes in the labor market in the United States is the growth of part-time employment. Between 1957 and 1991 the percent of the labor force that was part-time increased from 12 to 19 percent (Tilly, 1991). This expansion occurred because employers viewed part-time employees as a means to cut labor costs, particularly benefits costs, and because job growth in the economy has been in the service industries, such as the retail food industry, which traditionally employ many part-time workers.

Unfortunately, since 1979 involuntary part-time employment, consisting of individuals who prefer to have a full-time job, accounted for most of this growth. Also, involuntary part-time employment is not distributed equally among all groups; two-thirds are women, and another 16 percent are men aged 16 to 25 or 65 and older (Tilly, 1991). This raises the possibility that the part-time job market may be a "dual labor market," meaning that, for the same occupation or type of work, two labor markets exist at the same time, one a full-time labor market for older males and the other a part-time labor market for women and young men.

The positive side of this development is the mushrooming of opportunities for voluntary part-time or self-employment. Outsourcing of HRD work by firms, for example, has created a growing number of opportunities for self-employed HRD consultants. Likewise, the growth of part-time employment has made efforts to organize "job sharing." Job sharing occurs when a full-time job is divided in order to be shared by two or more individuals. Such an arrangement allows women in particular to continue their careers during child-bearing years.

Implications for Practitioners

When planning programs, workforce educators must consider the nature of the labor markets. Opportunity, measured by the number of projected openings for an occupation, may exist, but if they are going to be filled in the internal job market, it may not be an occupational area workforce educators may want to train. A good example is the area of robotics, in which most jobs that initially developed were filled by firms internally.

If graduates are likely to be entering a job market that is characterized by increasing numbers of self-employed, such as a specialized repair person, then the curriculum should reflect this reality. If the job market is a secondary job market characterized by involuntary part-time employment, low wages, and high turnover, such as cosmetology, then workforce educators must address this reality openly. This is not to argue that such occupations should be rejected as legitimate programs for workforce education. All employment is scarce, and involuntary part-time employment in a secondary job market may, in many cases, be the first step for some clients toward full-time employment in a primary job market.

A common and critical issue is how to help clients make the transition from education and training to work when vacancies are filled through the informal job market. Failure to crack the informal job market severely limits efforts to facilitate transition. This is particularly true when working with young or inexperienced workers. The reason is that most of these individuals are likely to work in small firms.

FIRM SIZE AND LABOR MARKETS

The stereotype of an employer, and the model too often used by amateurs who attempt to develop workforce education programs, is that of a large firm employing 500 or more workers, has a professional personnel department, conducts a formal hiring process, and provides most of its own formal on-the-job training. This stereotype is inaccurate, particularly for younger workers (Gray & Wang, 1989).

Figure 5.2 on page 78 shows the distribution of all workers and workers at the average age of 25 between the four firm-size categories typically used by researchers. Although the workforce in general is fairly evenly distributed among all four firm-size categories, young workers are much more likely to be found in small firms. Sixty-eight percent work in firms of fewer than 100 employees, 43 percent in firms of fewer than 20 employees.

Workforce educators whose clients are mostly teens and young adults, or those entering the workforce for the first time, should consider the unique labor market features of small firms. The differences between large and small firms are many, but three in particular are important to workforce education professionals, namely,

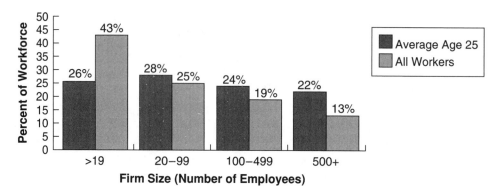

FIGURE 5.2   Distribution of Workers by Firm Size

the ability to provide formal training, the demographic differences of the work-force, and the resultant differences in hiring practices.

Training Practices in Small and Large Firms

As evidenced by the recent work of Carnevale et al. (1990a) of the American Soci-ety for Training and Development (ASTD), small firms are significantly less likely to provide formal training because they cannot afford the associated costs. Only 20 percent of the entire workforce ever receives any formal training in their entire ca-reer, and employees of small firms are even less likely to do so. Small firms cannot afford the direct (salary of trainee) and indirect cost (loss of productivity from tying up other workers or equipment for training) of formal training. They prefer to hire workers who are already trained, and those who have such training will have the advantage in competing for high-skills/high-wage work, particularly in small firms.

These realities make public sector workforce education more important to small firms. The ASTD study of skills training in the United States found that small firms were much more likely to expect employees to bear the cost of training at community colleges, for example. The relative greater importance of workforce ed-ucation to small firms is often overlooked by policy makers and workforce educa-tion designers alike. The danger in this oversight becomes more apparent when one considers the demographics of the typical workers in small firms.

Informal Hiring Procedures in Small and Large Firms

Although the largest percent of young workers are employed in small firms, the small-firm labor market is typically informal in nature and difficult to access. Most small firms avoid even advertising in the newspaper for the very practical reason that they do not have the staff to respond to the sometimes overwhelming re-sponse. Small firms rely mostly on the informal or word-of-mouth labor market, are less likely to require formal resumes, and are very interested in both occupational skills and previous successful work experience or teacher recommendations as an indicator of these skills. Although the ability to fill out a job application without misspelling is important, a formal resume is not. In many cases an interview suit will be much less important than owning a set of appropriate work clothes and tools of the trade.

LABOR MARKET PROJECTIONS

Workforce education programs in the public sector, particularly if state or federally funded, are typically required to document the fact that they are training individuals in occupations where there is unmet need for workers. Such forecasts of labor market demand and supply are called labor market projections. Systems that provide this information are typically called occupational information systems.

Workforce educators outside of HRD circles will find themselves using labor market projections fairly frequently. Twenty years ago it was common for public sector workforce educators to attempt to do labor market forecasts themselves by surveying local employers. They did this research out of necessity because good information below the national level was difficult to get and not very reliable. Fortunately, however, the situation has improved significantly; today's workforce educators seldom have to collect this type of data because federal, state, and even local agencies perform this service.

As outlined in Chapter 3, one universal mission of government is economic development. Arguably, almost all government policy and programs are related in some way to providing, directly or indirectly, an environment that is conducive to the creation of a high standard of living for its citizens. Governments pursue a variety of policies to accomplish this mission, one of which is to facilitate the equating of occupational supply and demand by sponsoring ongoing labor market projection research that provides data for occupational information systems.

Figure 5.3 on page 80 illustrates the supply and demand model for the labor market that is typical of those used by the Bureau of Labor Statistics and other labor market forecasting groups. It illustrates the variables that statisticians use to predict the supply side of the labor market. State and local agencies use similar models. Resulting data are published in a number of different sources ranging from, at the federal level, the *Occupational Outlook Handbook,* which is designed primarily as an occupational planning tool and published every five years, to data published in the *Monthly Labor Review.* At the state level virtually every Department of Labor and/or Commerce publishes monthly labor-force statistics, and in many states regional economic-planning agencies also compile labor statistics that include supply and demand figures.

Labor Demand Projections

While format and terminology may vary, the typical occupational information system provides a comparison of projected demand or job openings, with the projected supply of workers who are available to fill these vacancies (see Table 5.1 on page 81).

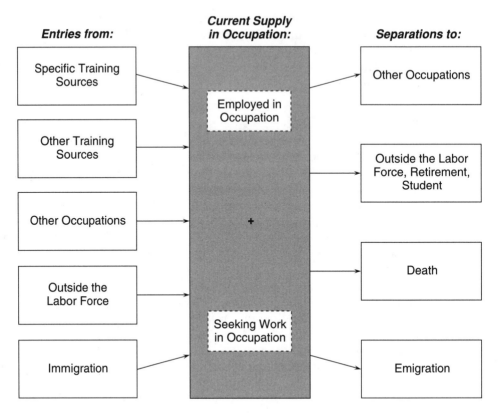

FIGURE 5.3   Estimating Labor Supply

Source: Passmore, D. (1989). Penn State University: State College, PA.

Demand data are a projection of job openings and can be listed by industry, region, or occupation. Demand projections attempt to predict growth or decline of employment due to overall health of the industry and historical employment trends. Demand projections also take into account the average age of workers and the number of those retiring who will need to be replaced. In some cases, an industry or occupation experiences little real growth, but the average age of the workforce is high, and therefore the need to replace workers is high. Because labor market demand is so highly influenced by changes in technology, the business cycle, and international competition, reliability is often suspect.

Labor Supply Projections

Labor supply is the number of workers who are available to fill vacancies. Typically labor market supply data are compiled only for skilled occupations—occupations that have relatively inelastic supply curves—or for national, state, or regional labor markets collectively. Labor supply data may be limited to a projection of individuals who complete formal training or credentialing programs, as is the case

TABLE 5.1   Average Annual Job Openings: 1990–2005

	Openings	Credentials Awarded	Net Openings
Professional			
Executive, Administration	436,000	506,830	–70,830
Construction Managers	7,000	825	+6,175
Marketing, Advertising, and Public Relations Manager	23,000	66,416	–43,416
Professional Specialty	623,000	1,120,063	–497,063
Physical Scientist	8,000	35,163	–27,767
Lawyers	28,006	44,314	–33,611
Technical			
Technicians	183,000	212,767	–27,767
Health	79,000	71,804	+7,196
Engineering	52,000	85,611	–33,611
Blue-Collar Technical			
Precision Metal, Craft, and Specialized Repair	455,000	133,057	+321,943
Mechanics, Installer, Repairman	160,000	91,758	+68,242
Service Occupation	882,000	237,062	+644,938
Operators, Laborers	477,000	41,504	+435,496
Farming, Forestry, Fishing	90,000	14,547	+75,453

Source: Compiled from Eck (1993), Monthly Labor Review KCG/PSU.

in Table 5.1. Such data, however, may underestimate the actual supply, because, as indicated in Figure 5.3, the actual number of workers available can be affected also by immigrants (legal or illegal), individuals who have the relevant skills or credentials but who are out of the labor market (such as students and mothers), and individuals with these skills who are working in other occupations but could be attracted to the industry if vacancies occur. It is not correct to think that workforce education is the only source of supply for a particular occupation.

Reliability of Labor Market Projections

As with any prediction, the reliability of labor market projections is always a concern. As the geographic region of prediction (for example, a county versus the nation), becomes smaller and the time of prediction shorter (for example, a 6-month outlook versus a fifteen-year outlook), the reliability of demand data decreases. A single plant closing or expansion can completely alter such data for a small locality, although having little effect on national projections. At the federal level, a change in government spending can have a significant effect on total employment and also on distribution of employment. When the U.S. Department of Labor's Bureau of Labor Statistics (BLS) made its 1990–2005 projections, for example, no one could have foreseen the sudden effort to balance the federal budget, or welfare reform, both of which will have some effect on the occupational distribution in the economy. The BLS and other agencies attempt to compensate for these events by making labor market predictions under assumptions of slow, moderate, and high economic growth.

Likewise, there are numerous challenges to predicting the actual labor supply. In particular, it is difficult to predict the number of individuals who are credentialed and work in other jobs or who are out of the labor market but would be available if vacancies occurred. The effects of immigration are also difficult to predict. The development of international labor markets has further complicated the picture. In many highly skilled occupations, such as engineering and computer science, there is a worldwide surplus of credentialed individuals. In the past, immigration restrictions have limited the impact of these surpluses on domestic labor markets. Now, however, the work can often be electronically sent anywhere in the world, and the labor market becomes worldwide.

Occupational Classification Systems

Because of the immense and ever growing number of different occupations in the economy, a prerequisite for effective occupational projections is a classification or coding system. The term "occupation" refers to a grouping of work tasks that are related and have had a name—such as masonry or computer repair technician—assigned. In the United States the system used to classify occupations is called the "Standard Occupational Classification" (SOC).

At the national level, occupations are clustered into larger occupational groupings for analysis purposes. This book uses classification systems currently employed by the federal Bureau of Labor Statistics. The major categories in this schema are provided in Table 5.1. This schema is used by the BLS to report many different types of occupational information and will be the format used in this and remaining chapters.

Using Labor Market Data

There are several common mistakes in interpreting labor market projections that should be guarded against. The first is the confusion between fastest growing employment and total employment. It is typical for government agencies and the press to report listings of occupations that have the highest percentage of change. Individuals think that these figures indicate where the largest numbers of jobs will be in the future. This may or may not be a correct assumption. For example, in the health field, on a percentage basis, hospitals are predicted to be the slowest growing employment segment in the industry, but in terms of total employment hospitals are still predicted to remain the largest center of employment. Without knowing the total employment for an occupation, percentage changes are meaningless. For example, both child-care workers and travel agents are predicted to grow 66 percent between 1990 and 2005, but that amounts to 451,000 child care workers versus only 76,000 travel agents.

The second mistake, and one frequently made by the public, is forgetting that employment projections are demand-side data only. They do not take into account labor supply. Table 5.1 provides both and illustrates the pitfalls. Note, for example, that in the category of professional employment the economy is projected to create 436,000 jobs annually in the executive/administrative occupations and only 7,000 in construction management occupations. Based on these numbers alone, the first category has a far greater number of opportunities than the first. However, when the number of individuals who will be getting credentialed or trained in these two occupations is taken into account a far different picture emerges. Now the outlook for construction managers is excellent with demand exceeding supply by 6,175 jobs, whereas the outlook for executive/administration is not good at all, with supply exceeding demand by 70,830 jobs.

Likewise, it is a mistake to discount occupations that are predicted to have negative growth, meaning that total employment at the end of the prediction period will be less. A typical example is the occupational group called Precision Metal, Craft, and Specialized Repair. This occupation group is predicted to lose workers. However, this decline is partly due to increasing sophistication of manufacturing processes resulting in fewer workers. However, the jobs that remain are mostly high skills/high wage, the occupational outlook is positive, and demand exceeds supply by 321,943 jobs.

EMPLOYMENT DATA

Whereas the nation's workforce education system is seen as a key system for reducing unemployment, it is useful for workforce educators to have a working knowledge of the terminology used in employment data. Whereas occupational projections attempt to forecast the supply and demand for labor, employment data measure the net result in a point in time in the labor force.

For measurement and descriptive purposes the total labor force is divided, typically, into two categories. The "civilian labor force" is an estimate of persons 16 years of age and over who are either employed or unemployed and includes everyone except those institutionalized, whether they are seeking employment or not. "Total employment" is an estimate of the civilian labor force that is employed (having worked at least one hour for pay or profit during the reporting period) including an estimate of unpaid family workers, self-employed workers, and agricultural workers.

Total unemployment is a parameter that estimates the number of workers who are not working but are actively seeking work and are currently available for suitable employment. Therefore, the unemployment figures are often an underestimate of the true number of unemployed because they do not count the "long-term unemployed" or discouraged workers who have been out of work so long they have virtually stopped looking and are technically out of the labor market though fit to work. These and other individuals, such as full-time students, who are neither employed nor unemployed are said to be not in the labor force. The "labor force participation rate" is the percentage of the civilian labor force that is currently employed.

Zero unemployment at any time is impossible because there will always be a certain percentage of the labor force that is between jobs. This phenomenon is called "frictional unemployment" and is thought to account for as much as 4 percent of unemployment. For this reason full employment is generally now considered to be achieved when the unemployment rate is in the 4 to 5 percent range.

A more thorny problem for policy makers and workforce educators alike is what is termed "structural unemployment." Structural unemployment is the difference between the total number of people seeking work and the number of jobs the economy is generating. In poor economic conditions the structural unemployment rate increases, but in some urban and rural areas the structural unemployment rate remains high all the time. This occurs because employers of the past who attracted families to these areas have either gone out of business or relocated. Workforce educators will have only limited success in areas of high structural unemployment because the basic problem may not be lack of worker skills but lack of jobs. A common strategy is based on the rationale that by improving the availability of workforce education in these areas of high structural unemployment the skills levels of the workforce will be increased, which will, in turn, attract industry into the area.

Unemployment figures since the early 1980s have run in the 5 to 7 percent range. Unemployment rates for people of color are typically twice the rate of whites, and the rate for high school dropouts is higher still (see Table 2.3). Also, considering that long-term unemployed could add another 5 percent, the true national unemployment rate could be as high as 11 percent. Factors complicating the issue further are the policies of the U.S. Federal Reserve Board, the agency charged with controlling interest rates and inflation. Typically, the Board views a falling unemployment rate as an early sign of coming inflation. When the rate falls below 6 percent, the agency historically attempts to slow down the economy. Therefore, the price of low inflation seems to be a structural unemployment rate of at least 2 to 4 percent because as soon as the unemployment rate falls within this range, the Federal Reserve board increases interest rates, which results in slower economic growth and less demand for workers.

LABOR MARKET MISCONCEPTIONS

While workforce educators use labor market data for program planning, the public uses it to make career planning decisions. Because of the dramatic economic changes that have occurred since the 1970s there has been a lot of confusion and anxiety regarding the labor market of the future. This anxiety has, in turn, led to a number of misconceptions by the public regarding the labor market. Some of these misconceptions have worked against workforce education by discouraging enrollment in programs the public incorrectly thinks hold little opportunity. With this in mind, workforce educators should understand these issues.

Misconception #1: In the future most jobs will require a college degree.

Fact: Of 147 million jobs that will exist in the year 2005, only 32 million, or 21 percent, will require a college degree.

There is a widespread misconception that in the future most jobs will require a college degree. This stems partly from general confusion about the fastest growing occupations and those that will generate the greatest number of jobs. While the number of jobs that will require a college degree will increase more quickly than the number that will not (39 percent versus 16 percent), the fact is that in the foreseeable future, for every job that requires a college degree, four will not (Shelley, 1992). What has changed is the percentage of non–college level employment that requires skill. In 1950, unskilled labor, that which typically requires only Level I basic job skills (see Chapter 4), accounted for 60 percent of all employment. By the year 2000, it is predicted to account for only 15 percent. The percentage of all work that is professional (requiring a four year or graduate level college degree) employment has, however, not changed at all and is predicted not to change in the future.

Misconception #2: Most high-wage jobs in the future will be in technical fields and all of these jobs will require a college degree.

Fact: The largest and fastest growing segment of the emerging technical workforce is occupations that do not require a four-year college degree.

Most labor market experts agree that the most promising segment of the future workforce comprises technical workers. Since 1950, the number of these new worker elites has increased 300 percent and will represent one-fifth of all employment by the year 2005 (Richman, 1994), or 29 million jobs. There is little doubt that aside from the traditional high-wage professions, the best opportunities for the future will be in the growing ranks of what Peter Drucker (1994) calls "knowledge workers." The public, however, has jumped to the conclusion that college training will be required for these jobs. Not so (Gray & Herr, 1991).

As illustrated in Figure 5.4, the largest segment of technical workers is "blue-collar" technical workers (Carnevale, 1990a). These are primarily workers who are technicians employed in the crafts, precision metals, and specialized repair occu-

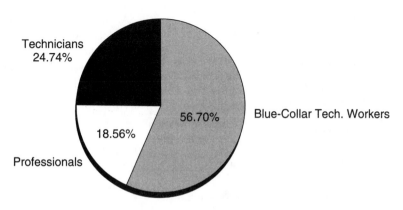

FIGURE 5.4   The Technical Workforce

Source: Compiled from Carnevale, et al. (1990a).

pations. These jobs do require special (Level III) skills, and in some cases they are best learned at the associate degree level, but they do not require a baccalaureate degree. In fact, among technical occupations, those that require a four-year college degree are the fewest in number and, on a percentage basis, the slowest growing (Carnevale et al., 1990a).

Table 5.2 lists some of the typical blue-collar, nonprofessional, worker elite occupations, none of which require a college degree. Noticeable are the variety of skills and diversity of work environments, suggesting that almost everyone could find rewarding careers in one or more of the occupations on this list. What is important for public sector workforce education is that already by the mid-1990s it was becoming apparent that more and more firms were giving preferences to those

TABLE 5.2   The New "Worker Elite" Blue-Collar Technical Occupations

Craft and Construction
   Construction Drafting
   Construction Project Manager
   Heating–Air conditioning Technician
   Plumbing–Pipe Fitting Technician
   Precision Welding
   Specialized Carpentry and Installation
   Specialized Interior Finishing
      and Installation

Health Occupations
   Dental Assistant
   Dental Hygienist
   Emergency Medical Technician
   Home Health Aide
   Licensed Practical Nurse
   Medical Laboratory Technician
   Medical Record Technician
   Optometric Technician
   Radiology Technician
   Surgical Technologist

Manufacturing
   Computer Controlled Equipment
      Operator
   Drafting Technician
   Electronics Engineering Technician
   Electronics Lab Technician
   Engineering Technician
   Manufacturing Systems Operators
   Manufacturing Technicians

Service Occupations
   Accountant
   Agribusiness Sales
   Automatic Office Managers
   Commercial Design
   Computer Graphics Specialist
   Criminal Justice and Corrections
   Data Processing Managers
   Fire Fighters
   Law Enforcement–Protection Occupations
   Library Technicians
   Paralegal
   Professionally Trained Chef
   Specialty Auto Mechanics

Technical Service, Repair, and Installation
   Airframe Mechanic
   Avionics Repair Technician
   Biomedical Equipment Technician
   Computer Systems Installation and Repair
   Electromechanical Repair Technicians
   Telecommunications Installations
      and Repair

with relevant technical associate degrees when filling vacancies. Thus, it can be predicted that the percentage of all employment that is technical will increase; this is an important labor market rationale for the education reform called tech-prep, discussed in Chapter 14.

Misconception #3: As the number of four-year college degree graduates increases, the economy will generate an equivalent amount of commensurate employment.

Fact: The U.S. Bureau of Labor forecasts that through the year 2005 one in three college graduates will not find college-level employment; among those preparing for the professions this number will be one in two.

In light of the rapid growth in enrollment in four-year colleges, one must conclude that they, parents, and advisors assume that the economy will generate increasing amounts of college-level employment to accommodate the increasing percentages of young adults who will earn a college degree (Gray & Herr, 1995). Unfortunately this is not true. According to U.S. Bureau of Labor forecasts, four-year colleges will graduate 497,000 more students with professional credentials alone than college-level jobs through the year 2005.

This suggests that literally millions of four-year degree holders will be underemployed by the turn of the century. As dismal as these forecasts sound for college graduates, however, they are a conservative estimate that, among other things, does not take into account migration into the United States by college graduates from abroad (thus increasing supply) or computer-related work that can be sent instantaneously anywhere in the world (thus decreasing domestic demand). Therefore, the actual supply of college graduates may, in a global sense, exceed the demand for their services to an even greater extent than conveyed by U.S. Bureau of Labor projections.

Misconception #4: As the number of four-year college graduates grows, a four-year degree will be needed to get even nonprofessional employment.

Fact: College graduates are likely to displace those with lesser degrees but only in low-skills/low-wage employment. They will not displace those with technical skills.

Another widely held myth is that, as the number of people who obtain a four-year college degrees exceeds the number of jobs that require this degree, these graduates will take the better-paying jobs traditionally held by those with less education. There is little evidence, however, to support this fear. In a national survey of employers in the thirteen largest industrial sectors, 10 of 13 industry groups ranked the need for workers with technical training higher than the need for those with a college degree (Adult & Continuing Education Today, 1992), confirming the importance of skill, not degrees, in the hiring decisions made by firms.

Of course, some college graduates will take jobs that do require a college degree. But only in low-skills/low-wage occupations. College graduates are already displacing high school graduates but mostly in secondary job markets in low-skills/low-wage areas such as retailing. Importantly, college graduates are not displacing, and will not displace, less educated individuals who have Level III occupational skills that are in demand. An individual, for example, with a baccalaureate liberal arts degree will not displace an individual with an associate degree in automated manufacturing technology or a professionally trained chef.

Misconception #5: Because higher education is correlated with future earnings, high wages are a labor market return for education.

Fact: In the labor market, above average wages are a return for occupational skills in demand, not education per se.

The widely held first four misconceptions discussed above have led to the seemingly universal belief that more education will guarantee high future earnings. Yet this is in reality a classic case of ex post facto thinking or confusing correlation with causation. Although education and earnings are correlated, in fact high-wage rates are paid in the labor market as a premium for specialized skills in demand. This explains why some occupations that do not require a college degree, such as those of electricians, specialized health technicians, and manufacturing technicians, pay more than many occupations that require a baccalaureate degree. The correct causal relationship for high wages is implicit in the term high-skills/high-wage employment. The key to earning high wages and economic security is obtaining occupational skills, not education per se (Gray & Herr, 1995).

The relationship between skill and earnings is illustrated in Table 5.3. In this table, the six major occupational groups are ranked highest to lowest by earning, by net opportunities, and then by the percentage of all workers in these groups that report prior training or experience as being a prerequisite for the job they held. Note the almost perfect correlation between the rank order for earnings and the

TABLE 5.3   Occupational Groups Ranked by Earnings, Net Opening, Required Training, percent Female

	Earnings	Net Opening	Required Training	% Female
Managerial–Professional	1	6	1	47%
Craft, Precision Metal, Specialized Repair	2	3	2	9%
Technical Support	3	1	3	64%
Service	4	4	5	25%
Operative, Laborer	5	2	4	60%
Farming, Fishing	6	5	6	16%

Source: Compiled from Eck (1993) and Statistical Abstracts of the United States, 1994.

need for prior training. This relationship confirms that skill, not education, is the key to high wages. Jobs that require high levels of skill typically pay high levels of wages.

A four-year college degree will equate to higher earnings only to the extent that it is interpreted in the labor market as indicating occupational skills in demand. The drastic cutback in middle management alone suggests that this automatic equating of college degrees to occupational skill is lessening, leading to the conclusion that those without degrees, but with job skills in high-skills/high-wage technical occupations (see Table 5.2), will outearn all four-year college graduates except those who will find jobs in the professional managerial ranks (Gray & Herr, 1995).

Misconception #6: The gender wage gap will be eliminated as more women go to college.

Fact: The gender wage gap will be eliminated only when women make up a larger percentage of the blue-collar technical workforce.

Presently, the wages of all women in the workforce are still only about 70 percent of wages paid to males, even though women now make up about one-half of the workforce. Previously it had been thought that this gap was due primarily to fewer women going to college and therefore having less human capital investment. Today, however, more women than men go to college and graduate from school. And although the increase in college attendance by women has resulted in improvements in the wage gap, analysis suggests that unless the educational attainment of women dramatically exceeds that of men in the future, the wage gap will not narrow further (Gray, Huang, & Jie, 1993).

The reason is illustrated in the last column of Table 5.3. Although women have just about reached parity in the professional ranks, they make up only 9 percent of the workforce in the second highest paying occupational category: craft, precision metal, and specialized repair. Meanwhile, women make up 60 percent of the unskilled operative or assembly workforce, leading Noel (1992) to conclude that the relevant issue for the majority of women is not the glass ceiling but escaping the sticky floor of low-paying assembly jobs. Undoubtedly workforce education should play a major role in effecting this change.

SUMMARY AND IMPLICATIONS FOR PRACTITIONERS

A clear understanding of labor market basics is part of the knowledge base of the workforce education profession. When the mission is creating individual opportunity, it is the labor market where this opportunity will be realized. Therefore, it is particularly important that professionals understand the sources of labor market advantage in the labor market. When the mission is to develop the nation's workforce, one role is to equate labor market supply to demand and by so doing prevent labor shortages or inefficient surpluses. Thus, it is useful to understand the sources of labor market supply-and-demand data and related validity issues and it is sobering to realize that the labor market will ultimately determine the success of some types of workforce education, regardless of its quality. Finally it should be realized that workforce education policy as well as the demand by the public for various types of workforce education is affected by conventional wisdom that the populace holds regarding the labor market. In many cases these perceptions are inaccurate. In these situations the workforce education professionals find themselves in the role of explaining labor market economics. In fact, one can observe that, although the product of workforce education is work-related instruction, the public expects professionals to be interpreters of labor markets as well.

6

SOCIOLOGICAL FOUNDATIONS OF WORKFORCE EDUCATION

Examining the foundations or knowledge base of workforce education is important because such a process emphasizes that work and preparation for it can be viewed through multiple lenses: historical, philosophical, economic, psychological, and, particularly, in this chapter, sociological. Each of these disciplines provides insights on how workforce education has been and is organized; the assumptions about human nature that underlie different approaches to workforce education; the market value of such preparation; individual action related to the choice and implementation of workforce education; and how workforce education is organized, who chooses it, and the network of roles that make up the occupational structure for which such students are preparing.

In the preceding chapters a number of concepts about the historical and philosophical foundations of workforce education were discussed (e.g., Taylorism, social Darwinism). Such concepts suggest that the philosophical perspectives that are accented in a given historical period and the political and economic trends comprising the external environment that exist during such periods are extremely influential in shaping how workforce education is conceived and implemented. Sociological perspectives advance such views by further focusing on contexts, organizations, and groupings of workers into which workforce education must be integrated and to which such education must be directed. These views are particularly vital to those persons preparing for or engaged in human resource development or management.

SOCIOLOGICAL PERSPECTIVES OF WORK

In broad terms sociological foundations emphasize several major themes. One is that sociological perspectives tend to accent the environmental factors that facilitate or constrain individual action. For example, as Hotchkiss and Borow (1990) suggest,

> *Psychologists are interested in how constellations of personal attributes, including aspirations, aptitudes, interests, and personality traits, shape subsequent job performance and satisfaction. Sociologists, by contrast, generally are more interested than psychologists in how institutional factors such as formal rules, informal norms, and supply and demand factors shape the settings in which individuals work. Sociologists have generally viewed paid employment and occupational choice as embedded in a broad system of social stratification. (p. 263)*

Thus, among other emphases, a sociological view is concerned with the structural factors that condition individual choices and their consequences, about the network of roles in which work takes place, and who plays what roles and why. Sociological perspectives also articulate the characteristics of the social environments in which work takes place, the normative culture that prevails in different workplaces, and how these affect individual behavior.

Implicit in sociological views of work is that work is a social institution, work is social behavior, and workers perform their roles within a network of social roles. In other words, a given worker interacts with other people: coworkers, supervisors, customers, managers, and more indirectly, stockholders and other investors. To accent this point and how various disciplines view work differently, Super and Bohn (1970) have contrasted sociological, economic, and psychological views of an occupation as follows:

> *Viewed* sociologically, *an occupation is a role with certain socially defined expectations, played in a network of related roles that constitute the systems of production, distribution, and service, for certain generally expected material and psychic rewards. Viewed* psychologically, *an occupation is a set of tasks and role expectations, the performance of which requires certain skills, knowledge, aptitudes, and interests and brings certain rewards. Viewed* economically, *an occupation is a means of assuring the performance of necessary work and therefore, also of securing a steady flow of income to individuals. (p. 113)*

A fundamental concept in the sociology of work is that work is performed by individuals who operate within a network of role relationships. As such, worker behavior is affected both by role perceptions held by the worker of how his or her job should be performed and by role expectations of what the worker should do as seen by those with whom the worker interacts or for whom he works. In some instances role perceptions by the worker and role expectations by others are in conflict. Such role constructs emphasize that work performance does not take place in a vacuum but occurs within an organizational culture, an environment in which job hierarchies, power and authority relationships, the division of labor, and related role dynamics between people, are played out (Hodson & Sullivan, 1990). These role dynamics organize the performance and organization of work and translate the work structure into rules, policies, and beliefs about how individual work should be done and why. These role dynamics indicate, clearly or less clearly, the relationship of each worker to the group.

Such role dynamics also provide possible responses to some of the major goals people hope to attain from work. In this case, their needs may include social affiliation, friendship, identity with something larger than themselves, a sense of contribution to a shared, organizational mission, and a feeling of being valued or needed by others to get the job done or to achieve mutual goals. Although not necessarily sought directly, work also confers social status on workers and their families. The money one is paid and the responsibility and title conferred on the individual in the workplace is, in many ways, the source of one's socioeconomic status, with all of its related aspects to be discussed later.

As suggested above, sociological perspectives describe work as complex and not confined to either its technical content or its economic implications. Landy (1989) has suggested that

> *work is something that happens to an individual. It is a treatment of sorts. People go to a work setting and are exposed to various elements. These elements include things such as heat, light, and noise. In addition, there are such elements as pay and supervisory style and coworkers. Even the duties and responsibilities that make up the job are treatments. Workers are exposed to a work pace, a certain demand for productivity, and accountability. (p. 600)*

Landy's view can be extended to suggest that when an individual chooses a job, a whole series of other choices are made with virtually no intent or information. In addition to the work content or technical tasks to be performed, one's choice of a job typically brings with it the choice of a work group of which one will be a part with all its support or hostility, its role expectations for each worker, and its definitions of the values and merits of an individual's work performance. Indeed, in most instances, the work role is not a solitary one. Workers perform in combination with others on whom they rely or who rely on them, in teams, in departments, or in other forms of collectives. Therefore, when a job is chosen, one also chooses the persons with whom one will work, the role expectations of others, the social status ascribed to the job, the types of leisure in which one will likely engage and with whom one will likely engage in leisure, how much vacation time will be taken and when vacations will occur, the types of continuing education or training required, the style of supervision, whether one's use of time is rigidly prescribed or discretionary, and the "work culture," the beliefs and traditions, in which the work group will function and work tasks will be performed.

Although sociologists are less concerned than psychologists and other specialists about how individuals make the choice of a job or why, they are concerned about most of the contextual dimensions named above as aspects of the work environment, how they vary across work settings and organizations, their implications for the organization of work, and the nature of the role relationships that support work as a goal-directed group activity. Industrial and organizational sociologists are also concerned with the factors and social forces that combine to alter the sociology of work or how the sociology of work differs cross-nationally or cross-culturally.

SOCIOLOGICAL CLASSIFICATION
OF LABOR MARKETS

A final area of particular concern to those engaged in workforce education and development is a vocabulary of the workplace and the interaction of access and mobility within it with issues of race and gender. Sociologists have introduced a
variety of interesting and important ways to classify both the nature of firms and
the types of jobs that exist within these firms. It is, then, a short step to classify the
types of persons who hold jobs within different types of firms and at different levels within them.

At a basic level sociologists concerned with structuralist approaches to resources available and their relationship to the distribution of the rewards of work
have advanced notions that have been technically described as *dual economy theory*
and *dual labor market theory*. In dual economy theory, firms have been classified by
economic sector as core or periphery (Hotchkiss & Borow, 1990) or by the more familiar notions of a *primary labor market* and a *secondary labor market* (Doeringer &
Piore, 1971). Core or primary labor markets typically refer to large firms that hold
major power in the markets in which they operate, are typically engaged at national or international levels, usually are technology intensive in their application
of advanced technology, provide high income and excellent fringe benefits (e.g.,
health care, education) for their employees, and have extensive career ladders that
provide multiple opportunities for advancement, movement to supervisory and
management opportunities, and security for workers. Periphery firms tend to be
smaller, with lower wages and fewer benefits, less security, shorter career ladders,
and fewer opportunities for advancement, and less opportunity for training or for
educational benefits than firms in the core or primary labor market. It might be
noted here that periphery firms may be divided into those that are essentially
"start up," or young firms that may be highly technological, creative and innovative, well on their way to becoming part of the primary or core economic sector, or
those firms that are more likely to be described as part of a secondary labor market.
These are often described as the world of fast-food restaurants with minimal career
ladders, a transient work force, often minimum wages, few health or other benefits, and work content that is designed to be achieved by workers who are primarily part-time and with limited education or technical training. Often this subset of
periphery firms is a place for young persons to establish their credibility as workers and obtain spending money or some income to apply to education.

In essence core firms and primary labor markets not only differ in terms of the
economic sectors they occupy, but they also differ in terms of the internal labor
markets, entry ports, and who is likely to be hired. Firms in the core or primary labor markets are likely to be larger and with greater resources to train workers. The
salaries, promotional opportunities they provide, and job security are likely to attract persons with good education, experience, and training. Core or primary labor
market firms also can afford to train those they employ and, indeed, repeat training as often as their industrial processes or equipment change and require work re-

learning. Often because of size, attractiveness to experienced and educated workers, and resources that allow training to be done in-house and by experienced workers, these firms have not historically required or supported workforce education. In contrast, many of the periphery firms, because they are small and frequently cannot afford in-house training departments or the loss of production that occurs when master workers train neophyte workers, have relied on workforce education to provide persons who have sufficient skills that reduce their need for training. These workers are less expensive to train and experience a shorter period of time to become productive than those with no technical skills and those who need extensive training before they can be productive.

As has been suggested, the characteristics of internal labor markets and career ladders are not independent of the description of firms as core or periphery or as in the primary or secondary labor markets. Internal labor markets are shaped and developed within these different work organizations as symbolic and as de facto mechanisms for advancement, in which earnings are related to the level of the job, its responsibilities, and technical skill requirements. Internal labor markets in firms in various economic sectors have, for example, different entry ports for persons employed in different occupations important to the firm and reflected in the career ladders detailing experience and skills or training prerequisites.

Although frequently cast as a dual labor market or dual economy, in fact it would be more realistic to speak of the occupational structure as comprising a continuum or range of firms that differ in size, command of resources, internal labor market characteristics, training requirements and availability, and other variables discussed earlier. But whether one thinks of more and less desirable employment organizations, a dual classification or a continuum of firms, a primary or a secondary labor market, who works in which of these firms and sectors differs by race and gender. Access to these firms, and to desirable positions within them has to do with institutionalized formal and informal rules, organizational culture, and often institutionalized beliefs about which classes of individuals are suited for specific jobs. For example, unionized core firms in urban areas tend to be dominated by white males in the internal labor force. Indeed, much of the empirical research on the subject suggests that minority group members are concentrated in low status occupations and earn substantially less than whites (Farley & Allen, 1987) and that women remain employed in a narrow band of occupations and consistently earn less than men (England & McCreary, 1987). Gender segregation by occupation is more apparent than racial segregation by occupation, although there have been declines in the gender composition and segregation of jobs and occupations (England & Farkas, 1986). However, sociologists have pointed out that there is a difference between job and occupational segregation in which it is possible for occupations to show less gender segregation, even though some jobs within occupational groupings remain segregated (Bielby & Baron, 1986). In the main, racial and gender differences cannot be accounted for by human capital variables such as training and ability but are primarily a function of structural barriers of stereotype, prejudice, and discrimination. Discrimination against women and minority group members is not confined to access to occupations or mobility within them. It is also reflected in income differences, which is a proxy for the quality of jobs available to minority persons and women and promotions attained and which suggests that the median family income for African American families is about 60 percent of that for white families and that full-time female workers make about 65 percent of the earning of full-time male workers (Hodson & Sullivan, 1990).

SOCIOLOGICAL PERSPECTIVES OF CONTEMPORARY WORK TRENDS

As sociological perspectives are applied to characteristics of contemporary work forces and work organizations, many factors arise from the emerging global economy and the resulting changes in the national economy that are affecting the sociology of work in the United States. Examples of these factors include the following:

The Downsizing and Reorganization of Work Organizations

Among the trends associated with downsizing are reductions in middle-level management and the reconfiguring of many jobs in order to use advanced technology in the workplace to its fullest advantage as a source of increased productivity. Such changes have affected the organizational structures of work, changing many from a pyramidal, centralized, and hierarchical structure to a more flattened and decentralized structure. In such circumstances traditional patterns of upward mobility are being modified to accommodate horizontal or lateral mobility as managers and skilled workers are frequently assigned to work teams, solving different types of organizational or production problems rather than specializing in one type of problem or process. In such cases, the sociology of work shifts its foci from the hierarchical structure of power relations to the diffusion of power through the organization, work-team consensus building, team building, quality circles, and other forms of shared decision making that include all workers who have relevance to a given production or organizational decision.

Just-in-Time Procedures

The search for efficiency in the workplace has led to such processes as "just-in-time inventories," which reduce the space and personnel necessary to warehouse and distribute parts, materials, and other elements important to particular work goals or processing. Just-in-time inventory procedures ensure that necessary parts and raw materials arrive at the production site just in time to be used, thereby dramatically reducing the costs of storage. Monitoring these production needs by advanced technology and tracking their convergence from suppliers at just the right time increase the importance of timing and the complexity of logistical planning, but they reduce the number of permanent workers required to manage inventory, keep it secure, or engage in related jobs.

Just-in-time inventory control is, in some ways, related to just-in-time workers. Although not described in those terms, corporations and industrial sociologists increasingly talk about the use of a "contingency workforce," which really means a part-time or temporary workforce, to augment a core, permanent workforce. The basic point of such an approach to personnel management is to reduce the permanent overhead costs of maintaining a large core workforce by supplementing the core workforce with temporary or part-time workers who do not receive permanent pension or health-care benefits and are less costly than permanent workers. In such situations part-time or temporary workers can be added at seasonal work peaks or when needs for labor surge for short periods of time. In some cases particular functions (e.g., data entry and other administrative tasks, recruitment of employees, employee assistance programs, and social services) can be outsourced to firms that provide such services under contract without adding to the corporation's permanent costs for functions that would otherwise require core employees and the long-term costs of housing them and providing them with individual benefits.

As these changes in work organization and personnel management unfold, they pose new challenges to the application of the sociology of work. Among them are concerns about the meaning of work for thousands, perhaps millions, of workers who may no longer anticipate having a lifelong career identity with a particular firm or the assurance of stable employment during their work life. They pose such sociological questions as, How will such potential instability affect work preparation patterns or work choice? How will economic uncertainty affect long-term spending patterns of persons who become part-time or temporary employees on an essentially permanent basis? What are the distinctions in characteristics, ability, and skills between those who become core, permanent employees and those who do not? Are temporary or reserve employees disproportionately members of minority groups or women? What are the effects for society of having large numbers of persons experience underemployment (e.g., part-time employment, jobs that do not fully use one's skills)? How do part-time and temporary workers satisfy their needs from work for social relations, affiliations, and personal identity?

The Global Economy

The rise of a global economy and the international economic competition that it spurs among nations have accented the fundamental importance of advanced technology as the element that makes such world economic structures possible. Satellite transmissions, computers, telecommunications, electronic mail, Picture Tel, and facsimile transmissions (faxes) are only part of the enormous array of mechanisms that permit work units for the same corporation to be located throughout the world and coordinated by electronic means. Such technologies allow huge sums of capital to be moved electronically overnight without respect to political boundaries. Advanced technologies permit industrial parks to arise in the Caribbean nations, in Ireland, or in India, to download from satellites electronically communicated work tasks involving information processing, data entry, and related activities and then upload the finished work to satellites and return it to the corporate location in the

United States, Western Europe, or Japan where it originated. Computer software development and information processing by electronic means are only examples of the many ways advanced technology has contributed to the globalization of the workforce, to the creation of what anthropologists are now calling the global factory (Blim, 1992: 1) in which industrial production for the capitalist world market is now found on every continent and in most regions of the world, incorporating "vast new populations of workers—peasants, artisans, industrial workers—in novel production or labor processes" and contributing as well to a global labor surplus and to global unemployment. All of these possibilities are present at the same time; they allow corporations in any developed nation to reach out across the globe to find talented and willing workers, and typically less expensive workers than exist in the United States, and to engage in what might be described as transnational outsourcing.

In such circumstances the sociology of work becomes increasingly internationalized as it examines the impacts of the economic and political events that have caused a restructuring of the world's economy. Among contemporary concerns are the shifts in the nature of the labor market in one nation or another as specific industries are moved from nation to nation. An example are the effects that result as multinational corporations acquire industries recently privatized in countries shifting from a communist form of economy to a market-driven, capitalist economy and as these corporations introduce a variety of new management and organizational dynamics to make the previously communist economies more dynamic, productive, and interactive with the rest of the world's economy. In such circumstances, sociologists have important concerns about how such major introductions of technology and knowledge affect the social rhetoric about work in countries where the work ethic had been stable and advanced technology was not a major part of the workplace. They are concerned with how various cultures embrace work identity, become innovative or marginal in the world economy (Hodson & Sullivan, 1990), make assumptions about workers and how work should be organized, and describe patterns of work meaning and outcomes in different nations. England (1990), for example, has demonstrated in his research that patterns of work meaning and related work outcomes are differently distributed among the workforces of Japan, Germany, and the United States. England has reported some eight patterns of work meaning in which work is more or less valued and more or less central to individual identity. The eight patterns are arrayed in Table 6.1.

TABLE 6.1   Cultural Patterns of Work Meaning

Pattern A—nonwork-centered, nonduty-oriented workers
Pattern B—nonwork-centered, high duty-oriented workers
Pattern C—economic worker pattern
Pattern D—high rights and duties economic workers
Pattern E—low rights and duties noneconomic workers
Pattern F—moderately work-centered, noneconomic, duty-oriented workers
Pattern G—work-centered and balanced work values workers
Pattern H—work-centered expressive workers

Each of these patterns represents different combinations of work centrality, economic values, levels of obligation and commitment, and entitlement. England's research showed that the labor forces of the United States, Germany, and Japan were represented differently by the proportions of workers in each of these patterns.

Although each of the three countries has workers in each of these patterns, they vary in the percentage or concentration of workers in particular patterns. For example, patterns E, F, G, and H are the most work-centered patterns and those in which workers define working in terms of "contributing to society," "something which adds value," "being accountable for one's work," and "basically interesting and satisfying." According to data presented by England (1990), Japan has 63.9 percent, the United States has 49.8 percent, and Germany has 30.6 percent of its workers in the four most work-centered patterns identified (E, F, G, and H). These are the patterns in which job satisfaction, company orientation, contributing to society, being accountable, and adding value have been found to be the highest in the definitions of work.

Such cross-national or cross-cultural views on work, meaning how work is perceived by workers and how central work is to individual worker identity, provide sociologists of work important insights into how workers in a particular nation are likely to incorporate perspectives about work into their personal psyche and the work behavior they manifest. Sociologists of work also study how the values and perspectives about human resources or individual behavior that predominate in a given society are likely to be accommodated in work organizations and, indeed, in national policies.

The classic work in this area has often contrasted the United States and Japan in their expectations of worker behavior, their organization of work, and in their related governmental policies. As has become axiomatic in discussions of social values and individual traits that are dominant in the United States, freedom, justice, liberty, and unfettered individual achievement tend to be frequently cited. In such perspectives the burden of achievement rests with individual action, aspirations, and skills; individual advancement is an individual responsibility, not a corporate one. Work organizations are organized around such assumptions about the primacy of individual responsibility to remain employable and to gain skills that allow one to be competitive for advancement and occupational mobility. These social values are not those that predominate in Japan. In that nation loyalty, conformity, hierarchy, duty, and obedience are dominant social values. To accommodate and reinforce these social values, work organizations and policies toward workers are different in Japan than in the United States. Japan's economic and political system related to work has increasingly been referred to as a "developmental model" rather than as a "regulatory model," the term that often tends to be used to refer to the United States and to the United Kingdom (Dore, 1987).

Developmental models of work organization are more prone than regulatory models to clearly define strategic economic goals, ensure that workers are constantly prepared to manage and implement the processes required to meet the economic goals of the work organization, and to reinforce worker identification with these goals and the personal contributions necessary to achieve such outcomes. It is within such contexts that Japanese work policies emphasize harnessing the tacit or latent skills of every worker from the factory floor to the executive office, to encourage all workers—whether custodian, machine operator, or manager—to diagnose problems they encounter and organize information and actions that will improve productivity and corporate knowledge. It has been suggested (Wood, 1990) that in a developmental model every worker is expected to "figuratively" think as an industrial engineer in order to find ways to seek continuous improvement in one's personal job and in an aggregate sense throughout the organization. It is within such a perspective that notions emerge of a corporate family in which everyone, whatever the job, has an important contribution to the whole. It is also why workers in Japan are trained in teamwork, multifunctional or cross-trained approaches, interpersonal skills, and problem-solving capabilities. It is assumed that such skills are critical to creating conditions that encourage cooperation rather than competition among workers, collective identity and commitment relevant to the organizational mission, and a personal sense of being responsible for and diagnosing the ways by which the organization can become more productive and effective (Wood, 1990).

A regulatory model, in contrast to the developmental model just described, is seen as being more concerned with the processes and rules of competition rather than the substance. Issues about antitrust regulations, antimonopolistic power in the marketplace, and the separation of government functions and influences from those of the private, corporate sector are addressed with intensity, legislation, and punishment, if breached. Certainly this is not so in the same ways in Japan. In the perspective of some observers the regulatory model assumes that individuals or organizations will constantly try to "beat the system," to abuse power, and, therefore, they must be regulated in order to promote equity, access, and fairness in competition (Fallows, 1989). But, somewhat paradoxically, in the United States and in a regulatory model, considerable expenditures occur in legal services and in the creation of bureaucratic structures by which to monitor, interpret, and implement regulations while at the same time developing mechanisms by which to stimulate a constant search for short-term profits in which individual workers are expected to be aggressive risk takers and to manifest relative autonomy as they pursue individual achievement and as they apply their personal ability to cope with market forces and the competition from other firms.

It would be inaccurate to argue that a developmental model and a regulatory model are extreme points of a dichotomy and as such they describe perfectly the differences that characterize the sociology of work in the United States and Japan. They are not. They are rather on a continuum of difference that emanates from historical, political, and cultural differences in beliefs about work and work organizations. Indeed, Hodson and Sullivan (1990) have examined in a comprehensive fashion work practices across the global economy. In doing so they distinguish industrial relations in the least developed nations and in the more advanced developing nations. Within these emphases they compare sociological perspectives in the developed economies through a variety of lenses: state-regulated capitalism, macroplanning, codetermination, autonomous work groups, state-planned economies, and worker self-management. Discovering and applying these differences in the work culture, in work groups, and in work outcomes, as these constitute the sociology of work in specific nations or cultures, are important foundational content for workforce education. This is true for many reasons but, perhaps significantly, because the sociology of work differs not only in selected cross-national comparisons but also across industries in the United States. The models of work organization, expected individual work behavior, and the network of roles in which workers perform is not the same in the construction industry, the transportation industry, the health care industry, or in retailing and financial services. Each of these industries manifests a somewhat different sociology of work that persons engaged in workforce education and development need to anticipate and study as relevant.

Technology, Information, and Power

A further example of a major emphasis in the sociology of work is how advanced technology has changed the distributions of power and information in organizations as well as how it has changed the preparation for work. For example, as more work activity is information-based and more workers are using computers and other forms of advanced technology to implement the work processes for which they are accountable, more persons in a plant or firm are sharing larger quantities of information. Because, in the past, power has frequently rested on possessing restricted information that was held only in the hands of managers or other executives, as information is more widely held by workers at lower levels in the work organization, there is a diffusion of power. In essence, the implementation of computers has redefined the social role of workers, modified the work environment, changed the social relationships among workers in organizations, and changed the flow and exchange of communications and information within organizations. For some workers the installation of computers in the workplace has engendered more autonomy, but for others it has placed them within new forms of monitored worker productivity, surveillance of worker behavior, social or organizational control, and an altering of employee and management relationships (Jackson, 1987).

The inclusion of computers and other advanced technology in the workplace has changed the mix of jobs available in the American occupational structure and blurred boundaries, not only between management and employers but also between different occupational classifications of workers. For example, by the year 2000, the automotive assembly plant and the tasks performed by workers on the assembly line will be dramatically different from what was true in the 1980s or even early 1990s. In the latter period, workers on the automotive assembly line were still installing automotive parts manually as a total car was assembled on the line. In the year 2000 much, if not all, of the fabrication, assembly, and finishing of an automobile will be done by robots, monitored and directed by computers. In most instances during these processes humans will rarely, if ever, touch an automobile as it is being assembled. Rather they will program and maintain the computers and robots that perform these tasks. In such contexts, even though the worker is still classified as engaged in manufacturing and automotive assembly, what that person is actually doing is akin to that of a service industry, to applying information and knowledge to program, operate, and service computers and other forms of advanced technology.

Stress in the Workplace

At a minimum, then, the intensity of the implementation of advanced technology has altered the work environment, the language of the workplace, communications among workers and management, the nature of the work organization itself, and the mix of jobs available in the United States and in other countries as the reach of advanced technology becomes worldwide. It has also introduced new forms of stress to the workplace and it has, in general, been responsible for a rise in educational requirements expected of workers in many occupations.

The Office of Technology Assessment (1988) has asserted that stress resulting from working conditions has become a major health hazard, resulting in stress-related absenteeism and medical expenses. In addition, alcoholism and drug abuse may be related to job-induced stress. Although uncertainty in the American economy has often been greater, pressures can increase in periods of rapid change. Rapid change in working environments and management practices can lead to stress. Many new office jobs result in increased responsibility without increased authority—a combination that easily leads to stress (390–391).

Another factor likely to increase stress in contemporary workers is the rise in educational requirements associated with emerging occupations and with those occupations being redesigned to become more technologically intensive. For more than a decade in the United States, the average education or skill level required for employment has steadily increased. This phenomenon has occurred, at least partially, because many unskilled and semiskilled jobs have been eliminated by the use of technology in the United States or they have been exported to overseas locations, thereby pushing up the levels of education required by the jobs that remain. Another factor is that, although there will remain many jobs requiring a minimum education, particularly in the service sectors, new jobs being created require functional competence in reading, writing, communications, and frequently in computer literacy. In these emerging jobs, knowledge is replacing experience as the basic requisite for employment throughout the workforce (Drucker, 1989; Toffler, 1990). Technical skills learned at a postsecondary level, not necessarily college, are becoming the expectation for high-skills/high-wage employment in many occupations, including skilled workers and technicians. These rises in educational requirements are occurring throughout the world as it has become increasingly accepted that the primary asset of a nation hoping to be a central player in the global economy is not its raw materials or even its capital resources but rather the literacy, numeracy, teachability, and flexibility of its workforce.

The modifications in the workplace, in communications, and in information flow among workers and among workers and managers in the amount and types of stress in changing work environments, in the shifting classifications and availability of jobs, and in the rising educational requirements in the workplace lend themselves to sociological study and explanation. Although each of these shifts ultimately has direct effects on individual workers and their family members, sociologists, by definition, are more likely to be concerned about the nature of these changing work contexts, the effects of social forces on the organization of work, and the social relations and communications among workers. Clearly, the new factors that have emerged as preeminent sociological problems in work as a social institution are the pervasive impact of advanced technology and a changing international and political environment to which domestic work organizations and workers must accommodate.

SOCIAL CLASS, WORKFORCE EDUCATION STUDENTS, AND WORK

However important sociological perspectives are on the organization of work and the contemporary forces affecting such organization, there are other important applications of such perspectives as well. For much of the history of workforce education, particularly as it has appeared in the secondary school in vocational education curricula, there have been concerns that vocational education was a dumping ground for students of low achievement (Aring, 1993) or that it tended to recruit students of low socioeconomic background into vocational education and thereby limit their opportunities for social mobility. Such views tend to be borne out when one views selected profiles of students who take academic or college preparatory curricula in high school in contrast with those students who major in vocational education. For example, Berryman (1982) reported that these contrasts showed the following for vocational students:

- They demonstrate substantially lower school performance and measured ability than academic students.
- They derive from families of much lower socioeconomic status than those of academic students.
- They show more self-esteem than academic students but have less sense of control over events that affect them.
- They value occupational security and family happiness more than academic students.
- They value occupational contacts and steady progress in work more than the academic group.
- They participate in extracurricular activities less than academic students.
- Their postsecondary plans differ substantially from academic students.

Berryman (1982) summarized her findings by stating that,

When we look at this array of variables, we see a group that, relative to one or both of the other curricula groups, comes from the economically lower-status families in the community; does not do well at what schools tend to define as their highest status mission—cognitive development. This group is not part of the high school's extracurricular structure except for that part directly related to the vocational curriculum, it rates the quality of the school positively, is not alienated from the high school, does not regard itself as having been channeled into its curriculum, wants money, steady work, and a happy family life, prefers to work after high school, selects practical (technical/vocational) postsecondary education, has higher postsecondary employment rates and a higher number of hours worked per week and is more satisfied with jobs as a whole and with their specific dimensions. (p. 184)

Other studies of vocational education students show some greater heterogeneity among such students than does the research of Berryman. For example, Dayton and Feldhauser (1989) have reported on the presence of gifted students in vocational education as defined by their high level of academic talent and ability, vocational talent, high level of motivation, persistence, study skills, and leadership. The National Center for Educational Statistics has reported that,

The vocational curriculum appeals to a diverse group of students. Individuals from all racial-ethnic backgrounds and all levels of academic ability and socioeconomic status take vocational "education courses." But, these data also show that participation in most vocational areas decreases as students, socioeconomic status, academic ability, and high school grades increase. Graduates in the highest socioeconomic, academic quartile, or those who mostly earn As in high school, are less likely than students with lower socioeconomic status, academic ability, and grades to participate in vocational education. (p. xxii)

A sociologist who looks at these data may interpret them in a number of ways. One would be to characterize students in vocational education as being predominantly from low socioeconomic environments, carrying out the implications of family influence to pursue blue-collar jobs in the trades and technical areas. This could possibly be because their fathers are engaged in such an occupation or because there are no role models in the students' environment that demonstrate how to pursue other occupations of a managerial or professional nature. Sociologists might suggest that these students lack information about possibilities other than vocational education or that employers, because of ageism or other prejudices against lower socioeconomic youth, have deliberately or inadvertently created obstacles to their mobility and further education. Such hypotheses would each be accurate for some students. Certainly, information about a spectrum of educational and occupational possibilities through role models in one's immediate environment, positive counselor contact, or systematic exploration opportunities has been shown to be less available for most students in vocational curricula than for students in college preparatory programs (e.g., Herr, Weitz, Good & McCloskey, 1981; the Business Advisory Committee, the Education Commission of the States, 1985; the Research Policy Committee, the Committee for Economic Development, 1985).

FAMILY INFLUENCES OF WORK
AND STATUS ATTAINMENT

In such contexts, existing research findings suggest that family socioeconomic status is comprehensively related to the career development, socialization, and career choices of children. This basic sociological postulate, called the status attainment model, contends that "the social status of one's parents affects the level of schooling one achieves, which in turn, affects the occupational level that one achieves" (Hotchkiss & Borow, 1990: 267). More recent studies have expanded this fundamental concept to include greater attention to socio/psychological processes and mental ability as parts of this model of family status and occupational attainment (Sewell & Houser, 1975; Alexander & Palla, 1984). In addition, there are a number of perspectives that relate the influence of parents' socioeconomic status to the assignment of the student to an ability group in elementary school and subsequently to placement within a curriculum track in high school. In turn, the track a student pursues in the secondary school has a great deal to do with the type of academic learning to which one is exposed, whether or not one is likely to drop out or persist to high school graduation, and the total amount of education one ultimately completes. These curriculum choices in the secondary school tend to be proxies by which parents' socioeconomic status is linked to students' learning and aspirations in elementary and secondary schools and ultimately to their adult attainments (Vanfossen, Jones & Spade, 1987; Gamoran & Mare, 1989; Lee & Bryk, 1988; Garet & DeLany, 1988). Embedded in the socioeconomic status of families are many other issues and possibilities. Socioeconomic differences are associated with differences in information one acquires about work, the types of work experience one has access to, and the development of occupational stereotypes that, in turn, affect the development of vocational interests.

These exploratory experiences and the attitudes toward types of work available and for which one is "worthy," start early and differ in the educational experiences and content pursued. For example, McKay and Miller (1982) found in their research that elementary school children from middle and upper socioeconomic backgrounds choose white-collar and professional occupations as goals more often than children from lower socioeconomic backgrounds; that these attitudes are firmly established by the time a child is in grade 3, and that there is a positive relationship between socioeconomic level and the complexity of the data used to make occupational choices.

Friesen (1986) has contended that in trying to understand the positive effects between socioeconomic status in families and the vocational attainment of children, it is necessary to consider both opportunity and process issues. In the first instance the higher the socioeconomic status (SES) of the family, the more likely parents are to have the resources to finance educational opportunities that lead to higher status occupations. In addition, different socialization patterns exist among SES groups. As examples, middle-class parents tend to value self-direction in their children, and lower SES parents tend to value conformity. Other research has shown that parents reinforce behaviors or goals differently in sons and daughters, which leads to differences in career development (e.g., Schulenberg, Vondracek & Crouter, 1984; Bloch, 1983). The family's influence, both in SES terms and in other ways, has shown that familial dynamics and the process of career decision making are intertwined and can be related to difficulty by their children in making decisions about their careers and to career indecision (Kinnier, Brigman & Noble, 1990) and that occupational preference is socially constructed and is highly influenced by the career decision maker's expectations of approval from significant others for making certain occupational choices (Rockwell, 1987). Obviously, depending on the family's vision of the acceptability of the choice of vocational or other forms of workforce education, that choice may or may not be reinforced by a particular family or, indeed, even allowed into consideration by the student as a viable possibility.

Implicit in such views of family influence on choices of occupations and educational pathways is the reality that socioeconomic classes, however defined, differ in their values and behavior. Persons whose social class backgrounds can be described as lower, middle, or upper class or some combination thereof (e.g., lower middle) are distributed differently across occupational types and levels. For example, Evans and Herr (1978: 120) observe that, "Managers and professionals tend to be upper class or upper middle class. Skilled workers, semiprofessionals, small proprietors, and white collar workers most frequently are lower middle class. Semiskilled workers are frequently upper lower class, and those people who work only when they choose to do so are usually lower lower class." Although they are not precise or without exceptions, such a relationship of social class to occupation has at least two dimensions. One, what is the social class of origin when a child or adolescent is making occupational and other career choices? Two, what is the likelihood that one can change one's social class through occupational mobility? Taking the second question first, it is clear that persons can exceed their parents' social class through substantial education, hard work, self-discipline, chance, and other factors related to occupational mobility. Opportunity for such occupational mobility and the higher income, material possessions, and status that accompany it have long been a professed article of faith in the historical and political metaphors that are used to describe the United States. Certainly, in comparison with nations in which class boundaries are more rigid or virtually impenetrable, the United States does allow for occupational and status mobility, even though it is not easy. The other issue has to do with the social class of parents or a family household at the point of an educational or occupational decision. Whether the parents have been born and remained in a particular occupational class or risen in social class through the factors described, the attained social class is related to what parents are likely to advocate for choice among their children or other family members. Thus, middle- and upper-class parents tend to desire that their children obtain white-collar, managerial, and professional occupations and to do so by attending college and graduate school. Within such perspectives vocational education, as a subset of workforce education, has historically been focused on occupations that lead people to lower middle-class status or, for adults, to provide the skills necessary to cope with technological change or other factors that, if such education and skills were not obtained, could reduce the occupational and socioeconomic status of the worker. Indeed, one of the unclaimed outcomes of vocational education has been its demonstrated ability to increase a student's social class (particularly from lower class to lower middle class) by providing the technical skills required of skilled workers, semiprofessionals, technicians, small proprietors, and many white-collar occupations (Evans & Herr, 1978).

From a sociological perspective, the family is a facilitator, and particular family members may be role models of experience that limits or expands the knowledge and support of family member choices of educational and occupational options. The family is also the locus of reinforcements, contingencies, and expectations that subtly or directly shape work choice and behavior, and the family is a conduit for the attribution of socioeconomic status to children. In addition, the home is a workplace, a center in which social and occupational roles are modeled and given validity by the members of the nuclear family or by the network of relatives, friends, and acquaintances with which this unit interacts (Herr & Lear, 1984).

From a sociological perspective, as suggested above, the breadth and the specific substance of the individual's family, culture, or social class boundaries have much to do with the choices that can be considered, made, and implemented. The specific factors that operate in the lives of an individual are likely to include some combination of social class membership; home influences; school achievement, values, and faculty or peer influences; community opportunities available and values; range and characteristics of exploratory opportunities and role models available; and role perceptions of the individual relative to leadership and technical self-efficacy. Although these operate with different intensity and content in the lives of individuals, a consistent finding is that social class factors create barriers or open possibilities that tend to overarch the other sociological factors identified. Members of lower social classes, and particularly those from a culture of poverty, experience more undesirable life events; are more vulnerable to life stressors; receive different information about the world of work and pathways to it; receive less education, training, and counseling; and have a more fragile sense of control than their more economically advantaged contemporaries. As a result social class and racial differences are found in the amount of unemployment, resources available, and in the transition from school to work. Strong and comprehensive programs of workforce education have the promise of neutralizing the types of deficits that many persons from lower socioeconomic backgrounds experience as they consider educational possibilities and occupational options.

WORK ATTAINMENT

Hotchkiss and Borow (1990: 262) have described the work of sociologists as investigating the characteristics and behavior of people in organized groups, for example, in the family and in economic groups, including the workplace, and in identifying "the principles that govern the beliefs and conduct of group members in each of these institutional settings."

With particular attention to how the sociology of work differs from the psychology of career development, which is discussed in Chapter 7, Hotchkiss and

Borow discuss three major dissimilarities. One is that sociologists, unlike most psychologists, are particularly concerned with power and authority as well as with how these are reflected in the status hierarchy in the workplace, how the work-socialization process occurs, the role of such mechanisms as labor unions and collective bargaining, how the labor market operates, and the related issues of job satisfaction, work alienation, and occupational mobility and career patterns.

A second difference between sociologists studying work and psychologists is where the major emphasis should be placed on the influences that affect individual choice making about work. Typically, psychological theories related to career development assign major importance to individual action and motivation in which individuals have at least some control over the choices they make in spite of the external obstacles that may prevail in given circumstances. Sociological theories, in contrast, would give much greater weight to the role of institutional factors, market forces, and the availability and timeliness of opportunity than to the power of individual action. It is in this context that some sociologists would argue that the developmental and psychological notions of individual choice that undergird some approaches to career guidance are unrealistic. Perhaps the classic sociological view of this matter has been captured by British sociologist Kenneth Roberts.

In Roberts's view (1977) most people do not choose, in any precise sense of that term. Instead, they are chosen or act when opportunities arise. He summarizes the point as follows:

> *The notion that young people possess freedom of choice and that they can select careers for themselves upon the basis of their own preference is pure myth. It is not choice but opportunity that governs the manner in which many young people make their entry into employment. (p. 145)*

Roberts goes on to contend that the factors that are of major consequence in implementing his opportunity model are mechanisms of educational selection, the patterns of recruitment into different types of employment, home background, and other social culture factors. Although he does not address these explicitly, his model would incorporate the importance of socioeconomic class and family characteristics discussed previously as major influences on who finds access to, and mobility in, work. Thus, Roberts's view, although of particular importance at the point of entrance to the workplace or the labor force, also has implications for human resource management at various transitions in the employee's working life as institutional or work organization shifts occur (e.g., downsizing and the use of contingency or temporary workers to replace core, long-term workers) and change the opportunity structure. In Roberts's terms these factors also affect who will be chosen to continue to work, to advance, or to be unemployed.

Whether one embraces the sociological perspective advocated by Roberts and others who share his view about the importance of social structure factors in work attainment, there are corollary perspectives. One is that social structure factors found in a complex socioeconomic stratification system, such as that of the contemporary United States, is also a complex generator, filter, and dispenser of information. In essence, one's position in the SES strata of the nation has much to do with the kind of information one gets; the alternative opportunities one knows about and can consider; the overt or subtle barriers that one will face in seeking access to, or mobility in, work; and the kind of encouragement for certain actions one is likely to receive from family members, schools, peer groups, or communities. Thus, persons are often, if not generally, selectively informed, reinforced, or rewarded for certain types of behavior, depending on the SES, gender, racial or ethnic, religious, or ability group to which they belong.

A third major difference has to do with how sociologists and psychologists view the cause and effect relationships that shape work attainment, job performance, and job satisfaction. Again, psychologists tend to focus on how individual differences in attitudes, aptitudes, values, and interests affect choice of success in training, work performance, satisfaction, and job. Sociologists take a more contextual view that gives emphasis to how supply and demand, formal rules, and informal and other institutional policies and actions shape what work is available for individuals and how they attain and perform it.

WORK AND SOCIAL STRATIFICATION

One of the major characteristics of the sociology of work is the emphasis it places on paid employment and occupational choice as functioning within, and interacting with, a broad system of social stratification. Such views are additional ways to emphasize the importance of structural factors that influence individual choices and that relate to status attainment in the labor force or a particular workplace.

Sociological research in social stratification, status attainment, and structural approaches has different emphases. An important one is the attempt to examine how occupational fields differ in the social structure, structural factors, and job structures that comprise them. For example, what are the rules of access or the educational prerequisites to entering one occupation as compared to another (e.g., becoming a physician versus becoming a construction superintendent)? What is the social status ascribed to each? Who gains access and typifies the characteristics of workers in the occupation? What are the barriers, real or covert, to minority member access or access by persons described in other ways? What are the structural steps in an occupational career that relate to social stratification (e.g., apprentice/intern, journey person/resident, master/fully licensed, supervisor/department head)? Some of these structures facilitate or impede individual status attainment. Some of these structures affect access to an occupation and performance of the work, whereas others affect one's sense of well-being or job satisfaction in work. The latter include the type of career ladder that is available, the chances of advancement, the intensity of continuing education required to do the job and the availability of opportunities to acquire it, the clarity of requirements needed to become a supervisor or manager, the sense of fit with and contribution made to an organizational mission, the prospects for future earnings and how they are achieved, benefits provided for oneself and one's family, job security, and the presence or absence of discrimination.

In some theoretical perspectives, sociological theory and economic theory interact, although with some tension because of the different emphases on structural barriers and influences on social stratification each represents. One of these conceptual examples is human capital theory, which essentially contends that individuals invest in their own productivity in order to maximize their lifetime earnings. Typically included are individual expenditures for education and delayed or foregone earnings during a period of investment, for example, while going to a postsecondary trade school or to college. Sometimes expenditures on health care and travel costs to another location to improve earning power are included as investments in human capital theory. But the primary investment of interest to theorists is education, its form and substance and its relation to subsequent earnings and other forms of productivity.

Sociologists both criticize and incorporate elements of human capital theory. In the first instance, they argue that human capital theory places too much emphasis on the ability of individuals to choose jobs, to choose in ways to optimize their work attainment and to make rational decisions by which to match their personal profile of attributes (e.g., interests, aptitudes) to those required by jobs and occupations. In such perspectives, economic approaches to human capital theory, as just described, have more similarity to many of the psychological concepts of career development that are major theoretical assumptions on which career counseling and career guidance rest than they do to sociological perspectives about contextual and structural factors in choice. But the utility of human capital theory to sociologists is that inherent in its depiction of individual investments in education and other costs to improve occupational attainment and productivity is the likelihood that certain structural barriers and attitudes will nullify the effects of such investments on the attainments sought. For example, women or minority males may invest in schooling that they expect will prepare them for entrance into occupations that allow them to acquire earnings that they desire. While this rationale is economically and psychologically viable, sociologists may say that such a view does not attend sufficiently to the likelihood that many desired occupations will impose barriers on the ease of women or minority male access or on their occupational mobility beyond a particular level of attainment. As an example of such phenomena there is the possibility that, for persons investing in workforce education rather than in some other form of education investment as their way to maximize their earnings and to acquire access to a desirable occupation, societal stereotypes about the value of workforce education or incorrect information about its clear and positive relationship to future earnings (see Chapter 4) will nullify the potential benefits of such a decision for an individual or be used as information by policy makers to make decisions to limit the workforce options available.

SUMMARY AND IMPLICATIONS FOR PRACTITIONERS

This chapter has focused on examining some of the major constructs and theories that comprise the sociological foundations of workforce education. Although deserving of a more exhaustive analysis of many of the sociological concepts that are important to workforce education, several major points are of particular relevance here. One is that sociological foundations emphasize that neither workforce education nor the types of work available, the stability of jobs, and who obtains access to, and mobility in, the workplace occur in a vacuum. Such processes and institutions occur within a complex set of social forces and structural elements. If workforce education is to be successful, it must be attentive to the social policies as well as to the social stereotypes that affect its function and substance.

Sociological foundations also describe work as occurring within a network of roles and social relations. Again, if workforce education, or human resource management, is to be effective, it must teach students that work preparation cannot be confined to technical content alone but must also attend to the interpersonal skills and understanding of organizational mission and context that are essential to the worker's ability to cooperate with coworkers, customers, and supervisors and to adapt to the organizational culture in which work takes place.

Sociological perspectives provide insight into the importance of parent and family characteristics, socioeconomic status, race, and gender in predicting how occupational preferences and interests are formed and how these factors operate in facilitating or impairing entrance to, and mobility within, the occupational structure. Workforce education can provide information and skills that can help workers to neutralize SES and other structural barriers to work attainment and advancement.

Sociological research about the characteristics of the occupational structure provides insights into its divisions into core and periphery firms, primary and secondary labor markets, and the different requirements each has for workforce education. Such occupational classifications carry implications for the different types of work performed, structural elements of income and fringe benefits, comprehensiveness of career ladders and mobility, and who is likely to be employed in each of these sectors.

Finally, sociological perspectives demonstrate that workforce education must be a dynamic, not a static, process. Analyses of the changes in the occupational opportunity structure, the requirements of workers, the nature of work organizations, the implications of integrating advanced technology into the workplace, and related processes accent the reality that workforce educators in their planning and implementation of instruction must be willing to respond to a world economic structure in significant flux.

7

CAREER DEVELOPMENT THEORY

A third area of foundational knowledge for workforce educators is Career Development Theory. To be accurate, there is not one career development theory per se; there are theories devoted to different aspects of career or work behavior. Some of these theories attempt to describe the influences or factors that shape and motivate career behavior; others describe the structural characteristics of career behavior (e.g., career maturity) that are sought in workforce education or in other approaches to human resource development. Some theoretical approaches to career development focus on the centrality or meaning of work in people's lives; how career behavior unfolds over the life span; how people choose certain kinds of work; how they are inducted into work and adjust to it in the workplace; and the types of problems that people experience as they choose, prepare for, and enter, and adapt to work.

As suggested above, the types of concerns that are addressed in career development theories are fundamental to the knowledge base for persons engaged in workforce education. If one is going to prepare for jobs in the workforce, it is important to think about such issues as how central work is in people's lives, what kind of career patterns there are in different occupations and workplaces, why career behavior differs among individuals, the implications of matching people and work environments, and the knowledge, skills, and attitudes of importance in employability and occupational mobility. In many ways, such knowledge about career behavior is as important in workforce education as is the technical content of work performance. This is so because career behavior, for example, one's attitudes about and understanding of the organization in which one works, mediates how well and how enthusiastically one performs one's job. Put somewhat differently, it is possible to train a person to be the finest machinist in the world from a technical standpoint, but if the individual does not value being a machinist, did not choose and make a commitment to this type of work, is unwilling to be punctual in getting to work and remaining at work all day five days a week, it is very unlikely that this particular person will be a successful or satisfied machinist. Career attitudes have, in this case, been more important than technical skills and, as such, have reduced the purpose and productivity of this individual in this job. Thus, the excellent technical training of this individual was nullified because the person's interests, values, commitments, and work habits did not meet the expectations of the work environment, nor did they reinforce being a successful machinist.

As this simple example suggests, career behavior and the broader processes of career development are complex. So are the theories that seek to explain career development. They occur with roots in many disciplines, including those in the foundational areas described in the preceding three chapters, namely, economics and sociology. But career development theories exist as well in various branches of psychology (e.g., differential, developmental), history, mathematics, political science, anthropology, and other branches of the social sciences. Because work and its pervasive effects on human identity, motivation, economic well-being, and self-worth are so embedded in all human societies, each of the major social sciences has viewed career behavior as a topic of significance to which a given discipline provides a lens through which its implications for human behavior can be appraised and understood.

The interdisciplinary nature of career development theory, as just described, has been characterized by Super (1990) as follows:

> *The pioneers of career development are people from four disciplines. They are differential psychologists interested in work and occupations, developmental psychologists concerned with "the life course," sociologists focusing on occupational mobility as a function of social class, and personality theorists who view individuals as organizers of experience.* (p. 197)

These and other interdisciplinary emphases suggest that each of the theoretical or disciplinary "windows" used to explain career or work behavior has its own contribution to make to understanding such behavior in a particular population, setting, or developmental period. It also means that no particular discipline or career development theory is sufficient to explain the totality of individual or group career behavior. Therefore, because of the large number of research studies and conceptual attempts to explain career behavior and the limited space in one chapter to explore all of this interdisciplinary material, it is helpful to classify the major career development theories into families or categories of theories that permit their major perspectives to be more easily understood and applied to workforce education. There are many ways to classify career development theories. One way is to divide them into those that are psychological in origin and those that are not. The latter would include those that are economic or sociological in origin. Or one might classify such theories into two main approaches—the developmental and the differential—as have Holland and Gottfredson (1976). Super has suggested that one can place these theories into three main categories: "those that match people and occupations, those that describe development leading to matching, and those that focus on decision making" (1981: 8). For the purposes of this chapter, however, a classification structure will be used that addresses both the disciplinary origins and the conceptual emphases of career development theories (Herr & Cramer, 1996) as they can be divided into five theoretical groups: trait and factor, decision making, situational or sociological, personality, and developmental.

CAREER, SELF-WORTH, AND MOTIVATION

Before turning directly to the different theoretical treatments of career development, it is useful to discuss a bit further the language and importance of such concepts as career, self-worth, and motivation.

In the United States and other industrialized societies the type of work one does is perhaps the most pervasive way people identify themselves: I am a welder, an accountant, a computer operator. In a technical sense these terms really describe jobs or occupations, not careers. A *job* is usually considered to describe paid positions or a similar group of tasks performed by one person that occur in a single organization. Thus, in these terms, the welder or computer operator just identified could be described as jobs in a single organization or workplace. However, they must also qualify to be identified as an *occupation*, a group of similar jobs found in different industries or organizations. Accounting is clearly an occupation that exists across industries or organizations. One of the important characteristics of jobs or occupations is that they occur independent of any individual. Jobs and occupations exist whether people occupy them, whether they are vacant or filled. Jobs or occupations can be classified in directories or work orders from employers, and they can be chosen by persons qualified to perform the tasks they represent. Jobs or occupations can be compared or contrasted in terms of the performance content or occupational activity they represent.

The concept of *career* is different from that of either a job or an occupation. Although we frequently use the term career interchangeably with "job" or "occupation," in a theoretical sense, these terms are different. For example, a career really is not independent of the person who constructs it. In this sense one does not select a career as one selects a job or occupation; one forges or creates a career over time by the decisions one makes about specific jobs, or occupations, or the firms for which one works. In such a view careers are unique to each person and are created by what one chooses or avoids choosing. They are dynamic and unfold throughout life. Careers are also seen by many observers as including the integration of work roles with those of family or community roles. Viewed in this way, the term "career" is a lifestyle concept that is comprehensive in the roles it includes at a point in time or across time.

While there are many definitions of career, one of the most enduring is that promulgated by Super (1976):

> *A career is the course of events which constitutes a life; the sequence of occupations and other life roles which combine to express one's commitment to work in his or her total pattern of self-development; the series of remunerated and nonremunerated positions occupied by a person from adolescence through retirement, of which occupation is only one; includes work-related roles such as those of student, employee, and pensioner together with complementary avocational, familial, and civic roles. Careers exist only as people pursue them; they are person centered. (p. 4)*

This combination of concepts that define career suggests several important emphases. One is that careers are longitudinal, they occur across the life span, and they include the various jobs, occupations, educational, prevocational and postvocational roles in which the individual engages. But this definition of career suggests that it is probably better understood after the fact as the various elements making up a career have already occurred. This is true, again, because a career is created from interim decisions; it is not chosen per se. But this definition also suggests that people engage in different types of career paths—some are linear and smooth, others are jagged and impaired—and that these variations are related to many individual factors such as preparation, confidence, ability, planfulness, information, and other important factors. Some career patterns reinforce job satisfaction, motivation to be productive and purposeful, and a positive self-concept. Other patterns, unemployment, jagged or uncertain employment, dislike of job and job place, inadequate skills, and a lack of desired information can lead to feelings of job dissatisfaction, unproductive and floundering behavior, and a negative self-concept. Such negative or positive circumstances and consequences can be confined to only one point in time, or they can be true throughout much of one's working life span or career. Thus, the concept of jobs and occupations as discussed above has much to do with what is to be chosen; the concept of career as we have described it has to do with the characteristics of the chooser as he or she considers and selects what is to be chosen and how such a job or occupational option interacts with personal motivation, self-concept, and feelings of self-worth.

The connections between career, motivation, and self-worth are assumed to be reciprocal and interactive. For example, if one has a career comprising jobs and other roles that one values and that gratify one's economic, psychological, and emotional needs, one is likely to be positively motivated, satisfied, have a positive self-concept, feel positive self-worth, and feel good about one's present and future. But, in some ways, we know more about the important interactions between career, motivation, and self-worth when one's career does not go well, when one is not satisfied with one's job, or when one loses it.

Most of the work in which people engage involves person-environment fit and the interaction of the individual and the organization. The ingredients of this interaction can yield satisfaction or dissatisfaction, feelings of competence or inferiority, and motivation to be productive or work-alienated. For example, Dawis (1984) has reported research results that show that job dissatisfaction is related to mental and physical health problems, including psychosomatic illnesses, depression, anxiety, worry, tension, impaired interpersonal relationships, coronary heart disease, alcoholism, drug abuse, and suicide. Other research has addressed the negative outcomes of work stress and difficult working conditions (Keita & Sauter, 1992).

Research findings such as those of Dawis about the negative effects of job dissatisfaction or Keita and Sauter about job stress are among the elements that have allowed links to be made between career development and mental health (Herr, 1989b). Just as the research has shown the variety of negative outcomes associated with job dissatisfaction, that research has also shown that job satisfaction leads to positive outcomes: tenure, longevity, physical health, positive mental health, and productivity.

Probably the most dramatic examples of the importance of work and employment to positive self-concept and motivation can be derived from the findings about unemployment. In addition to the social and fiscal costs of unemployment to nations around the world, there are major individual costs of unemployment. Like those described as related to job dissatisfaction, the outcomes associated with unemployment further make the connection between career, motivation, and self-worth. For example, in an Australian study (Feather & O'Brien, 1986) that followed a large sample of school-leaving students from high school to employment or unemployment, it was found that unemployment led to decreases in perceived competence, activity, and life satisfaction and an increase in depressive affect. Multiple studies of unemployed adults in the United States and in other nations have found that prolonged unemployment frequently is characterized by periods of apathy alternating with anger, sadness, sporadic optimism, few meaningful personal contacts, ominous feelings of victimization, lack of personal power, and low self-worth (Schlossberg & Leibowitz, 1980; Herr, 1989b). Borgen and Amundson (1984) depict the experience of unemployment as an "emotional roller coaster" that is comparable in its impact and stages to those found by Kübler-Ross (1969) in describing the grief process associated with loss of a loved one: denial, anger, bargaining, depression, and acceptance. In reviews of other studies of unemployment, there are reports of rises in first admissions to psychiatric hospitals; increased deaths from cardiovascular and alcohol-related diseases; imprisonment; sharp increases in suicide rates, chemical dependency and violence; and increased reports of depression, anxiety, and interpersonal problems by spouses as unemployment continues (Herr & Cramer, 1996).

Although many more studies could be cited which tie the status of individual career development to individual mental health, the findings reported here clearly affirm that career development, motivation, and self-worth are linked and interactive. Therefore, within this context, workforce education practitioners and students need to be aware of the importance of effective person-job fit, the power of decisions about jobs and occupations to either create or to impair career patterns, the impact of personality characteristics on choices made, and the importance of acquiring the opportunities for exploration, reality testing, career planning, and information relevant to the choices made. In brief terms, these are the types of emphases to be discussed in the career development theories presented in the next section.

CAREER DEVELOPMENT THEORIES

Trait-and-Factor Theory

The trait-and-factor approach is probably the approach to career development that is most familiar to the workforce educator. Actually this approach is not focused on the development of career behavior per se but on identifying and describing the factors by which people differ and the degree to which these factors are important in learning or in job performance.

The logic of this approach is that individuals can be conceived of as composing a constellation of traits, aptitudes, interests, values, psychomotor abilities, energy levels, and temperaments, which can be observed and reliably measured. The assumption is that these patterns of personal traits are more or less unique to each individual. The further assumption is that the individual, if he or she understands the personal characteristics possessed, can order these into some priority ranking and choose in accordance with them.

Trait-and-factor approaches also assume that different occupational choices are primarily conscious and cognitive rather than psychological and emotional as some other approaches assert. Such a view suggests that learning situations can be described in terms of their unique requirements for different combinations or "quantities" of these individual characteristics. In essence, different occupational or educational options can be profiled in terms of those levels of individual behaviors or potential behaviors that are essential to performing whatever is required in such situations. The information used is that which comes from such sources as trade-competency examinations, job analysis, occupational aptitude profiles, or work sampling.

In addition, trait-and-factor approaches assume that occupational choice is primarily a function of matching the person's profile of characteristics with that set of occupational or educational requirements most closely related to it. The prediction is that the closer the congruency between the individual characteristics and the requirements of occupational or educational options available, the more likely it is that adjustment and success will result.

These dimensions of the trait-and-factor approach really derive from a major conceptual model that originated in the first decade of the twentieth century and has been important to workforce education, human resource development, career guidance, and employment selection and classification throughout the ensuing decades. In 1909, Frank Parsons, the "father of vocational guidance," enumerated in his classic book *Choosing a Vocation,* his three-step process of vocational guidance. As he defined it, that process involved

> *First, a clear understanding of yourself, aptitudes, abilities, interests, resources, limitations, and other qualities. Second, a knowledge of the requirements and conditions of success, advantages and disadvantages, compensation, opportunities, and prospects in different lines of work. Third, true reasoning on the relations of these two sets of facts. (p. 5)*

What Parsons outlined beyond a process of vocational guidance was a trait-and-factor, actuarial, or matching approach to career behavior. Such an approach assumes that the individual can be described as having certain traits (e.g., interests, skills, aptitudes) that the different occupations or educational alternatives available to the individual require differing amounts and configurations of such traits, and that by matching individual traits and the requirements of different occupational or educational opportunities through a process of true reasoning (or decision making) a choice would occur.

Parsons' approach, which was originally focused on vocational guidance and is now integrated into many models of career guidance, is based on differential psychology, that branch of psychology that is concerned with identifying and measuring individual differences. This approach has both shaped and been shaped by the psychometric or testing movement in vocational/career guidance and in workforce education.

One can argue that vocational psychology, from its beginnings at the end of the nineteenth century until about 1950, was a psychology of occupations, not of careers. The occupation was the subject, and the persons in it were the sources of data on the occupation. Thus, from a trait-and-factor, actuarial, or matching approach, predictions can be made using individual traits as predictors and the degree to which these traits are possessed by successful persons in different occupations as the criteria. The techniques and results of the many studies combining different traits and different occupational requirements also provide a means of appraising an individual's possibilities. In essence, such concepts underlie the system of occupational analysis and classification from which results the Department of Labor's *Dictionary of Occupational Titles,* Occupational Aptitude Profile System, *Occupational Outlook Handbook,* and other tools by which to match persons and work opportunities.

Trait-and-factor approaches have been a mainstay of many career guidance and employment selection systems since the turn of the twentieth century. They have spurred the development of tests and inventories to assess individual characteristics, the use of occupational information, the creation of predictive systems for assessing the weights of importance of individual traits in the accomplishment of different occupational tasks, and the establishment of counseling systems.

Even though the trait-and-factor approach has had considerable influence on American educational and occupational thought, many critics believe it to be too simplistic and too deterministic. Specifically, many theorists contend that a major limitation of the trait-and-factor approach is its implied assumption that either personal traits or environmental requirements are constant and unchangeable. Some adherents of the trait-and-factor approach behave as though an assessment of an individual's traits at a specific point in life is predictive of all future observations; however, such a position does not take into account the amount of change possible in a person or in educational and occupational requirements over time. Extending the point further, considering individual traits as "fixed effects" tends to underestimate the degree to which many such traits are learned or the degree to which they are latent until triggered through encouragement and other social stimuli.

Finally, matching individuals and jobs on the basis of an observable fit is seen as overly deterministic unless the person involved is an active participant in the choice. Frequently, one finds that what appears to be the best fit is not valued by the person involved, and thus success and adjustment do not result. In such instances it is not a matter of which is the best literal fit between an individual's characteristics and the requirements of different alternatives but rather how the available choices accord with the particular person's assessments of what such a fit should be.

Regardless of the criticisms or the limitations of the trait-and-factor approach, the informational base about people and the options available to them, which this approach stimulates, is an exceedingly important influence on career development. Virtually all of the other approaches to career development that follow include trait-and-factor information or procedures, but the emphases they give to its use vary markedly.

There is evidence to suggest that the trait-and-factor approach is being rediscovered and reconceptualized by theorists in its implications for career guidance and workforce education. For example, Chartrand (1991) has contended that contemporary trait-and-factor models have evolved into "person x environment" approaches. Integrating historical and contemporary trait-and-factor approaches, Chartrand (1991) has summarized the person x environment fit approach as follows:

> *First, people are viewed as capable of making rational decisions. This does not mean that affective processes can be ignored.... Second, people and work environments differ in reliable, meaningful, and consistent ways. This does not mean that "a single type of person works in each job." ...Third, the greater the congruence between personal characteristics and job characteristics, the greater the likelihood of success.... This means that knowledge of person and environment patterns can be used to inform people about the probability of satisfaction and adjustment in different educational and work settings. (p. 520)*

Perhaps the overarching point is that both historical and contemporary trait-and-factor perspectives have stimulated important research studies, procedures, and assessments related to individual differences in the predictor variables that play important roles in the choice of, preparation for, and success in education, training, and employment. As such they have made important contributions to the development of workforce education.

Decision Theory Approaches

A second major emphasis in career development theory is decision theory. Approaches that fall within this category tend to be more concerned with the process of decision making, the process of how people choose, than with individual traits or with occupational or educational requirements. Decision approaches have evolved from an original base in economics. More recently mathematical, industrial/psychological, and motivation models have been applied to the decision-making process. Such perspectives have emphasized the interaction of personal expectations that one can perform the work required and that the likely consequences or outcomes of such work will be valued as major elements leading to occupational choices. Such models also emphasize the importance of personally held beliefs or perceptions of self-efficacy as major ingredients of both motivation and choice. Such approaches have evolved from a long line of models of motivation that have been important in industrial psychology. For example, Lawler (1973) has distinguished two types of expectancies that guide choice of work. They are portrayed as (E–P) and (P–O). The first, Effort–Performance, emphasizes the important role played by choice in the person's estimate of the probability that he or she can accomplish the intended performance (e.g., meet deadlines, learn or perform the necessary technical procedures) required in the particular job.

The second, Performance–Outcomes, has to do with the importance of choice in subjective probability estimates that, if a particular performance is achieved, it will lead to certain outcomes (e.g., greater prestige, a pay raise, promotion, or some other outcome). Lawler concludes that motivation or choice is a function of the interaction of these two expectancies: first, that one believes that one can do what needs to be done to learn or perform a set of tasks or a job (what Bandura [1977] has described as self-efficacy) and, second, if one is able to perform the behavior required, that a desired outcome will result. In the latter case there arises the expectation that the probable outcome will be attractive to the individual and/or that it will fit with the individual's preferred values from work.

Such important perspectives help workforce educators and others conceive of how motivation and related decisions are developed and how they interact. But decision theories also provide other important concepts of use to workforce educators. For example, in most decision theory approaches the assumption is made that one chooses an educational or occupational goal that will maximize one's gain and minimize one's chance of loss. Obviously, what each person values or considers to be gain or loss is likely to be different in degree and kind. The gain or loss is not confined to money but can be anything of value to a particular person. A given occupation or an educational opportunity might be considered as a means of achieving many different possibilities—among them greater income, prestige, security, social mobility, and leisure time—when compared with another course of action.

The specific notion of a decision approach is that an individual has several possible "alternatives" or courses of action from which to choose. In each of these alternatives certain events can occur. These events have different values to the individual and different likelihoods of occurrence that can be estimated. If each possible event is multiplied by its value to the person and its probability of happening, the person can determine the alternative that is likely to have the greater sum of value to him or her.

A major assumption of decision theory is that individuals can be helped to choose more rationally by predicting the outcomes of each alternative available as well as the uncertainty and risk each involves. Such a position acknowledges, however, that decision making is often based largely on subjective grounds, on what the individual's perceptions of events and alternatives are rather than on what some form of test data or another person would say they are. Given such circumstances it has become an accepted principle that the kind of information one has, its accuracy and timeliness, and the way he or she uses it will affect decision outcomes.

In an early model of decision making, Gelatt (1962) has argued that information is the required fuel for the decision maker. He suggests that the process of deciding requires a "predictive system" (determining possible alternative actions, outcomes, and probabilities), a "value system" (determining the desirability associated with outcomes), and a "decision criterion" (leading to integration and selection of an appropriate action). Clark, Gelatt, and Levine (1965) contend that the two requirements of good decision making are adequate information and an effective way of analyzing, organizing, and synthesizing this information in order to arrive at a choice. They further suggest that bringing these requirements together means that the individual needs appropriate information in terms of (1) possible alternative actions, (2) possible outcomes of the various actions, (3) the relationships between actions and outcomes, and (4) the individual's relative preference for the different outcomes likely to occur.

The individual's interpretation of different actions and outcomes present at a choice-point involves two other concepts typically included in decision approaches. First is the matter of risk-taking style. People differ in their willingness to cope with ambiguity or uncertainty of outcomes. Some people prefer the security of knowing what they will be paid and that they are likely to have a permanent position rather than the possibility of greater rewards and the unknowns of variety and tenuousness. Second is the matter of investment. Emphasized in this notion is the fact that any choice requires both tangible and intangible investments by the chooser, for example, capital, prestige, time, tuition, union dues, and deferred gratification, all of which can be deliberately considered and valued.

Decision theory indicates that the choices people make are really public testimonies about how they view themselves (good, bad, competent, incompetent), how they view their opportunities (attractive, negative, wide-ranging, limited), and the relationships between them. Decisions are like the tips of icebergs: they represent, but do not convey, all of the hidden meanings of a choice, the factors that shape it, or the hope or despair that is associated with a particular choice.

In practical terms decision theory has stimulated many paradigms of the choice-making process for use in vocational/career guidance or in workforce education to stimulate effective individual planning for work. One such paradigm suggests that any decision problem can be described in terms of four elements (Pitz & Harren, 1980):

1. The set of *objectives* that the decision maker seeks to achieve
2. The set of *choices*, or alternative courses of action, among which the decision maker must choose
3. A set of possible *outcomes* that is associated with each choice and
4. The ways each outcome might be assessed with respect to how well it meets the decision maker's objectives. (pp. 321–322)

Another major paradigm that integrates decision theory and the sociological, situational perspective explored in the next section is the social learning approach of Krumboltz and his colleagues (Krumboltz, 1979; Mitchell & Krumboltz, 1984). This approach emphasizes that "people learn their preferences by interacting with their environment in a long and complex series of experiences" (Krumboltz, 1994: 17). More specifically, this approach identifies four categories of influences on career selection. They include (1) genetic endowment and special abilities encompassing such factors as race, sex, intelligence, and special abilities; (2) environmental conditions and events including the special efforts of the geography in which one grew up and was socialized, social policies, family characteristics, natural disasters or events, and technological developments; (3) instrumental and associative learning experiences such as modeling by others, observational learning, career skills learned through instrumental and reinforcement learning; and (4) task approach skills planning. The further assumption is that these four categories of influences will lead to three classes of outcomes: (1) Self-Observation Generalizations (SOGs)—overt or covert statements that tend to appraise or evaluate one's actual or vicarious performance against some set of learned standards; (2) Task Approach Skills (TASs)—skills by which the individual copes with the environment through such processes as alternative generating, estimating, information seeking, planning, goal setting; and (3) Actions—entry behaviors such as applying for a specific job or training opportunity or changing a college major.

Although theoretically important as a model of career selection, Krumboltz's learning principles have been seen by others as fundamental explanations of processes and mechanisms embedded in other theories of career development as well (Subich & Taylor, 1994).

Certainly one of the many contributions of Krumboltz's work is to describe the task approach skills by which the career decision making of students and adults can be improved. They include the following (Krumboltz, 1979):

1. Recognizing an important decision situation
2. Defining the decision or task manageably and realistically
3. Examining and accurately assessing self-observations and world-view generalizations
4. Generalizing a wide variety of alternatives
5. Gathering needed information about the alternatives
6. Determining information sources that are most reliable, accurate, and relevant
7. Planning and carrying out the above sequence of decision-making behaviors (p. 39)

Decision theory, then, has provided important insights into the process of decision making as well as into the ways such a process can be analyzed and made more effective on an individual or group basis. Such models have been helpful in creating a rationale as well as program themes for inclusion in approaches to career guidance, career education, the creation of computer-assisted career guidance systems, and workforce education.

Decision approaches stress the importance of personal values in choice. Unlike a simple translation of the fit between traits and occupational requirements as the major structure of decision making, the decision approach advocates an active assessment by the individual of the odds faced in any alternative. Such a deliberation is seen as placing personal values at the forefront of the process of decision making. Decision making includes the identifying and the defining of one's values: what they are and what they are not and where they appear and where they do not appear (Katz, 1963).

Situational or Sociological Approaches

As they have been discussed thus far, trait-and-factor approaches demonstrate that individuals do differ in traits that are measurable and that have relationships to performance and to satisfaction in different educational, job, and occupational tasks. In some contrast, decision theories combine to explain the influences of, and the steps in, the decision-making process itself as well as how persons integrate self-knowledge, knowledge of alternatives available to them, and their own self-perceptions, values, and preferences into a plan of action, a choice. Situational or sociological approaches add a further dimension to available understanding of life style and of career development. Chapter 6 has discussed in some length the important insights that sociology contributes to a foundational base for workforce education. In that chapter relatively little emphasis was given to how sociological perspectives are included in career development theory. We deal with such emphases in this chapter.

It can be argued that as one examines the predominant theories of career development that guide national approaches to workforce education or, for example, career guidance, the disciplinary emphases that are most evident are psychology and sociology. In nations, such as the United States, where individual action is seen as the most important factor in career development, psychological determinants of such behavior are the primary explanatory systems. But in nations in which caste or socioeconomic class, social policies, or institutional barriers are seen as mediating and shaping individual behavior, the primary explanatory systems are sociological. Whether the explanatory system for individual behavior is primarily psychological or sociological, both disciplines have offered important insights into a total view of career development and the influences on it. In particular, sociological perspectives emphasize the reality that individuals do not develop their feelings about their own competencies or preferences, their commitment to work and knowledge about its meaning and options, or their attempts to choose, prepare for, and enter and adapt to work in a vacuum: The development of individual career behavior and the career pattern that evolves over the course of the individual's life are functions of the transactions that choosers or workers have with their personal environments—family, community, social class, and economic and political events.

Situational or sociological approaches to career development accentuate the reality that one's environments both provide the kinds of choices—educational, occupational, lifestyle—from which an individual chooses and also, directly or indirectly, shape the likelihood that persons holding membership in different groups are likely to make certain choices, not others. A sociological or situational view of career development suggests that the narrowness or the breadth of the individual's cultural or social class boundaries has much to do with the choices a person is likely to consider, make, or implement. In this sense the social structure of a family, a school, a community, a work setting, or a nation can be seen as both a generator and a filter of information ultimately communicated to an individual (Borow, 1966, 1984). Thus, the information and the encouragement that the poor receive as compared with that available to persons occupying middle or upper socioeconomic classes are likely to differ in kind and in degree. The sources of information, the role models of successful accomplishment of different educational or work choices, and the subtle forms of reinforcement, to value some alternatives or goals rather than others, vary throughout the socioeconomic continuum. Similar differences in the types of information and encouragement available vary across racial groups, ethnic and religious groups, the abled and the disabled, and between males and females.

Sociological approaches to career development emphasize the fact that one cannot choose what one does not know about, does not know how to prepare for, or does not know how to obtain access to. Such differences in information and encouragement affect choice making, work adjustment, and lifestyle patterns. Thus, the characteristics of the individual's culture or social class boundaries have much to do with the choices a person is likely to consider, make, or implement. As Herr and Cramer (1988: 115) observe: "The social structure represents the context in which each person negotiates his or her identity, belief system, and life course."

To understand the functioning of or, indeed, the latency of any given individual's psychological characteristics—traits—it is important to consider the characteristics of the social grouping, the geographical setting and/or the historical period in which the individual has been born and reared. It is these elements, as they combine to create the individual's social context, which influence the self-image or, in the words of decision theory, one's feelings of self-efficacy with regard to various types of performance, the ranking of the personal traits one is likely to use in work, the educational and occupational alternatives one is likely to know about or consider appropriate, and the financial and psychological resources one is likely to have available.

Sociological perspectives provide insight into the family and historical influences on risk-taking behavior and the choice outcomes that different people value. If one's basic survival needs—food and shelter—have been met erratically, it is easy to understand why that person chooses jobs that offer stability and a secure, if modest, income. If one's family values have constantly reinforced a set of behavioral standards to be achieved in order to avoid tarnishing the family name or being considered unworthy of the family's support, it is understandable that one's motivation will differ from another whose environment has reinforced other behavioral standards. If one's gender and one's race has been an obstacle to access certain opportunities, it takes an extraordinary amount of desire, persistence, and ability to gain access to such opportunities. Sociological perspectives address the probability that, while career and lifestyle preferences of people across social and economic class lines may be similar, their expectations of being able to achieve such preferences are likely to differ. The person raised in an environment that does not support planfulness or commitment to long-range goals, does not value deferred gratification as a price one pays to achieve better skills or to save for a better future, or does not provide knowledge of how to cope effectively with the environment is going to experience aspirations and career development of a different character than an individual who experiences another set of environmental characteristics.

Sociological perspectives have a long and important history in their probing of the effects of social class on occupations chosen and on other characteristics of the acquisition of work identity and career mobility (e.g., Hollingshead, 1949; Hoggart, 1957; Lipsett, 1962; Blau, Gustad, Jessor, Parnes, & Wilcock, 1956). As was discussed in the chapter on sociological foundations, recent sociological perspectives have raised questions about whether the emphases in many current career development theories on the primacy of individual action and value preferences are valid. Roberts (1977), taking a sociological perspective, raises the implicit question as to whether people choose or are chosen; the latter conditions are a function of their socioeconomic status, class boundaries against choosing certain opportunities, or levels of aspiration and related phenomena.

The probable answer to Roberts's question is that some people choose their occupational and lifestyle roles, others do not. Increasingly, research studies are reinforcing the view that the kind and quality of exploratory experiences, understanding of work opportunities, decision making, and related elements of career behavior are experienced differently by groups that differ on socioeconomic, gender, and racial terms (Herr, Weitz, Good, & McCloskey, 1981; Herr & Cramer, 1996; Herr & Enderlein, 1976). A large number of research studies using different explanatory systems and focusing on different populations have shown that career development is not a smooth, linear progression to upward mobility. Rather, there are different patterns of continuity and discontinuity, of delay and impairment associated with economic advantagement or disadvantagement, gender, race, differences in educational and intellectual level. These, again, are sociological phenomena.

In an important sense, sociological perspectives emphasize that individual behavior, however it is defined, always occurs in a context. Sometimes the context encourages and rewards people; sometimes it demeans people and reduces their information and feelings of power to implement their aspirations. Workforce educators, training and development specialists, and human resource management personnel who take seriously the implications of sociological perspectives on career behavior can create in their content and instructional climate, as well as in training or human resource development (HRD) programs in workplaces, ways to provide students or employees timely and accurate information that maximizes individual career development, that neutralizes the irrational beliefs and feelings of low self-worth that many persons who enter workforce education bring with them, and that allows people to avoid accepting stereotypes about the gender, race, or socioeconomic group to which they belong that limits their opportunities and decreases their feelings of self-efficacy.

Personality Approaches

Sociological approaches to career development are, in a sense, macro approaches. They describe the social and institutional mechanisms within which individual action is possible or by which it is blocked, impeded, or circumscribed. Personality approaches may be considered micro approaches, attempts to identify individual psychological characteristics, as opposed to group mechanisms, that shape career behavior.

Personality approaches, as compared with the four other categories of career development theory discussed in this chapter, emphasize needs and drives intrinsic to individual personality that choices of work are consciously or unconsciously intended to satisfy. For example, they contrast with the trait-and-factor approach, which emphasizes observable and measurable behavior (rather than inferred states as in the personality approaches) to explain the motivations of people to choose and to behave as they do.

The advocates of intrinsic need or drive motivation come from a variety of conceptual origins. For example, those who favor Freudian psychoanalytic approaches to the explanation of work choice and adjustment would favor intrinsic drive states as stimuli to select one form of work rather than another (e.g., Bordin, Nachman, & Segal, 1963; Brill, 1948).

A prominent characteristic of approaches to occupational choice or career development of psychoanalytic as well as some other personality theories is the use of classifications of personality types or needs and the relating of these to gratifications available in different occupational or educational options. Depending on the particular orientation of the theorist, such classifications have different emphases. For example, theorists who view career development through a psychoanalytic lens tend to view the particular form of work chosen by an individual as a sublimation or socially acceptable channeling of specific gratifications remaining from unresolved early problems in psychosexual development. Psychoanalytically oriented theories of career behavior would argue that adult occupations are selected, consciously or unconsciously, for their instinctual gratification as need for these is developed in early childhood, particularly in the first six years of life.

The views of Freud on the psychodynamic interaction between individuals and their work environments, as important as they are, do not comprise all the important conceptions of need-drive perspectives. For example, Bordin, Nachman and Segal (1963) have systematically analyzed different occupations to determine their capability to gratify various individual impulses. In their conceptualization, which is trait-and-factor in format but not in content, they substitute for traits like interests and abilities individual modes of impulse gratification, the status of one's psychosexual development, and levels of anxiety. The means by which occupations can satisfy the profile of individual needs are their instrumental modes—tools, techniques, and behaviors used—and the objects dealt with—needs of clients, pipes and plumbing fixtures, and money.

In addition to the focus on instinctual gratification by Freud or the classification by Bordin, Nachman and Segal of how occupations can meet individual impulses, other thinkers, who were originally psychoanalytic in orientation, have made contributions to personality approaches to vocational development. One of these is Alfred Adler. In strong opposition to Freud's major premise that human behavior is essentially determined by inborn instincts, Adler believed that such behavior was motivated by social urges. He believed that human beings are products of both heredity and experience, which results in the self-concept as a stimulus to behavior, the ability to hold and plan for goals, and a subjective, creative system of behavior through which persons search for experiences that aid in fulfilling their unique style of life (Adler, 1935).

But there are other theorists—for example, neopsychoanalytic, self-theorists—who also embrace a need-drive explanation for much of career behavior. The general assumption among such approaches is that, because of differences in personality structure, individuals develop specific needs and seek satisfaction of these needs through job or occupation choices and selection of work settings. The further assumption is that different occupational or educational areas are populated by people of different needs or personality type. In the personality approach one of the major features is a self-classification, either conscious or unconscious, by which persons seek out environments that are likely to gratify their particular need profile.

Roe (1956), for example, is a theorist whose personality approach to career development bridged psychoanalytic and self-theory approaches. Her approach had three major aspects. First, she adapted the theory of prepotent needs, formulated by Maslow (1954), to vocational behavior. Oversimplifying the matter, the assumption is that persons tend to select work that reflects gratification of the level of needs that they feel is most urgent or not routinely gratified from among such need categories as psychological, safety, belongingness and love, self-esteem, information, beauty, and self-actualization. A second dimension of Roe's work is an emphasis on the effect of child-rearing practices on adult orientations to or away from people and things. Her basic premise was that child-rearing environments that were overprotecting, democratic, or rejecting shaped differently the kinds of interactions people have with other people—toward or away from them—and with things. In turn, these interactions were seen as manifested in adult interest patterns related to choice of occupational families that either emphasized working with others or alone with ideas and things. The third aspect of her work was to delineate a two-dimensional classification of occupational groups by field and level. The eight fields in which all occupations were grouped across a horizontal axis included service, business contact, organization, technology, outdoor, science, general culture, and arts and entertainment. These fields were classified by the degree to which they gratify needs involving people or things. It is assumed that the major variable affecting choice of a group is interest and that interest focus derives from early childhood experiences in the family. The second dimension, that of level, includes six different levels of responsibility, training, or education including professional and managerial I and II, semiprofessional, small business, skilled, semiskilled, and unskilled. The assumption of Roe's theory was that the occupational level attained is a function of genetic endowment as reflected in intelligence, education attained, and capability for responsibility; the field chosen is a function of one's interest or noninterest in people or things.

Holland's approach (1973, 1985; Holland & Gottfredson, 1990) is currently the preeminent and most empirically based personality approach. It gives major and explicit attention to individual behavioral predisposition and personality type. A basic assumption of the Holland approach is that, as a result of the interaction between heredity and environment, the individual develops a hierarchy of habitual or preferred methods for dealing with social and environmental tasks; these preferences are reflected in one's modal personal orientation. This modal personal orientation, or behavioral style, is classified into one of six personality categories—artistic, conventional, enterprising, investigative, realistic, or social. Rather than being pure types, the theory advances the notion that most persons can be classified in some distribution of emphasis across two or three of the personality types, for example, Realistic–Enterprising–Investigative (RIE), and that one will then seek occupations or educational settings that satisfy and are compatible with the hierarchy of preferences the individual possesses.

The other part of the Holland equation is classification of the environment in ways comparable to classification of personality. The assumption is that, because people seek out and gravitate to settings where others are seen as sharing one's values and interests with regard to work activity, leisure time, and so on, specific occupations or educational units tend to attract persons of similar personality types. As a result, different occupations or curricula are populated to a larger degree than other occupations with persons of a particular personality configuration. Thus, occupations vary in the degree to which they are "loaded" with work habits, values, or work problems that are consistent with definitions of realistic, investigative, artistic, social, or other classifications of personality. In this sense, it is possible to consider occupations and other environments as being classified into the same six types as is personality: artistic, conventional, enterprising, investigative, realistic, and social. Changing career patterns, occupational or educational maladjustment, and other choice or adjustment difficulties could be explained by Holland's theory by suggesting that people who have certain patterns of preferences or certain behavioral styles achieve in some occupational or educational settings and not in others. Therefore, the role of career counseling or guidance is to match as congruently as possible the personality style and the characteristics of the work or educational setting. If this does not occur persons will either need to take on the characteristics or role requirements of the occupations they have chosen or leave it to continue seeking for a role which is congruent with their particular values, needs, and work habits. Workforce education has a role in helping students understand how occupations differ, both in performance content and in the organizational settings in which such work is performed as well as in the work norms and role expectations that describe different occupations and settings.

Holland, like Roe, also identifies level hierarchies within occupational environments. According to him the level of occupational responsibility or skill that one gravitates toward is dependent on the person's intelligence and self-knowledge. Self-knowledge refers to the amount of accurate self-information the individual possesses; self-knowledge is different from self-evaluation, which refers to the worth the person attributes to himself or herself.

Holland's theory (1973: 2–10) can be summarized by its emphases on individual behavior as a function of the interaction between one's personality and one's environment and on choice behavior as an expression of personality. Thus, persons inhabiting specific environments, occupational or educational, have similar personality styles, or modal personal orientations, and their responses to problems, work values, and interpersonal situations are likely to be similar. Therefore, the choice problem is how to locate and gain access to those environments that permit people to express their personality styles. As persons explore occupational or educational possibilities, they rely on stereotypes about themselves and about their choice opportunities to guide this search. If their preferences are clear and their information about self-characteristics or occupation is accurate, they will likely make effective choices. If their understanding of their personality type or appropriate occupational choices is unclear, they are likely to be indecisive and vacillate among possible choices.

Much more could be said about how need-drive or personality theory perspectives on career development explain the mechanisms of choice of and adjustment to work. But of growing importance are perceptions of how the work environment itself shapes some work behavior and frustrates other individual needs or styles.

Maccoby, (1976, 1980) for example, has studied how work influences the potential for pathological versus healthy developments and how work structures affect mobility within corporations. He speaks of corporate "psychostructures" that select and mold certain types of behavior in order to achieve congruence between the work requirements and the character of those who do the work. In essence, the corporate psychostructure reinforces some traits and restrains others. On the negative side, depending on the psychostructure operating, such environmental conditions can attract certain types of emotional disturbance or stimulate dependency, compliance, and other regressive behavior (behavior of a more primitive and childish nature), leading to substance abuse, underdeveloped feelings of compassion and affection, and other related phenomena. Hirschhorn (1988) has extended such analyses of the workplace and its effects on workers to show how bureaucratic inefficiencies, industrial accidents, superior-subordinate conflicts, destructive control systems, and other organizational events are understandable, perhaps even predictable, from a psychoanalytic perspective. Schaef and Fassel (1988) have addressed how work organizations reinforce or create conditions of worker pathology. In their analyses they describe addictive organizations, organizations that reflect the characteristics of individual addicts: denial, distrust, anger, manipulation, and coercion. These perspectives address various forms of organizational pathology that occur when dysfunctional managers negatively affect the climate of the organization or system they are administering and the employees with whom they relate. Such analyses also discuss how organizations can and do function as addictive substances in their centrality as organizations in employees' lives and in the loyalty they expect. Such views accent the overriding importance of how the needs, drives, and other psychological traits of the individual, however they originate, develop and are refined, and are, in turn, reinforced or frustrated by the work environment as a major factor in how individual career development is facilitated, thwarted, or arrested.

Developmental Theories

Each of the preceding perspectives focuses on some aspect of the implied assumption that individuals are better suited for some occupation or job family than for other occupational possibilities. The personality and trait-and-factor approaches attempt to identify the bases on which such individual differences in occupational fit might be identified. The decision approaches speak more directly to how people choose whatever they choose. The sociological approaches stress the importance of the social structure in determining what kinds of information and encouragement people of different socioeconomic, gender, or racial backgrounds are likely to receive, how this affects their likely awareness and consideration of alternatives, and how such social factors influence continuity and discontinuity in individual career development. The personality approaches address the types of needs or drives by which people classify themselves and for which they seek congenial environments.

The developmental approaches to be discussed in this section include many of the concepts advanced in each of the first four perspectives but do so with particular emphasis on the unfolding of career development across the life span.

The developmental approaches have expanded the vision of researchers and theorists from job or occupational choice as an *act* to occupational choice as part of an ongoing *process* of career development. Such a view reinforces the perspective that choice is not confined to a certain period of life but has its roots in the early life of the child and reoccurs throughout one's life span, changing the questions of importance to the individual in response to institutional, social, and economic pressures and to developmental tasks that the individual must negotiate at times of transition from job to job, employment to unemployment, and full-time work to retirement.

Ginzberg (Ginzberg, Ginsburg, Axelrod, & Herma, 1951) and his colleagues were among the first theorists to give a multidisciplinary voice to career development as a longitudinal process. As a team composed of an economist, a sociologist, a psychologist, and a psychiatrist, Ginzberg et al. asserted that "occupational choice is a developmental process; it is not a single decision but a series of decisions made over a period of years. Each step in the process has a meaningful relation to those which precede and follow it" (1951: 185) (see Table 7.1).

Using a developmental process as their organizing framework, Ginzberg et al. identified a series of life stages in which certain factors that ultimately relate to occupational choice are faced by preadolescents and adolescents. These stages were labeled *fantasy, tentative,* and *realistic,* and each of these was broken into substages. For example, the tentative period was divided into interest, capacity, value, and transition substages that emerge sequentially. Each of these factors tends to emerge in turn and serves to further filter the alternatives one will consider. The tentative period is followed by the realistic stage, which is broken into exploration and crystallization substages. A major point that emerged from these perspectives in the original Ginzberg et al. work was that, as children, adolescents, and adults cope

TABLE 7.1   Career Maturity through Young Adulthood

		Approximate Ages		
Preschool	5–9	10–14	15–18	19+
Formulation of Self-Concept ————————————▶			Translation into Postsecondary Plan	
Developing Preferences ——————————▶			Choice ——▶	Transition
Fantasy ——————————————————▶		Tentative ———————————▶		Realistic
			Exploration	Crystallization

Source: Gray, K., & Herr, E. L. (1996). *Other Ways to Win: Creating Alternatives for High School Graduates.* Thousand Oaks, CA: Corwin Press.

with the tasks, self-insights, and information about the alternatives available to them in these different life periods, there is a constant compromising between wishes and possibilities. This synthesizing and compromising process tends to define, filter, narrow, and make more specific and realistic the range of choices that a particular individual is likely to consider. Ginzberg and his colleagues originally viewed the process of filtering out alternatives as generally irreversible and as occurring predominantly during adolescence.

Ginzberg and his associates discussed implications for career development across the life span, but their work primarily focused on the period from birth to the early twenties. In this sense their work was consistent with much speculation at the time that assumed adulthood was a relatively static period of time that essentially represented a playing out of decisions about jobs, occupations, and career issues made in adolescence. Subsequent theorists, including Super and his associates, to be discussed next, broadened the perspectives of Ginzberg and his associates to greater attention on adult development as a dynamic period with issues and choices to be made that are different from those apparent during adolescence. But that important issue aside, Ginzberg et al. provided attention to the factors that influence career choice: in particular, individual values, emotional factors, the amount and kind of education, and the impact of reality imposed by environmental pressures.

In a restatement of his theory in 1972, Ginzberg modified his original premises in several ways. First he no longer emphasized that choice making ends in adolescence or young adulthood; he agreed that decision making is a process that continues throughout adulthood. Second he tempered his early view that the developmental processes of choice are irreversible. His 1972 work suggests that the individual may return to alternatives earlier rejected as personal circumstances change to accommodate such possibilities. Finally, he replaced the earlier notion of *compromise* as a major aspect of choice with the concept of *optimization*. Although subtle in their differences, optimization really suggests more individual power to constantly try to improve the occupational fit between changing selves and circumstances rather than subordinating or giving up one's goals in deference to specific reality factors.

Following the work of Ginzberg et al., the developmental approach, which has received the most attention and been the most comprehensive in its influence on research and theory in career development, is that of Super and his colleagues. Although the work of Super became visible at approximately the same time as that of Ginzberg and his colleagues and was, in part, a response to what Super felt were deficiencies in that approach (1953), Super's influence has been more wide-ranging and enduring. Many of the original propositions of Super's approach and refinements in these constructs have evolved from a longitudinal study of the career behavior of a group of ninth-grade boys that began in the early 1950s and followed these persons into adulthood. Known as the Career Pattern Study, this longitudinal research on the same individuals from early adolescence into the late thirties became the crucible in which many of the ideas of Super and his colleagues have been tested.

Super's approach (1957, 1969a, b, 1984a, 1990, 1994) is in many respects a multidisciplinary approach. Super (1969b) labeled it a differential-developmental-social-phenomenological psychology, which reflected a confluence of knowledge bases. In fact, in formulating his theoretical constructs, Super has integrated insights from differential, developmental, social, and phenomenological psychology with those from trait-and-factor, sociological, and personality approaches into an organized whole. He has also incorporated into various iterations of this theory insights from economics and political science.

Perhaps the best-known aspect of Super's theory is his life stage structure, which incorporates developmental tasks into five periods across the life span. This structure bears resemblance to some dimensions of the staging phenomena proposed by Ginzberg et al., but extends it across all phases of adulthood. These life stages, adapted from the earlier work of Buehler (1933), include *growth* (from birth to approximately 14 years of age), *exploration* (ages 14 to 25), *establishment* (ages 25 to 45), *maintenance* (ages 45 to 60), and *decline* (age 60 and beyond). Each of these stages is divided into substages that identify developmental tasks individuals must confront and master if their career development is to proceed effectively. For example, during the exploratory stage the developmental tasks of major importance are crystallizing a vocational preference, specifying it, and implementing it; and in the establishment stage, the years of early adulthood, the developmental tasks of importance are stabilizing in the chosen vocation, consolidating one's status, and, subsequently, advancing in the occupations. Each of these tasks and those in other life stages are broken down further into the behaviors and attitudes that comprise them.

In more recent refinements of his model of career development, Super has referred to the five major life stages cited above as *maxicycles,* and he has added the notion of *minicycles,* which describes the reprocessing or recycling of the decision-making elements (e.g., fantasy, tentative, realistic) that occur within a maxicycle at points of transition from one stage to another. Associated with this life stage/developmental task/maxi-mini cycle structure across the life span are several other important concepts. One of these is *career maturity;* another is *career adaptability.* These concepts convey the notion that there are certain behaviors that are descriptive of the individual's readiness for career decision making and of mastery of the developmental tasks associated with each life stage. The assumption is that the possession of these behaviors is related to whether one stabilizes or flounders in one's occupational life or career development. Specifically, Super's research demonstrates (1977, 1985) that the same five factors are important in career maturity in adolescence and career adaptability in adulthood: planfulness or time perspective, exploration, information, decision making, and reality orientation. His work suggests that while the type of information needs and the content of the developmental tasks in adolescence and adulthood differ, the decision-making principles and the skills that underlie readiness for decision making are the same at any age and in any life stage. As such, these constructs represent the content and topical sequence by which to design courses and programs in career education and workforce education focused on fostering student career maturity or career adaptability. Table 7.2 identifies the types of behaviors that have been found to represent the five factors that are indicative of either career maturity or career adaptability. These

TABLE 7.2   Selected Behavioral Factors Descriptive of Career Maturity in Adolescence and Career Adaptability in Adulthood

Planfulness or Time Perspective
　　Developing an attitude of readiness for planning a choice
　　Developing an attitude of independence of choice
　　Awareness of the need for choices
　　Awareness of the need to crystallize a career choice
　　Awareness of present–future relationships
　　Awareness of immediate choices
　　Awareness of intermediate choices
　　Awareness of ultimate choices
　　Specificity of planning

Exploration
　　Formation of self-concept
　　Translation of self-concept into occupational terms
　　Taking steps necessary to obtaining information relevant to possible next steps
　　Identifying needed data
　　Seeking needed data
　　Identifying and using resources
　　Reality-testing information obtained formulating a generalized preference
　　Differentiation of aptitudes, values, and interests
　　Evaluating exploratory outcomes
　　Implementation of self-concept into actions related to obtaining the education or training
　　　for the preferred occupation or in finding employment in balancing life roles

Information
　　Possession of information related to options available
　　Acquisition of information on the world of work, education and training, preferred
　　　occupational roles, other life–career roles
　　Specificity of information of immediate and more remote concern
　　Possession of information on the preferred occupation

Decision-Making Skills
　　Awareness of factors on choice and in formulating an occupational preference
　　Awareness of contingency factors which affect career goals
　　Identifying alternatives
　　Identify outcomes and probabilities associated with options
　　Evaluate and weigh old and new data
　　Specification of preference
　　Select preferred plan

Reality Orientation
　　Acceptance of responsibility for choice and its consequences
　　Reality testing of self-concept
　　Ability to compromise and synthesize among available options and self-concept, social
　　　factors and aspirations
　　Ability to learn from role playing and feedback
　　Ego-involvement
　　Personal endeavor
　　Achievement motivation

behaviors represent potential attitudes or skills that workforce education programs or career counselors might wish to design a program to facilitate.

A key construct that has been a constant throughout the evolution of Super's theory is the importance of the development and implementation of the individual's self-concept. In this sense he has argued that the individual is a socialized organizer of his or her experience and that, as part of such a process, the individual chooses jobs or occupations and forges a career that permits the expression of the self-concept as it has emerged from one's developmental history. In his later work Super emphasized the individual's dual focus on self and on the environment's social, economic, and political determinants of careers. In either case one of the assumptions that has been important to Super's theory is that the individual chooses a job or occupation that allows him or her to function in a way that is consistent with a self-picture. Thus, an occupational choice may be made to affirm and actualize a presently held self-concept or to attempt to actualize an ideal self-concept. In addressing such issues Super has stimulated the development of a comprehensive literature that links the person's view with the way he or she views occupations, educational opportunities, and lifestyles (1984a).

From such a perspective the self-concept shapes and, indeed, triggers individual behavior. Therefore, workforce education must be concerned not only with helping students learn occupational skills and how occupations differ in performance content, but also it must help students learn to view themselves in realistic ways. Just as it is possible to suffer from inaccurate, obsolete, or distorted information about occupational requirements and training expectations, one can also suffer from distorted and unrealistic estimates of one's ability and vague understanding of one's personal values and preferences.

In the later stages of his theory development, Super gave considerable emphasis to giving visual expression to many of the constructs about which he was concerned. One of the prime examples was his construction of a Life–Career Rainbow to depict what he came to label as a life-span, life-space approach to career behavior. Figure 7.1 illustrates his view that most people play nine major roles in life and that these emerge approximately in a chronological order that includes (1) child, (2) student, (3) leisurite, (4) citizen, (5) worker (including unemployed worker and nonworker as ways of playing the role), (6) spouse, (7) homemaker, (8) parent, and (9) pensioner. These roles are played in what he calls theaters: (1) the home, (2) the community, (3) the school (including college and university), and (4) the workplace. In his theory Super discusses the importance for the individual of the timing of entry into, and exit from, these roles, the possible conflicts among concurrent roles, and the relationship between specific roles and individual values. He further describes how playing several roles simultaneously in occupation, family, community, and leisure tends to affect them. In his view success or difficulty in one of these roles is likely to affect the other roles and lead to success or difficulty in them as well. As roles increase and decrease in importance in various developmental stages, they are conceived of in the following manner: "The simultaneous combinations of life roles constitutes the *lifestyle;* their sequential combination structures the *life space* and constitutes the *life cycle*. The total structure is the *career pattern* (Super, 1980: 288).

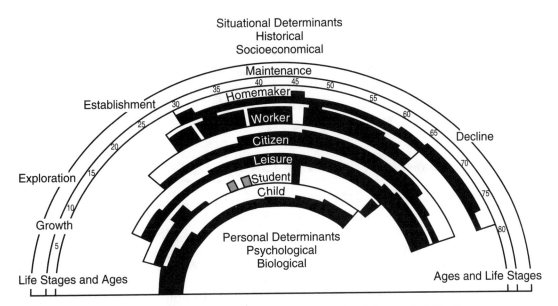

FIGURE 7.1   **The Life–Career Rainbow: Six Life Roles in Schematic Life Space.**

Source: Super, D. E. (1990). A life-span, life-space approach to career development. In D. Brown & L. Brooks (Eds.), *Career Choice and Development: Applying Contemporary Theories to Practice* (2nd ed., p. 212). San Francisco: Jossey-Bass. Used with permission.

Super's notions of the structure of career maturity and of career adaptability and his concept of the Life–Career Rainbow have provided the bases for the creation of several major assessment instruments. These assessments have served to convert his theoretical notions into operational forms that make the theory directly accessible to practitioners. Among the major instruments that are assessments of various aspects of Super's theory are the Career Maturity Inventory and the Career Development Inventory, which have been constructed to assess adolescent forms of career maturity; the Adult Concerns Inventory, which has been used to assess aspects of career adaptability; the Salience Inventory, designed to assess participation in, commitment to, and the values associated with the centrality of work or other roles reflected in the Life–Career Rainbow earlier described; and the Work Values Inventory and the Values Scale, which assess intrinsic and extrinsic values people seek to gratify in work and, indeed, how these profiles of values in work differ across nations (Super, Sverko & Super, 1995).

Assessments of career development in its different manifestations and in its different developmental task content are essential elements in Super's theory because they accent the importance of identifying and acting on instances in which career development has gone awry or, instead, demonstrates the maturity, adaptability, or readiness for choice that is important for an individual or group. The fundamental assumption of such a perspective is that, if persons experience a lack of information or a deficit in reality-testing behavior in a particular life stage, they are not likely to cope effectively with later developmental tasks that build on such earlier career behavior and thus their career development may be impaired or de-layed. Such adolescents or adults may flounder in one developmental spot, or they may prematurely close off their consideration of training opportunities or occupa-tional choices because of a lack of self-knowledge, planning, role conflicts, or an array of other possibilities. Such circumstances reduce the quality of the career de-velopment that persons are capable of achieving if such barriers are not offset by well-planned and relevant programs of workforce education.

SUMMARY AND IMPLICATIONS FOR PRACTITIONERS

While less than exhaustive, it has been the purpose of this chapter to illustrate the insights about the multiple factors that shape the processes and create the content of career behavior that are found in some of the major theories of career develop-ment. The richness of these insights suggests that the process of career develop-ment includes both subjective and objective elements that are interactive with environmental and self-learning. These insights affirm that career development is a process of learning about oneself and one's choice options and bringing these to-gether many times in the course of one's life in deliberate or inadvertent plans of action. These insights provide workforce educators ways to understand and frame problems in career behavior and to identify the types of content that can be use-fully included in workforce education curriculum as a way of increasing student career maturity and readiness. To meet the latter goals requires that, in workforce education and in human resource development, occupational skills must be taught in ways that reinforce student or employee attainment of self-efficacy and personal competence; and in ways that allow them to explore, to choose, and to apply these skills in ways that foster self-identity and self-worth.

DESIGNING WORKFORCE EDUCATION

Having established in Part I the historical prelude for workforce education, its missions, and its ethical obligations, and having reviewed in Part II the rudiments of the profession's knowledge base in economics, sociology, and career psychology, we now turn to the "practice" of workforce education. It is argued that being an educational endeavor, the "heart" of workforce education is its curriculum. The principal "product" of the practice is instruction. The component of this instruction is occupational subject matter. Were workforce education to vanish, it would become occupational-related instruction below the four-year college level, or in business and industry, employee training would vanish as well. Thus, a discussion of the practice of workforce education is actually an investigation of its curriculum, instruction, and content. These are the topics of Part III. Chapter 8 introduces workforce education curriculum design, Chapter 9 addresses instruction specifically, and finally, in Chapter 10 the content of workforce education is discussed.

8

WORKFORCE EDUCATION
CURRICULUM DESIGN

Among professional educators, a distinction is made between curriculum and instruction. Curriculum is the broader of the two terms. The purpose of curriculum is to give direction to instruction, whereas the purpose of instruction is to design various teaching strategies to promote learning.

A comprehensive workforce education curriculum can be viewed as a strategic plan that addresses six questions: *who* is the target clientele, *what* should be taught, *why* should it be taught or what is the mission, *when* or at what age or level should it be taught, *where* or in what educational setting should it take place, and *how* should instruction be designed to teach it? Although it is not correct to use the terms "curriculum" and "instruction" interchangeably, the terms "curriculum" and "program" can be used interchangeably because a comprehensive curriculum describes the program.

Generally, curriculum is determined by those responsible for governance or supervision, such as school boards or training directors, whereas often instructional design, and always the delivery, is the responsibility and—more often than not—the prerogative of individual faculty, teachers, and trainers. In many cases, broad curriculum decisions, such as deciding to offer an associate degree in electromechanical repair, are made by governing bodies, whereas most details of instruction are delegated to those who deliver instruction. Likewise, in business and industry, management typically approves broad proposals or a set of broad directions for training, while delegating the curriculum and instruction development and delivery to trainers or outsourcing it to training vendors.

In practice, the sharp distinction between the concepts of curriculum and instruction often becomes blurred. Although determining program content, scope, and sequence is a curriculum issue, and selecting instructional methods an instructional issue, developing student learning objectives occurs in both curriculum and instruction design. Nonetheless, keeping the two concepts distinct is still useful for the practitioner.

CURRICULUM PHILOSOPHIES

A comprehensive curriculum addresses the strategic question of who will be served and for what purpose. Content or subject matter selection and instructional design are driven by these initial decisions. Meanwhile, the practitioners' philosophical view regarding the purpose of curriculum or education in general will greatly influence or bias how he or she answers these strategic questions. It is useful to practitioners to become familiar with the major philosophical positions regarding the purposes of curriculum in order to identify their own individual preferences and, therefore, bias.

McNeil (1996) identifies four major philosophical points of view regarding the purpose of curriculum: humanist, social reconstructionalist, technologist, and academic. The *humanist* believes the purpose of curriculum and instruction is to help individuals maximize their human potential, whereas the *social reconstructionist* views its purpose as the means to create a better general, social, or organizational/professional good. The humanist views individuals and what is good for them as the key test of curriculum design, whereas the reconstructionist views the needs of individuals as secondary to the needs of a better social order for all individuals. *Technologists* view curriculum and instruction as neutral: curriculum and instructional design are viewed as a technology to be used to determine instructional objectives (needs assessment) and teach them (instructional design). Finally, those with an *academic orientation* view curriculum and instruction as the method employed to convey subject matter related to various fields of study. In a sense, this text is based on an academic orientation. But an argument could be made that the authors' call for a single workforce education profession with a common set of ethical imperatives suggests a reconstructionist point of view. Likewise, Dewey envisioned workforce education as a tool for social reconstruction, and many adherents to Dewey's educational philosophies have reconstructionist hopes for workforce education (see Kincheloe, 1995).

Clearly, these differing points of view regarding the purpose of curriculum are not necessarily mutually exclusive. Furthermore, the philosophical position of a curriculum and instructional designer depends to a great extent on the client to be served and the setting in which one practices. Among human resource and development (HRD) professionals, for example, most take a technologist point of view, whereas public sector practitioners take mostly a humanist position.

THE ETHICS OF CURRICULUM DESIGN

Chapter 1 stressed the critical role played by the four ethical obligations of the professions in guiding practice. In the case of workforce education, the four ethical imperatives are to promote learning, ensure health and safety, protect the public or private trust, and facilitate the transition from school or training to work.

Ethical curriculum development occurs when the design is consistent with these four points of the profession. Unethical curriculum development occurs, for example, when the selection of instructional materials and equipment is influenced by free dinners provided by vendors at conventions.

Very often, legitimate ethical dilemmas occur in curriculum design. For example, community support is always desirable, and one way to build such support is to do public service work. Invariably, however, requests are made that are not part of the curriculum objectives. Doing the project will not promote learning; rejecting the project may jeopardize community support. The aspiring workforce education professional, therefore, should be aware that curriculum or program design often involves ethical conflict.

MANAGING THE CURRICULUM DESIGN AND IMPLEMENTATION PROCESS

Designing and implementing comprehensive workforce education curriculum, and therefore programs, involve a great number of variables, ranging from establishing program missions to writing performance objectives to selecting instructional materials to finally delivering instruction. Managing this process successfully is a critical skill for the workforce education professional. In this chapter a four-phase management strategy for curriculum development and implementation is provided (see Figure 8.1) to guide the practitioner: curriculum strategic planning, implementation planning, implementation, and assessment. The reader is cautioned that although this four-step strategy suggests a structured sequential set of considerations, in practice unique local circumstances may change the sequence, add variables, or make still others inapplicable. Curriculum design can, in fact, be thought of as putting a puzzle together—one may start with any piece as long as in the end all pieces are accounted for.

Actually, in curriculum building, some pieces may be discarded altogether, depending on the situation: An HRD specialist who works on a contract basis can be expected to approach curriculum design differently from a community college dean of technology. Nonetheless, the comprehensive curriculum management strategy is recommended as a beginning template for all curriculum development, because all too often—and one reason why so many programs fail—the process used consists of a rather arbitrary selection of the occupation and content, gut feelings regarding enrollment projections, purchasing some instructional materials, hiring an instructor, and hoping for the best.

PHASE I: CURRICULUM STRATEGIC PLANNING

Curriculum Management
Phase I: Curriculum Strategic Planning

1. Establish institutional/program mission and vision
2. Establish institutional/program curriculum goals and objectives

Phase I: Curriculum Strategic Planning

1. Establish institutional/program mission and vision
2. Establish institutional/program curriculum goals and objectives
3. Conduct an environmental scan of
   a. Student/trainee characteristics
   b. Labor market projections
   c. Curriculum trends
   d. Constraints and opportunities

Phase II: Implementation Planning

1. Determine program type
   a. Level/type of workforce education
   b. Labor market analysis
2. Address articulation issues
3. Develop curriculum
   a. Determine format
   b. Select design methodology and execute

Phase III: Implementation

1. Select staff
2. Develop instructional design
3. Purchase instructional materials
4. Prepare instructional facility
5. Schedule instruction and enroll students/trainees
6. Deliver instruction

Phase IV: Assessment

1. Conduct implementation assessment
2. Conduct outcomes assessment
3. Revise curriculum

FIGURE 8.1   Curriculum Management

3. Conduct an environmental scan of
   a. Student/trainee characteristics
   b. Labor market projections
   c. Curriculum trends
   d. Constraints and opportunities

Phase I of the curriculum management process is curriculum strategic planning. This phase is best conceptualized as a specialized form of strategic planning that deals solely with curriculum and program. If this planning process is thorough, a defensible strategic plan for curriculum will result.

Strategic planning is organized by managers, involves all program stakeholders, and is often formally endorsed by a governing body. The process begins with obtaining consensus regarding institutional or program mission and vision.

Mission and Vision

The logical beginning of workforce education curriculum design is establishing the mission of the institution or unit. A workforce education mission statement identifies who will be served, in what manner, and for what purpose; it addresses the who and why in curriculum issues; and may, in broad terms, address the what question as well. The statement should be brief and specific. In the public sector the institutional mission is determined or shaped by public policy, legislation, and local custom. An example of a mission statement is given below.

> *The mission of Connecticut's Regional Vocational-Technical system is to provide intense, occupational-specific training below the associate degree level. The equal opportunity program is offered for youth and adults in collaboration with business, labor, and community groups in preparation for the demands of the twenty-first century. Academic instruction is provided to ensure that students will be career-directed and will possess communications, problem solving, and citizenship skills which allow them to be productive, adaptable, and satisfied individuals (Connecticut Regional Vocational Technical Schools, November 1985).*

Although to beginning practitioners a mission statement may seem a rather esoteric activity, the veteran knows that questions of mission can be political land mines, thus the value of having a mission statement that has been adopted by the governing body is not to be underestimated. A mission statement, in particular, is useful in debates regarding what types of programming are and are not appropriate for a particular institution, program, or department. Managers should also be sensitive to "mission creep." All too often workforce education programs, in their attempt to meet local needs, build enrollment or secure outside funding and continuously push the limits of their mission. The practitioner should be cautioned that trying to be all things to all clients has historically been a dangerous strategy.

Vision Statement

In the early 1990s, it became common for institutions to create a vision statement in addition to a mission statement. A vision statement describes the vision workforce education professionals have for their organization. Given the mission, the vision describes the overall goal of what the institution would like to become as it performs its mission. An example of a vision statement is provided by the following:

> *The vision of Alpha Technical College is to become recognized by the community it serves as an institution that cares, is responsive, and is effective.*

Institutional Curriculum Goals and Objectives

Once the mission and vision have been established, a set of broad curriculum goals and objectives should be agreed on that relate to all programming. In this book the authors have argued for two such goals and related tasks for the profession as a whole, namely, to *promote career opportunity,* with the objective of increasing individual labor market advantage, and to *develop the nation's workforce* with the objective of increasing worker productivity.

The Environmental Scan

A classic aspect of strategic planning is the environmental scan. The purpose of this scan is to gain insights that will lead to a curriculum that meets the institutional curriculum objectives. In the case of workforce education this scan minimally includes an investigation of the clientele, demographics, academic and career aspiration characteristics, labor markets and labor market projections, curriculum design trends, and community, state, and national constraints and opportunities.

Student/Trainee Characteristics.   Effective curriculum design requires precise knowledge regarding the target clientele. Although workforce education at the secondary and postsecondary levels has traditionally invested considerable effort to determine clientele program interests, very little effort goes into projecting the academic level of the clientele. Unfortunately, as a result, it is relatively common to find that the institutional vision and curriculum far exceed the academic talents and preparation of those enrolled. Similarly, in all too many cases the academic skills of entering students change over time, but the curriculum does not. It is an ethical imperative that mission, vision, curriculum objectives, and instructional strategies be consistent with clientele skills and abilities.

Labor Market Projections.   Effective strategic planning for curriculum design requires a consideration of labor market trends and developments. At this strategic planning stage, what is of concern are large scale developments that would affect all curriculum design. Some examples are the growth of part-time employment or self-employment in certain occupations, the growing preference of employers for employees with cross-skills, and the increasing use of work teams.

Curriculum Trends.   As part of the strategic planning process for curriculum, it is important to consider the curriculum reforms that are being debated in the field. In the 1990s these were such topics as youth apprenticeship, integrated tech prep, applied academic, all aspects of the industry, and school to work (see Chapter 14). In the HRD field they included formal on-the-job training and constructivism (see Chapter 15). Although some or all of these reforms may be rejected, it is important to consider them if the program in question is to stay abreast of the profession's efforts to continuously improve.

Strategic Constraints and Opportunities.   Finally, the environmental scan includes an overview of the local, state, and national arena to identify strategic constraints and opportunities. Constraints typically include such things as budget and state and federal regulations. Opportunities can include population growth and economic growth. Political realities can be both a constraint or an opportunity; the truly skilled workforce education manager is one who has the ability to sense both and determine what is possible.

PHASE II: IMPLEMENTATION PLANNING

Phase II: Implementation Planning

1. Determine program type
   a. Level/type of workforce education
   b. Labor market analysis
2. Address articulation issues
3. Develop curriculum
   a. Determine format
   b. Select design methodology and execute

Once the curriculum strategic planning has been completed, the next step is to plan the implementation. This planning involves two major activities: (1) determination of program type and then (2) curriculum development.

Determination of Program Type

The determination of program involves three types of decisions. The first is a determination of the type or level of workforce education that will be developed. The second is a determination of occupation(s) to be addressed. The third is to determine how the program will be articulated with academic classes, prior technical programs, and more advanced technical programs.

Levels of Workforce Education.   There are not one but three levels of workforce education and two different types within each. They differ according to the degree that specific occupational skills or tasks are addressed: see Figure 8.2 on page 146.

The broadest type of Level I workforce education is that group of programs whose purpose is career exploration or job readiness. One type of program is exploratory programs to help students make a career decision.

The second type of program in Level I is programs whose goal is job readiness. A typical example is school-based learning experiences for students who will participate in school-to-work programs. In such programs job skills are taught at the work site; the objective of prior instruction is to prepare students to benefit from this experience. This instruction could include some occupational-specific content, particularly one that is related to safety. At this level the objective is exploratory or teaching general (Level I) essential employability skills, not occupational preparation.

FIGURE 8.2   Levels of Workforce Education

At Level II of workforce education programming, the content becomes more occupationally specific and the objective is to provide labor market advantage in specific occupational areas by teaching Level I, II, and III essential skills. There are two types of programs at this level.

The first type of programming at Level II is occupational cluster programs. The program goal is to teach job-entry occupational skills relevant to a cluster of occupations, such as construction trades, allied health, and heating-ventilation-air conditioning (HVAC). The objective of occupational cluster programs is to provide a high degree of flexibility in entering the labor market by providing entry-level labor market advantage in a number of occupational areas (see Chapter 13). Programs of this type are most typically found at the high school level and are also preferable when the labor market has limited opportunity in any particular occupation such as one might find in rural areas.

The second type of programming at Level II is programs that prepare clients to compete for employment in a specific occupation. The content becomes occupational specific, such as inhalation therapist, automated machine technician, and computer systems management. The objective is to provide labor market advantage in a specific occupation. These programs are the most common type of programming in high schools, although some argue they are more appropriate at the postsecondary level or in robust urban/suburban labor markets (see Chapter 13).

Programs at Level III are typically found in business and industry or are specialized short-term programs for special populations in the public sector. The first type of programming at Level III addresses content specific to a particular job or task within an occupation. Milling machine operation, pastry chef, or accounts receivable clerk are job-specific programs. Workforce education of this type is often found in public sector employment and training programs. In the second type of programming at Level III, content is confined to a specific task. Training individuals to use a new software package and compliance with new federal regulations are typical examples. Usually workforce education at this level is for incumbent employees and is either provided or sponsored by employers.

Selection of the appropriate level of workforce education is dependent on a number of variables including mission, the clientele, the labor market, and the sponsor. The level or appropriate type of programs for high-school-age students is a matter of debate among workforce educators, some advocating cluster programs, whereas occupation-specific courses remain the typical program type. The decision of level is critical for the curriculum planning process, because it is the prerequisite to making all the decisions that follow in the process, beginning with occupational identification.

Occupational Identification. To varying degrees workforce education at all levels, from exploratory to task specific, is taught within some broad or narrow occupational context. What occupation(s) or clusters of occupations to develop curriculum for is perhaps the classic and defining workforce education curriculum/program development decision. The variables that affect this decision include workforce education level, clientele, sponsor, and labor market. At the exploratory level, occupations could range from all occupational clusters to those occupations offered at a particular institution or to an in-depth look at just one. At the other end of the spectrum, job-specific or task-specific workforce education typically is determined by either the employer or, in the public sector, by the immediate labor market. At the occupational cluster and occupation-specific level the decision becomes more complex and is typically a trade-off between the labor market, student or trainee interest, and budget, staff, or facility constraints.

Labor Markets Projections. Reflecting the technologist view of curriculum design as well as the dual mission of providing individual opportunity and developing the nation's workforce, the variable that gets at least the most lip service in determining what occupation(s) to prepare students for is labor market demand. Most programs at Levels II and III are determined at least in part by labor market projections regarding employment supply and demand data.

The sources, uses, and reliability of labor market data were discussed in detail in Chapter 5. Typically in the public secondary and postsecondary education sector, labor market data justification is required by funding or regulatory agencies. At this point in the process it is also advisable to contact local employers to gauge their labor market needs and level of support. Although it may be premature to establish an advisory committee until after an occupational focus has been made, this does not prevent contacting relevant employers to get input to make these decisions.

It is a professional axiom in workforce education that it is unethical to train for jobs that do not exist. There are, however, numerous ethical dilemmas that result, beginning with the reality that student or client interest often contradicts labor market projections. Another harsh reality is that there are far more individuals who aspire to professional high-skills/high-wage work than there are jobs. In many cases at all levels of education, if one compares enrollments with job outlooks, supply exceeds demand in the majority of fields. But should these programs be closed when so doing limits opportunity for individuals to prepare to compete for this desirable but scarce employment? The compromise is that workforce education and baccalaureate level professional preparation programs typically address occupations that show employment potential even if the total number of openings may be fewer than those credentialing themselves. The goals of workforce educators in these common situations is to prepare their clients to be competitive in striving to compete for those opportunities that exist.

Articulation Issues

A second implementation planning consideration is the issue of curriculum articulation. "Curriculum articulation" refers to the degree the curriculum is coordinated with previous education, or training course taken simultaneously in other departments, and more advanced education in the future. Integrating academic and vocational education is an articulate issue concerned with how to ensure that students receive math, science, and communications instruction that will provide the level of academic skill needed in the relevant occupation (see Chapter 10). Another articulation consideration is whether to develop tech-prep programs of study that provide formal connections between occupational programs of study at the secondary and two-year postsecondary education level. Typical articulation issues in HRD include ensuring the transfer of training into increased productivity back in the work setting or development of a sequence of human development experiences for employees in a way that forms a logical whole.

Curriculum Development

The third element in implementation planning is curriculum development. For obvious reasons the curriculum must be developed prior to implementing a program of study. This process begins with determining what format of curriculum documentation will be used, and then the formal curriculum development process is started.

Curriculum Format

Curriculum documentation refers to the format that will be used to document (write) the curriculum. Typical examples include a course of study, curriculum guides, course outlines, and a course syllabus (Duenk, 1993). These different types of documentation are not mutually exclusive: a well organized program will have all four.

A *course of study* typically states the objectives of the entire curriculum and outlines the sequencing of courses and modules that collectively make up the course or program. A high school course selection guide or a community college course catalog are examples of a course of study; the booklet in total represents the course of study for the institution as well as outlining various different courses of study related to different subjects or content areas.

A *curriculum guide* is a detailed description of the curriculum for a particular course. It is the most detailed of all types of curriculum documentation including not just learning objectives but often instructional design options and equipment requirements. In practice many curriculums used in education including work-force education are in fact "off the shelf" commercial materials that include a curriculum guide.

A *course outline* or *course syllabus* is typically the type of curriculum documentation provided to students or clients. A good course syllabus includes a course outline that lists the sequence of course content that will be addressed. In addition a course syllabus states student objectives, course requirements, methods of students' evaluation, and other information students or clients need to know regarding the course itself.

Curriculum guides can be organized according to, or can organize, the program content in a number of different ways. The two most common are *units of instruction* and *modules of instruction.* The unit of instruction documents the instruction of a body of content and often relates to a set number of class sessions (two weeks, for example). Units are most often associated with group instruction. *Learning modules* are most often related to individual instruction and are designed to be self-contained learning packets that outline learning activities.

WORKFORCE EDUCATION CURRICULUM DESIGN MODELS

Two curriculum design models are prevalent in workforce education. Those models are competency-based education (CBE) and instructional systems design (ISD). CBE is most often associated with secondary and postsecondary workforce education, whereas ISD is associated with human resource development (HRD) in the private sector. The difference in the methods reflects the differing curriculum objectives in these two environments. The CBE education method begins with the assumption that the goal is to provide instruction to students or trainees. The ISD model begins with a different assumption, namely, that there is a performance problem to be solved, but it may or may not be a training problem or one that will respond to instruction. The ISD model begins with analysis of the performance problem, whereas the CBE model begins with an analysis of the occupation or task to be taught. The characteristics of CBE are listed in Figure 8.3.

- The goal is to teach essential outcomes
- Outcomes are described in behavioral, observable, or criterion-referenced learning objectives
- Outcomes are taught in a prescribed sequence
- Instruction is narrowly focused on learning objectives
- Assessment is defined by the behavioral objectives and is typically in the form of demonstration or application
- A minimal level of competence is established which all students must obtain before continuing to the next behavioral objectives
- Students or clients are provided with frequent/timely feedback regarding their performance

---

FIGURE 8.3 Characteristics of Competency-Based Education

THE COMPETENCY-BASED EDUCATION (CBE) MODEL

The CBE curriculum design model is inherently technologist and behaviorist in nature. The process is based on the technologist philosophy that curriculum design must be methodologically rigorous in order to ensure that instruction is based on reliable and valid descriptions of the desired behavior to be taught. The goal is to replicate this behavior among students or trainees. Thus, CBE is sometimes referred to as performance-based education and is essentially the same as outcomes-based education. CBE has the five-step process listed in Figure 8.4 (McNeil, 1996; Finch & Crunkilton, 1995).

Task analysis. Task, or occupational, analysis is the term given to methodologies used to determine curriculum content. The various methods of task analysis are discussed in Chapter 10.

Performance/learning objectives. The purpose of task analysis is to enable the curriculum designer to write student performance objectives. These objectives define the behavior that must be demonstrated.

Performance/learning objectives in a CBE and ISD curriculum design system are written according to three criteria (Finch & Crunkilton, 1995). First, they must describe the *activity,* or what the student or client is actually expected to do. Second, they describe the *condition,* or circumstances, under which the activity is to be performed—typical examples include time, tools, and materials. Finally, the objectives establish the *standard,* or level of performance, that must be reached. In some

---

Step 1. Task Analysis
  What are the concepts and essential skills required?
  What is the minimum level of competence required?

Step 2. Performance Objectives
  Define activity, condition, and standard.
  Sequence performance objectives.

Step 3. Instructional Strategies
  Analyze characteristics of the students.
  Select instructional strategies.
  Design and/or purchase instructional materials.
  Prepare instructional facility or setting.
  Validate instruction.

Step 4. Implementation
  Conduct instruction.

Step 5. Evaluation
  Was the curriculum implemented as designed?
  Was it instructionally effective in improving performance?
  How should the curriculum be changed?

FIGURE 8.4   Five-Step Competency-Based
Curriculum Design Method

Occupation: 119   CHILD CARE AND GUIDANCE
     Duty: c   PROVIDING FOR THE PHYSICAL NEEDS OF CHILDREN
     Task: 002   Perform daily health inspection

Performance Objective
     Condition for Performance of Task
          Blankets, pillows, first aid kit, thermometer
     Performance
          Daily inspection
     Standard
          Child care worker must check daily for signs of illness or injury; if necessary, isolate, monitor and comfort the sick; treat minor injuries with first aid; and report serious situations to parents

---

FIGURE 8.5   Illustration of a Performance Objective

curriculum designs, learning objectives are divided into *enabling objectives,* which describe performance that must be mastered in order for the student to be able to successfully perform the *terminal objective.* An example of the performance objectives used by the Vocational Technical Education Consortium of the States (V–TECS) is given in Figure 8.5.

Performance or learning objectives used in workforce education are of three types: cognitive, psychomotor, and affective and can be ordered from simple to complex (Vogler, 1995). *Cognitive learning objectives* are related to facts and knowledge that students or clients are required to explain, apply, and contrast. *Psychomotor learning objectives* relate to manipulative observable skills that students are required to demonstrate. *Affective learning objectives* relate to interpersonal behaviors or beliefs that students are required to demonstrate awareness of or to acceptable practice.

Developing instructional strategies. Once the performance objectives have been written, the next obvious step is to design instruction to maximize the propensity of students to master the objectives. Instructional design is a field of study in itself and will be dealt with separately in Chapter 9.

Implementation and evaluation. The final step in the CBE model is to implement or conduct the course and evaluate the results. These topics will also be addressed separately in Chapter 9.

CBE and Individualized Instruction

CBE is typically associated with individualized instruction, meaning that instruction is designed to allow students to proceed at their own pace. Students do not proceed to the next instructional objective until they have performed at the level of mastery stated in the first objective. For this reason individual *learning activity packets* (LAPS), or modules, that allow a student to work individually and instructors to monitor individual progress, are often used in CBE. When CBE is individualized, it becomes important that before implementation some consideration is given to how student progress will be monitored and how the differential progress can be effectively communicated to employers and supervisors. In some workforce education settings, this monitoring is sometimes done via a computerized data management system that is available commercially.

Individualized instruction, although preferable, is not, however, a prerequisite of CBE. The defining characteristic of CBE is task analysis that leads to very specific performance objectives, not individualized instruction. The military, for example, uses CBE extensively but often also uses large-group instructional techniques. Whether CBE needs to be individualized depends on the importance of students mastering one task before going on to another, which, although always desirable, is sometimes unnecessary or impractical because of time restraints.

Criticism of the CBE Model

CBE has shortcomings. Although the focus on task analysis and the resulting student performance objective is its strength, CBE can also result in a curriculum that is inflexible and too narrow in scope. Although CBE lends itself very well to observable or procedural skills instruction, it is not as well suited to affective tasks (McNeil, 1996) such as the ability to function in work teams. Also, because of its reliance on rigid performance criteria, CBE seems to be a better fit when the objective is to train, not educate. And, although some students benefit from the lock step hierarchical sequence of learning objectives, others, particularly the more talented, may find the rigidity boring and thus counterproductive. Finally, CBE tends to be reactive, not proactive. Because CBE is based on an analysis of observable occupational tasks, the resulting curriculum content is based on what are the current skill requirements, often failing to be proactive in addressing what they will be in the future.

INSTRUCTIONAL SYSTEM DESIGN (ISD) MODEL

The instructional system design (ISD) model of curriculum development is most often used in business and industry or private sector workforce education and is popular among HRD professionals. Although ISD and CBE have many common elements, each is best suited for a different environment and different clients and therefore has different beginning assumptions and overall goals.

The typical goal of CBE curriculum design is to provide labor market advantage to the individual whose status is that of student. Thus, CBE begins with the assumption that instruction is appropriate. The typical goal of ISD curriculum, on the other hand, is to increase human performance of employees. However, it is *not assumed* that instruction is an appropriate solution, because training is only one way to increase human performance and will be successful only if the problem is, in fact, a human performance problem. If the problem is not lack of skill or knowledge or even attitude but, instead, inept management, an ineffective compensation plan, obsolete equipment, or just plain hiring the wrong people for the job, no amount of training will increase human performance. Thus, unlike CBE, ISD begins with an analysis, or *needs assessment*.

The ISD Process

Rothwell and Kazanas (1992) define ISD as a process associated with "analyzing employee performance problems systematically, identifying the root cause(s) of these problems, considering various solutions, and implementing the solutions in ways designed to minimize the unintended consequences of corrective action." The steps in the ISD process are listed below in Figure 8.6.

The defining characteristic of the ISD model is the needs assessment step that precedes task analysis. Typically, HRD professional preparation includes significant training in various needs assessment methods (Rossett, 1988).

Action Research Model

A variation of the ISD model needs assessment step is a process called "action research." Action research is a problem-solving process conducted jointly by HRD professionals external to the firm, in connection with internal managers. The two groups jointly conduct the analysis and plan an intervention or action to be taken.

Step 1. NEEDS ASSESSMENT
What is the gap between desired and current performance?
Is this a human performance problem with instruction being the solution?
What is the cost and probability of reducing the gap through instruction?
What are the characteristics of the learner?
What is the level of motivation of the learner?
What are the characteristics of the work setting?

Step 2. TASK ANALYSIS
Conduct task analysis of the job or procedure.
Describe desired human performance.

Step 3. PERFORMANCE OBJECTIVES
Write performance objectives.
Develop performance measures.
Sequence performance objectives.

Step 4. INSTRUCTIONAL DEVELOPMENT
Specify instructional strategies.
Design and/or purchase instructional materials.
Prepare instructional facility or setting.
Validate instruction.

Step 5. IMPLEMENTATION
Conduct instruction.

Step 6. EVALUATION
Was the curriculum implemented as designed?
Was it effective in improving performance?
How should the curriculum be changed?

FIGURE 8.6   Steps in the Instructional System Design Model

Whereas the focus of ISD is on curriculum to improve individual performance, the focus of action research is on *organizational development* (OD). Although the action research model can be used to solve all types of problems, it is often associated with HRD because a large percentage of OD problems are human in nature and may require an instructional workforce education solution. When action research determines that an instructional HRD solution is called for, the ISD model is typically employed to develop the instruction.

PHASE III: CURRICULUM IMPLEMENTATION

Phase III: Implementation

1. Select staff
2. Develop instructional design
3. Purchase instructional materials
4. Prepare instructional facility
5. Schedule instruction and enroll students or trainees
6. Deliver instruction

Phase III in the curriculum management process is to implement the curriculum. It involves four major activities. The first is instructional staff selection or reassignment. The qualifications of the instructional staff should logically flow from the curriculum design but also may be regulated by state certification regulations and collective bargaining agreements. The next step is to design instruction, which is the subject of Chapter 9. In practice, instruction is typically designed by the instructional staff that will deliver it, although in some cases, particularly in HRD settings, professional instructional designers perform this work. Also, during this phase, instructional materials and equipment identified in the curriculum and instructional design are purchased, the educational setting or facility prepared, a time schedule developed, and student or clients enrolled and assigned.

Again, the practitioner is cautioned that the sequence just outlined is the ideal; in practice budget restraints often prevent reassigning or hiring staff before the course is scheduled to begin. Likewise, often equipment purchasing is lengthy and must begin early in the implementation planning phase to ensure it arrives in time, and, therefore, it often occurs before the curriculum is written.

PHASE IV: ASSESSMENT

Phase IV: Assessment

1. Conduct implementation assessment
2. Conduct outcomes assessment
3. Revise curriculum

The final step in curriculum management is assessment. The focus of this assessment is on the effectiveness of the curriculum in achieving the institutional curriculum goals and the specific performance objectives of the curriculum. A detailed discussion of assessment is provided in Chapter 13.

CURRICULUM DESIGN ISSUES

There are a number of seemingly timeless workforce education curriculum design issues. The professionals in the field should be aware of the major disputes and form their own points of view. This chapter concludes with a discussion of two recurring curriculum debates.

Occupation-Specific versus Cluster Programming

A classic debate in workforce education curriculum design is the question of depth versus breadth, or whether programs should be specific to an occupation or address a cluster of occupations. Although this issue used to be mostly a high school workforce education issue, increasingly it is an issue at the two-year postsecondary level as well. The issue involves a number of philosophical debates beginning with whether individuals are best served by (1) a program whose objectives are to provide maximum labor market flexibility by teaching job-entry skills in a variety of occupations, or (2) a program that stresses depth by teaching as many increasingly higher level skills in a single occupation as possible. Parents, general educators, and the public endorse clustered programs; employers like occupation-specific curriculum.

It is suggested that there is no single answer to the depth versus breadth issue. Which is the superior model depends, for example, on the labor market students are being prepared for. In an urban or suburban market, significant employment opportunities in a single occupational area may well exist, thus justifying occupation-specific programs. But in a rural area the opposite is probably the case; thus, individuals are best served by providing them with entry-level skills and, thus, some labor market advantages in a number of related occupations. The age of the learner also must be considered. One can assume that most high school sophomores or juniors are still in the exploratory career development stage and best served by a clustered program, whereas students at the postsecondary level should have more focused career objectives and would benefit most from an occupational-specific program. Finally, the rate of change in the industry may be a deciding factor. In fields where technology and thus relevant cognitive and psychomotor skills change month by month, a curriculum that deals with specifics seems destined to be always behind.

On-the-Job Training versus Formal Training

The objective of workforce education in business and industry is to solve human performance problems. The goal is very specific: when training is complete, the employee should be more productive. The issue of transfer of learning to the job site is a critical one to HRD professionals. One option is on-the-job training (OJT), defined as "training that occurs at or near the work site" (Rothwell & Kazanas, 1990). In terms of transfer of learning, OJT is, or should be, superior, because the learner never leaves the work site. The problem with OJT is that it is unplanned, informal, and provided when time permits by supervisors or even fellow employees. Therefore, OJT generally results in less learning than formal classroom, laboratory, or off-the-job training, which lend themselves to the use of new instructional technologies. As a result, both OJT and off-the-job training have advantages and disadvantages, and thus the debate.

One solution offered by Rothwell and Kazanas is *structured on-the-job training* (SOJT). The key feature of SOJT is that it is planned using the ISD model. Therefore, SOJT differs from other types of training, not in the design process but at the point it occurs. An important element, in fact perhaps the key difference between OJT and true SOJT, is that in SOJT the instructors are trained in instructional effectiveness techniques and are familiar with the instructional objectives of the training.

SUMMARY AND IMPLICATIONS FOR PRACTITIONERS

Undoubtedly, the bulk of workforce education professionals either design or design and implement curriculum. Thus understanding the fundamentals of curriculum design is nothing short of a professional imperative. This chapter has outlined a format for curriculum design. In the next chapter, one aspect of this process, namely, instructional design, is dealt with specifically.

9

INSTRUCTIONAL DESIGN IN WORKFORCE EDUCATION

Instructional design is that aspect of curriculum development that focuses on organizing to deliver instruction. Although students and trainees are the clients of workforce education, instruction can be viewed as the "defining product" (Corcoran & Goertz, 1995).

Richey defines instruction as "the science of creating detailed specifications for development of evaluations and maintenance of situations which facilitate the learning of both large and small units of subject matter" (1986: 9). Instruction focuses on the design or selection of teaching strategies or methods that increase the likelihood of learning. It is the combination of teaching practices and assessment techniques used by teachers or trainers (Newman, Marks, & Gamoran, 1995). In practice, all workforce educators who provide instruction must, out of necessity, be instructional designers and, to some extent, one's professional effectiveness will hinge on one's design skills. Some, however, particularly in training settings or curriculum/program development and publishing jobs, often are full-time designers who are extensively trained in learning theory, computer-assisted instructional design, and multimedia. The purpose of this chapter is to provide the workforce education practitioner with an introduction to the key elements and issues in instructional design as a basis for advanced study.

PHILOSOPHIES OF LEARNING

Consciously or unconsciously, instructional designers will be influenced by their philosophical orientation regarding how people learn. There are three major schools of thought in vogue today (Cooper, 1995): behaviorism, cognitivism, and constructivism. It is useful for beginning practitioners to be familiar with these philosophies in order to recognize their own biases because this preference will influence their teaching.

Behaviorism

Behaviorists view learning as the product of responding to stimulus in the environment. For example, we learn not to run on ice the first time we fall down. In the behaviorist mind-set the learner is acted on by the environment. The key to instructional design is to arrange appropriate stimuli that will provide the desired response. Behaviorism has several important assumptions for workforce educators (Cooper, 1993): (1) the key to analyzing and therefore teaching human behavior such as occupational skills is "objective" observation, hence description of these skills in order to design the stimuli appropriately, and (2) learning these skills depends on the quality (intrinsic versus extrinsic, immediate versus delayed) of the feedback (assessment) or consequences. Instruction based on task analysis that leads to behavioral objectives assessed by criterion-referenced measures is a behaviorist approach.

Cognitive Learning Approach

Cognitive science research has led to a different view of learning, namely, that there are different ways to learn and that individuals have different learning preferences or styles. In the cognitive learning approach the emphasis is not on the stimulus but on the learner. It recognizes, for example, that humans are often stimulated to learn by curiosity, not by some external stimulus. In the cognitive approach the emphasis is on designing instruction that provides a variety of instructional activities to address different styles or, in individualized instruction, the dominant style.

Constructivism

A third philosophy of learning, and one that came into vogue in the later 1980s, is constructivism. Constructivist learning occurs when individuals "construct," or discover, a meaning of their own from the content presented. The preferred way to design instruction is to provide opportunity for learners to create or discover their own meaning from the material. An age-old example of constructivist instructional design is the Socratic method of guiding students to discovery by asking open-ended questions. In workforce education, trainers who design instruction that includes opportunities to trouble-shoot a mechanical or electromechanical system are providing an opportunity for discovery or constructivist learning.

Synthesis

Although workforce educators who engage in instructional design will probably have a bias in favor of one of the three philosophical points of view regarding learning, in practice they will, or should, find themselves resorting to all three at various times. Although discovery learning may be their preferred method, allowing an individual to "discover" how to safely use an arc welder is out of the question. Furthermore, in reality, the cognitive learning approach seems perfectly consistent with behaviorism in that it stresses diversity in instructional methods that address all learning styles, leaving the question of reinforcement and objective design open.

Education versus Training

Is there a difference between education and training? If so, when is workforce education "education," and when is it "training"? Or is it always one or the other, and, if so, which one? Finally, is one inherently more valuable in every situation? The position taken by the authors is that, in fact, there are important differences between education and training.

The important distinction between training and education is that the goal of training is to teach people to follow prescribed procedures and to perform in a standardized manner. The goal of education is to create independent problem solvers who have sufficient depth of understanding to figure out what to do when the procedures break down. Education is preparation that can be generalized to the unexpected. Training is preparation designed to ensure standardized responses to predicted situations.

Does this mean that education is superior to training? Not necessarily. There are many cases in real life where maximum productivity or minimizing error results in fewer accidents in the workplace and increased productivity. In the case of using computer software, there is typically only one way to perform a function; figuring out why a particular key sequence saves a document is beyond most of us, but knowing how a document is saved is important. Programs designed to teach these types of skills are termed "training." Meanwhile, the central definition of *technical occupations* are jobs that require workers to make multiple "decisions," using math and science principles; this definition alone implies that programs to prepare most types of technical workers should be designed to be education.

Sometimes it is a matter of debate as to whether instruction should be designed as training or education. For example, in the nuclear power industry it was believed that the appropriate mode for preparing plant operators was training because safety would be maximized if every decision was reduced to a standard operational procedure. Subsequent nuclear power near-disasters led to the conclusion that training alone was not adequate because sometimes procedures fail when unanticipated scenarios occur. As a result, teams that operate power plants now must include one person with an engineering degree because such persons have been educated to a level of understanding that allows them to figure out what is happening, even when procedures break down.

It is also worth noting that much workforce education currently labeled "education," on close examination, is really mostly training. All too often, for example, because of the legitimate need to ensure the safety of the learner, many occupational preparation programs, particularly at the high school level, require students to get the instructor's approval for taking the next step in a process. The result is that at the end of the program the students have learned not to think or take initiative but, instead, to ask the supervisor before doing anything; such an instructional outcome is training, not education. In order to be educational, one instructional objective must be the creation of independent problem solvers: if not, it is training.

Finally, instructional design as well as curriculum content will be different if the purpose is education or training. The goals of education are more consistent, for example, with the constructivist view of learning, the Socratic discovery method of instruction, and preparation for occupations such as electromechanical repair. Training is more consistent with the behaviorist philosophy, competency based education (CBE), and preparation in occupations where following procedures are critical, such as those in the health occupations.

VARIABLES IN INSTRUCTIONAL DESIGN

The objective of instructional design is to organize lessons in such as way as to maximize mastery of the learning objectives of the curriculum. Instructional designers have a variety of variables to consider, including time, learning styles, and cognitive styles.

Time

Time is an unavoidable consideration in instructional design because the time allotted to workforce education is not infinite, and instruction must be designed within the time available. There are always outside constraints on time—such as school year, class periods, time away from the job—and thus a designer's first question often is, "How much time do I have?" instead of perhaps the more important question, "How much time do I need, given the characteristics of the learner and the material to be mastered?" As suggested by this latter question, time is an important variable for reasons related to learning theory (Anderson, 1983). Time spent on learning a task is the essential element in learning models such as those of John Carroll and, later, Benjamin Bloom. These researchers theorize that, if motivated, all students can learn if given sufficient time.

There are different ways time can be defined within an instructional context, and it is important for the workforce educator to understand the distinctions. *School time* or *training time* is the total amount of time allotted for instruction, but typically it is greater than the total amount of *classroom time,* which is the time students or clients spend in the learning setting. *Instructional time* is that time in which actual instruction occurs and again is typically less than even classroom time. Most important, however, is *engaged time,* which is that portion of instructional time in which students or clients are engaged in the process of learning. A critical element in instructional design is to maximize engaged time; likewise, a key element of the effectiveness of any instructional modality, be it stand-up training or simulations, is the ability to maximize engaged time.

Because, in practical terms, time for instruction is limited, an inherent dilemma occurs when the time individual students need to learn exceeds the time available.

As Lorin Anderson (1983) succinctly states, "The larger the gap between subject matter difficulty and student aptitude, the longer time they will need to learn." Although workforce educators, along with all educators, may philosophically believe the adage that all students can learn, the practical implication is that, for some students, the time they need may far exceed that which is available, or is far outside the norm. In such cases workforce education professionals may need to determine whether the task or occupation is appropriate for the individual affected.

Learning Styles

As suggested earlier, one important implication of the cognitive learning research is that individuals have preferred learning styles, and instruction is most effective when the method is consistent with the learner's style. An important further consideration is that instructional designers and teachers also have preferred learning styles and are likely to stress that style in their design, even when it does not match the dominant style of the students or clients.

There are a number of different learning style formats that have been developed to guide the design of instruction (Dunn et al., 1981). In the Kolp model (Kolp & Smith, 1986), four different learning styles are defined, and it is theorized that every individual, while using all four in different situations, has a preferred style. These four styles can be operationalized as follows:

1. *Watchers*, who prefer to be shown and learn best when the content or task is demonstration.
2. *Readers*, who prefer to read written instructions and learn best when left alone with appropriate materials to figure it out for themselves.
3. *Doers*, who prefer to learn by a form of hands-on trial and error and learn best by employing this hands-on approach.
4. *Sensors*, who prefer to learn by intuitively sensing what is occurring and learn best when given the opportunity to construct their own meaning for a given task.

Obviously some of these learning styles are not appropriate at all for some kinds of knowledge acquisition. The sensing learning style, for example, may be an individual's preferred modality, but it is not effective in trying to assemble a child's toy on Christmas Eve. In this case, even though an individual's preferred learning style may be that of sensor, he or she must resort to a different learning style—typically the second preferred style—which could be reading the manual, or trial and error (*doer*), or seeking out someone to explain the task (*watchers*).

In an ideal educational environment, students or clients would receive instruction that uses only their learning style. In reality this is not possible unless it is a tutoring situation. The solution is to design instructional strategies that include elements of all four learning styles.

A final rather important implication for workforce education professionals is that there is some evidence that individuals select careers, or are most successful, in occupations whose tasks are consistent with an individual learning style. According to Kolp and Smith (1986), technicians are more apt to be doers, law enforcement officers, watchers.

Cognitive Styles: Serialist or Holist

Although learning styles describe individual preference for different approaches to learning, cognitive styles refer to the different ways individuals mentally organize data as they learn. The body of knowledge associated with cognitive styles is immense, and for a full discussion the reader should consult Jonassen and Grabowski's *Handbook of Individual Differences: Learning and Instruction* (1993). One cognitive style distinction, namely, serialist versus holist, is particularly important, however, to workforce education practitioners and is therefore discussed below.

Individuals who are *serialists* learn by combining information in a linear sequence focusing on small chunks of information. Serialists create a step-by-step approach in their mind as a way to learn and remember. *Holists* use a global, thematic approach that attempts to create broad descriptions (Jonassen and Grabowski, 1993). Holists attempt to understand the "big picture" of how things work and interact, finding the details created by serialists as being useless without this large picture.

The importance of the serialist/holist cognitive distinction is that researchers have found (Pask, 1976) that learning is maximized when instruction is matched to individuals' preferred cognitive style (serialist or holist). The problem is that most workforce education content generated from either the CBE or instructional system design (ISD) model is serialist in format. This creates a problem for holist learners who need to understand the whole in order to remember the pieces. The implication for the many learning styles and the serialist or holist cognitive style is that instruction must be designed in such a way that experiences are varied enough to appeal to individuals conversant with all learning–cognitive styles.

PREPARING EFFECTIVE INSTRUCTION

Ultimately, designing and delivering instruction comes down to (1) preparing and sequencing instructional materials or media, or modifying purchased materials in order to present the content of the curriculum, and (2), if necessary, getting the instructional equipment needed to use them. When instruction is guided by a well-prepared curriculum, the curriculum guide will provide alternative instructional approaches from which the professional can choose, based on the learning environment and the learner. In a practical sense the selection of instructional modalities often begins with a consideration of what is available to instructors or trainers.

In the *ASTD (American Association of Training and Development) Guide to Professional Human Resource Development Roles and Competencies*, Rothwell and Sredl (1992: 297) suggest instructional media can be viewed as teacher or trainer dependent or equipment dependent. Some examples of each are provided below (see Figure 9.1).

In designing instruction, many of these methods may be selected to teach a single learning objective. In fact, the effectiveness of any of these instructional modal-

Teacher/Trainer Dependent	Equipment Dependent
Lectures	Videotape
Case studies	View graphs (overheads)
Role playing	Computer assisted instruction (CAI)
Written simulations	Automated simulators
Chalkboards	Internet resources
Handouts	Interactive video
Socratic questioning	Instructional television
Group problem solving	Decision-making labs
Group brainstorming	Diagnostic trainers
Nominal group techniques	Scaled-down equipment

FIGURE 9.1   Types of Instructional Media

ities or media depends to a great extent on how they are integrated by the instructor or trainer into an effective instructional lesson, module, or experience. The pivotal point in instructional design is not just the selection of media or modalities but how they are integrated in a sequence of activities that are effective in promoting learning. This integration into a sequence that maximizes learning is the core challenge in preparing effective instruction

Principles of Instructional Design

Instruction is effective to the degree that it results in mastery of the learning objectives, in which mastery is defined as meeting the stated performance standards. There are three guiding principles of instructional effectiveness.

Consistency Principle.   The consistency principle teaches that effective instruction results when the instructional methods used are consistent with the learning objectives and course content and when the method of evaluation is consistent with both the content and these methods. For example, if the learning objective is to reduce defects in a manufacturing process by improving the techniques of assemblers, instruction that includes some manner of hands-on instruction and practice is preferable to lectures or written material. Likewise, assessment of learning should also be performance-based, not pencil assessment.

Adequacy Principle.   The adequacy principle is an extension of the consistency principle. It teaches that instruction is effective when the strategies employed are adequate to teach the content, depending on whether the material is facts, concepts, or procedures. If the objective is to teach concepts, instruction needs to include examples and nonexamples, as well as defining all the attributes associated with the concept. If the objective is to teach procedures, instruction should include all the necessary steps, as well as opportunity for demonstration and guided practice.

Mastery Learning and the Mastery Principle.   Finally, workforce education instruction is typically based on the instructional principle of *mastery learning*.

Mastery learning adherents believe that instructional effectiveness is maximized when content is organized or sequenced into a hierarchy of tasks of increasing difficulty or sophistication. An objective or objectives are written for each task and an instructional strategy devised to teach each objective. Assessment is *criterion referenced*, meaning that it flows from the learning objective and typically is performance based. Students or clients progress to the next task or learning objective when they have "mastered" the previous objective. The definition or criteria for mastery are stated in the learning objective. Importantly, mastery learning is the common instructional framework employed in competency based education (McNeil, 1996).

ONE MODEL OF INSTRUCTIONAL EFFECTIVENESS

Whereas the purpose of instruction is to cause learning to occur, instructional effectiveness is the degree this desired instruction occurs. How to best design instruction to maximize effectiveness is an ever-evolving area of educational psychology research, particularly as new forms of instructional media—such as the Internet—are developed. Among schema or formats for designing effective instruction, the technologist model developed from the work of the psychologist B. F. Skinner (1968) is among the more popular with workforce educators in both the public and private sectors. Perhaps the best known of the technologist models was promoted by Hunter (1984).

An eight-step adaptation of a technologist or behavioral instructional effectiveness model for workforce education is outlined below (see Figure 9.2).

The instructional effectiveness model outlined above is grounded in the concept of teaching or designing instruction to master an instructional objective that

1. *Motivate the Learner:* Explain how the content will be important for success on the job.
2. *Present the Behavior Objective:* Describe the skill to be taught, how it connects to those skills previously learned, what level of performance is expected, and how this performance will be assessed.
3. *Provide Information:* Using any one of the number of different instructional methods (lecture, reading assignments, video, guest speakers, or AC), the relevant information is provided.
4. *Demonstrate:* Using any number of instructional techniques, the skill or procedure is demonstrated.
5. *Check for Understanding:* Students/trainees are assessed, typically informally, by asking questions randomly to determine if rudimentary learning has resulted from Steps 1 through 4. If not, these steps are repeated before going on to Step 6.
6. *Provide Supervised Practice:* Students/trainees are engaged in guided practice of the material taught, meaning that close supervision is provided while they attempt to master the skill.
7. *Provide Independent Practice:* When the instructor or trainer is confident that the material has been mastered to the point at which error, particularly error that is a risk to safety, is unlikely, then students are engaged in independent practice of the skill or procedure, using equipment and materials as similar to those in the workplace as possible.
8. *Assess Mastery:* Assessment is conducted to determine mastery, which is defined as meeting the performance criteria in the learning objective.

FIGURE 9.2   Eight Steps to Effective Workforce Education Instruction

is correctly prepared. In this model all instructional activity is guided by the question of whether it promotes the learning or mastery of the objective. The model is particularly well suited to the typical occupational content of workforce education when the goal is to teach behavioral objectives developed in either CBE or ISD curriculum development. However, when goals of instruction are not predetermined—such as group problem solving or creative design or less technical material such as [...]p consensus and interaction is an [...] may not be as instructionally eff[...] [...]ariety of instructional technique [...] situation.

It also shou[...] [...]ectiveness model typically includ[...] [...]ad, do). Also, all steps need not [...] [...]nts. With experience, practition[...] [...]ing what steps to omit. When stu[...] [...]ng practice probably will not be [...] [...]. Like all instructional models, t[...] [...]t dictate practice. However, when [...] [...]uctional effectiveness and the ultimate point of the profession, namely, learning.

[Handwritten note: This is a good place to use another reference. Ask for instructional techniques.]

THE ADULT LEARNER

Although exact numbers are not available, it is certain that, aside from high school vocational education, the majority of those involved in workforce education beyond the high school level are adult learners age 22 or older. For this reason the adult learner is the most common client of programs that address the mission of providing career opportunities for individuals. Instructional design for adults involves unique considerations.

Surveys of adults enrolled in education beyond high school demonstrate perhaps the obvious, that for 80 percent motivation is work related (Zemke & Zemke, 1981). In general adults will be motivated by that which has obvious nexus to job advancement and security, job changes, or a return to full-time employment. One important implication is that adults will be more receptive and more successful in workforce education when the program is timely to these events. A newly promoted supervisor or newly displaced or newly transferred worker is more likely to be teachable than incumbents. In particular, those who work in human resource development (HRD) settings need to be sensitive to what Zemke calls these "teachable" moments and capitalize on them.

Curriculum and Instruction for Adult Learners

Cross (1981) points out in *Adults as Learners* that there are unique considerations in designing curriculum and instruction for adults. First, new knowledge, concepts, tasks, or behaviors are learned quicker when they are concrete to the occupational goal and when they relate to the previous experience of the student or client. Second, the instructor must be sensitive to the pace at which new material is taught if the goal is mastery. Often the adult learner will need more time but will be more accurate once mastery has been reached. Third, new material should be presented in small segments, and, fourth, it is important that material be reviewed often to facilitate retention and recall.

Finally, research suggests ways in which instruction should be conducted that promotes learning with adults. First, adults prefer self-directed learning to stand-up lectures. "Self-directed" does not necessarily mean solitary learning. Adults have been found to benefit from group learning experiences, such as case studies and presentations. When working in groups, adults prefer some latitude as to how the task will be accomplished. Like learners of all ages, adults in particular do not like long lectures about material that in their view is irrelevant to why they are there. Adults benefit from having a clear account of what is expected in terms of their performance in the program of study; they do not tolerate ambiguity well, and prefer a well-structured method of instruction.

Adults frequently bring significant knowledge to the workforce education experience, and often rigid values; many times it is necessary to allow individuals to share both in order to promote learning. At the same time, the instructor must be sensitive to minority opinions and prevent less than thoughtful confrontation to occur. Finally, just like all learners, adults have different learning styles (see Chapter 9), and instruction must be varied to meet the needs of all concerned.

SUPERVISION OF INSTRUCTION TO IMPROVE TEACHING

An ongoing professional responsibility of workforce educators is to work to improve their own teaching effectiveness and help colleagues do likewise. When workforce educators are in a supervisory role, this responsibility becomes their formal job task as a workforce educator. Two methods employed to improve teaching are called *reflective teaching* and *clinical supervision of instruction*.

Reflective Teaching

The reflective model for improving teaching is, as the name implies, the idea that the one way for professionals to improve their teaching is to reflect on their teaching (Walker, Adamsky, Brower, & Hart, 1992). The process involves asking oneself questions such as "What did I do that worked and what did not?" Implicit in this method is the individual recognition that instruction is the key process of the profession and, therefore, it is imperative that it be as effective as possible. This may seem self-evident, but in practice it is not accepted among educators as being ethically imperative. This view, for example, is in opposition to the view that the instructor's role is to cover the content and the learner is at it fault if the instructional method was not effective.

Clinical Supervision of Instruction

Clinical supervision of instruction has the same goal as reflective teaching but, as the term "clinical" implies, it involves colleagues watching colleagues teach and then providing objective feedback. As outlined by Acheson and Gall (1987), the word "clinical" suggests a one-on-one interaction between supervisor and instructor or between instructor and instructor, with a focus on the actual teaching behaviors in the classroom or formal training setting. The rationale is similar to having golf pros watch you swing and tell you what they saw. Two factors are critical to the process. First, both the observed and the observer must share, if not a common model of teaching effectiveness, then at least a common terminology (such as "guided practice"), so that they may communicate effectively. The second critical factor is the use of a supervisory cycle (Acheson & Gall, 1987). This process begins with a goal setting—planning conference—that takes place prior to the observation on teaching and at which time observers and observed agree as to what the focus of the clinical session(s) will be (anticipatory set, testing learning). In the second phase, instruction is observed using one of many classroom observation techniques. In the third and final phase, a "feedback" conference is held between the observers and the observed in which the former report on what they saw, followed by a period of discussion.

Clinical Supervision and Performance Appraisals

Although the purpose of clinical supervision of instruction is to help educators become more skilled, a similar process, particularly in public school settings, is used for performance appraisals or evaluation. Although the process is intended to be *formative* (to develop competence) or *developmental* (for individual improvement), it often serves the dual purpose of being a *summative* method of documenting performance (Acheson & Gall, 1987). In places where this is practiced, the interface should be clearly defined and communicated. Often workforce educators find themselves in a position of being both mentors and evaluators of teaching effectiveness, and the two tasks often seem contradictory and thus impossible. But one should also consider that the role of instructors is exactly the same: namely, they are both promoters and evaluators of learning. This brings up the final aspect of instructional design, assessment of learning.

ASSESSMENT OF LEARNING

In both the public and private setting, workforce educators are typically required to assess individual student or trainee performance in meeting the curriculum's learning objectives and communicate the result to multiple audiences. This task is often a professional challenge to both instructor and supervisor. In a CBE or ISD curriculum, student assessment would appear to be a rather straightforward, non-controversial process; students either achieve mastery, as defined by the wording of the behavioral learning objectives, or they do not. If, in fact, the purpose of assessment was to objectively report the number of competencies achieved, there would be little or no problems; a student can either perform at the level required or not, and this can be documented.

Problems in student assessment arise, however, because in many educational settings and in all credit or degree-granting institutions, letter (A, B, C) grades must be awarded. Now assessment takes on a new dimension, namely, the rank ordering of students. Student assessment in CBE or ISD now becomes more involved. The issues are not just what competencies a student achieved but how many must be achieved to get an A, B, C, and so on. Such grading seems inconsistent with the individualization implied by CBE or ISD, yet it is the common practice, and in today's litigation-happy society, workforce educators are advised to have written grading policies and procedures and give their students or clients a copy. One technique that can be used is the development of assessment rubrics.

In the 1990s, the concept of *authentic assessment* became popular among general education professionals. Considering that "authentic" means to demonstrate the application of knowledge, it seems fair to suggest that workforce education assessment, when it results from CBE or ISD, has always been "authentic." One development from the authentic assessment movement, however, is of practical value to workforce educators, namely, the use of *rubrics* to define, in detail, assessment that is associated with particular learning objectives. Goodrich (1996) defines a rubric as a "scoring tool that lists the criteria for assessing a piece of school work." Of course, a well-written performance objective also lists such criteria, but often it does not describe the sometimes involved procedure necessary to perform the assessment or how variations among those students who achieve the objective will be graded. A rubric can be useful in communicating to students how letter grades will be assigned to performance. Specifically, all students may achieve the performance objectives but some at a minimum proficiency and others at the expert level. An assessment rubric describes these variations, how they will be determined, and the letter grade associated with each. Thus, rubrics have the advantage of both "defining quality" and communicating these definitions to students so they can become judges of their own performance (Goodrich, 1996).

Legal Issues in Student Assessment

There are several legal issues related to student assessment that workforce educators should be aware of. They evolve around the issue of what can be counted in determining a letter grade. The issues arise when grading policies begin to consider behaviors that are not strictly related to the learning objectives—such as attendance, disruptive behavior, and dress.

Can a student's grade be reduced for poor attendance? In general the answer, according to the courts, is no. At the same time, the courts have ruled that poor attendance can be a just cause for denying credit. Specifically, the courts observe that the purpose of grading is to communicate learning and, thus, knowledge. The use of criteria that do not correlate directly—have a nexus—with knowledge as defined by the learning objectives is inappropriate. If a student never attends class but masters all assessments, the student obviously had knowledge that is independent of attendance. However, schools can make attendance a prerequisite for credit, because credit communicates institutional success, and students cannot be said to have been a success at a particular institution if they never attend.

A similar type of logic applies to using grades as a form of classroom management or disciplinary technique. Again, a school system has in place policies regarding student behavior. These policies are separate and distinct from grading policies. It is incorrect to use grades as a classroom management technique.

Can a student's grade be lowered for failure to come to class appropriately dressed or for not using appropriate safety equipment? In this case the answer is not as clear. Correct occupational attire and use of safety equipment may have a nexus to the objectives of workforce education programs. The key point is whether correct dress and use of safety equipment are actually written as learning objectives in the curriculum. If they are, then attire and the use of safety equipment probably would stand the nexus test and could be used in assessment.

Ethical Issues in Student Assessment

There are, of course, ethical issues in student assessment. It is clearly unethical to show favoritism or to discuss individual assessment with those who have no legitimate need to know this information. Both actions are a violation of the public trust.

A more thorny ethical consideration is excessive failure. Namely, is it ethical for a workforce educator to give all failing grades. In such cases instructors typically cite high academic standards as the reason. Are they justified? The answer lies, again, in the purpose of the profession. The ethical obligation is to promote learning. Excessive failures indicate excessive failure to learn and arguable incompetence or ineffectiveness of the instructor. Excessive failure may be the result, for example, of the instructor's setting learning objectives that are not achievable given student skill levels. On the other hand, the learning objectives may be beyond the control of the instructor, set by licensing boards, or be minimal qualifications for employment. In such cases the issue is not instructor incompetence but inappropriate placement of students in the class.

SUMMARY AND IMPLICATIONS FOR PRACTITIONERS

Whereas workforce education is a professional endeavor, the defining product of which is instruction, it is imperative that workforce educators in all roles have knowledge of instructional design. In particular, all should have a personnel model of instructional effectiveness. This chapter presented such a model that is grounded in both behaviorist and cognitive learning theory. The design of instructional systems is, of course, a field in and of itself, and workforce educators are urged to seek out opportunities to learn more. Equally important is the professional obligation of those who deliver instruction to constantly work to improve in either the delivery or the monitoring of the instruction. This chapter ended with a brief discussion of student assessment, which is typically the last step in an instructional effectiveness model. The discussion included a consideration of several legal and ethical issues. Practitioners are advised to pay particular attention to these issues because they are fraught with conflict. The purpose of instruction is to promote learning (mastery) of curriculum content. Part III of the book closes with Chapter 10, in which curriculum content is presented.

10

CURRICULUM CONTENT

Although the "product" of workforce education is instruction, the essence of this product is the content. Curriculum content is the knowledge that is to be delivered by instruction. Content is the "what" of the who, what, when, and where questions addressed by a comprehensive curriculum.

In workforce education, content takes three forms: cognitive (facts and concepts), psychomotor (manipulative occupational tasks), and interpersonal (work ethics). Determining and validating this content are major activities in the workforce education curriculum development process. It is a process that is mostly unique to workforce education; although the content of traditional academic courses is somewhat timeless, the content of workforce education courses is ever changing as technology and materials change in the workplace. This chapter discusses the methods of determining curriculum content in workforce education as well as the three major types of workforce education curriculum content. The chapter also discusses an aspect of curriculum content specific to workforce education, namely, safety and the related topic of liability.

THE PHILOSOPHICAL BASIS
OF CONTENT DETERMINATION

Philosophy, according to Miller (1995), provides a unifying theory for guiding education activity. Arguably, the selection of curriculum content should be guided by a philosophical point of view or school of thought. When workforce education conforms to the technologist or behaviorist instructional design model (see Chapter 9), the guiding philosophical point of view is that of *pragmatism*. As suggested by the term "pragmatism," the pragmatist philosophy teaches that the real world is the reality that should guide thought and action and thus curriculum content. The objective of pragmatic instruction is to promote the learning of content that mirrors the real world as much as possible. The emphasis is on learning by doing in order to replicate successful behavior that is observable in the workplace. Pragmatic curriculum is verified or evaluated through human experience (Miller, 1995). The philosophical school of pragmatism is the underlying philosophy of the most common method of curriculum content determination in workforce education, namely, "task analysis."

METHODS OF CONTENT SELECTION

All educators and trainers are faced with decisions regarding content selection, or what to teach. The selection of curriculum content, however, is considerably more complex in workforce education than in general education. An instructor teaching algebra begins with a body of knowledge that has been well defined over the centuries, and even the sequencing of the content is probably time proven. The workforce educator, on the other hand, particularly the human resource development professional, is often faced with the task of selecting content to improve human performance or individual labor market advantage when the desired performance or task is complex, variable, and changing. Because of the rapidly changing nature of materials, technology, and evolving occupational tasks, workforce educators are also constantly having to revise the content of their curriculum. For this reason the workforce educator, in contrast to many general educators, must be skilled in the content determination technique called task analysis.

TASK ANALYSIS

Task analysis is defined as steps taken to study an aspect of work in order to determine the "task" an individual needs to master to perform adequately on the job. Task analysis is the main methodology used for curriculum content determination in both the competency-based education (CBE) and the instructional systems design (ISD) methods of workforce education instructional development. There are a number of different approaches to task analysis (content determination) that span the continuum from subjective to objectives. The first relies only on the philosophical point-of-view design to determine content.

The Philosophical Approach to Task Analysis

The most subjective of task analysis techniques, and therefore the least reliable and valid, is the philosophical approach (Finch & Crunkilton, 1989). In the philosophical approach to task analysis, curriculum content is determined by the philosophical belief of the curriculum designer or instructor about what students "should" know instead of any formal analysis of the workplace to determine what workers "need" to know to be successful. An example of the philosophical approach to curriculum content determination occurred in the early 1990s when federal funding regulations for high schools and postsecondary vocational technical education required that curriculum include content called "all aspects of the industry." The "all aspects of the industry" approach to content selection called for going beyond, if not deemphasizing, essential occupational skills and knowledge in favor of a broad range of knowledge that might affect a particular occupation. All aspects of a particular industry could include, for example, the role of labor unions, the environmental impact of the industry, and the importance of international competition. Obviously such content would not result from a formal task analysis of an occupation that investigates what workers do on the job. It stems, instead, from a philosophical belief (as advocated by the educational philosopher John Dewey) that, including this "all aspect of the industry" as curriculum content, would better prepare youth to be democratic change agents and decision makers. A more common approach to curriculum content determination is the "introspective approach."

Introspective Task Analysis

A slightly more reliable and valid approach to task analysis is called the introspective approach (Finch & Crunkilton, 1989). The *introspective approach* is the process whereby instructors or trainers determine what to teach from introspectively recalling their own occupational experience. In the introspective approach designers and instructors rely on recalling what they had to know in order to be successful, and then they design curriculum content accordingly. Before more sophisticated approaches to task analysis were developed, the introspective approach historically was the most common method of content determination in workforce education and was one of the main reasons instructors with extensive occupational experience were preferred.

In general, however the philosophical and introspective approaches to curriculum content are not preferred because they are not based on a systematic analysis of the occupation or task and thus lack reliability and validity. The philosophical approach is devoid of any workplace verification, and all too often the introspective approach results in the course content being determined by what the instructor likes to teach or is familiar with, not what students need to know. Other more formal or systematic methods of task analysis are preferred.

Formal Approaches to Task Analysis

The objective of formal systematic task or occupational analysis is to describe and verify the duties and tasks of an occupation (Finch & Crunkelton, 1989) in order that valid instructional objectives can be written and instruction designed to teach them. A comprehensive task analysis results in a listing or codification of all behaviors including skills, knowledge, and attitudes that are necessary either to obtain labor market advantage or to maximize human performance in an occupation. Although there are a variety of methodologies employed in task analysis, a common element is a system or hierarchy used to organize the content. An example is provided in Figure 10.1).

The hierarchy used to organize the results of task analysis begins with the identification of an occupational title (sometimes called domains), which is often

I. Occupational Title/Classification/Domain (Carpenter)
II. Job Title/ Essential Duties (Rough Framing)
III. Tasks (Installing Floor Joists)
IV. Steps (Installing Cross-Braces)

FIGURE 10.1   Format for Task Analysis Results

taken from the *Dictionary of Occupational Titles*—an extensive occupational classification system developed by the U.S. Department of Labor. *Duties* are the major responsibilities associated with a particular occupation and are often synonymous with job titles within an occupation. *Tasks* are those steps that must be accomplished to perform the duty or job. In the case of hanging interior doors, tasks would include framing and installing lock sets. In some task analysis formats, tasks are further broken down into *steps* taken to complete the task. For example, in the occupation or domain called carpentry, one job or essential duty is rough framing; one task of this job is to cut and install floor joists, and one step of this task is to install cross-bracing. A curriculum designed to prepare carpenters would include instructional design to teach the installation of cross-bracing.

In an HRD setting, task analysis in industry would most likely begin at the task level. In either case the result of task analysis is a delineation of those behaviors necessary to be successful in the workplace and, therefore, is the content of the curriculum.

TYPES OF FORMAL TASK ANALYSIS

Although the term "task analysis" refers to a specific type of research, there are several research designs or methods that are employed to conduct formal task analysis. They differ in the methodology used to identify and/or verify the duties, tasks, and steps associated with a particular occupation or performance problem. There are two main approaches: interviewing and/or surveying incumbent workers or occupational experts and direct observation of workers on the job.

Survey Methods: DACUM and DELPHI

Because of cost and time considerations, the most widely used methods of task analysis rely on sampling incumbent expert workers to develop and/or verify a list of duties, tasks, and steps associated with a particular occupation or domain. Perhaps the most familiar of this type of methodology is the *DACUM* process originally developed by the Canadian government. The term DACUM stands for "Develop A Curriculum" and employs a team of eight to ten incumbent workers, instructors, and others who are considered to be experts in an occupation. The group meets face to face, develops the duties and tasks, and then organizes them into a sequential instructional profile.

A second common approach using incumbent workers or experts is the *DELPHI* methodology developed by the Rand Research Corporation. In this technique the identification and verification is done by mailed questionnaires. The DELPHI technique can be viewed as a variation of task analysis that focuses on reaching consensus and typically begins with a preexisting task analysis list or a beginning list developed by a panel of experts. This initial duty and task list is mailed to a panel with the request that they indicate the degree to which they believe each item is important and then add new items that they think should have been included on the original. The next mailing includes the items recommended by the panel but not items the panel believed were not important. Commonly three rounds of mailings are done.

Observational Methods: Critical Incident Technique

The most elaborate form of task analysis involves actually observing incumbent workers do their jobs. One such method is called the *critical incident technique*. As the name implies, the intent is to determine what knowledge, psychomotor skills, and affective behaviors are critical to success by watching workers do their job. This technique is particularly useful in identifying interpersonal behavioral aspects of job performance or in solving unique human performance problems where only watching will reveal the key factors.

Advisory Committee Methods

The most common method used to verify for a particular locality a task analysis that has been done professionally is the use of occupational advisory committees. Typically, occupational advisory committee members are local employers. One function of this group is to act much the same as the panel of experts does in the DACUM process. Working from an existing task analysis, such as V-TECHS materials, the group makes alterations in the task analysis in order to bring it in line with the local labor market.

One note of caution needs to be made, however, in the use of occupational advisory committees for this purpose, namely, that, depending on the makeup of the committee, an overly narrow-focused curriculum can result. It may be, for example, that in a particular locale metal studs are not used and thus would not be recommended by the advisory committee composed of only local contractors. However, in a neighboring locality the fire code may require metal studs, providing a significant labor market advantage to those who are skilled in their installation. The same type of bias can result if all the occupational advisory committee members are late adopters of technology. For this reason, it is important that when advisory committees are used for the purpose of task analysis verification, they represent a variety of employers including some who do business outside the immediate region and some who are early adopters of new technology and materials.

Limitations of Traditional Task Analysis Methods

Formal task analysis has its drawbacks. Conducting quality task analysis is a sophisticated, time-consuming, and expensive process. For this reason, national consortia have been formed to conduct this research, including the Vocational Technical Education Consortium to the States (V-TECHS) and the Interstate Distributive Education Curriculum Consortium (IDECC). With the advent of these and other groups, task analysis for the workforce education professional at the local level now typically involves verification of tasks for a particular locality, using a task analysis completed by a consortium or private vendor. Typically, local occupational advisory committees are used to conduct such verifications.

Task analysis is not without its critics. Perhaps the most common criticism is that the methodology focuses on what is the current occupational environment, not what it will be, or even what it should be. There is also the tendency of task analysis methods to focus on observable psychomotor skills and related knowledge, and it often fails to focus on less easily observable essential work habits, academic skills, or advanced literacy skills. For example, the essential new interpersonal skills associated with the increased use of work teams in industry might not be identified in a task analysis process because the practice of using such teams is only beginning to become prevalent. Because of these limitations a different approach to task analysis is recommended. Developed for this book, it is called the "essential skills approach."

In the essential skills approach to task analysis, the three levels of workplace essential skills—Level I, work ethics; Level II, academic skills; and Level III, occupational and advanced workplace literacy skills (see Chapter 5)—are used as a guiding template to direct task analysis methods, be they DACUM, DELPHI, or critical incident. In light of the relationship of all three levels of skill to labor market advantage and success on the job, it is essential that workforce education curriculum address all three levels of essential skills. Frequently task analysis methods result in duty and task lists that are predominantly observable tasks; conspicuously absent are work ethics and behaviors, essential academic skills, and even advanced workplace literacy skills such as the critical skill of being a self-learner.

Essential Skills Approach to Task Analysis

To compensate for the limitations of traditional task analysis as discussed above, an *essential skills approach* to task analysis is recommended. In the essential skills approach, the three levels of workplace basic skills (see Chapter 5, Figure 5.1) serve as a guide to task analysis, meaning that at each phase the question to ask is, "Are there relevant essential work ethics and behaviors, essential academic skills, and workplace literacy skills as well as occupational skills that need to be taught?" Specifically, it is recommended that once an occupational title or duty is identified, three key essential skill questions are asked of each task and step that result from the task analysis: namely, "What are the necessary work ethics or behaviors?" "What are the prerequisite academic skills?" and "What are the necessary occupational and advanced literacy skills" (see Figure 10.2). By using this format it is more likely that a task analysis results in all levels of essential skills being identified and thus included in the behavioral objectives that flow from the analysis.

I. Occupational Title/Classification/Domain (Carpenter)
II. Job Title/ Duties (Rough Framing)
III. Tasks (Installing Floor Joists)
    essential work habits required
    essential academic skills required
    essential occupational-specific skills required
    workplace literacy skills required
IV. Steps (Installing Cross-Braces)
    essential work habits required
    essential academic skills required
    essential occupational-specific skills required
    workplace literacy skills required

FIGURE 10.2   Essential-Skills/Task-Analysis Taxonomy

THREE CURRICULUM CONTENT AREAS IN WORKFORCE EDUCATION

This chapter now turns to a discussion of the different types of workforce education curriculum content. This content is organized by the three essential skill levels, beginning with appropriate work ethics.

LEVEL I: ESSENTIAL SKILLS: WORK ETHICS

In Chapter 5 it was pointed out that the foundation of employment is a set of behaviors that are appropriate to the workplace. These essential behaviors—termed "work ethics"—include both an individual work ethic and a set of behaviors referred to as work ethics and behaviors, which may be common to all employment or specific to a particular occupation.

Successful workforce education practitioners know that workforce education that fails to address the basic level of essential skills will likely fail (Buck & Barrick, 1987). Without appropriate work habits, individuals are unemployable, regardless of Level II and III skills. Miller and Coda (1984) found, for example, that an "enabling work ethic"—defined as a set of beliefs and resultant behaviors that allow individuals to adapt in the workplace and thus ensure "long term harmony" at the work site—is a prerequisite to career success.

A distinction is made between work ethic and work ethics. The concept of a *work ethic* draws from the Protestant belief that working hard and striving for excellence was a moral responsibility and that being nonproductive was evil. When employers state they want an individual who gives a day's work for a day's pay, they are talking about the work ethic.

Good attendance	Honest
Punctual	Cooperative
Follows directions	Willing to learn
Neat appearance	Dependable
Friendly	Loyal
Tactful	Positive
Dresses appropriately	Patient

FIGURE 10.3   **Work Ethics: Behaviors and Attitudes Conducive to Occupational Success**

The meaning of the term *work ethics,* on the other hand, differs, depending on whether the occupation is professional—meaning that it has a code of ethics—or nonprofessional. In professional occupations "work ethics" refers to behaviors that are consistent with the points of the profession (see Chapter 1). In nonprofessional occupations the term "work ethics" is typically used to refer to a group of behaviors and attitudes that are appropriate in the workplace (see Figure 10.3).

Work behaviors include punctuality, good attendance, appropriate appearance, and friendliness. Habits include honesty, dependability, and cooperativeness. Virtually every study of skills needed in the workplace identifies these attributes as being essential. When the nature of the work is low skills/low wage, employers often indicate they are the only skills needed because the tasks can be taught quickly on the job. Even in high-skills/high-wage work, employers typically rank work habits second only to technical occupational skills (Thomas, 1989; Bishop, 1995).

Teaching Appropriate Work Habits

Despite the timeless importance of appropriate work habits for occupational success, research indicates that most often teaching these habits is not consistently part of workforce education curriculum and that instructional efforts to teach this content is mostly "unintentional," meaning that it is addressed only when the opportunity presents itself in the instructional setting (Ford & Herren, 1995). Some professionals may doubt whether work habits, particularly ethics and attitudes, can be taught. Research demonstrates, however, that they can (Sichel, 1991).

Appropriate work habits are taught in two ways—informally and formally. Regardless of whether work habits are part of the curriculum content, students or trainees learn work habits informally from observing the instructor or trainer (see cognitive apprenticeship discussed below) and by the degree of importance the educational program or institution puts on these habits as communicated by its policies and procedures. In programs in which attendance and accountability for absences are stressed, these habits are learned; if they are not stressed, student or trainees assume, and thus learn, that they are not important. Sometimes the type of learning that results from "leading by example" is referred to as the "hidden curriculum" (Pucel, 1995), suggesting that many times what is learned is not a part of the formal curriculum at all. It is important that both instructors and institutions practice the habits and attitudes they are teaching.

The second way work habits are taught is by formal instructional methods such as discussions of problems on the job, role playing, written case studies, and visual technologies. Ford and Herren's (1995) research found that, in their sample of work-study coordinators, discussion of on-the-job problems was the most common technique preferred and used, but a wide variety of other methods were used as well, including lecture, text, and video.

Writing in the *Journal of Vocational Education Research*, Annette Ford and Ray Herren (1995) suggest the *cognitive apprenticeship* model of instructional design could prove successful in teaching appropriate work habits. This informal instructional design concept, as explained by Brown, Collins and Duguid (1989) as well as by Berryman (1991), stresses the importance of learning that occurs when students or trainees model the behavior of their instructors or trainers as they progress through the curriculum, much the same way the apprentice of old learned from the master. Teachers employing the cognitive apprenticeship model use a variety of teaching strategies including coaching, scaffolding, fading, reflection, and exploration (see Berryman, 1991).

Unique Work Cultures

It should be noted that, although many appropriate work habits are generic to all work environments, some occupations have unique settings and cultures that result in unique standards of behavior. Appropriate attire on the job is one obvious example, but others are more subtle. In some skill construction trades, for example, even a seemingly unimportant thing like what workers use to carry tools when they are reporting to a job site can make a difference in employers' first impressions.

The existence of appropriate behaviors is not unique to the crafts but exists to some extent in all occupations. Often, conforming to these unique cultures is critical to success and needs to be made part of the curriculum content. For this reason it is just as important that curriculum content dealing with work habits be based on a task analysis methodology as it is for academic and specific occupational manipulative skills. To be effective, a curriculum must deal with both appropriate work habits that are generic and those that are unique, and only a good task analysis will specifically identify the latter.

LEVEL II: ESSENTIAL SKILLS: ACADEMIC SKILLS

The second level of essential skills is the traditional academic skills of reading for comprehension, mathematics, science, and both writing and oral communications. These essential skills are always prominently mentioned in state and national workforce preparedness studies. They were considered to be the first of a three-part foundation that the U. S. Department of Labor's study determined were necessary prerequisites to workers developing essential occupational competencies (U.S. Department of Labor, 1991a). It is clear that, once an occupation progresses from extremely low skill, proficiency in basic academic skills is necessary. At the same time the role academic skills play in the workplace and how they should be addressed in the workforce education curriculum are often overstated and grossly misunderstood.

The Role Basic Academic Skills Play in the Workplace

Although a broad set of academic skills is essential for success in formal education, common sense, backed up by research (Pucel, 1995; Stricht & Mikulecky, 1994), suggests that a much narrower subset is necessary for success in a specific occupation, and these subsets differ according to occupation. For example, in technical occupations, researchers found that only mathematical reasoning was a strong predictor of either success in training or productivity on the job. The most important predictor was prior technical knowledge; much the same results were found for nontechnical occupations as well. In a 1987 survey by the National Federation of Independent Business of six ability groupings considered in hiring, the academic group was rated last; number one was having prior occupational skills (Bishop, 1995).

The intent is not to argue that sound basic academic skills are not important. Such skills are, for example, the basis of the ability to be an independent self-learner. What is suggested is that it is far more likely that such skills are more important to success in training than on the job. In light of limited instructional time, workforce education curriculum should be designed to "concentrate" on a subset of academic skills that are related to specific occupational or human performance problems.

A fundamental principle in basic academic skill instruction for the workforce education profession is the advice given by the American Association for the Advancement of Science (AAAS), namely, that instruction be concentrated on a well-defined subset of academic skills and that sufficient instructional time be allowed for this purpose to ensure they are mastered by students or trainees (Blackwell & Henkin, 1989). Although the AAAS was speaking specifically about mathematics, the principle holds true for the other basic academic skills as well. In workforce education these essential academic skills are identified through the essential-skills task analysis process.

Identifying Academic Skill Requirements

Identifying a subset of appropriate academic skills related to an occupation or human performance problem requires task analysis. The importance of using task analysis to identify academic skills is suggested by the work of David Pucel (1995), confirming that in any particular occupation only a subset of academic skills is used regularly. Pucel studied the mathematics tasks and related mathematics skills required in two distinct occupations—secretary and electronics technician. His research identified 34 different secretarial tasks that required mathematics, but only 17 out of a possible 63 mathematical operations were used to perform these tasks. Electronics technicians were found to do 45 different occupational tasks that required 38 mathematical operations. It is interesting to note that neither occupation included tasks that required all operations, and only 17 were common to both.

Unfortunately, little occupational task analysis of this type has been done. In fact, often, when asked, employers are hard pressed to identify the exact mathematical operations workers perform. Research regarding science principles is even more scarce. Although workforce education curriculum designers and instructors may be able to rely on public occupational task analysis for psychomotor skills, they may have to do their own task analysis of academic skills (see Pucel, 1995).

Teaching Essential Academic Skills

There are four methods of teaching academic skills. One is the common academic approach of using traditional teaching methods, mostly stand-up lecture, to the teach the skills independent of any context. This method is widely used, even at two-year technical and community colleges in which the academic faculty is separate from the technical faculty and students from a variety of different technical and nontechnical programs take the same courses. In general, however, this non-contextual approach is the least preferred in workforce education.

There are three preferred methods of teaching academic skills in workforce education settings—applied academics, integrated academics, and related academics. *Applied academics* is the practice of teaching concepts by using a real-world context. The focus is on teaching academic, not occupational skills; the traditional sequence and scope of the instructional content are still used, but an applied context is used in the information delivery, guided practice, and independent practice stages. The curriculums prepared by the Center for Occupational Research and Development (CORD) are excellent examples of applied academics. *Integrated academics* is a strategy that attempts to coordinate the teaching of occupational skills and traditional academic skills by using the former as the context for the latter. The objective is to drive students as high in the traditional curriculum as possible by using a context they are familiar with, namely, the occupation they are studying. *Related academics* differs from the latter two in that the academic content is determined by what skills are necessary to master the occupational learning objectives. Not all of these approaches are appropriate in all settings. In high school workforce education, in which mastery of a broad set of academic goals is an educational objective, the applied or integrated approach may be preferable. In most other settings the related approach is preferred because of its focus on those skills that are essential to success on the job.

Perhaps the best individual to teach related academics is the occupational instructor or trainer. Research suggests, for example, that the opportunity to teach academic concepts is frequent in workforce education. Unfortunately, the research also suggests few instructors take the opportunity when it arises. Some do not think it is their responsibility; others do not feel qualified.

Academic Skills and Success in Training

A very common problem related to academic skills faced by workforce educators at all levels is that many times the level of academic skills that students or trainees have when they begin training is inadequate to benefit from the program of study.

Cigola (1992) found, for example, that, although the reading level of students in a high school retailing class probably was sufficient to be successful on the job, it was lower than the reading level of the instructional materials developed for this course by a national association. As a result, the reading level was a prime predictor of academic success in class but not necessarily on the job.

This is not an uncommon event. In some states, a large percentage of all students enrolled in occupational programs is classified as educationally disadvantaged. In such cases it is clear that the students' academic skills and the curriculum do not match. There are two choices workforce educators can make—change the students or change the curriculum. Faced with enrollment pressures and/or a mission to serve all students, the latter option is often the only one.

In circumstances in which the academic abilities of entering students are insufficient to master the curriculum content as designed, the workforce educator has several options. If it can be assumed that the academic skills of students or trainees can be remediated and it is possible to provide such remediation, then the curriculum may need only minor revisions. Often, however, it is not realistic to try to remediate academic skills, and different instructional methods that have less dependency on academic skills, such as reading, may have to be employed. For example, it is often possible to obtain visual instructional materials or materials written at a lower reading level.

When students' academic skills are dramatically inadequate to master the content, more drastic curriculum changes are required. Many times the gap between the prerequisite skills necessary to master the curriculum content and be successful on the job and those the students have is so large that the appropriateness of the occupational level addressed in the curriculum must be reconsidered. One approach is to alter the scope of the curriculum to teach only lower-level tasks and the steps necessary to be successful in the original occupation. For example, students may not have the prerequisite academic skills to be licensed practical nurses but do have the skills required to be a nurses' aide. Similarly, a building construction program of study may need to be revised into a building maintenance program to create a better match between the academic talents and occupational requirements of the enrollees.

LEVEL III: ESSENTIAL SKILLS: OCCUPATIONAL AND ADVANCED WORKPLACE LITERACY SKILLS

The final level of essential skills is occupational and advanced workplace literacy skills. Occupational skills are those unique psychomotor, analytical, and, in some cases, specialized behavioral skills that are specific to an occupation. The skills result in labor market advantage in gaining employment and are directly related to the productivity of incumbent workers. Advanced workplace literacy skills are those cognitive and affective skills that have come to be associated with the characteristics of a "world class" workforce. They include such skills as self-learning and effective group participation.

Essential Occupational Skills

Occupational skills can be manipulative in nature—preparing blood samples for analysis—cognitive and analytical in nature—estimating construction costs—or unique behavioral skills—sales techniques used by salespersons. Some occupational skills are used in a cluster of occupations. Such skills are described as *transferable skills.* An example of a transferable skill is the ability to use a micrometer to make extremely precise measurements. Because micrometers are used in occupations ranging from automotive repair to precision manufacturing, their use would be labeled a transferable skill. Depending on the mission of the workforce education program and the labor market, emphasizing transferable skills associated with a cluster of occupations may be a preferable content design. This is particularly true in rural labor markets or with younger students or trainees in which one goal is to maximize the scope of their labor market advantage as it results from instruction.

Teaching Occupational Skills

Occupational skills are the tasks identified in the task analysis process used in both the CBE and ISD instructional design models. These tasks or steps are ultimately written in behavioral terms that state what is to be performed, the conditions under which it is to be performed, and the level of proficiency required. The task of the designer or instructor then is to develop an appropriate design (lesson plan or module). The classic six-step behaviorist instructional effectiveness model is almost always used when teaching occupational skills (see Chapter 9). In particular, instruction invariably includes information followed by live demonstration. Instruction then typically proceeds to guided practice, then independent practice of the task or steps, followed by assessment of learning.

Often unique instructional methods are employed to teach occupational skills—most notable is the use of *automated trainers and simulators* that are designed to replicate tasks and steps that must be performed on the job. A scaled down but fully operational CNC controlled lathe that cuts only soft materials and fits on a tabletop is a type of trainer. Another common type of trainer is designed to teach how various industrial and residential systems work and how to diagnose the cause of malfunctions. Often such trainers allow the instructor to create various malfunctions in the system to demonstrate troubleshooting and allow guided and independent practice. Perhaps the most sophisticated of trainers are simulators that attempt to exactly reproduce the workplace environment. An example most are familiar with is the flight simulator used to train and retrain airplane pilots.

Advanced Workplace Literacy Skills

During the 1980s in the United States, a number of studies were conducted to determine what new skills workers needed to ensure that the nation would have a world-class workforce. The typical methodology consisted of interviewing or surveying chief executive officers and other experts regarding their vision of the worker of the future. The results were highly influenced by other developments, especially by the total quality movement (TQM) and its emphasis on teams and decision making at the lowest possible level. In the past few years many industries

---

Ability to be a self-learner
Decision-making/problem-solving skills
Group/team participation skills
Ability to work in a multicultural environment
Computer software manipulation skills
Systems design and improvement skills

**FIGURE 10.4   Advanced Workplace
Literacy Skills**

have downsized middle management dramatically and have adopted the TQM management approach, particularly the concept of work teams of cross-skilled workers who are authorized to make decisions as needed. As a result of this change in management philosophy from the Taylorist top-down to the Demingist TQM bottom-up approach, the workplace, particularly in manufacturing, has changed. To be successful, high-skills/high-wage workers are expected to have an expanded set of new skills referred to in this book as "advanced workplace literacy skills." Figure 10.4 summarizes these skills.

Teaching Advanced Workplace Literacy Skills
The new advanced workplace literacy skills reflect the current empowered role of high-skills/high-wage nonprofessional workers. In this role, workers are expected to act independently, to be able to teach themselves new tasks, to make decisions, to improve systems, and to solve problems. At the same time in this new role, the worker will more than likely be part of a work team that will be multicultural in nature, particularly in terms of gender and race.

The first implication of these developments is that it requires the workforce education curriculum to nurture independence as curriculum objectives. This suggests a curriculum design that is more constructivist than behaviorist, allowing for students or trainees to make multiple decisions and invent or discover solutions. It also suggests that instructors and trainers will have to be able to tolerate a lower degree of control and a higher degree of error by students.

The second implication of the new workplace literacy skills for curriculum design is the need to increase the use of student team assignments and other cooperative learning techniques in which students or trainees learn skills of group cooperation to achieve a given task. In the past one could assume most teams would be mostly white males, but tomorrow's workers will most likely encounter teams that are gender and racially diverse. The implication is clear: individuals who are sexist or racist will not realize their potential in the new workforce. The best place to put these attitudes to rest is in workforce education. Research (Sanogo, 1995) shows, for example, that women in nontraditional trade and industrial programs were much more likely to be harassed by fellow students than by instructors. Those who carry these behaviors into the workplace will fail; confronting such behaviors must be addressed in the same way lack of cooperation and tardiness, for example, must be addressed.

SAFETY AND LIABILITY

A unique aspect of workforce education curriculum content is the emphasis placed on safety. This emphasis stems from two concerns. The first is the importance good safety habits play in individual occupational success and worker productivity. It is reported, for example, that a work-related injury occurs in the United States every 18 seconds, and many are career-ending injuries. For this reason willful neglect of safety rules in the workplace is grounds for termination. The second emphasis is the issue of instructor liability when a student or trainee is injured while in class. Safety must be addressed as both a curriculum content and design issue and as a student or trainee supervision issue as well.

Safety Curriculum Content

Safety curriculum content is of two types. The most common are safety rules and operating procedures associated with specific materials, equipment, or processes that students or trainees will encounter in the curriculum and on the job. Such content may range from appropriate use of individual safety equipment to the appropriate storage of hazardous materials. The second type of safety curriculum content is the large number of state and federal regulatory programs that relate to various occupations. Some, such as the Occupational Safety and Health Administration (OSHA), are generic to most occupations, whereas others may be specific to particular occupations. Curriculums to prepare individuals for occupations in which hazardous materials are used would include hazardous materials legislation and worker rights in this regard.

Liability and Negligence

The influence of safety and liability issues on workforce education curriculum design cannot be overstated. In workforce education, much of the instructional equipment and materials are potentially dangerous. This concern for safety and liability permeates both curriculum content and design. For this reason, liability and negligence are discussed in this chapter on curriculum content.

More often than not, in workforce education the curriculum designer or instructor is put in the position of having to make a trade-off between instructional designs that simulate exactly work site conditions, but at significant risk to students or trainees, and designs that promote less optional learning but also minimize risk of accidents. Although, in general, it is wise to err on the side of safety, it is also impossible to eliminate all risk of accident. To be effective, workforce education must replicate the workplace to some degree, and the workplace, associated with some occupations, is a potentially dangerous place. Rather than render instruction totally ineffective out of safety and liability concerns, workforce education must act prudently to strike a balance. In fact, it is this demonstrated prudence that determines questions of negligence and liability.

Despite Herculean efforts by workforce educators, accidents still happen, and sometimes they are quite serious. In such cases the question of possible negligence and liability can be anticipated. A full discussion of these issues is beyond the scope of this foundations text, and the reader is directed, in particular, to Gatherhaol and Stern's *Legal Issues for Industrial Educators* (1987). What follows is a summary of the fundamental concepts.

SAFETY AND INSTRUCTOR NEGLIGENCE

The question of instructor and program administrator liability in cases of accidents is based on establishing if negligence occurred. The legal test for negligence is whether the instructor involved exhibits the *standard level of care* expected. The standard level of care holds that it is the responsibility of instructors to anticipate situations that could reasonably be foreseen and to proactively design curriculum to minimize such possibilities through a plan of supervision and instruction. The burden of proof that such proactive measures were taken lies with the instructor and administrator; thus, documentation is a critical aspect of all safety programs. Figure 10.5 provides six general rules for workforce educators that, if followed, would constitute a prudent plan of supervision.

The six guidelines listed below, if instituted and subsequently enforced, would constitute a plan of supervision that would meet the "reasonable level of care" liability test. An emphasis is placed on the plan being enforced. Although it is rare that a workforce education program does not have a safety plan of supervision, it

---

1. Equip all instructional areas and instructional equipment with safety apparatus that meets industrial or regulatory standards.
2. Provide and/or require all students or trainees to use relevant personal safety equipment such as safety glasses and hard hats.
3. Establish, post, and enforce safety rules and procedures for all instructional areas and equipment.
4. Provide instruction for the use of all equipment, materials, and procedures that could reasonably be anticipated to pose safety threats, and document that students or trainees master the instruction before they are permitted to use these potentially dangerous instructional materials.
5. Develop a daily safety program (such as checking safety equipment or hazardous material storage).
6. Develop an internal procedure for periodical safety audits of instructional areas, equipment, and materials.

FIGURE 10.5   Workforce Education Instructional Risk Management Guidelines

is not rare to find that it is not regularly enforced. It should be kept in mind that evidence that the plan was not enforced is evidence of negligence. It is also worth remembering that tenacious enforcement of the safety plan of supervision has important educational benefits aside from minimizing the risk of accidents: namely, that it communicates to the learner the importance of safety and does much to ensure that safety will become a habit of thinking.

SELECTION OF INSTRUCTIONAL EQUIPMENT

Among the numerous unique aspects of workforce education instruction is the selection of instructional equipment. In workforce education, instructional equipment is commonly industrial-grade occupational tools and equipment that is used instructionally to provide "hands on" guided and independent practice of occupational tasks and steps. Such equipment is one of the defining characteristics of workforce education and the contextual instructional modalities that are employed. It is also one of the principal reasons that the cost per student or trainee exceeds general education instruction. This chapter on curriculum content concludes with a brief discussion of selection of instructional tools and equipment.

The fundamental principle of instructional tools and equipment selection is that it should be based first and foremost on the curriculum content and instructional design. Although the nexus between instructional equipment and instructional objectives that flow from the task analysis process may seem elementary, the experienced workforce educator can cite numerous examples of instructional labs being equipped with instructional equipment that ends up unused because it does not support instructional curriculum objectives.

Technology Adoption Strategy

A related rule of equipment selection is that it should be guided by the institutional mission as it relates to technology adoption. At issue is the question of at what point in the adoption curve of new technology in the workplace will the curriculum be revised and new equipment acquired. In both industrial and service sectors, firms can be placed in one of three groups in terms of how quickly they adopt new technology. The *early adopters* take the risks associated with being on the cutting edge of new technology. *Fast followers* adopt new technology as soon as the early adopters have proved its worth. The *late adopters* adopt new technology only when it is imperative to survival.

Just as firms must decide on a technology-adoption strategy, workforce education programs must also decide whether they will be early, fast-follow, or late adopters of new equipment and processes as well. In some cases, the institutional mission is to assist firms in adopting new technology. If *technology transfer* is the mission, the institution will follow the early adopter philosophy of curriculum revision and equipment selection. More typically, however, workforce education programs take the fast-follow approach—if they have the funds to do so—adding new technology and instructional equipment when it becomes widely used in industry.

Equipment Specifications

Another axiom of equipment selection is to take the time to develop good specifications before sampling the market. A wise practice is to involve members of occupational advisory committees in developing these specifications before contacting vendors and others. During this process one should pay particular attention to hidden costs such as additional tooling needed to use equipment but not included in base price, special installation costs such as the need for unique electric and ventilation service, consumable supplies needed to use equipment, and cost of training. In many cases, the cost of these four items will exceed the cost of the base price of the equipment itself, and all too frequently in workforce education programs one can find equipment sitting idle because of unanticipated costs that were not budgeted.

Escalating Equipment Costs

From the inception of workforce education, an axiom of instructional design has been that students or trainees should learn to use industrial-grade tools and equipment. This philosophy has always been expensive and, without large industrial donations, particularly of consumable instructional materials (welding rods, for example), it is doubtful this type of instruction would have been possible. It is questionable, however, how much longer this philosophy will continue to be viable. The gap between equipment costs and available funds is widening rapidly because of rising costs and how quickly equipment is now becoming obsolete because of technological advancement. An industrial-grade kitchen for twenty students can cost over a million dollars. A computer-assisted designed software package and the necessary computer platform are almost guaranteed to be less than cutting edge in a year and obsolete in five. The equipment cost for some programs, such as dental hygienist, is getting so high that many programs are closing.

These rising costs have dramatic implications for workforce education curriculum design. The reality is that high instructional equipment costs are already changing the instructional design of workforce education and will continue to do so. Already instructional areas are much more likely to be equipped with trainers and scaled-down instructional equipment rather than full-size, industrial-grade hardware. It is also likely that curriculum design will need to rely more on work-based learning sites such as the practice promoted by the 1994 federal School-to-Work Opportunity Act to provide instruction on industrial-grade equipment.

SUMMARY AND IMPLICATIONS FOR PRACTITIONERS

The central ethical obligation of the workforce education profession is to promote learning. This chapter discussed the content of this imperative by addressing the issue of what should be taught. Philosophically, workforce education content determination is guided by the school of thought called pragmatism: the idea that what is taught should be guided by the practical consideration of what is observable and essential to achieve the ethical imperatives and the instructional objectives. This chapter recommends that practitioners be guided by the essential-skills approach to content determination, thus ensuring that what is taught includes all three levels of essential skills: work ethics, academic foundations, occupational-specific skills, and advanced workplace literacy skills. The practitioner is reminded that these skills are hierarchical. Programs that focus only on Level II and III skills, while ignoring Level I skills, risk certain failure.

This chapter also dealt with the critical issues of safety and liability associated with workforce education instruction. Although sound safety practices are essential to occupational success of workforce education clients, a sound plan of supervision designed to proactively prevent accidents in instructional areas is an ethical and legal imperative.

11

THE TRANSITIONAL SERVICES: JOB PLACEMENT

Various perspectives have been advanced in the preceding chapters about the two major missions of workforce education—developing the nation's workforce and promoting individual opportunity. In a major sense, these two missions converge and find their fullest expression in job placement. The act of placing a person in a job, particularly if the individual performs effectively and is satisfied, is, from an accountability standpoint, the most visible measure of what workforce education is about—preparing persons with employable skills and helping them to find employment. By many existing criteria, workforce education would be a failure if it prepared people for jobs that were not available or that did not match the skills they were trained to perform. Similarly, workforce education could be considered incomplete in its effectiveness if it did not help the persons trained to bridge the chasm from school or postsecondary training to employment, or from learning to implementing the skills they had acquired.

As we will discuss in this chapter, job placement is not really an *event*. If programs of workforce education are to be comprehensive and systematic in their application, job placement must be seen as the end of a *process*, the conclusion of a seamless progression, a career ladder, from school to work. This process begins in the experiences and modeling of the family, is constantly influenced by educational content, behavioral expectations, and applications of academic subject matter to work-related problems in the elementary, junior, and senior high schools, and is supported by transition mechanisms between the school and the employer and by the induction processes (orientation, on-the-job training, supervision) by employers. Thus, neither job placement nor the school-to-work transition in which job placement is embedded is solely a function of the school or training program. Rather, it is a complex process in which the school, relevant community mechanisms, and employers share responsibility.

As the United States has become increasingly engaged in intense international economic competition from other nations who have developed technological prowess, economic systems, and competent workforces that challenge the historical U.S. supremacy in export/import trade and global market share, American policies and practices in workforce education and human capital development have come under increasing scrutiny. Such scrutiny has revealed that many other nations have created workforce education systems from which the United States can learn. And such analyses have revealed that one of the most serious voids in U.S. policy and practice relevant to workforce education is at the point of the school-to-employment transition and at the point of entry in specific job placement.

The importance of U.S. deficits in how the school-to-work transition and job placement is treated is captured in observations made by several major policy analysis groups. One of these is the Commission on the Skills of the American Workforce (1991) that stated the issue directly in the following manner:

> *The lack of any clear, direct connection between education and employment opportunities for most young people is one of the most devastating aspects of the existing system. (p. 72)*

According to Berlin & Sum (1988), we could say that

> *We have the least well-articulated system of school-to-work transition in the industrialized world. Japanese students move directly into extensive company-based training programs, and European students often participate in closely interconnected schooling and apprenticeship training programs. In Austria, Sweden, the former West Germany, and Switzerland, it is virtually impossible to leave school without moving into some form of apprenticeship or other vocational training. (p. 1)*

A similar statement of concern can be found in *From School to Work*, published by the Educational Testing Service (1990), that states:

> *There are two difficult life-time transition points—into the work force for young people and out of the work force for older people. Given the rapid shifts in the American economy, currently the more difficult transitions are into the U.S. work force. And the U.S. record in assisting these transitions is among the worst in the entire industrial world... School counselors are overburdened, and helping with job placement is low on their agendas. The U.S. Employment Service has virtually eliminated its school-based programs. Our society spends practically nothing to assist job success among those who do not go directly to college. On the whole, the answer to the question, who links school to work? is the young themselves, largely left to their own devices... In the United States the institutions of school and those of work are separate and almost always, far apart. There are quite limited arrangements to facilitate this transition [to work] (p. 4).*

A final set of observations about the consequences that arise from the lack of a systematic process of school-to-employment transition services that begin in the school and span the period to induction into entry job placement is found in statements of the U.S. Congress's Office of Technology Assessment (1995). Speaking to the perceived problems that have recently led Congress to reemphasize work-based learning and to pass the School-to-Work Opportunities Act, which we will discuss at length in the remainder of this chapter, the Office of Technology Assessment identifies the following three problems:

1. Because there are few clear pathways between school and careers in the United States, many students are unmotivated in school and spend years bouncing from one low-paying job to another as they look for career opportunities.
2. Many young people are completing high school with low levels of basic academic skills, dysfunctional attitudes and work habits, and little occupational training; as a result they are inadequately prepared for well-paid employment and career progression.
3. Because of technological changes and international competition, increasing numbers of mid-level jobs now require complex thinking, close teamwork, and the ability to learn continuously while on the job.

Although there are many other important scholarly observations and policy statements that validate the importance of transition services and job placement as central components of workforce education, there are related emphases that also need some brief attention before turning to the nature of transition services per se.

Transition Defined

In one form or another, dictionary definitions of transition suggest similar elements. For example, a standard definition of transition is "a passage from one state, stage, subject, or place to another: Change" (Merriam-Webster, 1983: 1254). Thus, although life is full of transitions or passages from one educational level to another, one age or developmental level to another, the fundamental issue in the context with which this chapter is concerned is the transition from school or other organized training program to employment. It is impossible to specify a time period to characterize this transition; if transitional services are fully effective and there is an excellent match between the individual to be placed and jobs available, the transition period could be very short. Indeed, as in some European and Asian models which we discuss later, there may be no discernible gap between school and employment. Or, for those persons who complete school with no transition assistance available, who are figuratively cut adrift when they complete schooling or training, the process of transition to employment may be long and jagged. For some people there may be no period in their work life in which their commitment to their job is secure and stable and they are clearly no longer in transition.

As suggested earlier in the chapter, one can also think of transition as more than the period between the completion of schooling and the actual entry into employment. A more comprehensive view of transition would encompass the experiences in schooling that ultimately inform the individual's choice making and preparation for work that begins in the elementary school and that continues after job placement through the induction into employment. Such a view would recognize mini-transitions that occur, for example, when the individual combines schooling and part-time work or transition from one type of curricular content to another. Such a view of transition would downplay many current perceptions that educational content is separate from what takes place in work and other life experiences or that work only occurs when education has been completed. As Cheek and Campbell (1994) have observed, such views are both elitist and unrealistic.

Transition and Economic Competitiveness

Although precise data do not exist about the costs associated with less than effective transition services for students or adults making the transition from school or training to employment, there is no doubt that there are economic implications for both individual and social competitiveness. Certainly the longer an individual student is in transition from school to employment, the longer he or she is denied a steady income and the benefits associated with stable full-time employment. If the same individual is eligible for welfare or unemployment compensation, these costs become part of the governmental costs associated with less than fully functioning transitional services, and, indeed, the government loses tax revenue for use in other economically productive activities. In such cases the individual's lack of productivity becomes part of the aggregate reduction in productivity associated with the period of floundering, however short or long, that individuals experience as they try to make the passage from school or training to employment.

For those young persons who have serious difficulties in entering the labor market, there is the possibility, if not the likelihood, that some will be chronically underemployed or unemployed far into adulthood because, without the experience of full-time employment, they will lose credibility with employers, they will lack information relevant to effective job access and adjustment, and they will lack identity as workers (Mangum, 1988). Mangum has reported that there is a substantial minority of American youth primarily from culturally and economically deprived backgrounds who are "permanently scarred" by their unsuccessful experiences in making the transition from school to work. For these youth, and others who have significant difficulty in making the transition to employment, the problems of early unemployment and difficulty in effectively entering the labor market do not "age out": they linger, perhaps throughout that individual's life. The early deficits these people experience in seeing themselves as workers and establishing their early credibility with employers put these persons at risk compared with their age cohorts, and the residual effects of such experiences on their career life may be reflected in different forms of social or governmental dependency, impaired productivity, and the costs of treatment for substance abuse, depressive affect, and other behavioral and emotional problems found to accompany unemployment or underemployment (Borgen & Amundson, 1984; Feather & O'Brien, 1986; Winefield & Tiggemann, 1989).

The future potential as well as the current reality of the enormous individual, social, and fiscal costs that accompany an extended period of floundering and the possibility that some persons will be continuously at risk because of their inability to successfully negotiate the transition process to employment have now become a matter of national concern. In response, there has been a reconsideration of the importance of work-based learning in schools, the development of legislative remedies related to the school-to-work transition, and the stimulation of a variety of evolving recommendations that emphasize making schools more career relevant, that address school–employer partnerships, and that articulate other possible approaches to improving the school-to-work transition.

SCHOOL-BASED MODELS

Depending on how the issue is framed, there are many ways by which schools can create career pathways for students, ways that involve progressive knowledge about possible educational and career options to consider in the future. Such transition services include assistance with career planning, the integration of academic and vocational skills development within curricula, experiential learning related to reality testing the expectations of adult workplaces, the infusion of career development concepts into academic subject matter, community service, cooperative education, and other work-based learning opportunities. However these are specifically implemented, they need to reflect the reality that the school-to-work transition is not an event but, rather, a process that unfolds over an extended period. Such processes need to be rooted in the concepts of self and of opportunity that begin to be acquired early in the life of the child and advanced through whatever career-relevant activities and planning processes occur in the school as the adolescent or young adult ventures into the short or long transition period that bridges the passage between school and employment and that ultimately culminates, in the most positive sense, in the successful induction into a job. At each of these periods the questions to be answered and the needs to be met, as the career development of children, youth, adolescents, young adults, and adults evolve, require different emphases of career guidance, career-relevant schooling, work-based learning, and transition mechanisms.

One such conception of a system of school-based transition that emphasizes work-based learning has been provided by the Office of Technology Assessment of the U.S. Congress (1995). Figure 11.1 portrays that perspective. This model suggests the timing, intensity, duration, and progression of work experiences for children, youth, and young adults. As suggested in this model, work-based learning activities, in this case field trips to workplaces, can begin as early as the first grade and extend through postsecondary education and into graduate school. Obviously the examples given are not exhaustive of all possibilities, but this figure illustrates some of the types of emphasis in work-based learning that can be systematically provided at different developmental periods. There are all types of variations on the themes provided here. Herr (1995: 97–102), in addressing possible learning processes that could be systematically incorporated to increase career relevant schooling for employment-bound youth, has identified the following possibilities that appear in a somewhat abridged and paraphrased form.

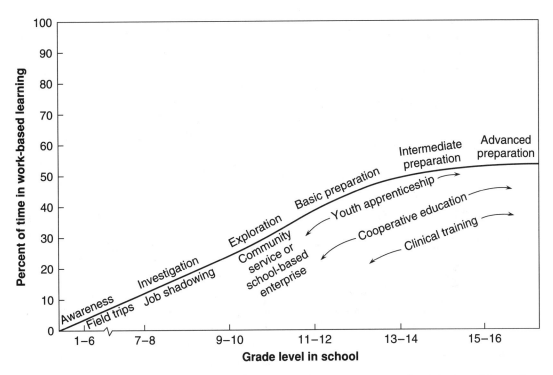

FIGURE 11.1   One Possible Progression through Several Types of Work-Based Learning

Source: Office of Technology Assessment of the U.S. Congress. (1995). *Learning to Work: Making the Transition from School to Work.* Washington, DC: U.S. Government Printing Office.

- Provide elementary students opportunities to learn that school is their work; that the work habits they develop in the elementary school are important indicators of the work habits that will be important in the junior and senior high schools and in the adult workplace. Also of significance in the elementary school are efforts to reinforce students' positive attitudes toward self and opportunities and their feelings of competence. In the elementary school, career guidance and work-based learning about the roles of workers and how personal interests, preferences, and abilities are reflected in classifications of jobs are not intended to force children to make premature choice but rather to avoid premature closure of future options. Provision of work-based experiences and knowledge in the elementary school requires extensive cooperation of teachers and parents to be effective. It is also important that elementary school personnel consider incorporating programs such as Kids and Power of Work (KAPOW, undated), in which employees of a participating business take classes of students on a tour of the business and then meet with them monthly, or at least periodically, throughout the school year to discuss characteristics of different jobs, work habits and attitudes, and the students' career interests. Teachers can build on these sessions as examples for use in academic course work.

- Make college and career options known to children beginning in the middle schools, if not before. Help them link what they are studying in academic areas to the occupational problems in which that subject matter is relevant or, indeed, critical. Help them to understand that they have options and the skills to address and master them.
- Provide a career guidance system, K–12, that focuses, among other goals, on helping students develop individual career development plans, the acquisition of self-knowledge and of educational and occupational opportunities, and the ways to explore and choose among these.
- Infuse career development concepts into academic subjects to help students understand how course work fits together and forms a body of knowledge and skills related to performance in work and other aspects of life.
- Promote schools-within-schools, career academies, and alternative preparatory academies. These possibilities provide special programs for students that promote student pride and participation as well as family and community involvement in schools. For example, career academies, in which students get work experience as well as course work that draws on a particular job family such as communications, computers, or teaching, help provide the kind of "real-world" experiences students need to better appreciate the education they are receiving. These schools-within-schools are part of a larger continuum of special programs that give students learning experiences outside, and in addition to, the traditional classroom structure (Massachusetts Institute of Technology, 1990).
- Develop clear expectations for student learning, including the use of competency based or outcomes-based education. In a study by the U.S. General Accounting Office of the strategies used to prepare employment-bound youth for employment in the United States and four competitor nations—England, Germany, Japan, and Sweden—several findings were particularly telling and relate to the area of clear expectations for learning (Warnat, 1991).

  1. The four competitor nations expect all students to do well in school, especially in the early years. In the United States, schools expect that many will lag behind.
  2. The competitor nations have established competency based national training standards that are used to certify skills competency. Practice in the United States is to certify program completion.
  3. All four foreign nations invest heavily in the education and training of employment-bound youth. The United States invests less than half as much for each employment-bound youth as it does for each college-bound youth.
  4. To a much greater extent than in the United States, the schools and employment communities in the competitor countries guide students' transition from school to work, helping students learn about job requirements and assisting them in finding employment.

- Require participation in community service programs for high school graduation.

- Provide educational opportunities that acknowledge that not only technical skills but multilinguality, leadership and social studies skills, and knowledge of cultural differences, national histories, political and economic systems of nations with whom we trade all become increasingly important in international trade.
- Focus on life skills. Secondary schools, including middle schools, should provide training in "life skills" such as formulating good work habits, interacting with public agencies, job hunting, appropriate behavior for the workplace, working in a team, completing applications and following instructions, looking for meaningful employment. Many of these skills can arise from helping young people understand that school is their work and that attitudes dealing with punctuality, accepting constructive supervision, honesty, and self-discipline are those valued as well in the workplace. Many of these skills and others can be gained through a variety of cooperative education and work-based learning opportunities. In this regard it would be possible to provide and use summer and academic year internships, apprenticeships, and cooperative work-site training (Massachusetts Institute of Technology, 1990).
- Enlarge the availability of cooperative education (which now enrolls about 5 to 10 percent of all students in high school and college) that structures students' experience in paid jobs to promote learning to extend what is taught in the classroom. The "co-op" method gives students direct practice in learning at the workplace. Many vocational-technical education programs also operate their own school-based enterprises, which likewise provide opportunities for students to learn through the process of producing real goods and services for community agencies. These options make deliberate use of work as part of the learning experience and bridge school and work directly.
- Provide certificates that recognize the demonstrated skills of students meeting articulated requirements for such skills in technical training or other program offerings in high school. Such demonstrations of skills will undoubtedly increase the use of portfolios describing examples of students' skills, more precise discussion of their skill development experiences, as well as greater clarity about their achievement of competency based career development experiences and associated attitudes.
- Increase tech-prep or 2+2 programs. These programs increase the availability of more rigorous course work tied to occupational skills and at the same time give more students the option to go on to postsecondary education. They help students see more clearly the connection between school and work, the importance of continual or lifelong learning, the integration of academic and vocational skills, and the need to bridge both work-oriented courses and those oriented toward further schooling. In their articulated structures they expedite student movement from high school programs to related community college programs and beyond with emphases on efficiency and equity.
- Modify the school curriculum to combine academic and vocational courses. Such an approach to an integrated curriculum, which like tech-prep and several other of the recommendations here are strong emphases in the Carl D. Perkins

Vocational and Applied Technology Education Act, gives students the benefit of occupational preparation and college preparation at the same time. It also potentially infuses academic courses with the task-oriented, problem-solving, and cooperative learning approach to learning that has been successful in vocational-technical education. These approaches incorporate the findings of research in the cognitive sciences, which suggest that abstract information is often best learned through authentic application in task or problem-solving learning (U.S. Department of Education, 1991).

- Apprenticeship schemes also need to be expanded in availability after high school in new ways that begin in the high schools and provide skill development opportunities during that period in ways similar to what is available in several of our competitor nations. Currently, apprenticeships in this country enroll hardly any students in high school and fewer than 2 percent of high school graduates, although in Europe, 30 to 60 percent of employment-bound students are likely to be in apprenticeships following high school (U.S. Department of Education, 1991). National and state youth apprenticeship legislation, which is now in place or to be implemented in the near future, is an excellent vehicle for this effort.

- Ensure that every secondary school graduate or school leaver is placed into a job, a school-to-work transition scheme, or postsecondary education.

Content Requirements in Work-Based Learning

Although some of these instructional processes are discussed more fully in a later section of this chapter, it is useful to think about what students should learn through these various work-based experiences. There are many ways to conceive such content, but some examples illustrate the possibilities. The point of these perspectives is that many of the work-based learning processes just noted are important as instructional delivery systems, but what is at least as important is the knowledge, skills, habits, and the attitudes that they should facilitate. Obviously, such content needs to be frequently reviewed and updated as shifts in job requirements occur in the occupational structure or as educational requirements to perform different jobs change. Wirth (1993) has effectively captured this concept in his observation that "When hammers and wrenches are displaced by numbers and buttons, a whole new kind of learning must begin" (p. 362).

Such a perspective was evident in Hull and Pedrotti's observations in 1983 that there are six educational implications common to all high-tech occupations. They were seen as including the following:

1. They require a broad knowledge of math, computers, physics, chemistry, electricity, electronics, electromechanical devices, and fluid flow.
2. They involve heavy and frequent computer use (including knowledge of practical applications of programming).
3. They change rapidly and require lifelong learning.

4. They are systems-oriented (and involve working with systems that have electronic, electromechanical, electrical, thermal, optical, fluidic, and microcomputer components).
5. They require a fundamental understanding of a system's principles as well as practical skills in designing, developing, testing, installing, troubleshooting, maintaining, and repairing the system.
6. They require substantial employee flexibility and adaptability. (pp. 28–31)

Although some of the six requirements stated may now be tempered by new innovations and technological developments, the core concepts developed by these two researchers has remained remarkably stable. Such content is of more relevance to technical occupations than to health care occupations or financial services, for example, but these perspectives are nevertheless important ways to emphasize particular subsets of learning that need to take place in selected instructional processes if they are to be effective and if career-relevant learning is to be maximized.

Another and somewhat more generic type of learning that has become well known among workforce educators is found in the content of the report of the Secretary's Commission on Achieving Necessary Skills (SCANS) entitled "What Work Requires of Schools" (U.S. Department of Labor, 1991). In identifying themes that tend to pervade workplace know-how, this report contends that schools should provide five categories of competencies and that these should be reinforced in three instructional emphases. The five competencies or forms of workplace know-how that schools should develop in students include the abilities to

1. Identify, organize, plan, and allocate resources such as time, money, materials, and facilities;
2. Work with others;
3. Acquire and use information;
4. Understand complex interrelationships; and
5. Work with a variety of technologies.

According to the SCANS report, these five areas of competency are developed through a complex interplay of three instructional elements that schools should teach: the basic skills, higher order skills, and the application of selected personal qualities. According to the SCANS report, demonstrating basic skills means that the student "reads, writes, performs arithmetic and mathematical operations, listens, and speaks"; demonstrating thinking skills shows that the student "thinks creatively, makes decisions, solves problems, visualizes, knows how to learn, and reason"; by effectively applying personal qualities the student displays responsibility, self-esteem, sociability, self-management, and integrity and honesty" (pp. 4–5).

From our colleagues in Canada has come a somewhat different perspective. Simon, Dippo, and Schenke (1991) contend that we must constantly keep before us in our planning, questions such as, "What do we mean when we say that someone is a competent participant in a workplace? What does it mean to say that someone has a good working knowledge of how things are done?" As they further suggest,

Working knowledge includes more than just the notion of a technical ability to perform certain tasks such as typing invoices, back-stitching upholstery, using micrometers, supervising outdoor play, washing hair, making cheesecake, and developing photographs. These are, of course, included in the meaning of the concept, but there is much more. Each and every task in a workplace is embedded in a particular set of social relations within which people define the facts, skills, procedures, values, and beliefs relevant to particular jobs in their own organizations. For this reason, job competency often means understanding how the particularities of one's workplace defines what one needs to know to get a job done. Perhaps more to the point, there is no work in the abstract; there is only work in context. "Learning work" often entails not only the development of technical and social skills, but also an ability to understand how and why such skills are used, modified, and supplemented in different situations. (pp. 27–28)

Within this context these authors employ the term "working knowledge" as a useful concept for the study of how people in different workplaces define what is important to know in order to be competent workers and to do competent work. The following is a partial list of different workplace features that Simon, Dippo, and Schenke (1991) suggest are some things it might be important to know in order to be an effective worker in any given workplace:

Workplace materials—material objects that are basic to a workplace. These include, for example, tools, equipment, decor, supplies, raw materials and finished products, and clothing.

The language of work—the specialized words and phrases, technical jargon, abbreviations, codes and forms as well as names, nicknames, slang, clichés, tones of voice, gestures, and modes of conversation.

Workplace facts—the information and beliefs taken as objectively true, incontrovertible, and accurate by at least some group of people in a workplace. These "facts" include not only task-related information but also reputations, workplace customs, rituals, and traditions.

Skills and techniques—the set of capacities and competencies necessary to perform certain procedures and complete certain tasks required by the organization of work in a particular workplace.

The frames of reference for evaluating workplace events—the principles used by workers to determine the good or bad qualities of things, people, events, and/or ideas; for example, the criteria used by others to determine a "fair day's work," "a job well done," "a good supervisor," or a "harebrained scheme!"

Rules and meanings—the implicit and explicit rules, understandings, and expectations that regulate interactions among people in various situations. Implicated in these are power structures, lines and areas of authority, questions of responsibility, status, prestige, and influence." (p. 28)

These components of "working knowledge" as proposed by Simon, Dippo, and Schenke (1991), are related to, and overlap to some degree with, the seven types of knowledge and skill necessary for most work that have been defined by Barley and Nelson (1995) and reported by the Office of Technology Assessment (1995). The latter are included in abridged and adapted form:

1. *Sensory interpretation* involves making inferences based on colors, shapes, patterns, sounds, smells, tastes, and tactile cues—perceived directly or with the aid of instruments.
2. *Sensorimotor dexterity* is the tactile sensitivity, the "feel" for the instruments, materials, and techniques used in a given occupation.
3. *Tricks of the trade* are plans of action that have been developed by practitioners in a specific occupation from a combination of experience, tacit understanding, and formal scientific knowledge.
4. *The local history of problems* is the accumulated knowledge of the causes, timing, and "fixes" of problems that recurred in a specific workplace over a period of time.
5. *Work style* is the set of work roles, social skills, norms, and customs that guide how work is conducted. Work styles vary considerably among occupations and organizations and sometimes across work groups within a single facility.
6. *Coordinating activities* organize and focus the general knowledge, technical expertise, and organizational status of different persons involved in a work task.
7. *Linguistic skills* involve the use of occupational jargon and its translation for nonspecialists.

In a final example of the type of content that needs to be reinforced in work-based and other career relevant learning, Lynch (1991) has extracted from various reports of skills needed in the future workforce the following considered to be important for both high school and postsecondary graduates. Under the term "skills workers will need," he has identified the following broad-based categories:

Computers and technology—programming simple jobs, using software extensively, maintaining equipment.

Problem-solving, critical thinking, decision-making—knowing how to learn, find answers, and solve problems.

Resource management—scheduling time and personnel, budgeting, using human and capital resources appropriately.

Economics of work and the workplace—understanding organization, profit, work relationships, work ethics, national and international systems.

Applied math, science, social science, and communications—using numbers, theories, and fundamental math and science principles, and effective language skills in the workplace.

Career and personal planning—setting priorities, taking advantage of continuing education and training opportunities, managing parenting and family life, maintaining personal health.

Interpersonal relationships—having appropriate values and attitudes toward teamwork and working effectively with customers.

Information and data manipulation—finding and managing information, using data, understanding systems and symbols, keeping records.

Technical skills—to the level required to sustain career employment. (p. 29)

There are many other compelling examples available of the types of career relevant knowledge, skills, and attitudes that are being identified as necessary to various sets of occupations or to the generalized expectations for which all workers need to be prepared to cope in the emerging global economy. It is important that such content be incorporated into the planning of curriculum and other work-based learning processes so that the latter can be sensitive to and reinforce the emerging requirements for workers in the twenty-first century. In its simplest form this knowledge, skill, and attitude base consists of three emphases: basic academic and technical skills, understanding of and ability to cope with the context or organization in which work is performed, and understanding of others and the interpersonal skills necessary to communicate and cooperate with supervisors, coworkers, and customers. The precise balance of each of these categories of "working knowledge" differs across occupations and settings, but the interaction among them in any particular occupation or workplace is likely to determine the success a young worker has in making the transition and adjustment to work. The opportunity to observe and to experience such interactions "in vivo," in a real work context, is one of the major advantages of work-based learning however it is defined—for example, cooperative education, apprenticeship, or internship.

WORK-BASED LEARNING

Work-based learning can be described in many ways, but at its core work-based learning is an application of ideas and actions to tasks and problems that originate in job performance and work settings. Such efforts restructure the educational experience so that students learn how academic subjects relate to the world of work and are provided opportunities to study complex subject matter as well as vital workplace hands-on tasks in real-life environments. Thus, as compared to traditional school-based learning, work-based learning is not abstract and removed from practical problems but uses the latter to help students learn to apply basic academic skills in problem solving. Work-based learning integrates academic and vocational skills. In addition, in school-based learning students frequently work alone; in work-based learning students frequently solve problems together in work teams in cooperative learning. In school-based learning, competencies are developed that are intended to be generalizable to a variety of life experiences; in work-based learning, competencies are more likely defined by specific tasks, equipment, and procedures, the familiarity with and mastery of which are essential in particular job families or settings. In school-based learning students tend to be removed from the settings in which they will ultimately practice the knowledge and skills they learn; in work-based learning the focus is on experiencing the authenticity of performing with others, using adult work role norms and expectations, under supervision, in an actual work environment, and using the tools of that occupation.

In the terms described above, work-based learning, whether it originates in the school (through vocational education, cooperative education, internships) or in another setting, has built-in transitional emphases. Not only may a student be employed by the employer with whom the work-based learning was undertaken, but, in more general terms, work-based learning provides an environment by which students can really test their knowledge, skills, attitudes, and habits as they interact with adult workers, organizational demands, equipment, work procedures, and work cultures. In such environments students have the potential to bring together abstract knowledge and hands-on activities and to use such experience in a focused pursuit of the school-to-work transition.

SCHOOL-SPONSORED WORKPLACE LEARNING

Although there are multiple approaches to facilitating school-based transition processes, the most comprehensive approach at the moment is defined and funded by the School-to-Work Opportunities Act. The School-to-Work Opportunities Act established a five-year effort to facilitate and nurture partnerships among schools, employers, and other stakeholders to create school-to-work transition systems. These systems are to include three components: school-based components, work-based components, and activities connecting the two.

On May 4, 1994, the U.S. Congress, on a bipartisan basis, made the School-to-Work Opportunities Act of 1994 (PL 103–239) a law of the land. Programs funded by the School-to-Work Opportunities Act combine classroom learning with real-world work experience. They fund the training of students in general job-readiness skills as well as in industrial-specific occupational skills. The School-to-Work Opportunities Act provides help to high schools and communities as well as colleges to create programs in cooperation with business, labor, and industry and to develop the academic skills and attitudes toward work that too many adolescents lack today and that both educational and community agencies have neglected.

The School-to-Work Opportunities Act introduces the term "career major" to mean "a coherent sequence of courses" or field of study that prepares a student for a first job and that (a) integrates academic and occupational learning, integrates school-based and work-based learning, establishes linkages between secondary schools and postsecondary educational institutions; (b) prepares the student for employment in a broad occupational cluster or industry sector; (c) provides students, to the extent practicable, with strong experience in and understanding of all aspects of the industry the students are planning to enter; (d) may lead to further education and training, such as entry into a registered apprenticeship program, or may lead to admission to a 2- or 4-year college or university" (Section 4, Definitions). The act also defines "career guidance and counseling" to mean programs (a) that pertain to the body of subject matter and related techniques and methods organized for the development in individuals of career awareness, career planning, career decision making, placement skills, and knowledge and understanding of local, state, and national occupational, educational, and labor market needs, trends, and opportunities; (b) that assist individuals in making and implementing informed educational and occupational choices; and (c) that aid students to develop career options with attention to surmounting gender, race, ethnic, disability, language, or socioeconomic impediments to career options and encouraging careers in nontraditional employment" (Section 4, Definitions).

The School-to-Work Opportunities Act encourages development of school-to-work transition systems that coordinate career orientation, academic and occupational education, high school and postsecondary schooling, work-based learning, and skill credentialing. The legislation specifically divides these emphases into the following three components and the elements of each as identified by the Office of Technology Assessment of the U.S. Congress (1995) from the act itself.

I. School-Based Learning
   1. Academic instruction in high school that meets the state standards for all students and the applicable standards of the National Education Goals;
   2. Career exploration and counseling, beginning no later than the 7th grade for interested students;
   3. Initial selection by interested students of a career major beginning no later than the 11th grade;
   4. Instruction that integrates academic and occupational learning;
   5. Arrangements to coordinate high school and postsecondary education and training; and
   6. Regularly scheduled evaluations of students' personal goals, progress, and needed learning opportunities.
II. Work-Based Learning
   1. Job training and work experiences aimed at developing pre-employment skills and employment skills at progressively higher levels and leading to the award of skill certificates;
   2. Broad instruction in "all aspects of the industry," to the extent practical; and
   3. Workplace mentoring.
III. Connecting Activities
   1. Activities to encourage employers to participate and to aid them in doing so;
   2. Assistance in the integration of school-based and work-based learning, and of academic and occupational instruction;
   3. Matching of students with the work-based learning opportunities offered by employers;

4. Liaison among the students, schools, employers, and parents;
5. Assistance for graduates in finding appropriate jobs, getting additional job training, or pursuing further education;
6. Monitoring of participants' progress after they complete the program; and
7. Linkage of these youth development activities with employer and industry strategies for upgrading the skills of incumbent workers. (p. 2)

The implementation of the School-to-Work Opportunities Act rests on and, indeed, embraces many concepts and recommendations that have been available for some time in American education but not fully implemented. For example, inherent in the school-based learning component are program emphases that resemble those that originated in models of career education that took shape in the early 1970s and that have provided possible methods by which the content and experiences of schools can be connected to the expectations and content of the adult work world. Particular techniques suggested embody the infusion of career development concepts and examples into academic subject matter; the use of adult resource persons to describe what they do in their occupation's system of job search strategies, career resource centers; field trips to, and shadowing of workers in, industry; or other techniques by which to increase students understanding of their own characteristics and interests and how these might be more effectively matched with job opportunities and requirements.

The School-to-Work Opportunities Act provides the support for and the viability of other school-based transition models that have been extant and quite important for many years. Cooperative education is one of these.

Cooperative Education

Probably the most common name for programs of work-study or school-based transition models has historically been "cooperative education." A specific definition of this term is found in Section 195 of Title II of the Education Amendments of 1976, in which the Vocational Education Act of 1963 is amended.

> *The term "cooperative education" means a program of vocational education for persons who, through written cooperative arrangements between the school and employers, receive instruction, including required academic courses and related vocational instruction by alternation of study in school with a job in any occupational field, but these two experiences must be planned and supervised by the school and employers so that each contributes to the student's education and to his or her employability. Work periods and school attendance may be on alternate half days, full days, weeks, or other periods of time in fulfilling the cooperative program.*

Cooperative education can vary significantly as to which students are served and for what purposes. In some schools cooperative education is available only to students in vocational education; in other schools it is available to students in any curriculum track. Although the formal cooperative education model is intended primarily to enhance occupational skills development for students by coordinating school-based and work-based learning, in many instances cooperative education is intended to enhance career exploration or academic skills development.

According to the Office of Technology Assessment of the U.S. Congress (1995), recent studies suggest that about half of all high schools offer a co-op program, but only about 8 percent of graduates have participated in them. About one-third to two-thirds of two-year colleges have co-op programs, but only about 2 percent of students participate. In community and four-year colleges participation in co-op programs is typically voluntary, although in some colleges and in some departments all students or all of those in particular departments are required to participate in cooperative education programs.

Cooperative education or work experience programs are essentially a process of behavioral change for students through experience. At one level, experience comes from immediately determining how what one learns in the classroom is applied at work. At another level it comes from being adult-oriented at the work station rather than adolescent-oriented. In this sense students have the opportunity to experience work norms as lived by adults rather than speculate about such things with their adolescent peers. Finally, cooperative education programs assist students to see themselves and the work done as a whole. Frequently, classroom study fragments employability traits, work habits, human relations, and communications into small increments for purposes of learning. In the real world all of these elements are part of a complete and constantly unfolding fabric that requires individual judgment and discrimination if career maturity is to result.

Work experience programs also allow students to test which career development tasks have already been incorporated into their behavioral repertoire and which still need honing. In this way work experience programs provide goal direction to learning and to student planning. A work experience in these terms is not just experience for its own sake but is related to employability. It represents a prime medium for career education and for developing effective work behaviors that help students acquire a positive career identity. Cooperative education also can be seen as a powerful tool in career guidance.

It might be noted here that elements of cooperative education are similar to those described in the literature on mentoring. For those school systems unable to develop cooperative education programs, mentoring programs may be a useful alternative. Mentoring is a process of providing role models from the community for students who will profit from being able to observe firsthand the work context and activity of a mentor. Mentoring programs are evident in business, in community colleges, and in other educational contexts.

Other School-Sponsored Workplace Learning Models

Beyond the comprehensive possibilities inherent in preparing students for the school-to-work transition through the legislation described above or cooperative education or mentoring, there are several other school-based alternatives that deserve brief mention.

School-Based Enterprises.   Historically, both comprehensive and vocational schools have provided school-based enterprises—stores, auto repair, construction, publishing, child care, manufacturing—in which students work part-time. Students in selected classes in retailing, business, or vocational education learn occupational and entrepreneurial skills pertinent to the school-based enterprise available. Sometimes students actually engage in the job application process and interviews relevant to participation in the enterprise. If employed, they may be required to meet certain criteria—punctuality, for example—to remain employed and to either earn credits toward graduation or to be paid for participation. Students usually start in entry-level positions and, depending on their continuing involvement with the enterprise and other requirements, they may move to more skilled, supervisory, or management positions.

School-based enterprises in school or in postsecondary education settings typically focus on academic reinforcement, career exploration, and occupational development. In many cases they are seen as "labs" in which students apply their school-based learning to occupational tasks for consumers who are in the community, not fellow students. Although the research on school-based enterprises has not been rigorous or wide-ranging, available anecdotal evidence and case studies have included evidence that participation in such school-based enterprises has resulted in some students becoming more engaged in school, has reinforced the importance of their academic skills, and has helped them to acquire basic work habits and specific occupational skills (Stern, et al., 1994).

Work Shadowing.   Another formal learning process related to mentoring or work experience is *work shadowing*. Although the term is virtually unmentioned in American career development literature, it has achieved increasing attention in British research. According to Watts (1986), "work shadowing describes schemes in which an observer follows a worker around for a period of time, observing the various tasks in which he or she engages, and doing so within the context of his or her total role" (p. 1). Although observation is critical to British models of work shadowing, this element does not stand alone. Rather, three other elements can be usefully added to observation: "*integration* with the work-guide (the worker being shadowed)—example given, asking questions about what he or she is doing; *participation* in the work-guide's work—example given, carrying out tasks for him or her; and *contextualization*—example given, observing or talking to other workers with whom the work-guide comes into working contact" (p. 40).

When one compares work shadowing to work experience and work visits, clear conceptual distinctions can be drawn among these processes. Herr and Watts (1988) have suggested that, "in work shadowing, the *prime* element is observation of work roles. In work experience, the prime element is performance of job tasks. In work visits the prime element is contextualization and observation of the range of work processes performed within the workplace" (p. 81). In particular, "the student engaged in work shadowing will learn about the *tasks* in which the worker engages, about the *processes* within the workplace in which he or she is involved, and—often particularly striking to the young visitor—about the *environment* of the workplace as a whole" (Watts, 1986: 41). Because work shadowing focuses on the work role(s) of a particular individual (work-guide), it can provide insight into informal aspects of human relationships at work, including power relationships. Such insights are obviously valuable within the broad context of workforce education, but the potential learning from work shadowing can also make it a powerful career-guidance mechanism.

Clinical Training.   Although primarily used in community colleges and other postsecondary educational settings, and particularly in the medical occupations, clinical training is a further school-based transition model. In such an approach students take academic and occupational courses and assume a series of positions that provide work experience and training. The course of study, the work experience, and a passing score on a licensure examination are all interdependent parts of the school-to-work transition approach exemplified by this model. This model has become the norm for training of students in the allied health occupations and is in format and procedure not unlike an apprenticeship model.

BUSINESS AND INDUSTRY COOPERATIVE EFFORTS

Although cooperation with business, industry, and labor is essential in any type of school-based transition model, it is likely to be more formalized in youth apprenticeships, apprenticeships, and compacts.

Youth Apprenticeships

Youth apprenticeships are a relatively new variation on the historical apprenticeship model to be considered next. Youth apprenticeships have been described as the newest form of work-based learning. They have been given impetus by the School-to-Work Opportunities Act, although there have been examples of youth apprenticeship approaches in selected locations around the nation since the early 1990s.

According to the Office of Technology Assessment (1995), "Youth apprenticeship is the most ambitious, coordinated, and sustained model of work-based learning in the United States. It is directed at serving the widest spectrum of students—in terms of academic performance and career interests. The objectives are broader than those of other models, encompassing the reinforcement of academics, exploration of careers, occupational skill development, and productive activities" (p. 161). The key elements of youth apprenticeships include "school-based learning that provides career counseling, integrates academic and occupational instruction, and extends from the later years of high school through some postsecondary education; progressively higher levels of paid work experience, accompanied by training and mentoring; and the opportunity to earn an industry-recognized skill certificate" (p. 161).

Youth apprenticeships differ from traditional apprenticeship models in several ways. The latter are typically operated by unions and employers. Youth apprenticeships serve students in high school and through at least one year of postsecondary education. Traditional apprenticeships usually do not include young adults until they have been out of high school for several years. In a youth apprenticeship, students usually work part-time, or they may rotate between full-time work and schooling. In some models, high school students go to school part-time and are apprentices part-time. In contrast, in traditional apprenticeships the enrollees usually work full-time and then attend classes for two or three hours each week. Finally, youth apprenticeships tend to provide the formal instruction involved through high school teachers or postsecondary education instructors rather than by the personnel of unions or employers as is typical in traditional apprenticeships.

In describing the characteristics of the Pennsylvania Youth Apprenticeship Program (PYAP), Wolfe (1993) indicated that this model is a school-to-work program that links the classroom to the work-site experience based on the premise that all students can learn. It stresses skills learned on a one-to-one basis, using mechanisms and processes that make academics relevant. PYAP grew out of a study done by the Pennsylvania Department of Commerce and the National Tooling and Machining Association, which showed that the most serious obstacle to competitiveness in the industry was a lack of skilled workers. At the local level the model is guided by local consortia of education, business, labor, and other community organizations. Model programs currently operate in six sites and include 79 firms sponsoring 100 students. Of the firms, 76 are manufacturers using metal working skills, and 3 are hospitals that provide training and education in health care occupations.

Although there are some differences in the models used in each site, the basic elements include a program designed around a four-year curriculum—approximately two years of high school and two years of postsecondary education. This is the format commonly known as tech-prep or 2+2. The assumption is that, to be successful in a technical environment, students must have some postsecondary skills. At the end of two years in the program the students receive a high school diploma and can choose to seek employment, continue the program for two more years and receive an associate degree at the completion of four years, receive an associate degree and go directly to a skilled job or a registered adult apprenticeship program, or continue in a four-year program.

Other program components include a paid wage for on-the-job training ($4.25 to $6.00 in 1993), which is negotiated at the local level; an integrated curriculum based on the needs of industries and one that provides academic skills that relate to the work site; broad-based skills that include critical thinking and problem solving; coordination between the teachers in the school and the mentors at the job site; and outcome, performance-based assessments, or portfolios for the students that serve as credentials that can be used to apply for jobs or to enter college.

Apprenticeships

Although apprenticeships are not school-based school-to-work transition models, they are certainly a major form of work-based learning. As suggested previously, they differ from youth apprenticeships in several ways. A major one is that traditional apprenticeship approaches begin after one completes high school and fully enters the adult work world.

In traditional apprenticeships, an apprenticeship is a formal, contractual relationship between an employer and an employee (apprentice) during which time the worker (apprentice) learns a trade. The training lasts a specified length of time and varies in time required, depending on the skills or learning expected by a particular occupation or trade. Apprenticeships usually last about four years, but they range from one to six years in length. An apprenticeship covers all aspects of the trade and includes both on-the-job training and related instruction, which generally takes place in a classroom. The teaching by experienced craftworkers and other skilled persons requires the study of trade manuals and educational materials.

During the period of an apprenticeship, apprentices work under experienced workers known as journey workers, a status obtained after successful completion of an apprenticeship. Apprentices are employees whose pay usually starts at about one-half that of an experienced worker in the trade being pursued. The apprentice's wage increases periodically through the apprenticeship as does the learning and skill level attained and the increasing ability to work with less supervision as the apprenticeship ensues. The sponsor of an apprenticeship program plans, administers, and pays for the program. Sponsors can be employers, employer associations, and unions.

The National Apprenticeship Act of 1937 (The Fitzgerald act) is the principal federal legislation identifying the criteria by which apprenticeship programs will be developed and evaluated and how the Secretary of Labor will work with appropriate state labor agencies and with state Departments of Education. Apprenticeship programs are commonly registered with the federal government or a federally approved state apprenticeship agency. These programs must meet federally approved standards related to job duties, wages, related instruction, and health and safety regulations. Currently, apprenticeships are offered in some 830 occupations. About 100,000 new apprentices are registered each year, with about 350,000 persons participating in approximately 43,000 apprenticeship programs. As of 1992, more than 22 percent of the apprentices were minorities, and more than 7 percent were women. In most states, or local level apprenticeship programs, outreach counselors are available to provide information about admissions to programs, the prerequisites and tasks involved, and related topics, and they counsel participants about preparing for interviews, how to get technical task training, and other issues (U.S. Department of Labor, 1991–92). Earlier in this chapter, some comparisons were drawn between the use of apprenticeships in the United States and other nations. Other comparisons can also be cited: The United States ranks 14 out of 16 developed Western nations in the share of the workforce enrolled in such programs (Glover, 1986); less than three-tenths of 1 percent of the workforce are currently enrolled in apprenticeship training programs (Elbaum, 1989). In comparison to such other nations, including Great Britain, in the United States, beginning apprentices will be at least 20 years of age rather than 16 or so (Glover, 1986), giving increased credence to the current rise in availability of youth apprenticeship in the United States; and the number of high school trade courses has a highly significant impact on obtaining apprenticeship training (Gittner, 1994).

Compacts and Collaboratives

Again, as stimulated by a variety of factors including concern about the quality of education and their desire to become involved in school improvement, concern about current or future skill shortages in industry, opportunity to train future employees for their company, opportunities to attract minorities and women to their company, and to observe and try out potential young employees, employers have become engaged in community collaboratives of different forms to provide work-based experiences for high school students. In some cases, these community-based employer-school partnerships have been called compacts, consortia, or collaboratives. The Boston Compact has received considerable attention as the prototype for such efforts. The Boston Compact Initiative includes a joint effort involving seven middle schools and some sixty businesses in Boston, Massachusetts. As a result of a variety of collaborative efforts between employers and the schools involved, both the school's academic and extracurricular programs improved. School participants gained better understanding of the private enterprise system, and students and teachers learned about the requirements and expectations of the business world. In addition, business people gained increased knowledge of the educational system. Other benefits accrued from the compact. One was the provision of adult worker literacy training. Soon after the initial compact provisions, extensive agreements developed between employers and colleges and universities in the Boston area (Marron, 1994; Pease & Copa, 1994). Given the early collaborative climate between schools and employers in Boston in behalf of school-to-work transition schemes, the Private Industry Council in Boston has used the relationships of the Boston Compact to create the Boston Jobs Collaborative and the ProTech Youth Apprenticeship Program for which employers are constantly recruited, career specialists coordinate student placements with participating employers, visit each student regularly, and provide troubleshooting and technical assistance (Hightower, Hollock, & Breckenridge, 1995).

Beyond the important school-to-work transition activities provided by the various initiatives in Boston, the Office of Technology Assessment (1995) has also cited the important work of the Kalamazoo Valley Education for Employment Consortium, which involves nine school districts, the local community college, the intermediate school district, and more than 100 employees. This consortium provides a variety of system components including career guidance, mentorship, work-site-based education, cooperative education apprenticeships, and business-industry work-site training programs. The Office of Technology Assessment has also cited the Cooperative Education Program in two-year colleges in Cincinnati as an excellent example of postsecondary-employer collaboration in support of the school-to-work transition.

TECH-PREP

A final major school-to-work transition model is that of tech-prep. As defined by the U.S. Congress in 1990, a tech-prep program means a combined secondary/postsecondary program that (a) leads to an associate degree or a two-year certificate; (b) provides technical preparation in at least one field of engineering technology, applied science; mechanical, industrial, or practical art of trade; or agriculture, health or business; (c) builds student competence in mathematics, science and communications (including through applied academics) through a sequential course of study; and (d) leads to placement in employment (Congressional Record, 101st Congress, 2nd Session, August 2, 1990). These programs increase the availability of more rigorous course work tied to occupational skills and at the same time give more students the option to go on to postsecondary education. They help students see more clearly the connection between school and work, the importance of continual or lifelong learning, the integration of academic and vocational skills, and the need to bridge both work-oriented courses and those oriented toward further schooling. In their articulated structures they expedite student movement from high school programs to related community college programs and beyond with emphases on efficiency and equity.

Tech-prep programs are designed to accomplish this agenda through strategies described as integration, articulation, and work-based learning. They typically require the introduction of new courses sequenced in a core curriculum that leads students to develop advanced skills for technical occupations that are focused on higher order thinking skills such as creative thinking, reasoning, communication, math, and science. Although articulation between secondary and postsecondary institutions is essential to ensure systematic and coordinated curriculums across institutions that will lead students to two-year or four-year degrees without duplication of effort and loss of credit, tech-prep programs also need to form partnerships with business, industry, and labor to validate that what is being taught in the program is relevant to what is needed in the occupations for which students are being prepared and to facilitate student transition between school and work in these occupations. Finally, tech-prep programs also need to be planned to be sufficiently flexible to accommodate other work-based learning initiatives including youth apprenticeships and traditional apprenticeships.

THE TOTAL PLACEMENT CONCEPT

Perhaps the overarching premise on which transitional services leading to job placement must rest is an inclusive, not an exclusive, one. In essence, such a view holds that no student should leave a secondary school, a community college, or other training program without planning his or her next step and the needed support to make a successful transition to employment. Just as college-bound students have traditionally been provided resources and counseling to make a considered, deliberate, and smooth transition from the secondary school to college or from a transfer program at the community college to a four-year college, students leaving the secondary school, a tech-prep program, or other training facility deserve no less as they seek job placement. That is the intent of transition services.

The Role of Employers in Transitional Services

This chapter has identified the role of employers in the school-to-work transition as a major factor in the success of this transition. The importance of employers in providing sites for work-based learning, in validating the content of tech-prep or technical course preparation, in providing mentors or resource people to help persons learn about occupational content and work role expectations, and in creating work-study structures by which to provide youth apprenticeship or traditional apprenticeship opportunities are all essential to the success of transition services. But employers also have other direct impacts on workforce development and on the transition to work as it relates to the services and the support systems they provide in the workplace.

Workforce development in these terms has to do with how new employees are oriented to their jobs, to the culture of the workplace, and to their contributions to the mission of the enterprise as well as the degree to which new or younger and older workers receive employer-provided training and the nature of that training. It has to do with how human resource development processes and systems are provided by an enterprise, the mentoring and information they provide to employees, the encouragement and training provided to have workers develop loyalty and commitment to long-term mobility within the firm, incentives to improve their competencies, and the ability to find ways to improve how their jobs are done, and how the individual worker can relate as a team player to coworkers and as a person of service to his or her customers, however they are defined. It has to do with whether individual enterprises make a connection between their human resource policies and business strategy (CPC Foundation/Rand Corporation, 1994: 59).

SUMMARY AND IMPLICATIONS FOR PRACTITIONERS

As this chapter has demonstrated, workforce education would be incomplete and its effectiveness significantly diminished without including as part of its purview the provision of transition services intended to implement job placement. In this sense, workforce education must be seen as a system of components that interact to equip students or adult workers with the knowledge, habits, and skills to perform jobs that are available and that are emerging. Much of this learning should occur in the schools in a progressive process from the elementary school forward. Much of the relevant learning is aimed at acquiring the literacy, numeracy, problem solving, and teachability that underlie the acquisition of the technical and employability skills required of workers.

Workforce education must also serve to integrate academic and vocational skills, particularly as these are integrated in work-based learning of different forms: cooperative education, school-based enterprises, youth apprenticeships, apprenticeships, and so on. To a large degree, these schemes represent structural transition models that span the chasm between the learning of work skills and their application.

To deal systematically with workforce education and the provision of relevant transition services, schools must become more career-relevant in their application of academic subject matter to the expectations and practices of work and in their valuing of students whose goals on graduation are the movement directly into employment. The School-to-Work Opportunities Act has defined a possible structure for such increased career relevance combining school-based learning, work-based learning, and connecting activities by which transitional goals for students can be identified and articulated. This legislation as well as that of the Carl D. Perkins Vocational Education and Applied Technology Act has emphasized many possible ways by which career pathways for students can be implemented to create a seamless progression, a career ladder, by which students can negotiate the passage from school to work. Tech-prep is one of the major possibilities to provide a systematic career path for many students, but, as this chapter suggests, there are a variety of other possibilities that can be implemented in the school and in cooperative activities with employers.

This chapter has emphasized the importance of transition models in schools as a part of workforce education. But it has also affirmed that in addition to cooperative efforts between schools and employers and the multiple responsibilities each of these partners has in implementing transition programs, employers have a particular responsibility in the processes they employ to induct new workers into their organization and to provide them mentoring and on-the-job training. Such transition mechanisms provided by employers in the workplace can also be extended to adult workers engaged in a variety of transitions that accompany their career mobility following their original entry, induction, and adjustment to work.

In sum, then, workforce education comprises a complex and wide-ranging set of components, processes, and purposes. To be complete, to bring closure to the various elements of workforce education, requires the planning and the implementation of systematic approaches to transition services and to job placement.

12

CAREER GUIDANCE

THE ORIGINS OF VOCATIONAL GUIDANCE

Contemporary forms of career guidance in the United States originated in the models of vocational guidance that arose in the late nineteenth and early twentieth centuries as a partner to vocational education. Both got their stimulus from the burgeoning dynamics of the industrial revolution as the national occupational structure was being transformed from one that had been primarily agrarian to one that was increasingly industrial and urbanized. The occupations that accompanied the transplantation of the new industrial era from England and other parts of Europe to the United States were characterized by a great hunger for workers and stimulated the mighty waves of migration from the country to the city in the United States and from nations abroad to this country.

As the industrial revolution flourished, the two major objectives for workforce education so frequently addressed in this text, economic development and individual opportunity, were seen in tandem, as two sides of the same coin. The separate components of identifying and selecting a job became the province of the emerging processes of vocational guidance, now career guidance, and the preparation for a job or an occupation became the role of vocational education, now workforce education.

Stephens (1970), a historian of education, has summarized the relationship between vocational guidance and vocational education at the beginning of the twentieth century as follows:

> To many leaders of the vocational reform movement...it was apparent that vocational education was but the first part of a package of needed educational reforms. They argued that a school curriculum and educational goals that mirrored the occupational structure created merely a platform and impetus for launching youth into the world of work. What was clearly needed to consummate the launch were guidance mechanisms that would insure their safe and efficient arrival on the job. Without guidance experts it was argued, other efforts at reform would be

> *aborted…. Therefore, in the name of social and economic efficiency, the argument continued, the youth who had been carefully trained would also have to be carefully counseled into a suitable occupational niche. (p. xiv)*

Although this important historical analysis provides the perspective of the time about the presumed interdependence of vocational guidance and vocational education, it is also important to think further about the context in which these two processes were to function. Many of the same questions and issues that now make up the national conversation about the ongoing transformation of the United States from an industrial to a postindustrial, information-age economy at the brink of the twenty-first century were present in different guises a hundred years ago as the industrialization of the United States rolled across the nation with particular intensity from the 1870s to the early decades of the twentieth century. Considerable attention was being focused on the need for adequate education for children so they would have the skills demanded in the emerging workplaces of the nation. The need for effective placement of adults into the work opportunities provided by the rapidly growing industrial complex was, like improved and more relevant education for children, considered to be a social imperative, a national priority. Many of the subquestions and tensions of the national political rhetoric of the time had to do with how potential workers, both immigrants and nonimmigrants, should be distributed across the increasingly diverse occupational structure of the United States and who should do it; how the gap between the existing content of schooling and the realities of the adult world should be bridged, and if the curriculum of the school should be differentiated for students with different goals in life or different talents; how the frequent job changes by workers who were not aware of either their capabilities or the jobs available to them could be stabilized by schemes to match people's characteristics with job requirements; and how the issues of general dissatisfaction of so many workers with the working conditions and general inhumanity of the workplace could be changed.

The substance and the implications of these questions were increasingly given voice by educators and, perhaps more powerfully, by the strong influence of the social reform movement of the time. Social reformers, settlement house staff in inner cities, and human rights activists at the beginning of the twentieth century were mounting local and national dialogues that focused on the terrible conditions in which many workers worked and lived and the national need to eliminate the view by many industrialists that workers were the chattels, the property of their employers, of industry rather than persons of worth and dignity who deserved the right to determine their own destiny by making choices about jobs and related matters.

The practical problem of the time, however, was that there was virtually no scientific knowledge base on which vocational guidance or approaches to workforce education could be constructed. This was a time in the history of the United States when palmistry, physiognomy, and phrenology (forecasting the future of an individual by the bumps on the head) were seen by many persons as valid methods to obtain insight into an individual's future. In essence, there had not yet developed beyond a very rudimentary form a measurement tradition by which to classify individual differences in intellect, aptitudes, and interests and to relate these to differences in individual requirements present in different types of work performance. There was no *Directory of Occupational Titles* or *Occupational Outlook Handbook*. There was no systematic classification structure that described the occupational structure of the nation.

Out of these challenging conditions and social reform movements came a variety of examples of vocational guidance processes and programs being put in place in some schools in eastern and midwestern cities in the late 1800s and the rise in urban areas of vocational guidance services in YMCAs, settlement houses, philanthropic organizations, and other settings. But most scholars of vocational guidance assign the major credit for conceptualizing the vocational guidance process that has endured and been refined through much of the twentieth century to Frank Parsons, an engineer, social reformer, and critic of the schools in Boston. Parsons believed that "it was better to choose a vocation than merely to hunt for a job." As the result of his search for a scientific basis by which to assist immigrants and others to deliberately and effectively choose work, he authored *Choosing a Vocation*, which was posthumously published in 1909. In this book Parsons described the techniques he used and found helpful in assisting adolescents to identify their capabilities and choose jobs with a reasonable probability of success. Among other techniques, Parsons advocated the importance of reading biographies, observing and interviewing workers, and reading existing job descriptions in newspapers and other media.

More important in the development of vocational guidance, and subsequently career guidance, than the techniques that Parsons described was his conceptualization of the process of "true reasoning" that provided a model, a paradigm, for vocational guidance. As such it stimulated the elaboration of the various elements of the model and subsequent research and refinement. According to Parsons (1909) vocational guidance leading to *true reasoning* in the counselee includes three steps:

> First, a clear understanding of yourself, aptitudes, abilities, interests, resources, limitations, and other qualities. Second, a knowledge of the requirements and conditions of success, advantages and disadvantages, compensation, opportunities, and prospects in different lines of work. Third, true reasoning on the relations of these two groups of facts. (p. 5)

This deceptively simple scheme stimulated research and theory throughout the twentieth century: first, individual differences, the measurement of such differences, and the predictive value of specific individual traits or combination of traits in determining who is likely to be successful in different types of training or job performance; second, differences in job or occupational content and activity, how these can be measured and classified, and the meaning of these differences for requirements for individual training, skills, and other characteristics; and, third, the elements and importance of true reasoning, which is currently seen as the synonym for decision making and includes concerns about choice-making styles, risk-taking behavior, indecision and indecisiveness, and knowledge about and use of information in shaping and acting on one's educational or job options.

As suggested above, the first step led to the development of many different types of tests useful in the classification of individual characteristics relative to other persons and to different educational and occupational options. The second step focused on the development and classification of information about jobs, training opportunities, curriculums, and other options from which persons could choose. This combination of the use of tests and information has continued to be a mainstay of vocational, and now career, guidance throughout this century. The third step, the making of wise and effective choices, has been increasingly viewed as the principal rationale for vocational guidance and the outcome to be sought from implementing the types of activities inherent in the first two steps of Parsons' paradigm.

Following on and implementing the approach to vocational guidance of Frank Parsons, several trends in the evolution of vocational guidance and vocational education are worth noting prior to examining contemporary approaches to vocational-career guidance. One is that during the course of the twentieth century, both vocational guidance and vocational education have become more formal and their practices and personnel more professionalized in their training and in their roles. Although both were seen at the turn of the century and into the 1930s and beyond as complementary partners in the preparation and distribution of students and adults across the occupational structure, those early bonds were frayed, and for several decades vocational guidance and vocational education tended to pursue very different processes and purposes. Vocational guidance became increasingly psychological, developmental, and personality-oriented rather than focused on skills preparation or occupational information; indeed, there were critics of the use of information in vocational guidance and advocates of its essentially therapeutic role rather than of its previous emphases on information-giving, performance, and the matching of students or employees to jobs. During this period vocational guidance, as practiced by school counselors and other mental health professionals, began to lose a central priority in their roles and diminish in importance. In large measure, this occurred because the role of school counselors had broadened and changed as schools went through a variety of educational movements (progressive education, life adjustment education). Although still a part of the repertoire of school counselors, the other demands for educational guidance and psychological points of view about the role differed significantly from the origins of vocational guidance and perceptions of it by vocational educators. Indeed, as will be discussed later, some of the thrusts of federal legislation since the 1960s have been to reconnect vocational education and vocational guidance. But, although vocational guidance had lost its major role for school counselors and related practitioners, its practice by vocational educators continued to be seen as integral to vocational education, whether school counselors or others saw it as a priority. Therefore, during the 1930s, 1940s, and 1950s, vocational educators tended to emphasize occupational information, vocational testing, and the increasing development of training programs tied to the growing technical character of the society.

THE ANTECEDENTS TO CAREER GUIDANCE

By the early 1950s, theory development and changing definitions of vocational guidance had set the stage for a transition in the terminology of the field from vocational guidance to career guidance. Perhaps the major marker of this transition was the redefinition of vocational guidance that had been adopted in 1937 by the National Vocational Guidance Association (NVGA) as a method of preserving the historical view of vocational guidance that originated at the beginning of the twentieth century and that was compatible with the view of vocational guidance that was held by vocational educators. The 1937 definition of vocational guidance was as follows: "the process of assisting the individual to choose an occupation, prepare for it, enter upon it, and progress in it" (Super, 1951). That definition embraced the traditional notions that had characterized vocational guidance. Such notions included the view that vocational guidance was concerned with predicting occupational choice or occupational success from an individual's test scores before entry into the labor market; the primary emphasis was on matching the aptitude for performance from the results of test profiles of those seeking employment to the requirements of available options, always attempting to maximize the compatibility or congruence between the two components. Vocational guidance was largely confined to one point in the life of the individual, that is, either initial entry into the labor market or reentry and readjustment to the labor market after occupational dislocations. And the major reference point for vocational guidance was the requirements of the occupational structure rather than of individual preferences or values (Herr & Cramer, 1996). These fundamental assumptions were cast into some doubt, if not dramatically altered, by the 1951 revision by the National Vocational Guidance Association of the 1937 definition of vocational guidance.

As advanced by the then NVGA president, Donald Super, the definition of vocational guidance as of 1951 was "the process of helping a person to develop and accept an integrated and adequate picture of himself and of his role in the world of work, to test this concept against reality, and to convert it into a reality, with satisfaction to himself and to society" (Super, 1951). This definition of vocational guidance essentially shifted the emphasis of the process from *what is to be chosen*, with its emphasis on occupational information and the matching of an individual to a job, to *the characteristics of the chooser.* For purposes of discussion the first emphasis can be called an occupational model—the second, a career model. This latter emphasis was a precursor to the growing use of the term "career guidance." In contrast to the emphases of vocational guidance identified in the previous paragraph, the new definition of vocational guidance was more psychological, blending the personal and vocational dimensions of guidance. The base of vocational guidance in its new conception focused on the importance of helping the chooser to clarify the self-concept and to increase self-understanding and self-acceptance as the evaluative base to which educational and occupational alternatives available to the individual can be related. The assumption is that, unless the individual has a relatively clear sense of his or her characteristics, goals, values, interests, aptitudes, and skills, he or she has no real basis on which to make a choice of a job or an occupation. To be fair, the latter conception did not so much reject the earlier view of vocational guidance as it did view that approach as too limited. Indeed, in practice the two emphases, what is to be chosen and the characteristics of the chooser, have tended to both be represented and blended in newer views of career guidance, particularly in new models of person-environment fit. In one analysis that suggests such blending, Chartrand (1991) has summarized the assumptions that are implicit in new models of person-environment fit, what some persons would likely label as contemporary trait-and-factor approaches to vocational guidance:

> *First, people are viewed as capable of making rational decisions. This does not mean that affective processes can be ignored.... Second, people and work environments differ in reliable, meaningful, and consistent ways. This does not mean that a single type of person works in each job.... Third, the greater the congruence between personal characteristics and job requirements, the greater the likelihood of success.... This means that knowledge of person and environment patterns can be used to inform people about the probability of satisfaction and adjustment in different educational and work settings. (p. 520)*

As career guidance models have increasingly influenced the language and practices of the field, several other differences between original (occupational) and contemporary (career) models can be observed. For our purposes, these include the following:

1. Career models embrace a longer time frame than occupational choice. They argue that career guidance is important across the life span, at points of developmental change (e.g., occupational entry, midcareer change, the transition from school to work, unemployment, preretirement, retirement). Thus, the concept of career embraces prevocational activity such as the effects on students of educational programs and options, the induction and adjustment of employees to work, as well as the postoccupational activity of the retiree working part-time or seeking compatible volunteer activity.
2. Career models emphasize development approaches to career guidance by providing programs that help students or adults to learn relevant skills: career planning, job search, assertiveness, anger management, stress reduction, and decision making.
3. Career models suggest that career guidance includes a continuum of activities that need to be tailored to the needs of particular counselees for help with exploration and choice, induction into the workplace, problems of work dysfunction, unemployment or underemployment, occupational reentry or occupational exit, or retirement.
4. Career models suggest that career guidance should be concerned not only about aptitudes and skills but also about the clarity of the self-concept, personal planfulness, exploratory behavior, the individual attitudes and knowledge that facilitate or impede the choosing, learning, and using of technical skills.

5. Career models emphasize the role of career guidance in systematically educating students or adults to the knowledge, attitudes, and skills that will be required of them at future choice points in planning their educational programs, in selecting and preparing for work, and in helping them anticipate and prepare for career paths available to them within a workplace. Such a view emphasizes that career guidance is not only a remedial or treatment approach that is used after it is clear that a person cannot choose or is in a situation with which they cannot effectively cope; career guidance is also an educative, preventive approach that attempts to help persons develop general employability and career-planning skills that will help them to manifest future career behavior that is positive and effective.

6. Career models emphasize that career guidance approaches need to move beyond a focus on slotting individuals into *what is* (a matching approach) to preparing them as well for lifestyle choices and options of *what might be*. Thus, career guidance needs to help persons integrate their work roles with those of family, parent, and other lifestyle roles to understand how conflict may occur among these roles, and ways by which to avoid such conflicts.

Inherent, then, in the historical evolution from vocational guidance approaches embedded in occupational models to career guidance embedded in career models have been growing emphases on a range of efforts to develop decision-making skills in students and adults; concern for the self-concept, aspirations, values, and self-understanding as central content in career guidance; attention to the interaction of education, leisure, occupation, and values in the creation of a lifestyle; the importance of flexibility and the ability to cope with change, contingency planning, flexibility in goals and routes for them, and positive uncertainty (Gelatt, 1989) as important attitudinal assets in a period of rapid change in social and occupational conditions.

These perspectives do not so much denigrate the importance of information in career guidance as broaden the types of information that are valuable to students and adults. In essence career guidance as compared with earlier views of vocational guidance is seen as more comprehensive in who should be served across the life span; its models are more longitudinal and use programmed, structured, and preplanned approaches designed to assist students and adults to deal with the changing questions and dilemmas they face across educational levels, life stages, and transitions; it is more likely to include developmental content useful in helping persons anticipate, plan, and act on a variety of career-related tasks; and career guidance emphasizes many interventions in individual career development (e.g., career guidance curriculum, computer-assisted career guidance systems, structured workshop, self-directed assessments) that can be used without confining counselors or career guidance specialists to a one-to-one individual counseling framework.

The perspectives just addressed about comprehensive career guidance have begun to permeate reports, position statements, and federal and state legislation addressed to needs for career guidance. Some selected examples follow.

CONTEMPORARY NEEDS FOR CAREER GUIDANCE

There were many pieces of federal legislation in the 1960s and 1970s that focused on the occupational preparation of the socially and economically disadvantaged, school dropouts, out-of-work youth, and the unemployed and the underemployed. Many of these programs failed because they frequently focused on meeting the needs of the labor market rather than on the needs of individuals (Herr, 1974). As this deficit in meeting legislative purpose became increasingly evident, federal policies began to undergo a metamorphosis in which developing a sense of personal competence in individuals touched by such legislation, as increasingly manifested by coupling technical skills training with skills in choosing and planning job choice, became increasingly apparent. Such trends began to be evident in legislation dealing with schools and with nonschool agencies as different pieces of legislation began to embrace the inclusion of counseling and placement activities as major components of programs. Of particular importance to federal affirmations that vocational education and vocational guidance are reciprocally related to each other, as was true at the turn of the twentieth century, were the Vocational Education Act of 1963 and the amendments to that act in 1968. As a conceptual base about career behavior and career guidance practice began to grow rapidly and comprehensively in the 1960s, these insights were increasingly reflected in federal legislation and in national policies and position statements. These perspectives argued that vocational-career guidance is important in its own right and in relation to success in vocational education.

In the 1980s and 1990s, a series of preeminent legislative pieces emerged that continued to reinforce the importance of career guidance, defined its elements, and affirmed its essential role in vocational education. One of these pieces of legislation was Public Law 98–254, the Carl D. Perkins Vocational Education Act of 1984. The Perkins act provided, on an annual basis, nearly one billion dollars in federal support to states to provide strengthened and improved vocational education to major segments of secondary school populations and to groups with problems of access to the occupational structure. Among its other purposes the Perkins act was concerned with two major goals—(1) providing equity and access to vocational education for subpopulations who have historically been underserved in educational, training, and occupational opportunities, and, (2) ensuring that the vocational education opportunities to which these subpopulations obtain access are excellent. Throughout the Perkins legislation, career guidance is mentioned time and again as an essential ingredient in addressing both excellence and equity issues.

In essence, in the Perkins act the Congress gave a resounding vote of confidence for guidance and counseling and for specialists in these areas, since in the Perkins act only certified counselors are able to be charged with the organization, administration, and conduct of the guidance and counseling programs the legislation supports. In addition, the law authorized funding for training and updating counselors, required that state advisory councils for vocational education include representatives of career guidance and counseling organizations, and specified support for state-level leadership for guidance.

Perhaps most important, the Perkins act authorized and specified guidance provisions for grants. For example, Title III, Part D authorized grants for "programs (organized and administered by certified counselors) designed to improve, expand, and extend career guidance and counseling programs to meet the career development, vocational education, and employment needs of vocational education students and potential students." Such programs shall be designed to assist students to

1. Acquire self-assessment, career planning, decision making, and employability skills;
2. Make the transition from education and training to work;
3. Maintain marketability of current job skills in established occupations;
4. Develop new skills to move away from declining occupational fields and enter new and emerging fields in high-technology areas and fields experiencing skill shortages;
5. Develop midcareer job search skills and clarify career goals; and,
6. Obtain and use information on financial assistance for postsecondary and vocational education and job training.

In addition, Section 332(b) elaborated the intention that programs of career guidance and counseling shall encourage the elimination of sex, age, and race bias and stereotyping and handicapping conditions.

One report that was published almost simultaneously with the enactment of the Perkins act was the 1984 report of the National Commission on Secondary Vocational Education (National Commission on Secondary Vocational Education, 1985). The report of this commission, entitled *The Unfinished Agenda,* was an attempt to correct the stereotyped image of vocational education and to propose a series of recommendations that would strengthen vocational education in American schools.

Although the report of the National Commission on Secondary Vocational Education offered recommendations in areas including access to vocational education, funding, curriculum, and leadership, only those most relevant to how career guidance should be viewed are noted here. For example, in contrast to the typical, narrow view that vocational education should provide entry-level occupational skills for students, the commission contended that vocational education in the secondary school should be, and generally is, concerned with the development of the individual student in five areas: (1) personal skills and attitudes, (2) communications and computational skills and technological literacy, (3) employability skills, (4) broad and specific occupational skills and knowledge, and (5) foundations for career planning and lifelong learning (p. 3). Obviously these five purposes strongly argue that vocational education is not only concerned with teaching the technical aspects of job performance but also with work habits, career planning, and job-access skills. They also argue for a strengthened role for vocational-career guidance as integral to vocational education and as important in its availability for all students.

More specifically, in its support for career guidance, the National Commission on Secondary Vocational Education stated:

Inadequate student knowledge subtly but formidably constrains student access to vocational education. Students and parents need to be accurately informed about what vocational education is, how it relates to their personal and career goals.... We need comprehensive career guidance programs that will provide this information and remove some of the subtle status distinctions involving vocational education.

Comprehensive guidance means counseling that is available to all students, covering all subjects, leading to all occupations.... We cannot achieve this goal of comprehensive guidance when counselors must deal, on the average, with 400 or more students. Nor can this goal be achieved unless counselors and teachers cooperate in new approaches to facilitate the career development of students and unless counselors expand their use of group techniques, computer-assisted career guidance, comprehensive career information systems, and other methods designed to provide assistance to all students.

Counselors must serve as a resource to integrate career guidance concepts and occupational information in the classroom. In addition, the amount of shared information between vocational educators and school counselors should be increased to reinforce the likelihood that counselors will effectively advise students to consider vocational education as an option. (p. 10)

Other national reports have also identified the role of career guidance and career counseling in addressing major national social problems. For example, the Business Advisory Committee of the Education Commission of the States (1985), in a national report dealing with the growing problem of alienated, disadvantaged, disconnected and other "at-risk youth," recommended "new structures and procedures for effecting the transition from school to work or other productive pursuits..." It also advised that, "young people need more and better guidance than ever before" (p. 26). The report goes on to specify the need for coordinated programs including career counseling, financial assistance, summer jobs, cooperative education, options, and role models if such at-risk youth are to be reconnected to schooling and to work.

The Research and Policy Committee of the Committee for Economic Development (1985), in a report dealing with business and the public schools, strongly recommended that schools provide employability counseling and exploratory programs to assist in career choice, job search, and general employability. In 1984, the National Alliance of Business and the National Advisory Council on Vocational Education, in a major analysis of the nation at work, argued for more school-to-work transition programs, including job placement assistance, career counseling, cooperative career education activities with business, and counseling about vocational-technical program alternatives to college degree programs. In 1988, the W. T. Grant Foundation, Commission on Work, Family, and Citizenship, in a report entitled *The Forgotten Half*, also argued for counseling for employment, career information centers in schools and communities, improved counseling and career orientation, monitored work experience, work incentives, redirected vocational education, and an increase in community and neighborhood services designed to assist at-risk youth and those students not going on to college.

In 1989, the Commission on Workforce Quality and Labor Market Efficiency, supported by the U.S. Department of Labor, strongly recommended in its report that attention be paid to the dynamics of the school-to-work transition, with state employment security agencies and private industry councils establishing school-based employment services with direct connections to employers. The report further encouraged employers, whether small or large, to provide information on job openings and to consider filling vacancies with recent high school graduates. The intent of these recommendations is to harness the possibilities of cooperation between government agencies in the community that are directly involved with job placement and job training with the school's efforts in career guidance so that concrete information on local job vacancies are provided to students in a timely and accurate fashion; to show that the system works for those who have the necessary skills (e.g., high school completion); and to argue that career guidance and counseling in schools must not only be active in educating students for choice but be directly involved in concrete steps to help place students in jobs in the local community as an important aspect of their effective transition from school to work.

In a large measure, the federal support for career guidance that appeared in the Carl D. Perkins Vocational Education Act of 1984 was reaffirmed in the reauthorization of the Perkins act, retitled the Carl D. Perkins Vocational Education and Applied Technology Act (1989). More recently the U.S. Congress included career guidance as a major emphasis in the School-to-Work Opportunities Act of 1994 (PL 103–239).

Programs funded by the School-to-Work Opportunities Act combine classroom learning with real-world work experience. They fund the training of students in general job-readiness skills as well as in industrial-specific occupational skills. The School-to-Work Opportunities Act provides help to high schools and community colleges to create programs in cooperation with business and to develop the academic skills and attitudes toward work that too many adolescents lack today and that both educational and community agencies have neglected.

The School-to-Work Opportunities Act provides for a school-based learning component, a work-based learning component, and a connecting-activities component. It introduces the term "career major" to mean "a coherent sequence of courses" or a field of study that prepares a student for a first job and that (A) integrates academic and occupational learning, integrates school-based and work-based learning, establishes linkages between secondary schools and post-secondary educational institutions; (B) prepares the student for employment in a broad occupational cluster or industry sector; (C) provides the students, to the extent practicable, with strong experience in and understanding of all aspects of the industry the students are planning to enter; and (D) may lead to further education and training, such as entry into a registered apprenticeship program, or may lead to admission to a two- or four-year college or university (Section 4, Definitions). The act also defines "career guidance and counseling" to mean programs: "(A) that pertain to the body of subject matter and related techniques and methods organized for the development in individuals of career awareness, career planning, career decision making, placement skills, and knowledge and understanding of local, state and national occupational, educational, and labor market needs, trends, and opportunities; (B) that assist individuals in making and implementing informed educational and occupational choices; and (C) that aid students to develop career options with attention to surmounting gender, race, ethnic, disability, language, or socioeconomic impediments to career options and encouraging careers in nontraditional employment" (Section 4, Definitions).

Although the School-to-Work Opportunities Act specifies the elements of the school-based learning component and the work-based learning component of a school-to-work opportunities program, for the purposes of this chapter it could be argued that the connecting activities component is most directly relevant. That component (Section 104) indicates that the connecting activities shall include

1. Matching students with the work-based learning opportunities of employers;
2. Providing, with respect to each student, a school-site mentor to act as a liaison between the student and the employer and the student and the school, teacher, school administrator, and parent of the student, and, if appropriate, other community partners;
3. Providing technical assistance and services to employers, including small- and medium-sized businesses, and other parties in (A) designing school-based learning components described in Section 102, work-based learning components described in Section 103, and counseling and case management services; and (B) training teachers, workplace mentors, school-site mentors, and counselors;
4. Providing assistance to schools and employers to integrate school-based and work-based learning and integrate academic and occupational learning into the program;
5. Encouraging the active participation of employers, in cooperation with local education officials, in the implementation of local activities described in Section 102, Section 103, or this section;
6. (A) providing assistance to participants who have completed the program in finding an appropriate job, continuing their education, or entering into an additional training program; and (B) linking the participants with other community services that may be necessary to assure a successful transition from school to work;
7. Collecting and analyzing information regarding postprogram outcomes of participants in the School-to-Work Opportunities program, to the extent practicable, on the basis of socioeconomic status, race, gender, ethnicity, culture, and disability, and on the basis of whether the participants are students with limited English proficiency, school dropouts, disadvantaged students, or academically talented students.

Although other national reports could be cited here, the examples given are sufficient to support the premise that the legislative mandates and the observations of national commissions have combined with federal legislation to enlarge the scope and function of vocational-career guidance, both in vocational education and outside of it. This momentum can be seen in the evolution of the practices of vocational and career guidance.

CONTEMPORARY PERSPECTIVES ON CAREER GUIDANCE

Although many of the current pieces of legislation and national reports cited tend to focus on career guidance processes for young persons leaving the secondary school and making the transition to employment, contemporary practice has become broader and more comprehensive than if applied only to this part of the life span. As career development theory (discussed in Chapter 7) has become more wide-ranging in its connections between influences on career behavior and the outcomes likely to result and in its attention to adult career behavior as well as to that of adolescents, career guidance systems have become more comprehensive in the populations served. In addition to the need to serve the special needs of women, persons with disabilities, and racial and ethnic minority groups, career guidance has also been directed to the larger needs of adult populations in mid-career change, occupational dislocation, unemployment, underemployment, and in other developmental transitions. As suggested in Chapter 7 in the explanations of career development theory given there, under the impetus of an expanding knowledge of adult development, it has become clear that as one ages, one reassesses choices and plots one's possibilities of still attaining certain idealized goals, sometimes with anxiety and despair, sometimes with confusion and inappropriate information, and sometimes with frustration and stress. Whichever the circumstance, career guidance is needed.

In an operational sense, career guidance systems and processes tend to appear under different names in schools (K–12), in colleges and universities, in community agencies, and in workplaces. The term "career guidance" is most frequently used in educational institutions, particularly kindergarten through grade 12. In colleges and universities, the term more likely to be used is "career development and placement services." In community agencies, the term might be "employment counseling" or "occupational counseling," or "job readiness services." In workplaces, the term may be "career services" as part of the larger context of human resource development.

Given this wide application of career guidance, there is no one definition that fits all settings or populations, although there are perspectives that have wide currency. One of these is that concepts such as career guidance, career development and placement, or career services include many processes that are combined in various ways to serve the needs of persons engaged in career planning and decision making. For example, when speaking of the needs of disadvantaged youth in secondary schools, the Employment and Training Administration of the U.S. Department of Labor (1993: 6–7) suggests that the following processes should be included:

- Outreach alerts students to services.
- Classroom instruction provides an integrated set of planned and sequential curricular activities.

- Counseling helps students explore personal issues and apply information and skills to personal plans and may be offered individually or in small groups.
- Self-assessment provides students with a clearer understanding of their values, skills, abilities, interests, achievements, aspirations, and needs.
- Career information—easily accessible, current, relevant, and unbiased—provides a solid framework on which to base decisions.
- Exploration activities are experiences designed to broaden horizons, test interests, and stimulate career planning.
- Work experience offers opportunities to test decisions and develop effective work abilities and behaviors.
- Career planning activities help youth learn the skills needed to make decisions and understand the future impact of choices.
- Placement services help youth make the transition to school, work, or the military.
- Referrals to other professional services allow youth to obtain assistance beyond the scope of the program.
- Follow-up activities provide opportunities to maintain contact and track progress.

In colleges and universities, as career development processes have been added to traditional models of placement, the career services offered in higher education vary by institutional type and mission and by the allocation of resources to such services. In broad terms, career development and placement services in higher educational institutions are likely to include, in addition to individual counseling, the following categories of career guidance:

1. Infusing academic subject matter systematically with information pertinent to career development (e.g., how the academic content is used in solving particular kinds of programs in work settings, the relationship between academic majors and the occupations in which graduates are employed);
2. Providing specific credit courses that have personal development and career information components (e.g., course content dealing with self-assessment, career evaluation, career planning, and decision making);
3. Use of external resources (e.g., speakers, field trips, internships, and so on) in classes, in dormitories, and in clubs or Greek organizations to provide direct communication of career-related information;
4. Integrating placement and transfer processes in support of career planning;
5. Opportunities for work-study/cooperative education with career information incorporated;
6. Decentralized counseling using academic departments as the location for counselors who, among their other responsibilities, coordinate the career and academic advisement of faculty;
7. Seminars on college life and educational and career planning;
8. Personal assistance groups or group counseling focused on self-awareness and career planning;
9. Human potential seminars;
10. Use of interactive, computer-based guidance systems.

Viewed somewhat differently, a survey of career services operated through career planning and placement services in colleges and universities for which there were 823 institutional respondents (College Placement Council, 1991*) (abridged and adopted here) suggested that, in descending order of frequency in 1991, the following services were provided by the respondent institutions:

Service	*% of Respondents*
Career counseling	94.2
Occupational and employer information library	93.7
Placement of graduates into full-time employment	93.4
Campus interviewing	91.6
Placement of students into summer and part-time employment	83.2
Placement of alumni	82.7
Credential service	71.9
Resume referral	71.6
Cooperative education, intern, experiential program	62.8
Resume booklets	56.3
Vocational testing	52.1
Computerized candidate database	48.2
Career planning or employment readiness course	31.6
Academic counseling	28.7
Dropout prevention and counseling	16.2

In the workplace, career specialists apply career services either as a part of such initiatives as human resource development or personnel development. Sometimes these are provided in-house by corporate employees; sometimes they are provided under contract by counseling psychologists or other career specialists in the local community. Again, depending on specific corporate philosophy, the career services provided may take a variety of foci. Included are such emphases as the following (Herr & Cramer, 1996):

- Classifying employees in efforts to maximize person–job fit,
- Providing assistance to plateaued workers,
- Identifying and providing information about career ladders in a particular firm,
- Providing information about job postings on vacancies within a firm,
- Facilitating wellness programs for workers, including information, workshops and seminars, fitness programs dealing with chemical abuse, managing job stress, nutrition, and so on,
- Outplacement counseling for workers being terminated as a mechanism to help them prepare for a new job search, assuage the personal and organizational trauma and anger associated with the termination, and engage in goal setting and self-assessment,

---

* Chart reprinted from the 1991 *Career Planning & Placement Survey,* with permission of the National Association of Colleges and Employers, copyright holder.

- Employee assistance programs that directly address or refer troubled employees to outside specialists, alcohol and drug rehabilitation facilities, mental health and social agencies, psychiatrists and psychologists, and self-help groups such as Alcoholics Anonymous,
- Retirement planning to help employees anticipate and plan for retirement,
- Training supervisors and managers in ways to facilitate employee career development, create more productive work environments, and identify and refer employees who are experiencing personal, family, and work adjustment problems.

Although there are many other types of services and processes that could be identified and included under the rubric of career guidance, these emphases in services offered tend to differ across institutions and populations. They have in common the recognition that most persons have multiple dilemmas, problems, or career needs that require multiple interventions. Therefore, contemporary forms of career guidance, career development and placement services, or career services usually include a program of counselor activities that go beyond one-to-one interaction between a counselor and a student or adult. For example, comprehensive career guidance programs are likely to include such elements as assessment; individual counseling; group guidance or workshops on such topics as anger management, communication skills, job search skills and decision making; placement of students into part- or full-time employment; and follow-through and support while students are getting settled in a job or adjusting to it. The development of planned and systematic experiences in didactic, simulated, and psychoeducational processes to teach students or adults certain types of information about themselves or about occupational alternatives, skills in decision making, or values clarification has become reasonably commonplace. Consultation about student career development or adult trainability or employability by counselors with teachers, employers, and others; the use of group processes in career guidance; the use of simulation and gaming as well as computer-based systems of information retrieval and analysis—all represent major emphases in the provision of career guidance and, indeed, career counseling by career professionals.

CAREER COUNSELING

As these expanding views of career guidance and career counseling have evolved, so has the importance of career counseling in its own right and the importance of the competencies required to engage in such services. Although there are many statements of required competencies available, the most authoritative one is that adopted by the National Career Development Association (1991). First developed in 1981 and significantly revised in 1991, the ten categories of competencies essential to the practice of career counseling include the following:

- General counseling
- Information
- Individual/group assessment

- Management/administration
- Program implementation
- Consultation
- Career development theories
- Special populations
- Supervision
- Ethical/legal issues

Each of these ten competency categories include a series of knowledge or skill competencies by which the training of career counselors or the evaluation of their ability to perform career counseling functions can be evaluated. Selected excerpts illustrate the types of knowledge and skills that undergird the various competency categories. They include, for example

- Ability to support clients and challenge them to examine the balance of work, leisure, family and community roles in their careers,
- Knowledge of information, techniques, and models related to computer-assisted career information delivery systems and career counseling,
- Sensitivity toward the developmental issues and needs unique to minority populations
- Ability to design evaluation programs that take into account the needs of special populations, minorities, the elderly persons with acquired immune deficiency syndrome (AIDS), and women,
- Ability to apply ethical standards to career counseling and consulting situations, issues, and practices.

These efforts to continue to professionalize the counselor engaged in career counseling and career guidance in schools, colleges and universities, and workplaces are reflected increasingly in state certification and licensure standards, in national certification efforts (e.g., the National Board of Certified Counselors, the Career Counseling specialization), and in state and national accreditation processes (e.g., the Council for the Accreditation of Counseling and Related Programs).

Professionalizing the training and the competencies of career specialists reflects the expanding roles expected of such persons as identified in changing federal legislation and the national commission reports cited previously as well as in professional organization perspectives and in the growth of theory and its effects on the techniques and processes that counselors use.

In broad terms the competency statements for career counselors that have been created by the National Career Development Association (NCDA) and cited previously reflect changing views of what career counselors do. Indeed, the consumer guidelines prepared by the NCDA under the title What Do Career Counselors Do? cite the following services (NCDA, 1985):

- Conduct individual and group personal counseling sessions to help clarify life/career goals.
- Administer and interpret tests and inventories to assess abilities and interests, and to identify career options.

- Encourage exploratory activities through assignments and planning experiences.
- Utilize career planning systems and occupational information systems to help individuals better understand the world of work.
- Provide opportunities for improving decision-making skills.
- Assist in developing individualized career plans.
- Teach job-hunting strategies and skills and assist in the development of resumes.
- Help resolve personal conflicts on the job through practice in human relations skills.
- Assist in understanding the integration of work and other life roles.
- Provide support for persons experiencing job stress, job loss, and career transition. (pp. 1–2)

What is apparent in this brief analysis is that the emphases undergirding the conceptions of the processes perceived as important in helping persons deal with career problems, whether labeled career guidance or career counseling or something else (e.g., career services), have changed in the labels ascribed to them and, perhaps more important, in the comprehensiveness of application with which they can be credited. For example, one can argue that, historically, models of career guidance and, more specifically, career counseling have focused more on issues of career choice than on work adjustment or unemployment problems, even though most people spend more of their life working at a job or occupation than they spend choosing it (Hershenson, 1996). This balance seems to be undergoing a process of reconceptualization as contemporary expectations of career counseling are being enlarged and applied to new or emerging sets of career issues. Indeed, when career counseling focuses on difficult work adjustment problems or the grieving and loss associated with unemployment, this process clearly fuses with personal counseling as a mental health modality.

The result is that career counseling is being increasingly seen as an important intervention in its own right and that it is also a continuum of interventions, not simply a single process (Herr, 1997). At one end of the continuum are the traditional approaches of career counseling to choice, to situational indecision, clarifying life-career goals, and administering tests and inventories to assess abilities and interests to clarify career options. But at the other end of the career counseling continuum is the application of career counseling to stress reduction, anger management, integrating and resolving conflict between career and other life roles, helping persons reconstruct and reframe past experiences, learn ways to reduce their indecisiveness, assist in modifying career beliefs, address underlying issues which lead to work dysfunctions being played out in the workplace, providing opportunities for occupationally displaced persons to vent their anger and their feelings about personal concerns and job loss, and the role or diffusion of personal identity.

In many ways the evolution and the expansion of concepts and techniques of career guidance and career counseling, as they have been discussed here, have paralleled the growth in theoretical perspectives about how career counseling can be implemented and the contributions that different approaches to career counseling can make as they relate to the career needs of students or adults. In Table 12.1, Herr

TABLE 12.1   Examples of Potential Contributions of Six Approaches to Career Counseling for Employment-Bound Youth

Approach	Major Contributions in Career Counseling
Trait and Factor	Matching of individual traits to the requirements of a particular job, occupation, or training opportunity.
	Helping employment-bound youth to examine the range of jobs for occupations for which their abilities, achievement, aptitudes, and interests would qualify them.
	Assisting employment-bound youth to understand the elasticity or transportability of their current knowledge or skills across jobs, occupations, industries.
	Providing employment-bound youth with a classification system of self-characteristics and language (e.g., interests, values, aptitudes, achievement, skills) and of jobs, occupations, and careers by which to facilitate identification of possible options to explore and information to secure.
	Facilitating individual assessment of the probabilities, the odds, of gaining access to and being successful in different jobs, occupations, or educational opportunities.
Client-Centered	Providing a safe and accepting environment in which to explore career planning and work adjustment issues.
	Encouraging employment-bound youth to take control of their lives and to set goals for action that can be rehearsed and tried out in counseling.
	Helping employment-bound youth develop insights into their personal priorities, personal patterns of behavior, and barriers to their achievement of goals.
	Establishing a sense of hope that conditions that brought the counselee to the counselor can change in positive ways.
	Reinforcing that the counselor views the counselee as a person of value who has the ability to identify issues and barriers in his career life and ways to change them.
Psychodynamic	Providing a connection between past experiences and present behavior that is relevant to career choices or work adjustment.
	Assisting the counselee to understand unresolved conflicts in the family or in other past relationships that may be hindering current interactions with co-workers or supervisors.
	Facilitating the employment-bound youth's understanding of messages from and expectations of others that have been incorporated into the individual's negative view of self, senses of self-efficacy, or feelings about opportunities.
	Helping the individual to examine past educational, employment, or social experiences that may clarify needs or gratifications to be sought from work.
Developmental	Providing insight for employment-bound youth about developmental tasks that they may need to explore, complete, or anticipate in their career-planning process.
	Helping counselees to clarify and integrate the role of work and its importance in comparison with other life roles: family, parenting, leisure, community service, and student.
	Assisting counselees to acquire awareness that work and occupation serve to provide a focus for personality organization for most men and women, although for some persons this focus is peripheral, incidental or even non-existent.
	Facilitating clarification of the counselee's self-concept and ways to implement it in work.
	Assisting counselees to identify and act on their work values, resources, self-concept in fashioning possible career patterns they wish to pursue.

Continued

TABLE 12.1 *Continued*

Approach	Major Contributions in Career Counseling
	Facilitating counselee understanding of the process of change across time and the ways to anticipate and cope with such change.
	Helping counselees understand that success in coping with the demands of the environment and of the person at any given life/career stage depends on the readiness of the individual to cope with these demands. In particular, this means helping the individual to understand and acquire the elements of career maturity or career adaptability: planfulness or time perspective, exploratory skills, relevant information, decision-making skills, and a reality orientation.
	Providing counselees awareness of the important roles played by feedback and reality-testing in the development of self-concepts and the translation of these into occupational self-concepts.
	Assisting counselees in understanding and acting on knowledge that work satisfactions and life satisfactions depend on the extent to which the individual finds adequate outlets for abilities, needs, values, interests, personality traits, and self-concepts. They further depend on establishment in a type of work, or work situation, and a way of life in which one can play the kind of role that growth and exploratory experiences have led one to consider congenial and appropriate.
Behavioral	Helping to demystify employment-bound youth's concerns about or problems with career planning or work performance.
	Facilitating clarification of goals that counselees hope to achieve in counseling, in work, and in social interaction and breaking them into increments that can be learned or relearned.
	Analyzing with counselees their environments to identify cues and reinforcers that are important in triggering and sustaining their behavior.
	Providing opportunities for social modeling, vicarious learning simulations, role playing, behavioral rehearsal, and feedback so that counselees can be helped to accurately understand and learn desirable behaviors or skills important to their goals, improved work performance or adjustment, job choice, and career planning.
	Assisting counselees to specifically identify behavioral deficits and create conditions or experiences that will provide reinforcement of appropriate learned responses important to goal attainment.
Cognitive Behavioral	Helping employment-bound youth to modify inaccurate or maladaptive cognitive sets about self, others, and life events.
	Assisting counselees to understand the cognitive bases of their moods, anxieties, or depression and the direct connection between thoughts and feelings.
	Facilitating counselee analysis of their automatic thoughts and irrational beliefs about their abilities, worth, work opportunities, or performance.
	Providing employment-bound youth help in cognitive restructuring or reframing their concerns about career planning, the school-to-work transition, or work adjustment.
	Identifying with counselees' tendencies to overgeneralize or use cognitive distortions as they assess problems, issues, or barriers related to the choice of and implementation of work.

Source: Herr, E. L. (1996). *Counseling Employment-Bound Youth*, pp. 200–205. ERIC–CASS. Greensboro, NC: University of North Carolina. Used with permission.

(1996) has addressed such perspectives to the career needs of employment-bound youth.

As Table 12.1 illustrates, the theoretical underpinnings of career counseling can be conceived in at least six theoretical approaches. None of these approaches offers the final solution to all career issues brought to the career counselor. Rather, it is more accurate to suggest that each of the six approaches cited make particular contributions to understanding and being helpful in assisting counselees with particular types of career issues. Obviously, while the application of career counseling theories illustrated in Table 12.1 are focused on employment-bound youth, these approaches could be equally well applied to other populations.

SUMMARY AND IMPLICATIONS FOR PRACTITIONERS

This chapter has provided a historical overview of the antecedents to contemporary forms of career guidance and career counseling in the United States. Also at issue have been descriptions of career guidance and career counseling as they have been increasingly supported and defined by federal legislation, national commission reports, and professional organizations. As the professionalization of career specialists and career counselors has ensued over the last two decades, the potential importance of career guidance and career counseling as important adjuncts to workforce education and development has grown. The value of career guidance or career counseling is no longer confined to the initial choice of a job but is also related to the school-to-work transition, the induction and adjustment to work, the resolution of work dysfunctions and conflicts, the involuntary exit from work through unemployment, and the dynamics of retirement.

Just as the early history of vocational guidance and vocational education saw these processes as a partnership, recent federal legislation has attempted to bring the processes of career guidance and workforce education into a new reconciliation and partnership. Both in terms of individual opportunity and economic development, it is to be hoped that such a partnership will continue to strengthen and to evolve.

THE NATIONAL WORKFORCE EDUCATION SYSTEM: POLICY, TRENDS, AND ISSUES

The final foundation for workforce education practitioners is an understanding of the public policy process that establishes direction for the field and an overview of the resultant national public and private workforce education system, particularly the trends and issues involved. The purpose of the final part of this foundations text is to provide this background.

13

WORKFORCE EDUCATION POLICY

The instigator of a majority of all workforce education is public policy. Even when workforce education is offered in business and industry, the content is often a reaction to public policy regulations such as those associated with OSHA, EEOC, or handling of hazardous material.

Because it is funded by government, arguably all public sector workforce education is instigated by public policy. Furthermore, because of the perceived link between poverty, social unrest, and employment, public policy dealing with a multitude of noneducational social issues frequently contains workforce education provisions that affect the profession. Welfare reform legislation, for example, always contains significant training provisions. Because of the impact public policy has on workforce education programs and workforce education professionals, having an understanding of public policy fundamentals is an important foundation for effective practice. Particularly those practicing in the public sector will more than likely find themselves attempting to influence public policy in order to improve their programs.

PUBLIC POLICY DEFINED

Public policy is defined as decisions made by governing bodies or public officials, the intent being to create a public benefit (Quade, 1989). In a majority of cases, public policy takes the form of legislation. When a group of elected or appointed officials make decisions that affect others and have the authority to implement these decisions, they are making public policy. The fundamental example is when elected officials set tax rates; few are involved in the decision, yet all are affected.

In the United States, most public policy comes from the legislation process at the federal, state, and local level. Often government employees, covertly or overtly, make policy through the regulations they develop; less frequently the judicial system will make rulings that, in effect, become public policy. Although all laws are public policy, not all public policy are laws. A decision by a community to build a regional area vocational school instead of adding vocational-industrial education programs in each county high school, in effect establishes the public policy regarding how workforce education will be provided.

Public Policy Characteristics

Public policy has a number of unique characteristics that, when understood, assist in understanding the process, its successes, its failures, and even how to influence its development. What follows are six important characteristics drawn from the work of the late Edward Quade of the Rand Cooperation, a U.S. firm that specializes in public policy research.

Public Policy Exists within the Public Domain.   Public policy can affect and regulate only those situations that are within the public domain, meaning events that government has some direct or indirect power to alter. The extent of the public versus private domain is a function of a nation's tradition and values. In countries with a centralized planned economic system, the public domain is very broad, whereas in an unplanned laissez-faire capitalist system, such as exists in the United States, the public domain is more limited. This is a particularly important point for workforce education policy development, because, for example, in an unplanned laissez-faire capitalist system all private sector training is generally not within the public domain. If the federal or state government wanted to make private firms invest more in the training of its employees, its options to effect this change are limited because this is a private decision of firms and thus not within the public domain.

The limits of the public domain are always in flux and hotly debated in the United States. Rhetoric in the 1990s regarding overly intrusive big government was really a negative reaction to increasing the public domain. Very often workforce education public policy tests the limits of public domain as policy makers seek ways to solve economic and social problems, such as requiring welfare recipients to enroll in training in order to receive benefits.

The issue becomes more complicated when one considers that different governing bodies have different public domains. The issue of states rights versus local or federal control in the United States is a debate over both the extent of the public domain and who controls what domain. Workforce education officials at the state level, for example, are criticized for usurping local control when they develop statewide performance standards; the issue is whether determining standards and/or curriculum is within the state's domain or that of local school boards.

Public Policy Is Intended to Create a Public Good.   The objective of public policy is to create, through government action, a greater public good for its citizens. Public policy intended to provide unemployment compensation and retraining for workers displaced due to plant closings is an example of such a policy and one that has general support. Often, however, there is not a public consensus as to what constitutes a greater good. In such cases, public policy can be controversial and divisive. Federal school-to-work legislation was, for example, viewed as intrusive by some family rights groups.

Public Policy Reflects Society Values.   Public policy reflects the values of policy makers and, to the extent that the democratic process works, the values of society as a whole. When values change, policy ultimately changes. The increased importance placed on work as part of welfare reform in the 1990s reflected a change in values from mothers should be home with their children to mothers should work to support their children.

Often more efficient public policy options are not possible because they conflict with the values of the electorate. An example is the "open admissions" higher education system that has developed in the United States. Most industrialized nations limited higher education enrollment to conform to their labor market. The U.S. system, on the other hand, allows virtually anyone to enroll, and government provides financial aid to ensure income is not a deterrent, despite labor market projections. In terms of results, the U.S. system is inefficient; at best only about one-half who start a postsecondary degree graduate. However, open admissions are very unlikely to change because they reflect how much Americans value opportunity, and, so far, the taxpayers are willing and able to pay the price. Finally, values affecting public policy often conflict. For example, although most Americans agree that balancing the budget should be a national priority, 95 percent also believe the government should provide financial aid to students.

Public Policy Involves Multiple Parties and Perspectives.   Public policy is unique in that it typically involves four different groups who are involved in different ways and affect its outcomes.

First there is the *target group,* or those whose status is hoped to be improved by legislation or policy. The target group can be high school students, young adults, or adults returning to the workplace. Second are the *influencers* (special interest groups, lobbyists, and so on), or those who are to gain or be hurt financially, those who do not make policy decisions but attempt to affect the decision. Workforce educators are, or should be, part of this group. The third group is the *decision makers* themselves; in the United States they are almost always elected government officials. In reality, however, much of the actual drafting of policy is done by a fourth group, namely, the legislative staff. The fourth group is the *implementors,* public employees charged with implementing the policy. Often this group is faced with the formidable task of attempting to interpret the "intent" of public policy legislation and make it happen through regulation.

The dynamics among these groups can often become bizarre and unpredictable, and often the result is policy that, when finally implemented, looks foreign even to the decision makers who voted for it. This is often the case because how legislation is implemented is determined by regulations developed by the implementors, efforts by the influencers to affect these regulations, and subsequent actions by the courts to modify them. Also, it is always wise to keep in mind that public policy in the United States is a result of the political process, and what emerges is often not what is totally desirable but what was politically possible.

The Results of Public Policy Are Often Unpredictable.   Perhaps the most intriguing characteristic of public policy is that, because the social and economic system involved is so complex and because it often is only partly in the public domain, policy makers can only speculate (hope) that the desired result will happen.

A classic example were the federal efforts in the 1970s and 1980s to ensure that at-risk youth would have access to secondary vocational education. The intent certainly was not to create a high school vocational education program that was only attended by at-risk youth. However, by the early 1990s, this policy had become so successful that the vocational education systems in many states were in danger of becoming special education systems, partly because a majority of students abandoned the curriculum as it became stigmatized by growing special education enrollments (NAVE, 1994).

Another classic case of the unpredictability of public policy was the movement in Congress to consolidate and fund a variety of workforce education efforts at the state level through block grants. Although the concept was very popular in Congress, no one really knew what effect it would have on the nation's workforce education system because it was impossible to predict how the block grant would be handled in the fifty states. In the realm of public policy, the best laid plans often do go astray.

TYPES OF WORKFORCE EDUCATION POLICY

There is such a variety of workforce education policy in the United States that a framework to organize it into some logical order is helpful. Such a framework is provided in Figure 13.1. This schematic portrays federal workforce education policy. A schematic for state and local efforts would look quite the same, adding only unique state policy efforts. The purpose of this diagram is not to provide an exhaustive review of all federal workforce education policy or programs (there were, in the mid-1990s, well over 100 federal programs alone) but to provide a framework for understanding the U.S. workforce education system.

As indicated in Figure 13.1, federal workforce education emanates from the president and the Congress and is typically implemented by the Departments of Education, Labor, and Commerce. However, workforce education activity can probably be found in every federal department. These policies or programs can be divided into one or the other of the two missions of workforce education—workforce development or promoting individual opportunity. Each category is discussed below.

Workforce Development Policy

It is useful at this point to recall the human capital development theory explained in Chapter 4. The theory predicts that investment or inputs in human capital (people) will result in more productivity, allowing higher wages, increased consump-

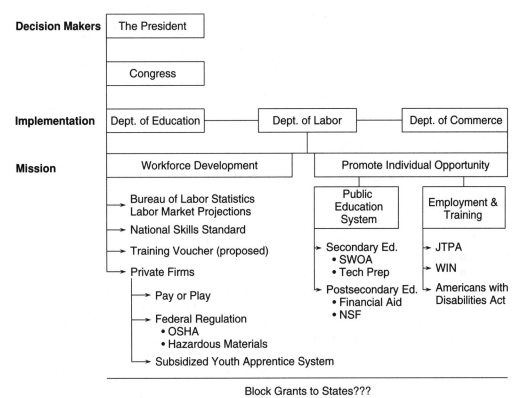

Decision Makers

The President

Congress

Implementation

Dept. of Education — Dept. of Labor — Dept. of Commerce

Mission

Workforce Development

Promote Individual Opportunity

Bureau of Labor Statistics
Labor Market Projections

National Skills Standard

Training Voucher (proposed)

Private Firms

Pay or Play

Federal Regulation
• OSHA
• Hazardous Materials

Subsidized Youth Apprentice System

Public
Education
System

Employment &
Training

Secondary Ed.
• SWOA
• Tech Prep

Postsecondary Ed.
• Financial Aid
• NSF

JTPA

WIN

Americans with
Disabilities Act

Block Grants to States???

FIGURE 13.1   U.S. Workforce Education Policy Schematic: Federal Level

tion, and a higher standard of living. As public policy makers explore various options to improve the economy through workforce education, they are, in effect, considering different alternative types of human capital inputs or investment. These policy options are limited by the existing boundaries of the public domain, social values, conflicting national goals, multiple constituents, and other political realities.

Included in Figure 13.1 under the broad category of workforce development are some examples of present U.S. workforce education policies in which the intent is to improve the quality of the national workforce in general. The objective of these policies, or more specifically the programs these policies create, is to help the nation's firms be more productive by improving the overall quality of the labor force; the focus is not on individuals but on groups of workers and firms that employ them.

Some policies or programs, such as the Bureau of Labor Statistics' labor market projections, are designed to make the nation's labor market operate efficiently, thereby preventing labor shortages. A program with similar objectives is the *National Skills Standards* program. This program, which is based on the policy rationale that the lack of national occupational skills standards, as exist, for example, in Germany, hurts the economic competitiveness of the country because it inhibits the effective mobility of labor to areas of the country with labor shortages.

An overarching federal goal is to stimulate more workforce training of employed workers. Yet these decisions are made either by individuals or by firms and are outside the public domain, thus creating a policy challenge. How does one get individuals or firms to invest in training when government has no authority to make them do so?

One proposed policy is to motivate employed workers to seek additional training provided by community and technical colleges to create a financial incentive for individuals. Specifically, through tax codes or directly, workers would be provided a "voucher" that could be used to pay for training related to their occupation; in this case the voucher is a strategy to affect behavior that is not within the public domain to control.

Private firms present similar challenges to policy makers who hope to stimulate increased spending on training. When the objective is to stimulate a higher investment in training by firms in general, the government must rely on those few strategies it has that can affect corporate behavior. One such tool is the tax code. An example, proposed in the 1990s, was the *play or pay* program. In the play-or-pay scheme, policy makers would use the tax codes to encourage increased private sector investment in training by requiring all firms to provide training as a fixed percentage of total revenue, or the firms would be taxed for the equivalent of what they did not spend. It is not surprising that the play-or-pay concept has not gotten much support; government intervention into the decision making of firms is contrary to the value of many legislators, opposed by business, and therefore politically impossible. Another policy option is for the government to directly reimburse firms for training costs. Federal subsidies to firms to provide apprentice programs is one such example.

Federal Policy to Promote Individual Opportunity

Although intervention into the training decision of private business firms is controversial, government's role in sponsoring public workforce education is not. As discussed in Chapter 1, since the turn of the twentieth century, government has taken an activist role in developing policy aimed at providing workforce education. The purpose of this policy is to help individuals become employed and upwardly mobile. Such efforts can be divided into two categories—"public education" (both secondary and postsecondary) and "employment and training." Several examples of each are listed in Figure 13.1.

Beginning in the late 1980s, pushing all students higher in the math and science curricula (integration of academic and vocational education), encouraging greater use of the industrial apprenticeship model (youth apprenticeship), encouraging greater attendance at two-year technical education (tech prep), and a better school-to-work transition program for youth (School-to-Work Opportunity Act) were federal priorities for secondary workforce education (all discussed in Chapter 14). Many of these policy initiatives were also aimed at the two-year postsecondary education community as well. The second group of federal policies designed to promote individual opportunity are targeted to groups that are typically underrepresented in the labor force or displaced because of economic restructuring. These programs are given many labels; in this text they are called *employment and training programs*. A discussion of all these programs is provided in Chapter 14.

Block Grants

In 1994, the new Republican party majority in Congress made the proliferation, lack of coordination, and cost of federal workforce education policy a part of its legislative agenda. The principal piece of secondary and two-year postsecondary workforce education legislation, the Perkins act, was due for reauthorization, and the opportunity was used to propose a dramatic change in policy direction. The goal was to combine all, or mostly all, programs in the general area of promoting individual opportunity into a single piece of funding legislation and use one or more block grants to distribute money to the states (Dykman, 1995).

The block grant concept, although partly a guise to send less money to the states and thus balance the budget, signaled, in fact, a rather dramatic change in federal workforce philosophy. The proposed block grant legislation rescinded virtually every existing workforce education federal program and put very few stipulations on the states as to how to use the money it was sending to them in the grant. With the convening of a new Congress in 1997, support for block grant legislation has diminished. Nonetheless, this development will be watched closely by public sector workforce educators because, if nothing else, these programs are often directly supported by federal and state dollars; thus, a change in funding mechanism could affect them dramatically. For example, it could change the focus of workforce education policy development from the federal to the state level in which practitioners have the potential for greater influence.

THE PUBLIC POLICY ANALYSIS PROCESS

As the workforce education profession matures, workforce education professionals should become, and are becoming, more and more involved in developing as well as implementing a public workforce education policy. Toward this end, and as a way for the reader to gain greater insight into workforce education policy itself, this chapter now turns to a discussion of workforce education policy analysis and formulation. The nine steps in the process are listed in Figure 13.2 on page 246. In order to focus discussion on the analysis and development process, we will use as a policy topic the need for an improved system to facilitate the transition from school to work. Before beginning, it should be noted that, while these steps are listed in a sequence, in practice, the steps overlap and even change sequence, depending on the issue and the understanding of the problem.

1. *Define the Problem.* The first step in the policy analysis and formulation process is to clearly define or understand the problem. For example, in the early 1990s, it was widely believed that among developed countries the United States had the

1. Define the problem
2. Identify the causes
3. Define the desired outcome
4. Identify multiple constituency perspectives
5. Identify criteria to evaluate alternatives
6. Develop policy alternatives
7. Analyze policy alternatives
8. Implement
9. Evaluate

**FIGURE 13.2   Steps in Public Analysis
and Formulation**

worst system for tying the outcomes of its educational system, namely, its graduates, to employment. In fact, when contrasted with the elaborate transition system
for those who go from high school to college, it can be easily argued that the nation
had no system at all. In this case the problem seems well defined. But is it? Is the
problem confined to high school graduates who want to go to work or to higher education graduates as well? Is the problem mainly an adolescent/young-adult issue,
or is it a problem for all ages? The reader should begin to see that, depending on the
answer to each of these questions, different policy alternatives could be developed.

   2. *Identify the Causes.* The next step in the policy development process, and perhaps the most difficult, is an attempt to understand the problem well enough to hy-
pothesize its causes. As suggested earlier, one major challenge of public policy
development is how to influence a complex interaction of economic, social, and
psychological variables—which often even the best of analysts can only speculate
about regarding cause and effect.
   In the case of the need for an improved system to transition from school to work,
one essential question is why such an elaborate system exists for the college bound
and none at all exists for those who go to work. Undoubtedly, most readers could
offer a hypothesis, but in doing so, one begins to understand that insight into the
workings of U.S. high schools, the historical relationship between high schools and
employers, attitudes of school personnel regarding postsecondary education, demographics of students who go to work, and common community values is required. Perhaps the single most important reason public policy fails is that the
environment is never clearly understood, not because of lack of expertise on the
part of policy makers, though all too often this is the case, but because of the complexity of the situation. In many cases, policy alternatives are numerous, but little
evidence can be found to suggest they will work to solve the problem.

   3. *Define the Desired Outcome.* Even when the policy problem is well defined, the
desired outcome still may not be. In our particular example, it is all well and good

to say the desired outcome is a better school-to-work transition system, but it is not specific enough to develop policy alternatives to create such a system. Is the objective one system that accommodates all students, both those who go to work and to further education, or just those who are employment bound? Is the desired outcome a system that is based in educational institutions or in some other agency such as the Department of Labor's field offices? Is it desirable to have a single national system or one that varies between states or even communities? Is it desirable that the system include the concept of "one stop shopping," meaning that the system should provide all related employment services including child care references? Should the policy attempt to improve academic and occupational preparation before transition or concentrate just on job placement? Again, how one defines the desired outcome affects what policy alternatives are developed.

4. *Identify Multiple Constituency Perspectives.* As outlined earlier, one characteristic of public policy is that it involves multiple actors. For this reason, successful policy analysis requires identification of the multiple constituents and their multiple perspectives because these groups ultimately may determine whether a particular policy alternative is politically viable. It is, however, often difficult to identify the multiple players and the perspective they may have. A classic case occurred in the early 1990s when Congress developed a transition policy called the School-to-Work Opportunity Act. The purpose of the act was to provide a better system to help students make the transition to the labor market on graduation. Family rights groups unexpectedly opposed the bill, however, arguing it was anti-family because it interfered with parental rights to guide the education of their children (Brustein, 1995). Parent groups in some states opposed accepting federal funds for this effort, concluding it was an attempt by Washington insiders to channel their kids into the secondary job market. Had the opposition of these groups been anticipated, the legislation might have included provisions to ensure their support.

5. *Identify Criteria to Evaluate Alternatives.* Assuming that the problem and the desired outcomes have been defined as clearly as possible, the environment understood, and multiple perspectives of the influencers anticipated, the next step is to identify the criteria for evaluating various alternatives. It should be mentioned that some might argue for developing the alternatives at this point before developing the criteria so as not to stifle creative alternatives. We argue instead that first identifying the criteria focuses policy development toward the problem as defined, meaning that identifying the criteria for evaluating alternatives requires a thorough review of the previous steps in the process.

Of course, one criterion such as cost ($) is universal. Others are specific to the problem and desired outcome. Using the case of a better school-to-work transition system, one criterion would be increasing the numbers of high school graduates who make the transition to the primary job market. Another important key to success is acceptance by parents of teenagers.

6. *Develop Policy Alternatives.* At this point in the policy analysis or formulation process, various alternatives are developed. As an example, two possible alternatives for establishing an improved system for the transition from high school to work would be a public school-based comprehensive total placement model or a Department of Labor field-office-based placement model to which work-bound high school students would be referred.

7. *Analyze Policy Alternatives.* The next logical step is to evaluate the policy alternatives against the criterion established in Step 6. The objective is to make a recommendation to the policy decision makers who would, in turn, take appropriate legislative or authoritative action. The policy analysis can be very sophisticated, using, for example, computerized economic models that can forecast economic changes that might result from increased investment in training or, in turn, forecast what increased training needs might result from changes in nontraining economic variables. But as Quade (1988) reminds us, "policy analysis is not an exact science," and seldom are the systems sufficiently understood for precise evaluation of alternatives.

To illustrate the analysis process, a very simple format for analyzing policy alternatives is provided in Figure 13.3 that uses simple pluses or minuses to indicate whether the alternative does or does not meet the criterion. In this case, we evaluate the two alternatives (a school-based and a Department of Labor field-based model) using three criteria: potential to increase job placement in the primary job market, parental acceptance, and costs. In this case, the result of using only three criteria is inconclusive, which is typical. Note that analysts have concluded they really cannot determine whether one model would be better than another in achieving the desired outcome, namely, increased job placement in the primary job market. Analysts recognize that the Department of Labor–based program would cost less because they have field offices in place that provide this service. At the same time it has been concluded that parental acceptance of the program would be better if it were school sponsored and staffed. Hopefully, the reader begins to see what Quade had in mind when he cautioned that policy analysis is as much an art as a science.

8. *Implement.* The next step is implementation of the chosen policy alternative. Implementation is as challenging as any other step because, more often than not, those who must do the implementing are far removed, in the sense of both a supervisory span of control and physical distance, from those who formulated the policy. Taking our transition from school-to-work scenario, even if the school-based

Policy Alternatives	Increased Placement	Parents' Acceptance	Costs
1. School-Based Model	?	+	−
2. Dept. of Labor–Based Model	?	−	+

FIGURE 13.3   **Policy Analysis: School-to-Work Alternatives**

model was considered superior, how can policy makers at the federal level get the nation's high schools to change?

One strategy would be to mandate it, but mandates are not popular, particularly when they are not accompanied with funds to implement them. Even if mandated and the funds subsequently provided, experienced policy makers know that compliance will still be an issue unless the state has an effective and, thus costly, method of compliance review.

If mandates are politically unrealistic, then a totally different strategy must be developed. One typical strategy employed at the federal level is to provide development money to states. In some cases, they are competitive, meaning that not every state receives a grant. In other cases, they are more of an entitlement, with each state receiving monies based on some funding formula. Another common implementation strategy of federal and state government is to require an agency to submit a comprehensive plan as a condition to receiving funding.

9. *Evaluate.* Evaluation of public policy takes two forms: implementation evaluation and outcome evaluation. Implementation assessment is the process of determining to what extent the provisions of the policy have been implemented. Outcomes assessment is the process of evaluating the results to see if the policy has been implemented. Assessment is discussed in detail in Chapter 14.

AFFECTING PUBLIC POLICY

Because of the historically high levels of state and federal involvement in the public sector of workforce education, professionals have a long history of working to influence workforce education legislation, regulations, and funding levels. The methods employed are those used by all groups who attempt to influence legislation. At the federal level, professional organizations such as the American Vocational Association, American Association of Community Colleges, and the American Association of Training and Development all employ government relations specialists (lobbyists) to ensure that their membership is represented in the formulation process. Similarly, state-level workforce education professional groups employ executive directors and lobbyists to affect state policy.

In recent years, the importance of lobbying at the local level has grown as the number of professional lobbyists has multiplied. Quite simply, legislators are often more responsive to persuasive arguments from their constituents than from national or even state level organizations; they want to hear from the people in the districts. The methods employed are straightforward—personal letters and contacts. Practitioners should not underestimate the power of such efforts, particularly if coordinated across a state or the nation. A prime example occurred in 1995 when the U.S. Senate attempted to combine workforce education with the welfare reform bill in order to provide more flexibility to governors in using workforce education funds for welfare. By all accounts, this was a "done deal." However, in a matter of weeks the proposal was dropped despite strong support from the state governors because of an overwhelming response from workforce educators from across the nation who, to put it mildly, found the proposal to be offensive.

The importance of local workforce practitioners becoming involved in the state legislative process may become even greater if the block grant approach to federal funding of workforce education is adopted. In the block grant approach, how funds are spent will be decided to a much greater extent at the state level. This could work to the advantage of local workforce educators if they seize the opportunity, because every workforce education program resides in some legislator's district. Therefore, getting legislators involved in seeing programs at work becomes more important as the specific policy formulation moves from the federal to state level.

Attempts to influence the policy development (legislative) process, of course, are not limited to those who practice workforce education in the public sector. Legislation such as "play or pay," if formulated, could have dramatic effects on human resource development (HRD) professionals. For this and other reasons, HRD professional groups also are heavily involved in the policy development process. It is no accident that the headquarters of the ASTD is located in Washington, D.C.

SUMMARY AND IMPLICATIONS FOR PRACTITIONERS

This chapter has provided a foundation for understanding the workforce education policy-development process. Although all education is influenced by public policy, workforce education, because it is more frequently funded totally by state or federal funds, is particularly sensitive and vulnerable. Workforce educators in the public sector will find themselves having to be more attuned to what is happening in the state and federal capital than most other educators. It is important, therefore, to have the skills to be one of the "players" in the process. In particular, it is important to be active, not just when the issue is funding but also when decision makers seek workforce education solutions to perplexing social problems. It is interesting to observe, for example, that none of the public education workforce education reform initiatives of the 1990s, such as tech-prep or school-to-work—was the result of proposals by workforce education professionals but instead was developed by the congressional staff. This is not a good omen for the profession; the field needs to be more proactive lest we be viewed as part of the problem and not part of the solution.

14

PUBLIC SECTOR PROVIDERS OF WORKFORCE EDUCATION: PROGRAMS AND ISSUES

Workforce education providers can be divided into two groups: public sector programs—those that are publicly supported—and private sector programs—primarily those that are financed by business and industry for their employees. The purpose of this chapter is to provide an overview of publicly supported programs in the United States. In Chapter 15, privately sponsored programs, especially business and industry funded human resource development (HRD) programs, will be discussed.

The intent in this chapter is not to provide an exhaustive listing of all programs supported with public tax dollars. Instead, public sector programs will be examined in three broad categories—high school, postsecondary, and state and federal employment and training efforts. The intent is to describe the basic types of programs offered and examine several major trends and issues facing each. The chapter begins with a discussion of the public sector workforce education delivery structure in general and related trends and issues.

WORKFORCE EDUCATION IN THE PUBLIC SECTOR: TRENDS AND ISSUES

Workforce education is a major effort of government. In the mid-1990s, the federal government spent 16.4 billion dollars on workforce education in areas such as counseling and assessment, remedial and basic skills training, classroom occupational training, on-the-job training, job search training, job placement training and even job creation/development (National Youth Employment Conditions, 1992). This dollar amount does not include related federal expenditures such as student financial aid. The recipients of the programs and services include high school students, postsecondary two-year technical education students in community and technical colleges, returning adults seeking to make job changes, displaced workers hoping to return to the primary job market, displaced homemakers, and unemployed bilingual adults.

Usually federal programs are funded via specific appropriations to the states based on funding formulas that typically were based on population and some indication of poverty. In most cases, these funds were entitlements, meaning that each state received money. States receiving these monies were obligated to spend them according to federal regulations, to submit state plans regarding how they intended to use the funds in compliance with these regulations, and conduct/submit evaluation/accountability reports. The states, in turn, ran some programs such as vocational rehabilitation services themselves but more typically funded local agencies such as school systems, private industry councils, and community-based organizations and community colleges to provide workforce education and services.

Although public sector workforce education programs are numerous—the U.S. General Accounting Office reported that the number of programs supported by federal funds alone was 125. Collectively, however, they could hardly be called a national workforce education system because these programs are administered by 14 different federal agencies with little or no coordination between them. The federal Department of Education administers 49, for example, and the Department of Labor administers 30. Often programs are designed to serve the same clients, and coordination between agencies is rare. The federal hodgepodge of programs mirrors the situation in most states where workforce education programs are typically found in Departments of Commerce, Education, and Labor, and, more recently in some states, directly administered by the governor's office.

Accountability of workforce education in the public sector has been both a constant priority and a perplexing issue in public sector workforce education as government seeks data supporting the public investment. One reason accountability has been controversial is due to significant differences of opinion regarding appropriate criteria (Stecher and Hanser, 1995). The traditional criteria have been performance based, namely, job placement. Workforce education professionals typically are not comfortable with this single criterion because it is easily influenced by instructional factors outside of their control such as labor market variations and/or does not reflect the unique challenges of working with "at risk" populations. By 1992, the emphasis swung to outcome assessment, meaning that added to job placement were assessments of learning objectives as well. In this assessment mode, the criteria now included assessment of gains in academic skills, mastery of occupational skills, and other demonstrations of competence.

Regardless of the methodology, however, the results of formal assessment efforts were troublesome both to the workforce education profession and to government because the results regarding effectiveness were, at best, mixed, some showing programs to be effective, others finding the opposite.

CHANGING PUBLIC POLICY DIRECTIONS

By the early 1990s, growing economic uncertainty stemming from international economic competition, worsening distribution of wealth among Americans, welfare reform, and efforts to balance the national budget, along with partisan politics, led to national and state efforts to improve the public sector workforce education system in the United States. One early indicator of reform direction was the 1990 amendments to the Carl Perkin's act that funded high school and two-year postsecondary vocational-technical education. A new emphasis was placed on improving the academic skills of vocational students, preparing students to continue to postsecondary technical education, and accountability systems that assessed multiple student outcomes.

A more important bellwether of the changing direction of the public sector of workforce education was the 1994 School-to-Work Opportunities Act. As indicated in the "Findings" section of the Act,

> *the United States lacks a comprehensive and coherent system to help its youth acquire the knowledge, skills, abilities and information about access to labor markets necessary to make an effective transition from school to career or higher education (Sec. 2.8), and Federal resources fund a series of categorical work-related education and training programs, many of which serve disadvantaged youths, that are not administered as a coherent whole. (Sec. 2.9)*

The federal intent was to reform public workforce education into a comprehensive coordinated system that assisted graduates in making a smooth transition from preparation programs to the next level of preparation or to relevant careers. Reflecting the concern regarding lack of coordination in the existing system, the act was to be administered jointly by the Department of Labor and the Department of Education. Inherent in the bill was the philosophy that such a system could be developed only when business and industry and providers of workforce education worked closely together.

The School-to-Work Opportunities Act signaled a new programmatic emphasis, at least as envisioned by federal policy developers, namely, work-based learning. Based on the German tradition of apprenticeships and earlier demonstration-site experiments with "youth apprenticeships," it was concluded that the necessary close relationship between providers of workforce education and business and industry, and the most effective transition from school to work could be accomplished through work-based learning rather than the traditional classroom/instructional laboratory approach. In particular, the act called for a system of (1) school-based career exploratory and preplacement education, (2) connecting or placement activities, and (3) work-based learning opportunities.

Perhaps the most significant implication of the School-to-Work Opportunities Act was a change in emphasis from workforce education that called for formal preparation, particularly of occupational skills in classroom/instructional lab settings, to an emphasis on initial general preparation including academic skills, and on transition accomplished through on-the-job learning. The focus was on placement in the workforce, and the rationale was that this would be best accomplished if a majority of the skills development took place at the work site as was the tradition in the apprenticeship system in Europe.

Proposed Changes in Funding Mechanism: Block Grants

In 1995, the focus of public policy debate regarding workforce education swung from programmatic concerns to dollars. In a quirk of fate—one that the workforce education profession may well have considered historic to their profession—two things happened simultaneously. First, the Republican Party became the majority party in both houses of Congress. Its agenda included fiscal conservatism and a smaller, less intrusive federal government. Second, the Carl Perkins act was scheduled for reauthorization and was one of the first major pieces of legislation to be debated by the new majority. What would have normally been debates regarding only those workforce education programs funded by Perkins quickly became debates regarding the total federally funded workforce education effort. The agenda switched from reauthorizing the Perkins act to repealing all existing federally funded workforce education programs and combining them into a funding mechanism called "block grants."

Federal funding for workforce education has been categorical, meaning that specific appropriations were made for specific programs and services. Part and parcel of the funding mechanism was the philosophy that the federal government would be very prescriptive regarding how funds could be spent.

The "block grant" approach reflected a quite different philosophy. Congress would send funds to each state via a block grant, giving the states significant latitude in how the funds would be spent. The downside was the total appropriation for the block grants would be less than the combined appropriations for those programs consolidated under the block grant. Therefore, states have more flexibility—in fact one proposal called for a flex account—in how federal workforce education could be spent, but they would get less money to spend. For example, one proposal was to combine 80 employment and training programs under a single block grant to the states and reduce funding by 15 percent. In effect, the block grant served to address several agendas: consolidation, increased flexibility at the state level, and reduced overall federal spending. As it turned out, however, the congressional legislation to put such a "block grant" system in place did not pass and Congress adjourned in 1996 without any Perkins act reauthorization. Furthermore, it seemed unlikely, following the results of the 1996 presidential election, that the block grant proposal would gain sufficient support to be become law in the next session of Congress that convened in 1997 (*Vocational Education Weekly*, Nov. 11, 1996).

National Skills Standards

One outcome of the national workforce competitiveness debates of the 1980s was the conclusion that the nation suffered from a lack of skills standards in training. Unlike Germany, for example, where national standards exist for almost every major occupation, in the United States standards exist for only a handful. The lack of training standards was seen as a deterrent because it led to significant nationwide variation in training even within the same occupation. This variation, in turn, led to difficulty in labor force mobility and hiring.

As a result of concern regarding the lack of national standards, the Departments of Education and Labor awarded 22 pilot skills standards projects, most of which were completed by 1995. The occupational areas ranged from grocery service/stock associate to advanced high-performance manufacturing. In each case, the result was a national set of skill level standards for entry level occupations. Based on the success of these pilots, the National Skills Standards Board (NSSB) was established to coordinate and expand the effort. In order to bring some structure to the effort, NSSB established 16 broad clusters (see Figure 14.1).

Agriculture and natural resources management
Business and administration
Communications
Construction
Education and training
Energy and utilities
Financial services
Health and social services
Hospitality and tourism
Manufacturing, installation, and repair
Mining and extraction
Public administration, legal and protective services
Property management and building maintenance
Research, development, and technical services
Transportation
Wholesale/retail sales

FIGURE 14.1   National Skills Standards Board: Categories of Skills Standards

Reminiscent of the structure used in task analysis results, it is proposed that within each of the 16 skills categories, skills would be identified as either core (essential to the entire skills category), concentrations (essential to a particular occupation within a category), or specialties (essential to a particular job within the occupation). Skills identified within each of these three groups would further be identified as either academic, occupational, or employable (advanced workplace literacy skills) (*Vocational Training News*, Dec. 5, 1996).

Although use of these standards is not mandated and industry groups will not be forced to develop standards, it is clear that workforce education programs should be quick to adopt those standards that are developed for their programs. In a sense these standards become a national task analysis for the occupation and thus an insurance that curriculum content meets industry needs and results in labor market advantage to workforce education clients. A good example of the use of such standards is the rather widespread adoption of the Automotive Service Excellence (ASE) certification standards by automotive workforce education programs. Offering students the opportunity to become ASE certified as part of the program of study is quickly becoming the standard of excellence of automotive training programs.

HIGH SCHOOL WORKFORCE EDUCATION: TRENDS AND ISSUES

Arguably, public supported workforce education designed for the general citizenry began with high school vocational education. Even before passage of the Smith-Hughes Act of 1917, which provided federal funds for kindergarten through twelfth grade education for the first time—specifically vocational education—many urban high schools had already begun programs in commercial education and manual arts. Responding to concerns from both industrialist and progressive reformers, high school educators differentiated the high school curriculum in the early 1900s by adding industrial arts, home economics, commercial/business education, industrial education, and, in rural America, vocational agriculture. Vocational education has been a traditional part of the high school program of study ever since.

Traditionally, high school vocational education programs include business education, vocational agriculture, marketing/distributive education, and trade and industrial education (T&I). These programs focus on skills related to a wide range of occupations in the crafts, precision metals, specialized repair, health, foods, and service industries. A student who concentrates in one of these programs of study, meaning those who take a complete sequence of courses, would likely complete a minimum of four credits of traditional classroom/instructional laboratory education in the junior and senior year of high school.

A second type of vocational education can be categorized as work-study or on-the-job training that utilizes supervised work-based learning to provide occupational preparation; the most universal title of these programs is cooperative education. Sometimes consumer and family science (formerly home economics) and technology education (formerly industrial arts and, before that, manual arts) are also included as vocational education. Preparation for employment is, however, generally not considered the main instructional mission of these programs of study and many professionals in these programs do not consider themselves vocational educators.

Vocational education is offered either within the comprehensive high school or at separate area vocational schools. Typically, business education and vocational agriculture and cooperative education are offered in the high schools, whereas trade and industrial (T&I) education are often housed in regional schools in order to provide these equipment intensive and therefore expensive courses on a more cost-effective regional basis. T&I programs are typically occupationally specific in that the instructional mission is to teach mastery of skills related to single occupational titles, whereas programs such as vocational agriculture more generally address skills related to a wide variety of agribusiness environments.

Programs also differ according to teacher preparation. All states require vocational education teachers to be certified. In all states, agriculture, marketing, and business education teachers must complete a four-year college degree program. Conversely, in most states, T&I teacher certification requirements are different. Four-year college degrees are typically not required; instead, four to six years of successful relevant trade experience, and in some states a trade competency test, are required for initial certification.

Declining Enrollment and Changing Demographics

Enrollment in high school vocational education programs peaked in the early 1980s. Since that time enrollment has declined. The main reason for this decline is the dramatic increase in the percentage of high school students going on to higher education, beginning in the mid-1980s (Gray & Haung, 1991). As a result of the changing aspirations of American teens, enrollment in college preparatory programs of study has increased and enrollment in vocational education decreased. Public high school graduates in 1992, for example, took three more academic courses and two fewer vocational courses than in 1982. This decline in enrollment is somewhat universal; white, black, and Hispanic 1992 graduates all earned fewer vocational education credits than in 1982 (NCES, 1994).

Special Needs Students

Declining enrollment has had several significant effects on high school vocational education. The most obvious is that fewer students are enrolled in vocational programs or courses and thus fewer programs are offered and fewer professionals are employed. The most significant impact, however, is less obvious. As enrollment declined the percentage of special needs students increased. As reported in the 1994 National Assessment of Vocational Education (NAVE), the only population that has shown an increased participation in high school vocational education since the mid-1980s has been special needs students: the physically/mentally impaired, those from impoverished homes, or those deemed educationally handicapped due to poor academic skills.

Ironically, although access to high school vocational education by special needs students was a federal priority during the 1980s, by the mid-1990s, the concern was that only these students were electing vocational education. The impact on high school vocational education is perceived to be dramatic. The 1994 NAVE study reported that many high school vocational educators had reported that, as the percentage of special needs students increased, high school vocational education came to be viewed by other high school students as programs for the less able or less motivated, and it was not something in which they would participate. This negative image works against enrolling students who are not special needs (NAVE, 1994). In some nations, vocational education is education for the handicapped, and many vocational educators worry that the same situation could occur in the United States. Clearly, this would not be in any one's better interest, particularly special needs students, who would end up isolated in vocational programs of study. Thus, recruiting a more diverse student body to high school vocational education has been a major effort of the profession.

The second challenge resulting from increased percentages of special needs students enrolled in high school vocational education is the curriculum. Both in the selection of occupational programs and in instructional level, the curriculum is now often inconsistent with the academic ability and skills of those who attend. As a result, a classical curriculum and ethical debate have developed in the profession: namely, is it a case of having the right curriculum but the wrong students, or the right students but the wrong curriculum? On the one hand, data suggest that the percentage of skilled to unskilled workers in the labor market is increasing and the need for high-skills/high-wage workers in technical areas is central to international economic conditions. Therefore, curriculum that addresses these labor force realities is valid. On the other hand, special needs students who may lack the skills to benefit from this curriculum do have a right to an effective high school education program of study and vocational education. Furthermore, data suggest that the relative size of this population of school-age students is growing; between 1989 and 1995 the percentage of children who live in households in which one parent held a full-time job decreased 30 percent (Manning, 1995).

In general, the profession has taken a middle ground by changing the occupational focus of programs and revising curriculum behavioral objectives in order to meet the needs of those currently enrolled. All the while, there are increased efforts to market the programs to attract students with higher academic talent by instituting programs such as integrated tech-prep.

Curriculum

Beginning in the mid-1980s and continuing through the 1990s, curriculum reform in public education, including vocational education, became a national priority. As explained by Grubb, "the claims that schooling ought to better prepare workers for the twenty-first century (termed vocationalism) have become increasingly strident since the publication of *A Nation at Risk*" (1996: 535). One aspect of this new vocationalism was federal and state policy efforts to "address the deficiencies of the old vocationalism," namely, high school vocational education (Grubb, 1996: 538). Beginning with the Perkins act amendment of 1990 that required integration of academic skills with vocational training and supported tech-prep, and then in 1994 the School-to-Work Opportunities Act, which emphasized work-based experiences, a number of vocational curriculum reform initiatives and issues have developed in the 1990s; four are discussed below.

1. *Career Guidance.* The new vocationalism has led to the rediscovery of an old idea, namely, the importance of career guidance for students before and during their participation in vocational education. The School-to-Work Opportunities Act specifically calls for "career exploration and counseling" for students. The responsibility for career guidance activities, however, remains an unresolved issue. Vocational education professionals typically view it as a responsibility of high school guidance counselors. An examination of the counselor-to-student ratio suggests, however, that this is unrealistic. High school vocational educators must address the reality that if they wish students to make more informed program selections they themselves must begin to provide students with exploratory experiences. The Connecticut Regional Vocational Technical School system, for example, requires all students to explore all programs of study before they make a program selection.

2. *Curriculum Scope* (depth versus breadth). Traditionally, the curriculum design or scope of high school vocational education, particularly T&I, has been *occupational specific*. Programs of study are focused on specific occupations, such as residential electrician, machine drafting, or automotive repair. The instructional objective is to teach mastery of as many skills unique to the occupation as possible; thus, the emphasis is on a depth of skills in a specific occupation. An alternative approach, often referred to as the *clustered* approach (Maley, 1975), is a curriculum organized around a group of related occupations such as health occupations, power mechanics, and metal trades. The instructional objective is to teach mastery of entry level skills or of skills that cross between occupations, the emphasis being on a breadth of skills.

Although data are limited, it is probably fair to say that currently occupational-specific programming prevails. This is true despite the fact that by the mid-1990s most state and federal policy makers were calling for broad-based programs that stressed cross-skills and flexibility. There are numerous reasons the profession has been slow to react; most of them are systemic to public education. In some states, vocational teacher certification is occupational specific, and the certification required for cluster programs is unclear. In other cases, existing staff are not cross-skilled themselves, not eager to change, and administrators not eager to take on the stress of making them change. Finally, in many cases, funds required for the necessary redesign of instructional laboratories, for new instructional equipment, and for retraining of staff do not exist.

3. *Integrated Tech-Prep.* In what amounted to a dramatic change in mission for high school vocational education, the 1990 amendments to the Perkins act endorsed a program of study called "tech-prep." The objective of a tech-prep program of study was to prepare students to go not to work but on to postsecondary technical education after high school graduation. For the first time the federal and state perspective regarding the mission of high school vocational education included preparation for postsecondary prebaccalaureate education.

The Perkins act also called for the integration of academic and vocational education. The objective of this initiative was to make applied or vocational education more academic and, hopefully, make academic education more applied. Of specific concern was evidence that the academic skills of high school vocational education students were below average and often inadequate for success in the occupation they were studying. In the early 1990s, the National Center for the Study of Vocational Education (NCSVE) led a movement to combine these two initiatives into the integrated tech-prep model. The rationale was that, if students were to prepare for postsecondary two-year technical education, their academic skills would need to improve, thus the need of tech-prep programs of study to ensure that participants received integrated academics instruction taught in a contextual format.

The importance of integrated tech-prep to high school level workforce education cannot be overstated. It may well be a question of survival in a form other than a program of study for teens with no hope. The reason is that national survey data indicate that 95 percent of all teens want to go on to higher education (see Chapter 2). Nationally, approximately 70 percent do continue their education, and it is estimated that at best only 20 percent of high school graduates seek full-time employment immediately. In some states it is closer to 10 percent. If high school workforce education remains only a program for those preparing for work, which are those with the lowest academic skills, enrollment declines will continue. Integrated tech-prep holds the promise of high school workforce education being an alternative route.

4. *Work-Based Learning.* Work-based learning programs, most commonly called cooperative education, have traditionally been an alternative to laboratory- or classroom-based high school vocational education. Students spend part of the week or day in class and part learning on the job. Most states have specific state regulations regarding cooperative education or similar programs, along with unique teacher certification requirements for staff who supervise these programs. Theoretically work-based learning is a cost-effective way to provide workforce education when funds for formal on-site programs are limited or, as in the case of rural high schools, when the job market is characterized by a number of different small employers. The quality of these programs has, however, been suspect because often they are mechanisms to provide a work-released alternative for at-risk youth with little or no monitoring of performance at the work site. In the future, however, work-based learning may be more prevalent and of better quality. Work-based learning was, for example, the central element of the 1994 School-to-Work Opportunities Act. Quality was to be ensured by providing to students both related school-based education and transitional services as well as close supervision of their work site by school personnel. Also by the mid-1990s, there were signs that the reauthorized Perkins act, the act that provides federal funds for high school and postsecondary occupation education, would require all funded programs to have a "capstone" work-based learning experience.

Effectiveness of High School Workforce Education

Beginning in the 1970s, as federal appropriations for vocational education grew and revisionist historians argued that vocational education was some sort of a plot against students from working class backgrounds, numerous researchers sought to determine if, in fact, vocational education led to labor market advantages. Early studies, such as the work of Grasso and Shea (1979), found little advantage from high school vocational education. By the mid-1990s, however, both improvements in methodology and better longitudinal data sets led to a consensus that those who complete a vocational education program of study—called concentrators—are (1) more likely to graduate from high school, (2) experience less unemployment, and (3) earn high wages provided they work in the field they studied in high school (Boesel et al., 1994). These benefits occur for both minority and majority students.

The key aspect of these research findings is that students' workforce education is beneficial only if students are successfully placed in occupations related to their field of training. Therefore, the profession should be concerned that a 1989 study conducted for Congress (NCES, 1995) reported that less than half of vocational education students were placed in related jobs. The implication for workforce educators is clear: unless considerable effort is invested in transitional (job placement) services and, as a result, the percentage of students who end up working in the field they studied, the programs are not cost-effective when labor outcome criteria are used.

In the late 1980s, federal policy makers concluded that because so few students actually ended up working in the field they studied and because of increased volatility in the labor market, a greater emphasis should be placed on academic skills in high school workforce education programs. As a result, assessment efforts turned to the performance issue of whether high school vocational education increased students' academic skills. Using National Assessment of Education Progress (NAEP) data, researchers documented an inverse relationship between taking vocational education and NAEP test scores (NCES, 1995). However, the researchers did not provide an answer to whether lower scores were the result of taking vocational education or, instead, that students with low academic skills in the first place were more likely to take vocational education. Meyers (1992) did find, however, that taking vocational courses that had a high math content did increase math scores. Workforce educators in the public sector should take special note of this research trend. It signals that funding agency assessment can be predicted to expand beyond outcomes such as placement to performance academic skill gains while in vocational education.

Preparation of High School Workforce Educators

T&I certification in the majority of states is nontraditional (see *Vocational Education Journal*, 1993). Teachers are not required to have a four-year college degree; work experience is required instead. This alternative route can be traced to the original Smith-Hughes Act of 1917 and the philosophy that only individuals who were experienced craftspersons would have the knowledge to teach. This rationale is debatable in the 1990s. The increased importance of teaching academic skills, the increased number of special needs students, and the movement toward cluster-designed instruction suggest a more formal process would be advisable. Although some work experience is desirable if for no other reason than credibility with students, some higher education that includes pedagogy also seems appropriate (for a full discussion of this issue see Gray, 1990).

If high school T&I education is to be truly integrated into the mainstream, then the preparation of its teachers needs to be more mainstream as well. The complicating factor is the effect a more traditional certification requirement would have on the supply of teachers. Some states that have attempted to make the transition to a more traditional approach, for example, have had to backtrack due to teacher shortages.

Professional Teaching Standards

In 1987 a National Board of Professional Teaching Standards (NBPTS) was established in the United States to "improve student learning by establishing high and rigorous standards for what accomplished teachers should know and be able to do" (NBPTS, 1996). Groups of professionals were formed to develop standards for public school teachers in the major academic areas including vocational education. The plan was that, once standards had been developed, an assessment process would be developed and professionals could voluntarily submit their credentials to be reviewed for eligibility to receive a nationally recognized NBPTS certification. The Vocational Education Standards Committee draft standards were distributed in 1996 (see Figure 14.2 on page 263).

The proposed standards were to apply to all workforce educators, defined by the NBPTS to include T&I, technology education, business education, family and consumer science, agriculture and marketing. The ultimate impact of these standards remains to be seen. Two issues are not clear. First, it can be anticipated that professional groups, such as family and consumer sciences and technology educators, may want their own set of standards. The second and more difficult issue and one that exists for all standards is how and where an individuals who seeks NBPTS certification will be assessed and who will bear the costs. Regardless, the standards do provide an excellent template for the preparation of beginning workforce education professionals at the high school level.

POSTSECONDARY COMMUNITY COLLEGE AND TECHNICAL EDUCATION: TRENDS AND ISSUES

The second major type of publicly sponsored workforce education in the United States is one- and two-year programs of study offered as part of the nation's higher education system. Such programs are offered at community colleges, junior colleges, and technical colleges and often are also offered by universities as well. Programs of study are typically one-year certificate programs and two-year associate degree programs. Often the certificate program of study is the occupational component of the associate degree program without the associated academics.

Creating a Productive Learning Environment
    I. Knowledge of students

    II. Knowledge of subject matter

    III. Creation of an effective learning environment

Advanced Student Learning
    IV. Advanced knowledge of occupational content

    V. Workplace readiness

    VI. Managing and balancing multiple life roles

    VII. Social development

    VIII. Assessment

Professional Development and Outreach
    IX. Reflective practice

    X. Collaborative partnerships

    XI. Contributions to professional community

    XII. Family and community partnerships

FIGURE 14.2 **National Board of Professional Teaching Standards Proposed Standards for Vocational Education**

Source: National Board of Professional Teaching Standards. (May, 1996). *Vocational Education: Standards for National Board Certification.* Washington, DC: NBPTS.

Programs of study at this level are wide ranging and address virtually all of the high-skills/high-wage nonprofessional occupations, particularly those in technical areas in which prior training leads to significant labor market advantage in competing for employment. Typical examples are dental hygienists, precision manufacturing technicians, electromechanical repair technicians, paralegals, and professional chefs. Programs can be classified as occupational, such as cosmetology and nurses aide; technical, such as electrician and electronics technician; and technology programs, such as mechanical or civil engineering technology. The latter, namely technology programs, deserves some elaboration.

Arguably, one key aspect of international competition for scarce high-skills/high-wage production such as electronics and precision manufacturing is a commensurate cadre of highly skilled technicians at the production level. These occupations require not only a sound background in relevant science and engineering concepts but also relevant manipulative skills. When policy makers refer to the technical workforce, they are describing graduates of technological two-year associate degree programs. Most engineering technology programs in the United States are offered at the two-year associate degree level, and some are transferable to four-year degree programs. Typical program titles are biomedical equipment technology, materials engineering technology, and computer engineering technology. As pointed out previously, the opportunities in these fields are tremendous. Preparing individuals for these occupations would seem the logical mission of postsecondary prebaccalaureate workforce education, but actually this role is one of considerable debate.

Debates Regarding Mission

A fundamental issue in postsecondary prebaccalaureate workforce education is the question of mission; specifically, should the mission be primarily preparation for full-time employment or primarily preparation for transfer to four-year baccalaureate programs of study? Although most institutions currently do both, the question of which is the preferred mission is a matter of considerable controversy. As suggested by Brint and Karabel (1989),the original mission of the community college in particular was to provide access to baccalaureate education, and, clearly, data suggest that a majority of students in these and similar institutions are enrolled in general studies transfer programs. As the capacity of the four-year college system continues to grow, however, and with the advent of open admissions, students typically do not need to go to community colleges first, and thus enrollment has been declining. More important, NCES data reported in the 1995 *Condition of Education* (p. 44) that only about 12 percent of all students who start at a two-year college end up in a four-year college two years later. Meanwhile, as discussed later in this section, the economic returns to two-year prebaccalaureate workforce education are similar to those for a four-year college degree. Although some members of the two-year postsecondary education community may prefer the transfer mission, clearly the data suggest that the workforce education mission is a better investment of public funds.

Enrollment

The data suggest that enrollments at the two-year postsecondary level have been increasing nationally. However, because many programs offered at this level are general-studies transfer programs and a large percentage of recent high school graduates are enrolled in these programs as opposed to occupational, technical, or technology engineering programs, these data do not portray an accurate picture of the enrollment situation for postsecondary prebaccalaureate workforce education. The information that is available indicates that full-time day workforce education programs at the two-year postsecondary level are facing enrollment problems similar to those experienced at the high school level. In 1995, of the 1.07 million who took the Scholastic Aptitude Test (SAT) fewer than 1 percent indicated they planned to enter a technical field (College Board, 1995). Between 1972 and 1992, the percent of high school seniors who planned to go on to higher education increased, but the percentage who planned to pursue two-year technical education decreased. In 1972, almost 20 percent indicated they would attend a two-year technical college; in 1992 only 11 percent were planning to take this option (NCES, 1994). In 1995, 61 percent of Florida's postsecondary scholarship money set aside for those planning to attend technical programs went unused (West, 1995).

At the same time it is somewhat ironic that enrollments in technical programs at the two-year postsecondary level are growing among one group of young adults. Called "reverse transfers," these are student who transfer out of four-year degree programs or have completed a four-year degree and then enrolled in an associate degree technology program so that they can gain labor market advantage in competing for high-skills/high-wage work. It could well be that in the near future reverse transfers will dominate postsecondary two-year technical education; to a certain extent they have already done so in some states such as California. Clearly, however, it is an extremely inefficient route for both the nation and those paying tuition bills.

There was, in the mid-1990s, one bright note regarding enrollment in two-year education programs. During the 1996 presidential debates, Clinton, the successful candidate, proposed a goal of two years of postsecondary education for all citizens. It is predicted that this theme will be part of the agenda of the president in his second term (Newsweek, Dec. 30, 1996). If nothing else, this agenda will serve to highlight this level of education to high school students and parents and stimulate a greater acceptance of this type of postsecondary education. Whether it will translate into increased enrollment in workforce education programs as opposed to general education transfer programs remains to be seen.

Postsecondary Remedial Education

A related enrollment problem is the inadequate basic academic skills of students enrolling in two-year postsecondary vocational and technical education programs. In 1995, the average student who planned to pursue this form of higher education had obtained SAT scores of only 357 verbal and 407 math (College Board, 1995). In light of the technical nature of these programs of study it is clear that many who enroll lack adequate academic ability or skills. As a result in most cases more than half must take remedial courses at the postsecondary level. It is not uncommon to have 70 percent of the entering freshman taking remedial education at a community college. At one urban/suburban community college, 95 percent of all entering full-time day students were taking remedial math.

Although remedial education is clearly effective and justified for returning adults, it is ineffective for recent high school graduates. In fact, for recent high school graduates remedial education is a predictor of dropping out. The graduating rates of those who require remedial education typically are 20 to 30 percent lower than those who enroll with adequate skills. It is not surprising that many who start vocational-technical programs with inadequate academic preparation fail to continue to graduation.

Postsecondary Workforce Education Curriculum Issues

In light of the enrollment and remedial education issues discussed above, it is understandable that one curriculum issue of some importance to providers of two-year postsecondary vocational-technical education is tech-prep because it holds the promise of both increasing enrollment and the academic/technical skills of those who matriculate. Yet many obstacles exist, beginning with the need for secondary and postsecondary educators to collaborate. *Articulation agreements*—written agreements regarding what level of competence high school graduates need to have to be admitted and what benefits will be given to those who possess them—are often difficult to negotiate. Equally challenging is the issue of what incentives can be offered to students to complete a tech-prep program of study versus taking the regular college prep or general program. Obvious incentives include preferential admissions status and waiving certain postsecondary course requirements based on competencies gained at the secondary level. The latter arrangement could allow students to take more advanced courses (the approach preferred by educators) or to complete the program quicker. The latter approach is termed "time shorted" and is preferred by tuition-paying students.

A second curriculum issue is the degree to which postsecondary workforce educators will be able or willing to adapt to whatever curriculum provisions are attached to future state and federal workforce education funding legislation. For example, with the exception of the health fields, few postsecondary occupational, technical, or technologies programs provide any work-based learning (cooperative education, clinical experience). Likewise, few institutions have attempted to *integrate* the academic courses in math and science that are required for a particular technical program with the technical course instruction. If these programs wish to be eligible for federal funding, they will soon have to make progress in these areas.

Funding of Postsecondary Workforce Education

Most institutions of higher education, except those blessed with huge endowments, face severe financial problems. Most, therefore, rely to varying degrees on tuition for part of the operating revenue. Thus, programs with low enrollment and high cost are in jeopardy. Many vocational-technical programs fall into this category. Even fully enrolled programs are not immune. Dental hygienist programs, for example, typically turn students away but are also very expensive to run and are declining in number. Postsecondary occupational, technical, and technology engineering programs are inherently more expensive than general studies courses. In times of declining state and federal resources and soft enrollments these factors can be predicted to continue to exert institutional pressure to close programs.

A second economic threat to postsecondary technical education is the rising cost of providing remedial academic education. Faced with limited resources, some states in the mid-1990s began to debate funding of remedial education courses in higher education. Considering the high percentage of two-year postsecondary education students who must take remedial courses, such a change in policy can be predicted to have a negative effect on enrollments and, subsequently, on revenues.

On a more positive note, by the presidential campaign of 1996 there was evidence that a two-year associate degree would perhaps become the new educational goal for all American youth. In a 1996 graduation speech, President Clinton called for a $1500 tax credit for up to two years of college. Such a proposal, were it ever to become law, would serve both to reduce the cost of a two-year postsecondary technical education, but, more importantly, serve to remind the public of the value of this type of postsecondary education.

Program Effectiveness

Because the two-year postsecondary workforce education system is largely publicly funded—20 percent of all Pell Grants and 10 percent of Guaranteed Student Loans go to community college students alone (Kane & Rouse, 1993)—the question of economic returns to individuals from attending two-year postsecondary education is a continuing issue. As with secondary workforce education, results are mixed. To begin with, the persistence rates of students who graduate or complete a program are typically low: NCES (1995) data suggest that only 23 percent who start a two-year program return the second year. And although it is argued that often individuals fail to complete or graduate because the course work they have taken allowed them to leave to take full-time employment, data to support this argument are mixed. Using National Longitudinal (NLSY) data for young workers of average age 24, Grubb (1992) found, for example, no earning benefits from taking community college courses unless students complete the entire program of study. Using current population data (CPS), Kane and Rouse (1993), however, found positive benefits from course taking but little additional benefit from holding the degree or certificate. Specifically, it was found that, on average, 30 credits of both four-year college or community college course work increased earnings by 5 percent over those of high school graduates. However, although results differ, both researchers did find positive economic gains from attending two-year postsecondary workforce education. It is also worth noting that Grubb's results are similar to Bishop's (1989b), namely, that economic returns to workforce education increase dramatically when individuals are successful in finding employment related to the field studied and that the returns are best for programs in the health, technical, and T&I programs.

STATE AND FEDERAL EMPLOYMENT AND TRAINING: TRENDS AND ISSUES

The third major type of workforce education programs in the public sector are those designed to provide what is generally termed "employment and training" programs for special populations. Table 14.1 on page 268 depicts the major categories of programs and targets clientele that existed in the early 1990s.

Estimates regarding the total number of programs vary. The General Accounting Office reports over 160. Most of these programs, however, were relatively small in terms of funding; 72 programs received, for example, only 6 percent of the funding. Obviously, with such a number, a detailed discussion of even a few is beyond the scope of this text. The reader can get a basic understanding of this type of workforce education, however, from examining what is arguably the centerpiece of federal employment and training efforts, the Job Training Partnership Act.

TABLE 14.1   Federal Employment and Training Programs

Targeted Groups	Counseling and Assessment	Remedial/Basic Skills Training	Classroom Occupational Training	On-the-Job Training
Youth: under 22 years old	37	36	27	17
Physical or mental disabilities	29	21	21	16
Educationally disadvantaged	10	22	9	5
Unemployed or dislocated workers	20	12	18	13
Veterans	15	11	8	7
Ethnic/racial groups and women	18	8	14	10
Migrant or seasonal farm workers	8	9	5	3
Economically disadvantaged	40	34	37	23

Communication from Human Resources Division, General Accounting Office to Chairman, Committee on Labor and Human Resources, U.S. Senate, July 24, 1992.

Job Training Partnership Act (JTPA)

Enacted in 1982, JTPA became the focal point of federal efforts to prepare youth and unskilled adults for entry into the labor force, principally by providing cost-free job training to those economically disadvantaged individuals and others who face serious barriers to employment. The JTPA program was a refinement of the original Manpower Development and Training Act and later the Comprehensive Employment and Training Act (CETA). Typical priorities of JTPA included adult literacy, skill training, high school drop-out prevention, and school-to-work transition (job placement). Training is typically aimed at the semiskilled level in occupations that had openings in the primary job market such as a clerk typists, welders, machine tool assistants, and medical assistants.

The administrative structure of JTPA is typical of this type of effort. The program was administered at the federal level by the U.S. Department of Labor, which allocated funds to each state department of labor. One unique feature of the program, and a harbinger of things to come, was funds allocated to local administrative units called Private Industry Councils (PICs). Legislation required that a majority of members of the PIC come from industry. This group, in turn, supervised the use of the funds to contract with a variety of providers of workforce education such as community based organizations, for-profit proprietary schools, vocational-technical schools, and community colleges to provide services to the target clientele. The act also signaled joint administration of workforce education funds, and many times the state grant was administered jointly by the state's labor and education department.

A second unique feature of the JTPA program was the use of outcome standards to evaluate the program. Criteria included placement and retention in full-time paid employment and reduction in public assistance. JTPA was perhaps the first, or one of the first, workforce education public efforts that experimented with performance contracting, meaning that providers of workforce education, such as area vocational schools, community colleges, private proprietary schools, and community based organizations were paid only for students who were successfully placed in jobs.

Beginning in the early 1990s, political energy built to reform what was largely viewed as an overlapping, wasteful, and generally ineffective employment and training system, including JTPA. Subsequently, legislators tried to put block grant legislation into effect in an attempt to repeal the JTPA legislation. This effort failed, however, and it seems likely that JTPA or a JTPA-type program will remain in each of the fifty states, with many of the same elements, particularly in the areas of local governance, and outcome performance accountability.

The Mission of Employment and Training Programs

An ever-present issue in government employment and training efforts are questions of mission, and therefore control. The debate is a classic argument over the two missions of workforce education: providing individual opportunity or preparing a world-class workforce. As Guttman (1992) argues, "the question is whether job training is a second chance system for those, mainly the poor and disadvantaged, who have not been well served by the mainstream education system or an adjustment of the mainstream education to serve the changing job market needs of an internationally competitive system." Clearly, in the mid-1990s, there were two systems, one to address the need to prepare the workforce in general and a second to provide a safety net for the poor and disadvantaged. Guttman argues that more energy was spent by these systems in competing for funds than was spent seeking effective ways to help clients. Such a dual system is now seen as counterproductive to the needs of the public and wasteful, and combining these systems was implicit in later block grant legislation that failed to pass. It remains to be seen, however, whether the programs will ever be combined, because the professionals who run them and the clientele served are dramatically different.

Employment and Training Program Changes

In the early 1990s, the Bush and then the Clinton administration proposed legislation that would revamp the federal employment and training effort. Two proposed programmatic changes, although not enacted into legislation, continue to dominate debate through the 1990s, namely, one-stop shopping and vouchers.

One-Stop Shopping.   One universal criticism of the present collection of employment and training programs is that they duplicate each other, are fragmented, are physically dispersed, and lack any coordination between them (Dykman, 1995). As a result, potential clients of the system frequently have to physically go to several locations for related services and all too often fail to learn of important programs that might exist elsewhere. The concept of "one-stop shopping" is that all referral services would be located at a single site. Unemployment compensation, information regarding job training, and skill assessment would be available at the same location. Early efforts to develop these centers have shown the benefits of housing them at high schools and postsecondary workforce education institutions. In addition training programs are also available on site.

Vouchers for Training.   After relatively unsuccessful efforts to improve what was viewed as a largely ineffective employment and training effort, a new consumer approach was proposed in the early 1990s. Instead of contracting with agencies to provide employment and training programs, government would give qualified individuals "vouchers for training" that they could use to purchase job training at any eligible program. The hope was that just as the competitive "free market" system results in only the best and most efficient firms surviving, similar benefits would result from instilling a free market in the employment and training market through vouchers. Voucher recipients would select the best programs, and the worst would disappear. As of the mid-1990s and despite rather widespread bipartisan endorsements, the practice has yet to be tried at the federal level.

Employment and Training Program Effectiveness

A continuing and often politically charged debate revolves around the question of whether state and federal employment and training programs are effective. Basically, do participants demonstrate labor market advantages over their counterparts who do not participate? Considering that the Clinton administration proposed spending $8.8 billion on JTPA and other Department of Labor training programs alone in fiscal 1997, the effectiveness of such expenditures is a matter of some significance, and the issue is unlikely to go away.

As with similar studies regarding the efficiency of high school and two-year postsecondary workforce education, results regarding the effectiveness of employment and training programs are mixed and therefore subject to political interpretation. By way of example, a 1996 study by the General Accounting Office concluded that federal job training programs were initially effective in that the employment rates and earnings of youth who participated exceeded those of nonparticipants from similar backgrounds. However, five years after the program, participants and nonparticipants had the same employment rates and earnings. Similarly, the employment rate for all men in job training was found to increase from 78 percent to 87 percent but then so did the employment rate for similar men who did not participate (GAO, 1996). In the short run, programs may be effective, but in the long run, ineffective, leading legislators to ask the question, "Why fund them at all?" (GAO, 1996).

Results regarding programs for high school dropouts are also mixed. A 1994 U.S. Department of Labor report indicated that job training programs for high school dropouts did not boost initial earnings but did have a slightly positive impact in later years (U.S. Department of Labor, 1994). Critics of these studies suggest the data are not timely, being based on a 1986 survey, and thus do not reflect changes made to improve the program. Yet the Secretary of Labor was reported as admitting that the department lacked sufficient data regarding the effectiveness of employment and training efforts (*Vocational Training News*, May 9, 1995).

As efforts to balance the federal budget continue into the next century, scrutiny of the billions of tax revenue dollars spent on workforce education can be taken for granted; the results have the potential to affect funding levels and, ultimately, public confidence in the profession. The workforce education profession must be involved in such research, take the results objectively, and be proactive in improving the quality of the programs.

Employment and Training Staff Credentials and Program Accreditation

With the exception of workforce education professionals in the field of vocational rehabilitation, individuals who teach, design, or administer employment and training programs are largely untrained. Nor is there any agency that accredits such programs. Although high school teachers must complete a training program in order to be permanently certified and postsecondary teachers must meet the criterion of accrediting boards, staff of employment and training programs do not. Although high school vocational education programs are usually accredited, as are postsecondary programs, typically employment and training programs are not. This situation does little to help the workforce education profession's reputation. It also may be one very important variable in the ineffectiveness of employment and training efforts.

PRIVATE CAREER COLLEGES AND INSTITUTES

At the prebaccalaureate level, the major providers of occupational and technical workforce education, measured in terms of number of institutions and enrollment, are, in fact, not public but private institutions. Although private—for profit—career colleges and institutes are not technically in the public sector, the programs they offer and the clientele they serve are very similar to public institutions, and therefore they are discussed in this chapter.

The magnitude of workforce education provided by private one- and two-year career colleges and institutes is typically underestimated. Often termed *proprietary schools*, National Center for Education Statistics data indicate that 5333, or 69 percent, of all postsecondary institutions providing vocational or technical education are private career colleges and institutes. Although most private institutions award certificates, 811 are certified by states to award associate degrees. As a group they tend to be smaller than public institutions, averaging only 220 students annually, and 95 percent are located in urban or standard metro areas. But, totally, they enroll 1.2 million students annually and award 681,000 degrees and certificates, 200,000 more than public institutions offering similar programs.

The performance of private versus public institutions, less than two-year institutions, is, and continues to be, an issue of some debate. Data suggest, for example, that the completion rate of private institutions is higher than that of public institutions. At the same time, the cost of private institutions is higher, and the student loan default rate is significantly higher than that of public institutions. For example, in 1992, the student loan default rate for one-year private institutions (21.5 percent) was twice that of public institutions (10.6 percent), but the placement rates of the private institutions tended to be 10 to 20 percent higher than that of public institutions (Greenawalt and Gotwalt, 1995).

To a certain extent, the student loan default rate issues and the dubious practices of some fly-by-night institutions have overshadowed the contribution made by private career colleges and institutions. In particular, private institutions are often the sole providers to post–high school workforce education in inner cities and thus are important providers for minority and majority urban poor. Also, in many states private institutions are the only providers of occupational-technical education in specific fields, ranging from aviation to truck driving.

ASSESSMENT METHODS FOR PUBLIC SECTOR WORKFORCE EDUCATION

Accompanying the programmatic and funding reforms in the 1990s was an increased emphasis on evaluation (see *Vocational Training News*, Nov. 9, 1995). This chapter concludes with a discussion of evaluation issues in public sector workforce education. The intent is not to report on the results of evaluations but on the methods employed and issues involved.

McCaslin (1995) traces the increased emphasis on evaluation of public sector workforce education to six factors: decreased financial resources, increased public dissatisfaction, regulations requiring outcomes assessment, professional interest in improving evaluation methods, interest in downsizing government, increasing coordination between agencies, and increased use of private vendors to provide training. To this list could be added the rising cost of providing financial aid to those who attend postsecondary workforce education and the associated student loan default rates.

Of these factors, the first two, less money due to efforts to balance the federal budget and increased skepticism regarding the effectiveness of the public investments in workforce education, are symbiotic and the dominant factors driving increased state and federal evaluation efforts. At the same time, dramatic and sometimes politically charged changes in delivery, such as contracted programs with for-profit organizations and joint administration of programs by different state and federal agencies, have raised new evaluation issues as opponents and advocates hope for results proving their point of view.

As a result of the increased interest in data indicating the effectiveness of public sector workforce education, there has been a simultaneous interest in the evaluative methods. McCaslin (1995) argues that there are currently three strategies or methodologies in vogue: outcomes assessment, performance assessment, and value-added assessment.

Outcomes Assessment. The traditional method of evaluating workforce education is outcomes assessment. Outcomes assessment evaluates the degree to which a given intervention results in the stated outcome (Bragg, 1992). In workforce education the desired result is typically full-time, paid employment, preferably in the field of preparation. This outcome has been the traditional evaluative criterion.

Performance Assessment. In 1993, Congress passed the Government Performance and Results Act, which required that federally funded agencies use performance assessment methods. The emphasis of performance assessment is on how well participants can "perform" as a result of the intervention (workforce education). Such terms as *authentic assessment* and *direct assessment* are typical outgrowths of the performance assessment movement of the early 1990s. Applying this concept to workforce education, evaluation would expand beyond job placement rates to methods that measured directly what concepts and skills students or clients had mastered by having them demonstrate their use. Arguably, performance assessment has always been an essential part of the two primary instructional design methods used in workforce education—competency based instruction and instructional system design (see Chapter 8). In reality, little formal data of this nature have been collected in the past, if for no other reason than collecting statewide performance data is both expensive and fraught with reliability and validity problems.

Value-Added Assessment. Value-added assessment focuses on the "positive differences" that result from a particular intervention or program. The typical methods employed are of the pre- and post-test type, the intent being to measure change in knowledge and skill level of students or clients. Value-added assessment goes beyond performance assessment, which may be heavily influenced by the prior skill levels of students or clients, to determining the degree that knowledge and skills have improved as a result of the program. Again, value-added research has methodological problems that result from the inability to control noninstructional variables that, in effect, result in gains in knowledge and skills.

Implementation Assessment. Another important evaluation methodology, not listed by McCaslin, is implementation assessment. The purpose of implementation assessment is to determine the degree to which the intervention or program was implemented as designed before moving on to outcomes, performance, and value-added assessments. All too often, workforce education evaluation efforts skip implementation assessment. Thus, often it is not known whether programs or services, as designed, were delivered or only partially delivered in the first place. Therefore results of outcomes, performance, or value-added evaluations may not be valid indicators of a program's potential because the program or service may not have been delivered as intended.

Assessment Issues

Federal regulations now mandate performance assessment. Yet, as the executive director of the Center on National Education Policy suggests (*Vocational Training News*, Nov. 9, 1995), this system was, and is, largely undeveloped and unproved. The initial concern was about the performance standards. A listing of possible performance standards included the old outcomes standards—reductions in dropout rates, job placement, and graduation rates—as well as new performance criteria such as academic skills assessment and meeting industry skill certificate standards.

A second evaluation issue being debated in the mid-1990s is whether states that did not meet the performance standards would be penalized. Among the strategies discussed was reducing funding to states that were low achievers by 5 to 10 percent, requiring states to provide technical assistance to low-achieving locales, and a two-year grace or remedial period followed by penalties. Other ideas included increased funds or incentives to states that showed progress.

As suggested by Stecher and Hanser (1995), there are other accountability issues, some of which are of a philosophical nature. To whom, for example, should programs be accountable, the clientele or the funding agency? As a case in point, if a voucher system were implemented, the perceived effectiveness of the system could differ dramatically between those who get the vouchers and the government that provides them. The states' interests and thus the assessment criteria might include the degree to which vouchers are used to train in technical areas, but from the individual's perspective the program is most effective when the vouchers can be used for any type of education.

As of the mid-1990s a melding of outcomes and performance assessments seems likely but not certain. What, if any, penalties would be assessed also remains undecided. Yet the potential impact for workforce education of future developments in the assessment criteria, methods, and penalties imposed by funding agencies in the future remains significant. Just the selection of outcome and performance criteria could, for example, alter all curriculum design in the future.

SUMMARY AND IMPLICATIONS FOR PRACTITIONERS

Professionals in any field need to be aware of the multiple facets of the practice. In particular, they should be conversant regarding the issues in the profession and the trends in the practice. This chapter provided the level of understanding in public sector workforce education for which practitioners should strive. Issues of mission, enrollment, curriculum design, funding, assessment, and the preparation of new professionals are common to all workforce education settings in the public setting. The chapter concluded with a review of assessment practices in public sector workforce education. Obviously, trends in assessment will impact workforce education practice. What the regulators choose to count will drive what is taught. For this reason, workforce education professionals need to take an active role in debates regarding assessment techniques and criteria.

15

HUMAN RESOURCE DEVELOPMENT IN BUSINESS AND INDUSTRY

Many of the factors cited elsewhere in this book as stimuli to changes in workforce education, and perhaps more directly to individual opportunity and economic development, are also important in corporate settings, whether profit or nonprofit, large or small, just as they are in schools and in other settings. In the adult workplace particularly, many current functions related to the adjustment and mobility of workers are combined under concepts such as human resource development (HRD) or human resources management. As typically used, these two terms are umbrella terms that include corporate emphases such as organizational development, training, personnel, and career development (or career services). To be somewhat more precise, human resources management includes such activities as training, education, appraisal, recruitment, selection, career development, succession planning, workforce planning, employee assistance programs, job enrichment, and organizational staffing.

If one thinks of human resource development as a particular application of workforce development in the corporate setting, this concept can encompass virtually anything that has to do with human activity in the workplace. It has to do with the services and the support systems for employees that occur in workplaces and in the advocacy of workers' needs by employers. Human resource development, as workforce development, has to do with how new employees are oriented to their jobs, to the culture of the workplace, and to their contributions to the mission of the enterprise as well as the degree to which new, younger, and older workers receive employer-provided training and the nature of that training. At issue in any particular work setting are the human resource development processes and systems provided, the mentoring and information available to employees, the encouragement and training provided to workers to reinforce their loyalty and to help them establish commitment to lifelong learning that facilitates their mobility within the firm, incentives to improve their competencies, and ways by which employees are encouraged to improve how their jobs are done, to relate to coworkers as team players, and to act as persons of service to his or her customers, however they are defined. It can be argued that human resource development is what bridges workplace policies and procedures regarding an employer's workers and business strategy (CPC Foundation/Rand Corporation, 1994: 59).

One of the human resource dimensions of particular importance in contemporary workplaces is how and the degree to which workplaces are involved in job training. In a report to the U.S. Congress by the Office of Technology Assessment (Hilton, 1991), it was concluded that only a few U.S. firms use training as part of successful competitive strategy, in contrast to firms in Germany and Japan. But, like many other nations, the United States has begun to develop new models of training and a variety of other nations are also pursuing training systems to help ensure international competitiveness and rising living standards. For example,

> *skill intensive Singapore obliges big companies to set up training systems, then measures their success. The French [in response to Germany's ability to produce skilled workers] have made a sustained attempt to improve their vocational education. In its most recent budget, the British government unveiled a scheme for reintroducing apprenticeships."* ... *Other British spokespersons on the economy are advocating creation of a university for industry, which would link workers and trainers electronically in a sort of permanent technology seminar. (The Economist, p. 20)*

But, as has been noted in a variety of contexts, "Improved training is not the royal road to success in all places at all times; for a growing number of people, the real problem lies not in a lack of job-specific skills, but in a surplus of social pathologies—too many people with too little self-discipline, self-respect, and basic education to fit easily into any workplace" (*The Economist*, 1994: 20). There are many explanations for such individual and workplace problems: insufficient career counseling before job choice, poor person-job fit, insufficient career exploration and planning while in the secondary schools, little prior exposure in the family or the schools to the attitudes and skills that make up general employability skills or industrial discipline. There are, as well, personality styles that tend not to fit well within a particular work context or are reflected in work-related dysfunctions (e.g., life-role conflicts, situational stress, anxiety and depression, patterns of under- or overcommitment to work) (Lowman, 1993). Where reconciliation of worker behavior and workplace needs does not occur, the result is frequently seen in the dismissal of workers, in jagged early labor market experiences, in poor productivity and purpose, and in other problems of work stability or adjustment.

These are areas about which training, induction, career counseling, employee mentoring, and other human resource functions can do something. But, if such is to occur, managers in business and industry must perceive workers as whole persons who do not leave their family or personal problems at the door when they enter the factory or office nor leave problems on the job when they go home. They also must be seen as persons whose productivity and purpose ebb and flow as they experience transitions (e.g., divorce, loss, parenthood) and traumas that affect their commitment to work. As such understandings of the human dimension of the workplace become more apparent and included in business strategies, terms such as human resource development, employee assistance programs, and career development services are rapidly entering the vocabulary of business and industry. From these perspectives, workers are seen as corporate resources to be nurtured, not used up and cast away. Workers are seen as human capital, which needs its own preventive maintenance in the forms of education, training, counseling, information about mobility within the firm, and preparing oneself for such opportunities.

As such perspectives are becoming operationalized in models of human resource development, there has been a steady, if uneven, rise in career services for adults in industrial and corporate settings. The intent of these services varies but they often include assistance in the classification and support of young workers to facilitate their induction and adjustment to work; counseling of plateaued workers as they consider career change and other options; mentoring, support, and counseling of women reentering the workforce or coping with the demands of childrearing and homemaking as part of a dual-career family; helping workers select training and education programs that are most relevant to their career goals in the firm; assisting workers to identify career ladders and career paths of interest to them and the skills and experiences required to progress in them; making referrals or providing other forms of support to workers dealing with substance abuse problems; promoting or providing programs by which to enhance workers' physical and mental wellness; providing outplacement counseling for workers being terminated; holding workshops and providing relevant information for workers engaged in retirement planning; and counseling workers and their families about the dynamics of geographic or international transfers. While there are other career services that could be identified, however these are defined and by whom they are delivered, in-house or by outsourced contracts, these services augment the provisions for training and retraining of workers, the supervision of workers' technical performance, and the implementation of other human resource development processes.

In many ways, human resource development or management, whichever term one prefers, is a contemporary and extended perspective on traditional personnel functions. Historically, workplaces have relied on personnel departments to recruit, interview, hire, classify, compensate and, if necessary, terminate employees. One can think of these emphases in terms of personnel management. Increasingly, however, in "high-tech," "high-touch" information-based organizations, it has become increasingly clear that employees are the major assets, the knowledge base, of the organization. Thus, they need to be nurtured, developed, and given opportunities for creativity, participation in decision making, and other ways by which to gain their institutional identity and loyalty. In this sense, then, rather than practicing traditional forms of personnel management per se, a growing number of firms are practicing personnel development, which typically includes the functions subsumed in personnel management—hiring, classifying, compensating, terminating—but emphasizes, in addition, the career development and training of the employee. Given such a perspective, this chapter will briefly discuss two of the major components of human resource development—career development and training—since they have both been discussed elsewhere in this book more comprehensively as major dimensions of workforce education and development.

CAREER DEVELOPMENT SERVICES AND HUMAN RESOURCE DEVELOPMENT

Several factors have begun to combine to increase the availability of career development services or programs in business and industry, in government agencies, and in other organizations outside of education. One factor is the reality of international economic competition in which the quality of a nation's workforce is a central element in competing successfully. A second is the relative shortage of adolescents available to enter the workforce, as the larger numbers of persons born during the high birth rate of the Baby Boom period following World War II have moved through the educational system and are now in mid-career. A third is the growing reality that it costs large amounts of money to hire, train, and terminate workers. Therefore, as suggested previously, more and more workplaces are changing their emphases from those of personnel management to those of personnel development. Each of these factors in its own way stimulates the provision of career development initiatives in human resource development. In many instances, workforce education, particularly in community colleges and technical institutes as well as in higher education programs designed to prepare persons for training and development positions or to provide customized training courses in industry, has parallel contributions to those of career development programs. This is particularly true when such programs combine training or retraining for workers with attention to their career mobility needs as reflected in career information and planning processes.

Career Information

Basic to the provision of career development services in organizations is the importance to employees of information about opportunities open to them in the firm, how they can prepare themselves to become eligible for such opportunities, how to use available educational benefits or training options (e.g., on-the-job, workshops, seminars, special courses in community colleges, and so on) to help them develop the skills that they need to realize their career aspirations in the firm. As career theory and career practice have long proclaimed, information is the fuel for decision making. Thus, career development services in business and industry have a primary responsibility to provide information that helps employees understand how their firm is doing, its expectations of workers, the career ladders and career lattices that constitute how the firm is organized, and the steps available for promotion and supervisory opportunities, job postings of vacant positions, upcoming workshops or educational opportunities, information on funded courses available in the local area, pay classifications, and how benefits are determined.

Information for workers can be provided in many ways: directories, catalogs, bulletin boards, electronic bulletin boards, computer-assisted career guidance systems tailored to the career ladders and lattices of a particular firm, career resource centers and career specialists who are available to help employees determine what information is relevant to them and how to use it. There are many types of career information delivery systems that can be included in a career development emphasis in human resource development. Table 15.1 on page 280 suggests examples of those from which a particular firm or career development unit might select.

From another perspective, Gutteridge (1986) has identified organizational career development tools that can be used for a variety of purposes in human resource development (Table 15.2). Again, these are excellent examples of a range of possible approaches and techniques that could be adopted for use in different firms depending on the emphases of the career development services to be implemented.

Career Development Services as System

Implicit in Tables 15.1 on page 280 and 15.2 on page 281 is the wide range of activities in career development services in which career development specialists in business and industry might engage. Some of these activities are primarily informational, some are developmental, and some are remedial, concerned with attempting to rehabilitate, refer, or assist troubled employees. Such approaches can be highly systematic or much more fragmented. Experts in human resource development advocate creating career development systems rather than providing a disconnected and uncoordinated set of career activities for workers.

Leibowitz, Farren, and Kaye (1986) have defined a career development system as "an organized, formalized, planned effort to achieve a balance between the individual's career needs and the organization's workforce requirements....It is an ongoing program linked with the organization's human resource structure rather than a one-time event" (p. 4). This is an excellent summary of the role of career development services in its attempts to bridge individual career needs and the work organization's requirements. Derr (1986) has taken the view that career development is a set of activities and resources that a company provides to help its employees achieve their career objectives (career enhancement), coupled with the organization's own attempts to recruit, develop, and move its employees according to its own short-term and long-term human resource needs (career management). It would be less than accurate not to suggest that there are often tensions between individual needs and organizational expectations, which persons in leadership roles in human resource development and the career specialists must be cognizant of and sensitive to resolving so that such career development services do not become coercive of workers or quasi-disciplinary processes (Cummins & Hoggett, 1995).

TABLE 15.1   Examples of Career Information Delivery Systems

Career Resource Center
   Devoted to acquisition, storage, retrieval, dissemination of information
   Technical assistance including career counseling to help identify and use
      relevant information sources

Printed Matter
   Directories
   Occupational briefs
   Occupational Outlook Handbook
   Vocational biographies

   Descriptions of workshops and other training
      provisions in-house
   Course catalogs related to funded training opportuni-
      ties in local educational institutions

Job Postings
   Information about available job openings

Media Approaches
   Bulletin boards and displays
   Television
   Slides
   Films
   Microfiche
   CD Rom

   Records
   Cassettes
   Filmstrips
   Microfilm
   Videodisks
   Electronic bulletin boards

Interview Approaches
   Discussions with assigned mentors
   Job clinics for immediate job placement
   Information interviews with prospective department heads
   Career counseling

Simulation Approaches
   Role-playing
   Problem-solving kits
   Job sampling
   Work shadowing

Support Groups
   Women
   Persons with disabilities
   Minority persons

Formal Curriculum Approaches
   Subject matter information related to either   Workshops
      specific academic or industrial skills   Seminars
   Modules

Computers
   Discover
   Computer program tailored to the career
      ladders and lattices of a particular firm
   SIGI Plus

TABLE 15.2   Organizational Career Development Tools

A. Self-Assessment Tools
   1. Career planning workshops
   2. Career workbooks
   3. Preretirement workshops
B. Individual Counseling
   1. Personnel staff
   2. Professional counselor
      a. Internal
      b. External
   3. Outplacement
   4. Supervisor or line manager
C. Internal Labor Market Information/Placement Exchanges
   1. Job posting
   2. Skills inventories
   3. Career ladders/Career path planning
   4. Career Resource Center
   5. Other career communication formats
D. Organizational Potential Assessment Processes
   1. Assessment centers
   2. Promotability forecasts
   3. Replacement/succession planning
   4. Psychological testing
   5. Other testing
E. Development Programs
   1. Job rotation
   2. In-house human resource development workshops
   3. External seminars/workshops
   4. Tuition reimbursement/educational assistance
   5. Supervisor training in careering counseling
   6. Dual-career programs
   7. Mentoring systems

Source: Gutteridge, T. G. (1986). Organizational career development systems: The state of the practice. In D. T. Hall (Ed.), *Career Development in Organizations*, p. 61. San Francisco: Jossey-Bass. Used with permission.

CAREER DEVELOPMENT FUNCTIONS IN WORK ORGANIZATIONS

Although in the preceding paragraphs the importance of information, the variety of ways by which such information can be conveyed to workers, and the concept of organizing career development as a system have been discussed, there are several other perspectives that are useful to consider. These give increased validity to the importance of human resource development and, more specifically, to career development services. One of these is the importance of job satisfaction and job stress in the lives of workers.

Job Satisfaction and Job Stress

Work serves many different purposes for people. In some instances, it is primarily an economic process that provides the means for a livelihood, for meeting wants or needs, or the acquisition of physical assets. In other instances, work serves to define social status for oneself and one's family, and as an opportunity to take responsibility and to be valued by others for what one can produce. In addition, work also serves psychological purposes: a place in which to achieve self-esteem, identity, a feeling of mastery, competency, or enhanced self-efficacy. Such multiple purposes, which work serves for different people, are linked in complex ways to job satisfaction and its corollaries.

The importance of helping workers obtain job satisfaction has grown over the past twenty-five years as more knowledge has become available about the relationship of job satisfaction to life adjustment in broader terms. Stimulated by Palmore's findings in 1969 that job satisfaction is the best predictor of longevity (better than physician's ratings of physical functioning, use of tobacco, or even genetic inheritance), the meaning of job satisfaction has been defined and redefined in the last two decades.

In perhaps the most comprehensive review of the research on job satisfaction, Dawis has suggested that, "From a cognitive standpoint, job satisfaction is a cognition, with affective components, that results from certain perceptions and results in certain future behaviors. As a cognition, it is linked to other cognitions, or cognitive constructs, such as self-esteem, job involvement, work alienation, organizational commitment, morale, and life satisfactions" (1984:286). Dawis further contends that, "from a behavioral standpoint, job satisfaction is a response (a verbal operant) that has behavioral consequences. On the positive side are tenure, longevity, physical health, mental health, and productivity; on the negative side, turnover, absenteeism, accidents, and mental health problems" (p. 289). Dawis also reports that job dissatisfaction is related to mental and physical health problems including psychosomatic illnesses, depression, anxiety, worry, tension, impaired interpersonal relationships, coronary heart disease, alcoholism, drug abuse, and suicide. The implications of job satisfaction and dissatisfaction for worker adjustment and productivity are major elements underlying the rationale for expanding human resource development and, more specifically, career development services in business and industry. So is worker stress in its various forms.

Job stress like job satisfaction is an extremely complex subject, but it has increased as an element of work life and in its importance to those who plan programs of human resource development and career services. Landy (1992) has placed work stress in the context of many of the changes in work that we have discussed throughout this book. He suggests the following:

Part of the difficulty in dealing with the topic of stress in the workplace is that it will not stand still long enough to give us a good look. The nature of work is changing rapidly. No one can ignore the revolution in work that is represented by computer technology. Everyone from the teenager operating the French fry machine at McDonald's to the psychiatrist diagnosing affective disorders has been affected by the introduction of the computer into the workplace (Garson, 1988; Zuboff, 1988).... It has become abundantly clear that the introduction of a video display terminal at the work site is not simply placing a screen on a desk. The correlative changes in work methods, social interaction patterns, patterns of supervision, and productivity goals are extensive.... Coupled with such technological changes, there are also dramatic changes occurring in the work force (Greller, 1990). Work groups are becoming older. Additionally, new members of the working population are more demographically diverse and possess skill sets and value systems that are not identical to those possessed by earlier generations. These changing skills and values also have implications for understanding stress in the workplace. It is becoming increasingly clear that the gap between skills demanded in new technological environments and skills possessed by the workforce is growing (Herold, 1990). This gap is bound to make itself felt in increased worker strain resulting from performance problems that represent increased demands coupled with diminished resources. This is likely to be just as true of existing workers whose skills are becoming obsolete as it is with new workers whose skills are deficient. (pp. 120–121)

Thus, just as specialists in human resource development are concerned with promoting job satisfaction by trying to maximize person-job fit, providing accurate and timely information to workers and support groups, and mentoring to persons as necessary, they are also concerned about ameliorating the factors related to job stress. As Landy has so aptly described, they include role conflict, a changing psychology of work, which because of the pervasive influence of advanced technology in the workplace has diffused information and responsibility for job decisions to a wider range of workers, inability of some workers to learn and perform the skills required in the new workplace, growing concern about working in polluted and potentially toxic job environments, working as part of a team and meeting the expectations of coworkers, changing interpersonal relations with supervisors, work overload, ambiguity in work roles and work expectations, time urgency and other such matters. These stressors and their resolution are career issues for many workers and for human resource development specialists.

It is a short step from job dissatisfaction and job stress to mental health problems at work. Providing outplacement counseling for those about to be terminated, for those who are underemployed, and those who are truly troubled employees becomes a challenge to human resource development and to the career development specialists and career counselors who are expected to address such issues. They are not insignificant issues. As Millar (1992), Director of the National Institute of Occupational Safety and Health, has described the issue: "Today mental disorders are the leading cause for social security disability claims in the United States. In the 1980s, they surpassed awards for musculoskeletal disorders.... There is no doubt that job-related stress and other psychological disorders are rapidly becoming one of the most pressing occupational safety and health concerns in the country today" (p. 5). Millar goes on to cite a number of representative findings from studies by government and corporate researchers. They include the following:

- The number of workers' compensation claims resulting from mental disorders has increased between 1980 and 1990.
- Approximately 1 in 10 workers are suffering from depression, and the cost to society and business is nearly $27 billion annually.
- Electronic monitoring of workers exacerbates job stress.
- The issue of greatest prominence to the workplace in the 1990s would be stress, and if some major corporations had one thing to do to improve production, it would be to institute a marriage maintenance program, since divorce is "killing" many workers.
- What the worker brings to the job may be as important as what the job brings to the worker. Stress off the job can play an important role in stress on the job. (p. 6)

These findings are of concern to human resource development programs and to systems of career development services. They reinforce the importance of the use of techniques in career programs that help workers manage stress and learn healthy living patterns. They also reinforce the importance of having places and persons who have the training and expertise to refer workers who are clearly troubled to services that would be beneficial to them. Frequently, the latter involve referral to contracted employee assistance programs in communities. These are typically organizations that are staffed with psychologists, psychiatrists, occupational health nurses, drug and alcohol specialists, and others who can address in an intensive and sustained way the physical and mental health problems of workers.

Much more could be said about job satisfaction or dissatisfaction, the personal effects on individuals working in less than optimal work environments and about worker turnover, employee morale, working conditions, work productivity, and individual worker needs and characteristics. One could analyze at length the growing issues concerned with alcohol abuse as it spills into the workplace and affects the tangible outcomes of accidents, absenteeism, and productivity as well as the private effects on self-esteem, commitment, and flexibility. Further, one could emphasize the work-stress connection or the creation of work environments that are mentally healthy as elements of a rationale for developing more comprehensive provisions of employee assistance or career development programs in the workplace.

Further analyses of the bodies of theory and research that point to the need for career development services in organizations is not necessary here. Suffice it to say that the current focus on preserving and extending human skills in workplaces through personnel development has economic and pragmatic roots as well as roots in a relatively long process of research on the dynamics of job adjustment and satisfaction, on the worker as a human being with multiple demands on his or her time, energy, and skills as these flow in and out of the workplace and spill from one life setting to another. Consequently, the workplace becomes by analogy a theater in which positive and negative, healthy and unhealthy, good and bad behaviors are played out in both individual and collective terms.

TYPES OF CAREER DEVELOPMENT SERVICES IN WORKPLACES

In any instance in which education, training, or counseling is implemented, they become interventions in the lives of persons or environments designed to change them in certain preplanned ways. So it is with career services in the workplace. Given different conceptions of employee needs, organizational purposes, profit margins, or resources available to be committed to career services, the latter take on different forms and objectives. Such services, for example, may be implemented by contracting with counselors, trainers, or human resource specialists in a community to provide career interventions with particular populations of workers referred to these specialists, or career services may be provided on-site by employees who are members of a personnel, human resource development, or training and development unit. In the first instance, employers may retain on a fee basis a firm that specializes in working with persons who abuse alcohol or with other types of problem workers. Through some confidential mechanism, workers may be referred to or encouraged to avail themselves of these contracted services in the community and outside the workplace per se. In other instances, comprehensive programs offering education, treatment, and information across the entire spectrum of workers may be available in the workplace, for employers and their families, during or after work hours.

Career development services, then, can be limited or extensive depending on their mission and the resource commitments made to them. As a result, the range of possible career services may be quite large but the application of actual provisions made in a specific setting may be limited. There are a number of surveys of the rank or the availability of career development or planning services in different forms of organization. Many of them suggest that such services as the following are provided: support for external training, alcohol/drug counseling, retirement planning, support groups for minorities and women, job separation counseling, career exploration, career ladders, teaching of advancement strategies, personal financial planning, and family/marital counseling. Analysis of this range of services by frequency suggests that most employers first provide services that appear to have the most direct impact on the functioning of their workforce—training and alcohol/drug counseling—and then they provide services that are likely to be of more personal concern to the worker in terms of his or her career development.

It is likely that the provision of career development services will change as the economic health of the particular corporation is altered. For example, during a period of merger with another firm, or "downsizing" of a workforce as automation replaces some jobs, the employer is likely to be more concerned with job separation counseling or what has come to be called "outplacement counseling" than would be the case in periods of expansion and high profits. Outplacement counseling is a process of helping workers who are being terminated find new employment, sharpen their job search and access skills, deal with the psychology of job loss, and otherwise make the transition from employment to unemployment and back to employment more successfully than they would if they were cut off abruptly without specific attention to their economic and psychological needs during such a difficult time in their life. Depending on the size of the group of workers to be terminated, employers will sometimes contract with consulting firms that specialize in "outplacement" to conduct group workshops as well as provide individual counseling for employees to help them cope with the multiple problems associated with unemployment they may experience. In other instances, firms may use their own personnel specialists, career counselors, or counseling psychologists to provide such outplacement counseling.

TRAINERS' ROLES IN CAREER DEVELOPMENT

Aside, then, from why and how organizations can provide career services, there is the issue as well of what roles vocational or career counselors and counseling psychologists can play either as consultants to or as in-house specialists in career planning and career services for employees. These are in support of or in addition to supervisors or other management personnel being active in the provision of such services. Leonards (1981) has suggested that counseling psychologists are particularly useful in a corporate setting because of their emphasis on working with normal populations experiencing developmental conflicts. He would see these specialists working on such matters as organizational development, program evaluation, and general psychological consultation as well as on the individual provision of career services such as those dealing with resolution of midcareer issues, preretirement planning, and other specific concerns about vocational or career development.

Osipow (1982), too, has suggested roles for counselors and counseling psychologists in industry, which span a range of career-related activities. The following are selected paraphrased examples from his list of suggested possibilities:

- Helping employees and managers identify hazards in work.
- Training employees to identify their work styles (especially those that might be deleterious to them) and teaching them to change such styles.
- Helping workers deal with the effects of repetitive work.
- Assisting workers and their families to anticipate and cope with transfers to new locations, especially if there is no choice.
- Counseling two-career couples about the special stresses and strains they experience.

- Helping workers in jobs with high interpersonal demands or boundary spanning roles (e.g., jobs that require employees to split allegiances across units or supervisors) to deal with the special problems such circumstances create.
- Providing information and support for workers anticipating retirement.
- Counseling employees about the problems of job loss, health care issues, self-help and self-care.
- Assisting workers to deal with the process of job evaluation.
- Providing family counseling.

Given the broad range of training needs that employees require to further the lifelong learning that their job necessitates, to learn new skills in anticipation of the shifting job content that accompanies the adaptation of advanced technology, or to acquire basic literacy and numeracy skills prerequisite to learning new job skills, Papalia and Kaminski (1981) discuss other needed counseling skills for an industrial environment. In particular, they argue that counselors or career specialists in industry should advise and counsel on programs offered by local and regional institutions of higher education. Among other roles is tuition reimbursement, matriculation, admission, or assessment of prior learning. In addition, counselors might be expected to negotiate for a particular firm the offering of special credit and noncredit courses, either in-house or at a campus location, locating special resource personnel needed to offer special programs, and renting space and equipment from area educational facilities so that industry can conduct its own programs in these locations. Obviously, in many instances, the negotiations for educational programs needed by a firm or industry will involve workforce educators in secondary schools and community colleges as the potential providers of the needed training or facilities. More will be said about this matter in the section that follows.

The examples cited of possible counselor roles in the provision of career services to workers in industries suggest many possibilities: program development, management and supervisory training, career planning, career counseling, equal opportunity efforts, resource utilization/networking, career information, counseling for special worker problems (e.g., alcohol/drug abuse), and counseling for families or individual family members. How such possibilities are placed in priority, arranged, and displayed can take many forms and respond to many assumptions about the role of career development in organizations. For example, with regard to assumptions about the importance of career services in organizations, Hall and co-workers (1984) has summarized a number of conclusions that he derived from reviewing the state of career development in organizations. They suggest in essence that although most work organizations have neither the resources nor the information to manage employee's careers, it is in the organization's best interests to encourage the employee to assume most of the responsibility for his or her own career development. To that end, the organization should provide information and support to facilitate the worker's assumption of career responsibility. Such a goal also means that employees need new career competencies, not just job skills, which allow them to be teachable, adaptable, tolerant of ambiguity and uncertainty, and able to anticipate and incorporate new job skills as these are stimulated by new production or other work performance systems. In his most recent work, Hall and his associates (1996) have extended these ideas to the need to facilitate in workers what is called protean careers—self-invented, self-managed, and relational. Counselors and workforce educators or trainers in and out of the organization have important roles to play in helping employees learn such skills. Of fundamental importance, however, is an organizational environment that is supportive of good career planning and career management, one which incorporates career development activities into a good strategic human resource management process.

TRAINING AND HUMAN RESOURCE DEVELOPMENT

One of the human resource development emphases in business and industry that is fundamental to the changing needs of work organizations for literate, flexible, and well-functioning workers is that of education and training. In the previous section, we briefly identified the role of the counselor in brokering or negotiating for training programs external to the organization. Whether in or out of the workplace, the availability of a range of education and training programs is necessary in any modern organization. This is true because the workforce of virtually any industry or work setting is composed of persons who vary widely in their work responsibilities and in the level of skills that they bring to their work. Therefore, a range of training from basic remediation in reading or mathematics, to training in supervisory and management skills, technical and communication skills, new employee orientation programs, performance appraisal, leadership, word processing, interpersonal competencies and time management, hiring and selection, and stress management, among others, may be uniquely important to individuals or to groups of workers.

Changing Content of Training

Training will be needed and differently focused for new workers, workers undergoing job changes, workers seeking to prepare themselves for advancement in the organization, workers with significant problems at work, and workers preparing to exit the workforce. Lo Bosco (1985) has suggested that the purposes of training include helping workers to perform better in their current jobs, to achieve self-improvement that is not necessarily job-related, to prepare for a higher level position, and to make lateral moves and/or to be retrained for emerging changes in their job content.

Training necessary in a work organization is likely to be technical for some workers and more psychological or affective for others. In either case, career development specialists or workforce educators are likely to first engage in some form of needs assessment or job analysis to determine the particular training or mix of training necessary in a particular setting. Then in-house staff or external experts, workforce educators and others, are likely to be placed on contract to deliver the specific content required. The training procedures used are likely to be similar to those used in other educational settings with the content tailored to the needs of selected workers within a specific firm. Thus, lecture, discussion, demonstration, role-playing simulation and gaming, computer-aided instruction, videotaped presentations, and other pedagogical techniques are likely to be employed to achieve the training objectives.

Different groups of workers will likely need different types of training. Managers, for example, will need training in supervision techniques, job performance appraisal, coaching and counseling skills relative to encouraging maximum career development among their workers. Such training is in addition to the technical information needed by managers about the implementation of new production processes, organizational procedures, and shifts in the structure of how work is done in the corporation.

Another function of training and education is to provide workers with different types of information that are relevant to their career opportunities and mobility. As suggested earlier in this chapter, most large, and many medium or smaller, organizations implement systematic ways of informing employees about career-related matters through some type of career resource center, newsletters, job postings, or other methods. Depending on the size of the firm and the resources committed to such information dissemination, methods used may include brochures, computer-accessed data, workshops, videotape presentations, general reference libraries, and other processes that can be useful to diffusing information about career opportunities within a company. The actual content of this information is likely to include such career-relevant material as educational and training opportunities available on-site or at other local institutions, job postings, career paths relevant to different departments, divisions or job families within the company, family benefits available from company or union resources, and the nature of career services available.

Growing Importance of Technical Skills and Technical Training

Although education and training in the forms described above is important, such processes are less likely to be as abundant as training specifically directed to the retraining of workers in new technical skills or the provision of remedial education for those workers who do not have the basic academic skills—reading, writing, mathematics—to learn the new job skills associated with the introduction of advanced technology or other production methods in the workplace. The context for changing learning requirements in work has been identified by many scholars. Toffler (1990), for example, has argued that knowledge has now become the world's prime commodity. As such, knowledge is rapidly replacing cheap labor and raw materials as the primary requisite to effective international competition. Drucker (1989, 1993), too, has accented the importance of worker knowledge. He suggests that knowledge is now a necessity for many, if not most, workers. He contends that in the twentieth century, knowledge has become the economy's foundation and its true capital. Knowledge has replaced experience as the primary requisite for employability. In turn, work organizations are evolving into new forms; they are becoming knowledge-, information-, and idea-based. They require employees in all settings who can work smarter and who can understand the various forms of knowledge exploding across disciplines relevant to their jobs, their central concerns and theories, the major new insights they can produce, and their application to problem solving. Against such perspectives, the trends in the content of work are clear. The new jobs in both the manufacturing and service industries will demand higher skill levels than the jobs of the past or present. Very few new jobs are being created for those who cannot read, follow directions, or use mathematics. Even though there will continue to be jobs with minimal education requirements, the persons who hold them will be more vulnerable to joblessness and unemployment than persons who have basic academic skills (Berlin & Sum, 1988). As jobs are relocated from one nation to another because of the dynamics of the global economy, or as a function of changes in the occupational structure in a particular nation because of the effects of the introduction of computers, automation, and other technologies, they transform the training and learning requirements throughout the economy and the spectrum of skill requirements necessary to maintain that structure. In the United States, it is expected that from now until the end of the century and beyond, jobs that are currently in the middle of the skill distribution will be the least-skilled occupations of the future, and there will be very few new jobs for the unskilled (Hudson Institute, 1987).

As technological adaptation continues to be implemented in the nation's occupational structures and workplaces, the economic development of individual firms will suffer if employees are not able or willing to learn new production systems or new management strategies. Thus, there is a growing and pervasive need in the workforce for basic academic skills as the base to learn new technical skills. The problem as stated in a joint publication of the U.S. Department of Education and the U.S. Department of Labor (U.S. Department of Education/U.S. Department of Labor, 1988) is that, "new technology has changed the nature of work—created new jobs and altered others—and, in many cases, has revealed basic skills problems where none were known to exist." Such realities have created the need for literacy audits among workers and the results have been unexpected in the magnitude of workers found to be functionally illiterate, without the basic academic skills that allow them to be effectively retrained for new and emerging jobs.

In essence, the current American workforce can be dismantled into those workers who are functionally literate and those who are not, those who have an adequate command of basic skills and those who do not. The number of those who do not is extremely troublesome. It is estimated that there are 23 million functionally illiterate people in the United States, 10 percent of the population (U.S. Department of Education/U.S. Department of Labor, 1988; Passmore, 1994). For the past 20 or more years, studies have shown that perhaps 40 percent of the adult population is coping inadequately with typical life problems (e.g., getting work, holding a job, buying things, making changes, managing economic life, and parenting). Other studies link deficits in basic academic skills to reduced productivity among workers. For example, one national study of employers found that 30 percent of those surveyed reported that secretaries have difficulty reading at the level required by the job; 50 percent reported managers and supervisors unable to write paragraphs free of grammatical errors; 50 percent reported skilled and unskilled employees, including bookkeepers, unable to use decimals and fractions in math problems; 65 percent reported that basic skills deficiencies limit the job advancement of their high school graduate employees. In another example, the New York Company, in a major recruitment effort, found that from January to July 1987, only 3,619 of 22,888 applicants passed the examination intended to test vocabulary, number relationships, and problem-solving skills for jobs ranging from telephone operator to service representative. In one final example, a consortium of New York City banks made a commitment to hire 300 high school graduates from five inner-city schools, but found that only 100 students were able to meet entry requirements that included an eighth-grade test of reading comprehension and mathematics skills (Berlin & Sum, 1988, U.S. Department of Education/U.S. Department of Labor, 1988).

In 1989, Lieberman Research Incorporated conducted a research study of the beliefs of corporate executives about American public education for *Fortune* magazine and for Allstate insurance. The findings suggested that two-thirds of the more than 400 executives who responded to the survey reported that their firms were having difficulties hiring employees because of basic skill deficits of the job applicants and that this situation was worse than had been true in the previous decade. Holzer's study (1996) in four metropolitan areas of the United States focused on the nature and characteristics of jobs in the central cities of these four metropolitan areas, the market for less-educated minority workers, and the requirements of the jobs available. Several findings emerged that have implications for training, particularly as they relate to the mismatch between the jobs available and the skills of those who apply. Among these findings are the following: "There appears to be both a shortage of available jobs for unemployed workers in the central cities and at least some difficulty in filling jobs that are available...." "The vast majority of jobs available to less-educated workers are in the retail trade and service industries and are white-collar or service jobs, especially in the central cities." "Most jobs available to less-educated workers require the daily performance of one or more cognitive/social tasks, such as dealing with customers, reading and writing, arithmetic calculations." "Employer skill requirements appear to limit the hiring of both Hispanics and Blacks for many kinds of jobs" (pp. 127–128). These data suggest, among other things, that while there are some job shortages in inner cities there are also skill shortages among the job applicants available. Thus, if available job applicants are hired, employers will need, in many cases, to provide those employed with basic academic, communications, and interpersonal skills that had not been acquired in their public school education or in other experiences.

One could dismiss the examples cited above of basic academic skill deficiencies as simply negative indictments of the school systems of the nation. However valid that may be, it misses several other realities. One is that for many jobs, basic academic skills and job or technical skills are essentially the same skills. Therefore, persons with poor academic skills are not able to perform a growing number of jobs, either current or emerging; their productivity is likely to be low if they do perform the jobs; and they will be difficult to retrain for new jobs. The point of concern, then, is that many existing workers requiring retraining do not have the basic academic skills that permit them to learn new tasks and procedures. Therefore, the training problem for business and industry related to the matter of the technical skills of workers becomes a two-tiered one. If many workers are to be retrained, the first necessity is to provide them with a form of remedial education to help them acquire the functional job-related literacy "to do" and "to assess," not simply to remember for future academic purposes. Such skills are going to have to be provided in either the workplace per se or by contractual agreement between business and industry, community colleges, private industry councils, area vocational-technical schools, community-based organizations, or comprehensive high schools. In such conditions, workforce educators must be seen as a major resource to provide such contracted services.

The second tier of technical training is that focused on training or retraining workers to acquire new skills required in the changing workplace. Such skills are wide ranging depending on the industrial processes, equipment, or customer services at issue. In some cases, the training period may be a short one, for example, as word processing operators are introduced to a new piece of hardware or software or a new networking system. Or the training may be much longer if, for example, workers are trained to move from some manual assembly line process to serve as troubleshooters or programmers of robots that will be doing what was previously done manually. In either case, workforce educators serving as contracted teachers or as industrial trainers on-site will have major contributions to make to the technical training process or to the assessment process by which needs are identified and training curriculum developed.

In either short- or long-term training situations, the workers involved are faced with the need to know and to be able to do things that they never knew or did before. They are in a world in which the need to acquire skills frequently arises out of the dynamics of the job itself as well as from the employer's need to increase the flexibility or adaptability of the workforce itself.

In an information society in which learning and knowledge are the key to competition for the employer as well as for the employee, training needs to be seen as a major part of the organization's commitment to human resource development. Training in such a paradigm does not stand apart from career services because frequently workers need help in understanding why they should engage in training, what retraining would be best for them, and how to cope with the anxieties they may experience in regard to their feelings so that they can successfully cope with the training requirements. Thus, workforce educators, industrial trainers, career counselors, and counseling psychologists will need to be seen as partners in the planning and provision of training and the career services that support such efforts.

In dealing pragmatically with the needs of the workers for whom they are responsible, some human resource development specialists will have to help their organizations view training as both a commitment and as a human resource development strategy. This observation is occasioned by the current reality that certain types of organizations seem receptive to employee training, while others, even when offered incentives to upgrade their workforce, appear resistant. For example, Hudson, Hooks, and Rieble (1994) surveyed 20 manufacturing plants that had received state funding to stimulate training of their labor force. They concluded that

> *...organizational inertia inhibits a dramatic change in labor training. Plants with an already skilled labor force are continuing a longstanding tradition of training employees, and plants introducing Japanese management systems are investing in training in team-oriented production processes. However, plants with a semi-skilled or low-skilled labor force typically are making few investments in training.* (p. 113)

Given the diversity of worker needs for training or retraining or for remedial education, in many cases the structure of training will need to be multidimensional in order to reach various subgroups of workers whose needs for functional literacy or for skills enrichment differ. In such a paradigm a continuum of training from the fundamentals of basic academic skills in a remedial education format to much more rigorous technical training, which can be tailored to the needs of various worker subpopulations at differing levels of employment development, needs to be present in many corporate environments. When overlaid with an academic advising service or extended to include career information about career paths, job postings, and other information on potential opportunities for mobility linked to mental health provisions for chemical dependent or troubled workers or stress-management and wellness for other subgroups of workers, then a comprehensive inventory of human resource development services unfolds in a tailored and systematic response to the diversity found in the learning, psychological, and advancement needs of the workforce.

These observations suggest that education, training, employability, and mental health issues are interactive and complexly linked. Such circumstances are made more complex as the forces affecting the occupational structure are found to be increasingly dynamic in their influence and as the workforce itself becomes more diverse in its needs for training, retraining, and employability and work adjustment skills. In such contexts, human resource development, career services, and training become bridging mechanisms that link workers to opportunities, broker possibilities for mobility and advancement, and assist the dispirited and the dislocated to find new purpose and direction.

HUMAN RESOURCE DEVELOPMENT: TRENDS AND ISSUES

The HRD field has undergone and will continue to experience significant changes as the workplace and corporate structures continually evolve. What follows are six issues that are predicted to be consistent concerns in the years ahead.

Performance Technologist, Human Resource Development, or Organizational Development?

An enduring issue for private sector workforce educators in business and industry will be the question of their appropriate role. There are at least three alternatives. First is the traditional role of *performance technologist*. In this role, the practitioner's job is to improve human performance; the focus is on changing behavior as dictated by learning objectives that flow from a formal needs assessment process. Second is the human resource development role. In this case, the job is to develop the firm's human capital with an equal emphasis on the individual's career development and his or her job skills. In the mid-1990s practitioners began debating a third role, namely that of trainers as *organizational development facilitators*. In this role the practitioner's job is expanded to include working with management to integrate human performance with the overall business strategies of a firm; the goal is to improve the organization, not just its employees. These roles, of course, are not mutually exclusive. A practitioner may be asked to do all three while working for the same firm. No doubt, however, some practitioners long to become closer to the strategic business decision making and no doubt, as a firm's human capital becomes the only lasting source of market advantage, this new involvement will be welcomed and necessary. Thus, it can be anticipated that while beginning practitioners may find themselves mostly in the performance technologist role, senior professionals may find themselves more involved in linking training with business strategies.

Flavor of the Month Training

Flavor of the month training, a term introduced by Dirk Cjelli (1994), refers to the growing practice of training content being determined by fads and CEO whim instead of needs assessment and other forms of analysis. As suggested by Cjelli, flavor of the month training occurs when the content of training is chosen because it is the current favorite or "flavor" on the training circuit. In this "cookie cutter" approach, fads—such as integrated work teams, total quality management (TQM) and others—are selected by management as topics for training without any clear idea of what outcome is hoped for. As suggested by the title, training conducted in this vein tends to be ever changing and trendy. It leads to a cynical attitude among managers when they are required to attend training on an ever changing range of topics that seem unrelated to their job. Flavor of the month training also often raises ethical questions when trainers attempt or are ordered to design training in areas in which they themselves have no background.

Moving Target Training

Moving target training, a term coined by Rothwell and Kazanas (1993), is perhaps the opposite of flavor of the month training in that the objectives intended are well documented but ever changing. The problem is that business conditions and technology change so rapidly that training can become obsolete before it can be designed: specifically, between the time a needs assessment is conducted and instruction delivered, the situation—thus the nature of the performance problem—changes. In a survey conducted by Rothwell and Kazanas (1993) "accelerated rate of change" ranks second only to "quality and service" as the most important trend affecting management development training efforts. This trend can be predicted to continue. Human performance technologists will need to develop quicker responses. Tobin (1996) reminds trainers that often timeliness is more important than methodology: sometimes methods must be streamlined in order to provide "just-in-time" training. Likewise, trainers will need to be ever alert to the reality that performance problems that exist today may be replaced by new ones tomorrow, thus the need for constant communication with front-line managers and work teams.

Behaviorist versus Constructivist Design

By the early 1990s, the debate between behaviorists and cognitive psychologists regarding how individuals learn began to spill over into instructional design, particularly among university instructional systems design faculty in higher education. The most popular instructional design model used by HRD professionals is the linear instructional system design (ISD) model. At the heart of the ISD model is the needs assessment process that leads to the written behavioral objectives that in turn guide instructional design. This behaviorist/technologist approach has become a matter of some debate among instructional systems designers and led to some calling for a different "constructivist" paradigm (Jonassen, 1991). By the mid-1990s, anything associated with behaviorism was considered to be, by some, out of sync with the times (Wilson, 1993). At the heart of the issue is the practice of designing instruction to achieve behavioral/performance objectives that are predetermined by the trainer or management versus letting the learners determine their own objectives (Cooper, 1993). Braden (1996) argues for an accommodation of different points of view but points out that behavioral/performance objectives are at the heart of the ISD process; without them, or some other way to identify the objective of instruction, design is meaningless. Perhaps more important, beginning practitioners should keep in mind that the "results" or change in behavior focus of ISD seems to be more consistent with the "return on investment" mentality of management; when CEOs ask what will be the outcome of a proposed training program, it is unlikely they will be receptive to hearing that it is up to the participants to decide.

New Instructional Technologies

An obvious trend in HRD are the ever-expanding alternatives to deliver training. Many fall into the general category of distance education (Wagner, 1993) in the form of interactive video, which can be delivered via compressed video, satellite, or the Internet. Pioneering work in the use of the Internet for training by David Passmore of Penn State University demonstrates the potential of the latter medium, particularly when the ability to use interactive video (see you—see me) becomes refined.

On the horizon is the promise of the "virtual reality" classroom. Pantelidis (1993) defines virtual reality as a highly interactive multimedia environment in which the learner and computer interact with each other at such a high level that the effect is the creation of a "real" situation in the eyes of the learner. The potential is immense for using this technology to develop real situations for training purposes.

Another instructional development that will continue to have a profound effect on training is the continued sophistication of "expert" or "electronic support" systems. Using all the technological developments discussed above, these computer-based systems provide instant job-related help to workers while they are working (Geber, 1991). Grabowski and Harkness (1996) have found that not only are these systems effective in increasing performance, but they are particularly effective when the learners are involved in developing them. Thus, a work team that develops its own expert system will likely benefit from both a deeper understanding of the process or procedure as well as have quick references to support them when they need it on the job.

Assessment

Among the many things private sector workforce education practitioners share is the reality that they will continue to be under pressure to demonstrate the effectiveness of their effort. In the private sector, such analysis is typically termed *return on investment* (ROI). Donald Kirkpatrick (1975) suggested that there are four basic types of training assessment: (1) reaction of the learner, (2) improved performance of the learner, (3) increased knowledge of the learner, and (4) how did training affect the organization. In the latter case, the effect typically looked for is increased profit or return on the money spent on training. From the beginning, HRD professionals have found it difficult to develop assessment methods to meet this level of accountability. As pointed out by Hassett (1992), many things (variables) affect profits at any given time, and it is difficult to isolate gains resulting only from training. Importantly, methodologies that could provide such refined information are also costly and time consuming; often by the time the results from such studies are known, they are also irrelevant because training needs and/or business conditions have changed.

SUMMARY AND IMPLICATIONS FOR PRACTITIONERS

This chapter has provided an overview of workforce education in the private sector. Most commonly referred to as human resource development (HRD), the field, when allowed to practice as it should, has two functions—functions that are similar to the two missions of workforce education. One is the career development of employees. The second is technical training to solve human performance problems and improve productivity. Of the two functions, the latter, especially in smaller firms, is probably the most prevalent. The chapter concluded with six issues or trends that are predicted to persist into the twenty-first century, beginning with the question of what, from a practitioner's point of view, is the appropriate role for human resource development and HRD professionals. While undoubtedly the answer will be dictated, in many cases, by management, the profession can influence their outlook.

Those who practice workforce education can be expected to benefit from increased opportunity if, as predicted, in the future the skills of a firm's workers are its only lasting competitive advantage. Whether human resource development becomes an integral part of organizational development remains to be seen. Regardless, constant changes in skill requirements of workers will ensure that the professional HRD specialist will be in high demand, and the challenge will be to keep up with the "moving targets" of training needs.

REFERENCES

Acheson, K., & Gall, M. (1987). *Techniques of Clinical Supervision of Teachers* (2nd ed.). Longman: NY.

Adams, A., & Mangum, G. (1978). *The Lingering Crisis of Youth Unemployment.* Kalamazoo, MI: W. E. Upjohn Institute for Employment Research.

Adler, A. (1935). The fundamental views of individual psychology. *International Journal of Individual Psychology, 1,* 5–8.

Adult & Continuing Education Today. (June 29, 1992). Employer survey. Vol. 22, No. 25.

Alexander, L., & Palla, M. (1984). Curriculum reform and school performance: An evaluation of the new basics. *American Journal of Education, 92,* 391–420.

American Council on Education. (1994). *The American Freshman National Norms for Fall 1993.* Washington, DC: Author.

American Society for Training and Development. (1991a). *America and the New Economy.* Alexandria, VA: ASTD.

American Society for Training and Development. (1991b). *Fundamentals of Quality.* Alexandria, VA: ASTD.

Anderson, J. (Winter, 1978). Foundations and the shaping of southern black rural education. *History of Education Quarterly,* p. 18.

Anderson, L. (Dec., 1983). Policy implications of research on school time. *The School Administrator,* pp. 25–28

Aring, M. K. (1993). What the 'V' word is costing America's economy. *Phi Delta Kappan, 74*(5), 396–404.

Auberbach, J. (1991). Education and training for a competitive workforce: overview. In *Looking Ahead,* XIII, 2, pp. 2–7. Washington, DC: National Planning Association.

Bandura, A. (1977). Self-efficacy: Toward a unifying theory of behavioral change. *Psychological Review, 84,* 191–215.

Barley, S. R., & Nelson, B. J. (May, 1995). *The Nature and Implications of Infrastructure Technological Change for the Social Organization of Work.* Unpublished contractor report prepared for the Office of Technology Assessment, U.S. Congress, Washington, DC.

Barlow, M. (1990). Historical background of vocational education. In Paulter, A. *Vocational Education in the 1990's: Major Issues,* pp. 5–24. Ann Arbor, MI: Prakken Publications.

Berlin, G., & Sum, A. (1988, February). *Toward a more perfect union: Basic skills, poor families, and our economic future.* Occasional Paper Number 3. Ford Foundation Project on Social Welfare and the American Future. New York: Ford Foundation.

Berryman, S. E. (1982). The equity and effectiveness of secondary vocational education. In *Education and Work.* Eighty-first Yearbook of the National Society for the Study of Education (pp. 169–203). Chicago: The University of Chicago Press.

Berryman, S. (1991). Summary of the cognitive science research and its implications for education—designing effective learning environ-ments. *Solutions.* Washington, DC: National Council on Vocational Education.

Bielby, T., & Baron, N. (1986). Men and women at work: sex, segregation and statistical discrimination. *American Journal of Sociology, 91*, 759–799.

Bishop, J. (May, 1989b). Making vocational education more effective for at-risk youth. *Vocational Education Journal*, pp. 14–17.

Bishop, J. (1995). *Expertise and Excellence.* Working Paper 95–13. Center for Advanced Human Resource Studies. Ithaca, NY: Cornell University.

Blackwell, D., & Henkin, L. (1989). *A Project 2061 Report: Mathematics.* Washington, DC: American Association for the Advancement of Science.

Blau, R. M., Gustad, J. W., Jessor, R., Parnes, H. S., & Wilcock, R. C. (1956). Occupational choice: A conceptual framework. In *Industrial Labor Relations* (rev. ed.), *9*, 531–543.

Blim, M. L. (1992). Introduction: The emerging global factory and anthropology. In F. A. Rothstein & M. L. Blim (Eds.), *Anthropology and the Global Factory* (pp. 1–30). New York: Bergin & Garvey.

Bloch, H. H. (1983). Differential premises arising from different socialization of the sexes: some conjectures. *Child Development, 54*, 1335–1354.

Boesel, D. (1994). *Final Report of the National Assessment of Vocational Education, Vol. II.* Washington, DC: U.S. Department of Education.

Bordin, E. S., Nachman, B., & Segal, S. J. (1963). An articulated framework for vocational development. *Journal of Counseling Psychology, 10*, 107–116.

Borgen, W. A., & Amundson, N. (1984). *The Experience of Unemployment: Implications for Counseling the Unemployed.* Scarborough, Ontario: Nelson Canada.

Borjas, G. (Dec., 1994). The economics of immigration. *Journal of Economics Literature*, pp. 1668–1670.

Borow, H. (1984). Occupational Socialization: Acquiring a Sense of Work. In N. C. Gysbers (Ed.), *Designing Careers: Counseling to Enhance Education, Work and Leisure.* San Francisco: Jossey-Bass.

Braden, R. (Mar.-April, 1996). The case for linear instructional design and development: A commentary on models, challenges and myths. *Educational Technology.*

Bragg, D. (1992). *Alternative Approaches to Outcome Assessment for Postsecondary Vocational Education.* Berkeley: National Center for Research in Vocational Education.

Brasher, K. (Aug. 28, 1995). Skilled workers watch jobs go overseas. *New York Times.*

Brill, A. A. (1948). *Psychoanalytic Psychiatry.* London: John Lehman.

Brint, K., & Karabel, R. (1989). The diverted dream: community colleges and the promise of educational opportunity in America, 1900–1985. New York: Oxford University Press.

Brown, J., Collins, A., & Duguid, P. (1989). Situated cognition and the culture of learning. *Educational Researcher, 18*(1), 32–42.

Brustein, M. (Dec., 1995). *Education for Employment*, p. 4.

Buck, L., & Barrick, R. (1987). They're trained but are they employable? *Vocational Education Journal, 62*(8), 29–31.

Buehler, C. (1933). *Der Menschliche Lebenslau als Psychologiches Problem.* Leipzig: Hirzel.

Business Advisory Committee, The Education Commission of the States. (1985). *Reconnecting Youth.* Denver, CO: Author.

Carnevale, A., Gainer, L., & Villet, J. (1990a). *Training in America: The Organization and Strategic Role of Training.* San Francisco: Jossey-Bass.

Carnevale, A., Gainer, L., & Meltzer, A. (1990b). *Workplace Basics.* San Francisco: Jossey-Bass.

Cassidy, J. (Oct. 16, 1995). Who killed the middle class? *The New Yorker*, pp. 113–124.

Center for Public Resources (1983). *Basic Skills in the U.S. Work Force. Corporate Roles in Public Education Project.* Washington, DC: Author.

Chartrand, J. M. (1991). The evolution of trait-and-factor career counseling: A person x environment fit approach. *Journal of Counseling & Development, 69*, 518–524.

Cheek, G. D., & Campbell, C. P. (1994). *Improving the School-to-Employment Transition with Lessons from Abroad.* In A. J. Paulter, Jr. (Ed.), *High School to Employment Transition: Contemporary Issues*, pp. 115–127. Ann Arbor, MI: Prakken Publications, Inc.

Chisman, F. (1992). *The Missing Link: Workplace Education in Small Business.* Washington, DC: Southport Institute for Policy Analysis.

Cigola, J. (1992). A comparison of first year marketing student reading ability with readability levels. Unpublished doctoral dissertation, Penn State University at Univerisity Park.

Cjelli, D. (Jan., 1994). In praise of the flavor of the month (after all Baskins-Robbins has 31). *Performance and Instruction.*

Clark, R., Gelatt, H. B., & Levine, L. (1965). A decision-making paradigm for local guidance research. *Personnel and Guidance Journal, 44,* 40–51.

College Board. (1995). *College Bound Seniors: 1995 Profile of SAT Test Takers.* New York: Author.

College dropout rate hits all-time high. (July 11, 1996). *USA Today.*

College Placement Council. (July, 1991). *1991 Career Planning & Placement Survey. Spotlight.* Bethlehem, PA: Author.

Commission on National Aid to Vocational Education. (1914). *Report of the Commission.* Washington, DC: U.S. Government Printing Office.

Commission on the Skills of the American Workforce. (1990). *America's Choices: High Skills or Low Wages.* Rochester, NY: National Center on Education and the Economy.

Cooper, P. (May, 1993). Paradigm shifts in designed instruction: From behaviorism to cognitivism to constructivism. In *Emerging Issues in HRD Source Book,* pp. 231–239. Amherst, MA: Human Resource Development Press.

Corcoran, T., & Goertz, M. (1995). Instructional capacity and high performance schools. *Educational Researcher, 24*(9), 27–31.

CPC Foundation/Rand Corporation (1994). *Developing the Global Work Force—Insights for Colleges and Corporations.* Bethlehem, PA: The College Placement Council, Inc.

Cross, P. (1981). *Adults as Learners.* San Francisco: Jossey-Bass.

Crutsinger, M. (Feb., 1994). Trade deficit with Japan tops record by $3 billion. Associated Press.

Cubberly, E. (1909). *Changing Concepts of Education.* Boston: Houghton Mifflin.

Cummins, A. M., & Hoggett, P. (1995). Counseling in the enterprise culture. *British Journal of Guidance and Counseling, 23*(3), 301–312.

David, H. (1976). *Education Manpower Policy.* Paper presented at the Bicentennial conference sponsored by the National Advisory Counsel on Vocational Education, Minneapolis, MN.

Dawis, R. V. (1984). *Job Satisfaction: Workers' Aspirations, Attitudes and Behavior.* In N. C. Gysbers (Ed.), *Designing Careers Counseling to Enhance Education, Work and Leisure.* San Francisco: Jossey-Bass.

Dayton, J. D., & Feldhauser, J. F. (1989). Characteristics and needs of vocationally talented high school students. *Career Development Quarterly, 37*(4), 355–364.

Deming, W. E. (1986). *Out of Crisis.* Cambridge, MA: Center for Advanced Engineering Study.

Derr, C. B. (1986). *Managing the New Careerists.* San Francisco: Jossey-Bass.

Dewey, J. (1916). *Democracy and Education: An Introduction to the Philosophy of Education.* New York: Macmillan.

Doeringer, P. B., & Piore, M. J. (1971). *Internal Labor Markets and Manpower Analysis.* Lexington, MA: Heath.

Dore, R. (1987). *Taking Japan Seriously: A Confucian Perspective on Leading Economic Issues.* Stanford, CA: Stanford University Press.

Drucker, P. F. (1989). *The New Realities. In Government and Politics/in Economics and Business/in Society and the World View.* New York: Harper & Row.

Drucker, P. F. (1993). *Post Capitalist Society.* New York: HarperCollins.

Drucker, P. F. (Nov., 1994). The age of social transformation. *The Atlantic Monthly,* pp. 53–78.

Duenk, L. (1993). *Improving Vocational Curriculum.* IL: Goodheart-Wilcox.

Dunn, R., DeBello, T., Brennan, P., Krimsky, J., & Murrain, P. (1981). Learning style researchers define differences differently. *Educational Leadership,* pp. 372–375.

Dykman, A. (Nov/Dec., 1995). One-stop shopping. *Vocational Education Journal,* pp. 34–38.

Eck, A. (Oct., 1993). *Job-Related Education and Training: Their Impact on Earnings.* Monthly Labor Review. Washington, DC: U.S. Department of Labor.

The Economist (1994, March 12). Training for Jobs. 330(7584), 19–20, 26.

Educational Testing Service. (1990). *From School to Work.* Princeton, NJ: Author.

Eisen, P. (Oct., 1993). A new game plan for American workers. *Vocational Education Journal.*

Employment & Training Administration, U.S. Department of Labor. (1993). *Finding One's Way: Career Guidance for Disadvantaged Youth.* Research and Evaluation Report Series 93–0, Washington, DC: Author.

England, G. W. (1990). The patterning of work meanings which are coterminous with outcome levels for individuals in Japan, Germany and the U.S.A. *Applied Psychology: An International Review, 39*(1), 29–45.

England, P., & Farkas, G. (1986). *Households, Employment, and Gender: A Social, Economic, and Demographic View.* New York: Aldine DeGruyter.

England, P., & McCreary, L. (1987). *Gender in Equal-
ity in Paid Employment.* In B. B. Hess & M. M.
Ferree (Eds.). *Analyzing Gender: A Handbook of
Social Science Research.* Newbury Park, CA:
Sage, 1987.

Elbaum, B. (1989). Why apprenticeship persisted in
Britain but not in the United States. *Journal of
Economic History,* 337–349.

Evans, R. N., & Herr, E. L. (1978). *Foundations of Vocational Education* (2nd ed.). Columbus, OH:
Charles E. Merrill Publishing Company.

Fallows, J. (1989). *More Like Us.* Boston: Houghton
Mifflin.

Farley, R., & Allen, W. R. (1987). *The Color Line and
the Quality of Life in America.* New York: Russell
Sage Foundation.

Feather, N. T., & O'Brien, G. E. (1986). A longitudinal study of the effects of employment and unemployment on school-leavers. *Journal of
Occupational Psychology, 59,* 121–144.

Finch, C., & Crunkilton, J. (1989). *Curriculum Development in Vocational Education* (3rd ed.). Boston: Allyn and Bacon.

Fletcher, W., & Robison, J. (1991). Worker training:
Competing in the new international economy.
Looking Ahead, (XIII) 2, pp. 26–33. Washington,
DC: National Planning Association.

Ford, A., & Herren, R. (1995). The teaching of work
ethics. *Journal of Vocational Education Research,
20*(1), 79–95.

Friesen, J. (1986). The role of the family in vocational development. *International Journal for the
Advancement of Counseling, 9*(1), 5–10.

Gamoran, A., & Mare, R. D. (1989). Secondary school
tracking and educational inequality: Compensation, reinforcement, or neutrality? *American Journal of Sociology, 94,* 1146–1183.

Garet, M. S., & DeLany, B. (1988). Students,
courses, and stratification. *Sociology of Education, 61,* 61–77.

Gatherhaol, F., & Stern. S. (1987). *Legal Issues for Industrial Education.* Ann Arbor: Prakken Press.

Geber, B. (Dec., 1991). Help! The rise of performance support systems. *Training.*

Gelatt, H. B. (1962). Decision-making: A conceptual frame and reference for counseling. *Journal of Counseling Psychology,* 240–245.

Gelatt, H. B. (1989). Positive uncertainty: A new decision-making framework for counseling. *Journal of Counseling Psychology, 36*(2), 252–256.

General Accounting Office (GAO). (1996). *Job
Training Partnership Act: Long-Term Earnings
and Employment Outcomes.* HEHS–96–40.
Washington, DC: U.S. Government Printing
Office.

Ginzberg, E. (1972). Restatement of the theory of
occupational choice. *Vocational Guidance Quarterly, 20*(3), 169–176.

Ginzberg, E., Ginsburg, S. W., Axelrod, S., & Herma,
J. R. (1951). *Occupational Choice: An Approach to a
General Theory.* New York: Columbia University
Press.

Gittner, R. J. (April, 1994). Apprenticeship-trained
workers: United States and Great Britain.
Monthly Labor Review, pp. 38–43.

Glover, R. W. (1986). *Apprenticeship Lessons from
Abroad.* Columbus, OH: National Center for
Research in Vocational Education.

Goodrich, H. (Dec., 1996). Understanding rubrics.
Educational Leadership, pp. 14–17.

Grabowski, B., & Harkness, W. (1996). *Journal of
Statistics Education,* (4) 3.68K

Grasso, J. T., & Shea, J. R. (1979). *Vocational Educa-
tion and Training: Impact on Youth.* Berkeley,
CA: The Carnegie Council on Policy Studies in
Higher Education.

Gray, K. (1988). Vocationalism revisited: The role of
business and industry in the transformation of
the schools. *Journal of Vocational Education Research, 13:4,* 15.

Gray, K. (April, 1990). Increased education now
needed in credentialing secondary level trade
and industry teachers. *School Shop 49*(9): 42–
44.

Gray, K. (Jan., 1993). Why we will lose: Taylorism in
America's high schools. *Phi Delta Kappan, 72*(5),
370–374.

Gray, K., & Huang, N. (1991). Quantity or quality:
An analysis of the impact of increased graduation requirements on students moving
higher in the math and science curriculum.
Journal of Vocational Education Research, 16(2):
37–50.

Gray K., & Huang, N. T. (1992). Sub-baccalaureate
postsecondary education: Does it pay off for
vocational education graduates. *Journal of Industrial Teacher Education, 29*(1), 9–20.

Gray, K, Huang, N., & Jie, L. (1993). The gender gap in yearly earnings: Is it lack of education or occupational segregation? *Journal of Vocational Education Research, 18*(3).

Gray, K., & Herr, E. (1995). *Other Ways to Win: Creating Alternatives for High School Graduates.* Thousand Oaks, CA: Corwin Press.

Gray, K., & Wang, D. (1989). An analysis of the firm size variable in youth employment using the NLS–Y data base. *Journal of Vocational Education Research, 14*(4), 35–49.

Gray, K., Wang, W. J., & Malizia, S. (1995). Is vocational education still necessary? Investigating the educational effectiveness of the college prep curriculum. *Journal of Industrial Teacher Education 32*(2), 6–29.

Green, T. (1987). The conscience of leadership. In *Leadership Examining the Elusive.* 1987 Year Book of the American Society of Supervision and Curriculum, ASSC. (pp. 105–115).

Greenawalt, C., & Gotwalt, E. (Sept., 1995). *Outcomes and Results: The Impact of Private Career Schools in Pennsylvania.* Harrisburg, PA: The Commonwealth Foundation.

Gregson, J. (1995). The school-to-work movement and youth apprenticeship in the U.S.: Educational reform and democratic renewal. *Journal of Industrial Teacher Education, 32*(3): 7–27.

Grubb, N. (June/July, 1992). Correcting conventional wisdom: Community college impact on students' jobs and salaries. *Community, Technical, and Junior College Journal,* 10–14.

Grubb, N. (Ap., 1996). The new vocationalism. *Phi Delta Kappan,* 535–546.

Gutteridge, T. G. (1986). Organizational Career Development Systems: The State of the Practice (Chapter 2). In Douglas T. Hall (Ed.), Career Development in Organizations. San Francisco: Jossey-Bass.

Guttman, R. (1992). *Bring Job Training Into the Mainstream.* In L. Harris (Ed.), *An Assessment of American Education: The View of Employers, Higher Educators, The Public, Recent Students and Their Parents.* Sponsored by the Committee for Economic Development. New York.

Hall, D. T. (Ed.) (1984). *Career Development in Organizations.* San Francisco: Jossey-Bass.

Hall, D. T., et al. (1996). *The Career is Dead—Long Live The Career. A relational approach to careers.* San Francisco: Jossey-Bass.

Hassett, J. (Sept., 1992). Simplifying ROI. *Training*

Herr, E. L. (1974). The decade in prospect: Some implications for vocational guidance. In E. L. Herr (Ed.), *Vocational Guidance and Human Development* (chap. 22). Boston: Houghton Mifflin.

Herr, E. L. (1989a). *Counseling in a Dynamic Society. Opportunities and Challenges.* Alexandria, VA: AACD Press.

Herr, E. L. (1989b). Career development and mental health. *Journal of Career Development, 16,* 5–18.

Herr, E. L. (1995). *Counseling Employment Bound Youth.* ERIC/CASS Publications. Greensboro, NC: University of North Carolina at Greensboro, School of Education.

Herr, E. L. (1997). Career counseling: A personal view of a process in process. *British Journal of Guidance and Counseling, 25*(1), 81–93.

Herr, E. L., & Cramer, S. H. (1988). *Career Guidance and Counseling Through the Lifespan: Systematic Approaches.* Glenview, IL: Scott, Foresman.

Herr, E. L., & Cramer, S. H. (1996). *Career Guidance and Counseling Through the Lifespan: Systematic Approaches* (5th Ed.). New York: Harper-Collins.

Herr, E. L., & Enderlein, T. (1976). Vocational maturity: The effects of school, grade, curriculum and sex. *The Journal of Vocational Behavior, 8,* 227–238.

Herr, E. L., & Lear, P. (1984). The family as an influence on career development. In S. H. Cramer (Ed.), *Perspectives on Work and the Family* (pp. 1–15). Rockville, MD: Aspen Systems.

Herr, E. L., Weitz, A., Good, R., & McCloskey, G. (1981). *Research on the Effects of Secondary School Curricular and Personal Characteristics upon Postsecondary Educational and Occupational Patterns.* (NIE-G-80-0027). University Park, PA: The Pennsylvania State University.

Herold, D. M. (1990). Using technology to improve our management and labor market trends. *Journal of Organizational Change Management, 3*(2), 44–57.

Hershenson, D. B. (1996). Work adjustment: A neglected area in career counseling. *Journal of Counseling & Development, 74*(5), 442–446.

Hightower, A., Hollock, R., & Breckenridge, J. S. (July, 1995). *Employer Participation in Work-Based Learning.* Unpublished contractor report prepared for the Office of Technology Assessment, U.S. Congress. Washington, DC: U.S. Government Printing Office.

Hilton, M. (March, 1991). Shared training: Learning from Germany. *Monthly Labor Review, 114*(3), 33–37.

Hirschhorn, L. (1988). *The Workplace Within: Psychodynamics of Organizational Life.* Cambridge, MA: The MIT Press.

Hodson, R., & Sullivan, T. A. (1990). *The Social Organization of Work.* Belmont, CA: Wadsworth Publishing Company.

Hoggart, R. (1957). *The Uses of Literacy.* London, England: Chatto and Winders.

Holland, J. L. (1973). *Making Vocational Choices: A Theory of Careers.* Englewood Cliffs, NJ: Prentice-Hall.

Holland, J. L. (1985). *Making Vocational Choices. A Theory of Vocational Personalities and Work Environments* (2nd ed.). Englewood Cliffs, NJ: Prentice-Hall.

Holland, J. L., & Gottfredson, G. D. (1976). Using a typology of persons and environments to explain career: Some extensions and clarifications. *The Counseling Psychologist, 6*(3), 20–29.

Holland, J. L., & Gottfredson, G. D. (1990). *An Annotated Bibliography for Holland's Theory of Vocational Personalities and Work Environments.* Baltimore: Johns Hopkins.

Hollingshead, A. B. (1949). *Elmtown's Youth.* New York: Wiley.

Holzer, H. J. (1996). *What Employers Want. Job Prospects for less-education workers.* New York: Russell Sage Foundations.

Hotchkiss, L., & Borow, H. (1990). *Sociological Perspectives on Work and Career Development.* In D. Brown, & L. Brooks & Associates (Eds.), *Career Choice and Development: Applying Contemporary Theories to Practice* (2nd ed., pp. 262–307). San Francisco: Jossey-Bass.

Hudson, R., Hooks, G., & Rieble, S. (1994). Training in the workplace: Continuity and change. *Sociological Perspectives, 37*(1), 97–118.

Hudson Institute. (1987). *Workforce 2000.* Indianapolis, IN: Author.

Hull, D. M., & Pedrotti, L. S. (1983). Meeting the high-tech challenge. *VOCED, 58*(3), 28–31.

Hunter, M. (1984). *Knowing, Teaching and Supervising.* In P. Hasford (Ed.), *What We Know About Teaching,* pp. 169–97. Washington, DC: Association for Supervision and Instruction Development (ASCD).

Iron Age. (Jan., 3, 1909). Industrial education in danger from its friends.

Jackson, L. A. (1987). Computers and the social psychology of work. *Computers in Human Behavior, 3*(314): 251–262.

Jonassen, D. H. (1991). Objectivism versus Constructivism: Do we need a new philosophical paradigm? *Technology Research and Development.*

Jonassen, D., & Grabowski, B. (1993). *Handbook of Individual Differences: Learning and Instruction.* Earlbaum.

Kane, T., & Rouse, C. (1993). Labor market returns to two-and four-year colleges: Is a credit a credit and do degrees matter? Working Paper No. 4268. Cambridge, MA: National Bureau of Economic Research, Inc.

KAPOW: Kids and the Power of Work. Arlington, VA: Fu Associates, undated.

Katz, M. (1963). *Decisions and Values: A Rationale for Secondary School Counselors.* New York: College Entrance Examination Board.

Keita, T. R., & Sauter, S. (1992). *Work and Well-Being: An Agenda for the 1990s.* Washington, DC: American Psychological Association.

Kincheloe, J. (1995). *Toil and Trouble.* New York: Lang Publications.

Kinnier, R. T., Brigman, S. L., & Noble, F. C. (1990). Career indecision and family enmeshments. *Journal of Counseling & Development, 68,* 309–312.

Kirkpatrick, D. (1975). Evaluating training. *Training and Development.*

Kolp, D., & Smith, D. (1986). *User Guide for the Learning Styles Inventory.* Boston, McBer & Company.

Krafcik, J. (1990). *Training and the Automobile Industry: International Comparisons,* pp. 8–9. Office of Technology Assessment (N3–1910). Washington, DC: U.S. Government Printing Office.

Krugman, P., & Lawrence, R. (Ap., 1994). Trade, jobs and wages. *Scientific American,* pp. 44–49.

Krumboltz, J. D. (1979). A social learning theory of career decision-making. In A. M. Mitchell, G. G. Jame, & J. D. Krumboltz (Eds.), *Social Learning and Career Decision Making* (pp. 19–49). Cranston, RI: Carrole Press.

Krumboltz, J. D. (1994). Improving career development theory from a social learning perspective. In M. L. Savickas & R. W. Lent (Eds.), *Convergence in Career Development Theories: Im-*

plications for Science and Practice (pp. 9–31). Palo Alto, CA: CPP Books.

Kübler-Ross, E. (1969). *On Death and Dying*. New York: Macmillan.

Landy, F. J. (1989). *Psychology of Work Behavior* (4th ed.). Pacific Grove, CA: Brooks/Cole.

Law, C. J. (1975). *A Philosophy for Vocational Education*. Columbus, OH: National Center for Vocational Education.

Lawler, E. E. (1973). *Motivation in Work Organizations*. Monterey, CA: Brooks/Cole.

Lee, V. E., & Bryk, A. S. (1988). Curriculum tracking as mediating the social distribution of high school achievement. *Sociology of Education, 61,* 78–94.

Leibowitz, Z. B., Farren, C., & Kaye, B. L. (1986). *Designing Career Development Systems*. San Francisco: Jossey-Bass.

Leonards, J. T. (1981). Corporate psychology: An answer to occupational mental health. *Personnel and Guidance Journal, 30*(1), 47–51.

Lind, M. (1995). *The Next American Nation: The New Nationalism and the Fourth American Revolution,* New York: Simon & Schuster Inc.

Lipsett, L. (1962). Social factors in vocational development. *Personnel and Guidance Journal, 40,* 432–437.

LoBosco, M. (1985). Consensus on training programs. *Personnel, 62*(12), 55–59.

Lowman, R. L. (1993). *Counseling and Psychotherapy of Work Dysfunctions*. Washington, DC: American Psychological Association.

Lynch, R. L. (1991). Teaching in the 21st Century. *Vocational Journal, 66*(1), p. 29.

Maccoby, M. (1976). *The Gamesman*. New York: Simon & Schuster.

Maccoby, M. (1980). Work and human development. *Professional Psychology, 11,* 509–519.

Maier, M., & Grafton, F. (May, 1981). *Aptitude Composites for the ASVAB 8, 9 & 10 Research Report 1308*. Alexandria, VA: U.S. Army Research Institute for the Behavioral and Social Sciences.

Maley, D. (1975). *Cluster Concept in Vocational Education*. Chicago: American Technical Society.

Mangum, G. T. (1988). *Youth Transition from Adolescence to the World of Work*. Paper prepared for youth and America's Future: The William T. Grant Foundation Commission on Work, Family and Citizenship. Washington, DC: The William T. Grant Foundation Commission.

Manning, A. (June 3, 1995). 5.6 million kids live in working-poor families. *USA Today*, p. A1.

Marron, P. J. (1994). New York State: Compact for learning and its role in school-to-employment transition. In A. J. Pautla, Jr., (Ed.), *High School to Employment Transition: Contemporary Issues* (pp. 257–262). Ann Arbor, MI: Prakken Publications.

Maslow, A. H. (1954). *Motivation and Personality*. New York: Harper & Row.

Massachusetts Institute of Technology, Quality Education for Minorities Project (1990). *Education That Works: An Action Plan for the Education of Minorities*. Cambridge, MA: Author.

McCaslin, N. (October 30, 1995). *Evaluation: An Imperative for Public Education and Training Programs*. Professorial Inaugural Lecture Series. Department of Agriculture, Ohio State University. Columbus, OH: OSU.

McKay, W. R., & Miller, C. A. (1982). Relations of social-economic status and sex variables to the complexity of work functions in the occupational choice of elementary school children. *Journal of Vocational Behavior, 20,* 31–39.

McNeil, J. (1996). *Curriculum: A Comprehensive Introduction* (5th ed.). New York: HarperCollins.

Merriam-Webster, Inc. (1983). *Webster's Ninth New Collegiate Dictionary*. Springfield, MA: Merriam-Webster Inc., Publishers.

Merva, M., & Fowles, R. (Oct., 1992). *Effects of Diminished Economic Opportunities on Social Stress*. Washington, DC: Economic Policy Institute.

Meyers, R. (1992). *Applied Versus Traditional Mathematics: New Econometric Models of the Contribution of High School Courses to Mathematics Proficiency*. Madison: Institute for Research on Poverty, University of Wisconsin-Madison.

Millar, J. D. (1992). Public enlightenment and mental health in the workplace. *Work and Well-being: An Agenda for the 1990s*. Edited by G. P. Keita & S. L. Sauter. Washington, DC: American Psychological Association.

Miller, M. (1985). *Principles and Philosophy for Vocational Education*. Columbus, OH: National Center for Vocational Education.

Miller, M. (1995). *Philosophy: The Conceptual Framework for Designing a System of Teacher Education*. Teacher Education Monograph. University Council for Vocational Education.

Miller, P., & Coda, W. (1984). *Vocational Ethics: Toward the Development of an Enabling Work Ethic.* Springfield: Illinois State Board of Education.

Miller, V. (1996). The History of Training. In *The ASTD Training & Development Handbook* (4th ed.). New York: McGraw-Hill.

Mitchell, A. H., & Krumboltz, J. D. (1984). Social learning approach to career decision making: Theory. In D. Brown & L. Brooks (Eds.), *Career Choice and Development: Applying Contemporary Theories to Practice* (pp. 145–196). San Francisco: Jossey-Bass.

National Assessment of Vocational Education (NAVE). (1994). *Interim Report to the Congress.* Washington, DC: U.S. Department of Education.

National Association of Corporation Schools. *Annual Convention Papers.* NY: Troy Press.

National Board for Professional Teaching Standards. (May, 1996). *Vocational Education: Standards for National Board Certification.* Washington: DC: NBPTS.

National Career Development Association. (1985). Consumer guidelines for selecting a career counselor. *Career Development 1*(2), 1–2.

National Career Development Association. (Jan. 11, 1991). Position paper approved by the Board of Directors.

National Center for Educational Statistics (NCES). (1992). *Vocational Education in the United States.* Washington, DC: U.S. Department of Education.

National Center for Educational Statistics (NCES). (1993a). *Adult Literacy in America.* Washington, DC: U.S. Department of Education.

National Center for Educational Statistics (NCES). (1993b). *The Condition of Education: 1993.* Washington, DC: U.S. Department of Education.

National Center for Educational Statistics (NCES). *Vocational Course Taking and Achievement: An Analysis of High School Transcripts and 1990 NAEP Assessment Scores.* NCES 95–006. Washington DC: U.S. Department of Education.

National Center for Educational Statistics (NCES). *Condition of Education: 1994* (p. 72). Washington, DC: Author.

National Youth Employment Coalition. (1992). *Making Sense of Federal Job Training Policy.* Washington, DC: National Youth Employment Coalition and the William T. Grant Foundation Commission on Youth and America's Future.

Newman, F. M., Marks, H. M., & Gamoran, A. (1995). Authentic pedagogy: Standards that boost student performance. *Issues in Restructuring Schools, 8,* 1–4.

Newsweek. (Dec. 30, 1996). The vital center, p. 4.

Noel, B. (Nov., 22, 1992). And now the sticky floor. *The New York Times,* p. 23.

Osipow, S. H. (1982). Counseling psychology: Applications in the world of work. *The Counseling Psychologist, 10*(3), 19–25.

Palmore, E. (1969). Predicting longevity: A follow-up controlling for age. *Gerontologist, 9,* 247–250.

Pantelidis, V. S. (1996). Virtual Reality and Education Laboratory. East Carolina Unv. Greenville, NC. In Rothwell (May, 1995), W. Emerging Issues in HRD Source Book. HRD Press.

Papalia, A. S., & Kaminski, W. (1981). Counseling and counseling skills in the industrial environment. *Vocational Guidance Quarterly, 30*(1), 37–42.

Parsons, F. (1909). *Choosing a Vocation.* Boston: Houghton Mifflin.

Pask, G. (1976). Styles and Strategies for Learning. British Journal of Educational Psychology. 46.

Passmore, D. L. (1994). Expectations for entry-level workers: What employers say they want. In *High School to Employment Transitions: Contemporary Issues* (pp. 23–30). Edited by Albert J. Pautler. Ann Arbor, MI: Prakken Publication.

Passmore, D. (1997). *Cost of Technical Skills Deficits in a Pennsylvania Community.* Unpublished research report. Penn State University.

Pease, V. H., & Copa, G. H. (1994). Partnerships in the School-to-Work Transition. In *High School-to-Employment Transition.* Ann Arbor, MI: Prakken Publications.

Pitz, G. F., & Harren, V. A. (1980). An analysis of career decision-making from the point of view of information processing and decision theory. *Journal of Vocational Behavior, 16,* 320–346.

Pucel, D. (1995). Occupationally specific mathematics requirements and application contexts. *Journal of Industrial Teacher Education, 32*(2), 51–75.

Purple, D. (1991). Moral education: An idea whose time has gone. *The Clearing House, 64,* 309–312.

Quade, E. (1989). *Analysis for Public Decisions.* New York: North Holland.

Reich, R. (1995). The frayed-collar workers. *Los Angeles Times.*

Research and Policy Committee, Committee for Economic Development. (1985). *Investing in our Children, Business and Public schools.* New York: The Committee.

Richman, L. (Aug., 1994). The new worker elite. *Fortune,* pp. 56–66.

Richy, R. (1986). *The Theoretical and Conceptual Bases of Instructional Design.* New York: Nichols.

Rifkin, J. (1995). *The End of Work.* New York: Putnam Books.

Roberts, K. (1977). *From School to Work. A Study of the Youth Employment Service.* Newton Abbott, England: David and Charles.

Rockwell, T. (1987). The social construction of careers: Career development and career counseling viewed from a sociometric perspective. *Journal of Group Psychotherapy, Psychodrama, and Sociometry, 1*(1), 93–107.

Roe, A. (1956). *The Psychology of Occupations.* New York: John Wiley & Sons.

Rossett, A. (1988). *Training Needs Assessment.* Englewood, NJ: Educational Technology Publications.

Rothwell, W., & Kazanas, H. (1990). Structured on-the-job training (SOJT) as perceived by HRD professionals. *Performance Improvement Quarterly.*

Rothwell, W., and Kazanas, H. (1992). *Mastering the Instructional Design Process.* San Francisco: Jossey-Bass.

Rothwell, W. B. & Kazanas, H. (Sept., 1993). Developing management employees to cope with the moving target effect. *Performance & Instruction.*

Rothwell, W., & Sredl, H. (1992). *The ASTD Reference Guide to Professional Human Resource Development Roles and Competencies,* Vol. II, 2nd ed. Amherst, MA: HRD Press.

Sanogo, C. (1996). *Facilitators and Barriers to High School Female Participation in School-to-Work.* Unpublished doctoral disseration, Pennsylvania State University.

Schaef, A. W., & Fassel, D. (1988). *The Addictive Organization.* San Francisco: Harper & Row.

Schlossberg, N. K., & Leibowitz, Z. (1980). Organizational support systems as buffers to job loss. *Journal of Vocational Behavior, 17,* 204–217.

Schulenberg, J. E., Vondracek, F. W., & Crouter, A. C. (1984). The influence of the family on vocational development. *Journal of Marriage and the Family, 46,* 129–143.

Sewell, W. H., & Houser, R. M. (1975). *Education, Occupation and Earnings: Achievement in the Early Career.* Orlando, FL: Academic Press.

Shelley, K. (1992). The future of jobs for college graduates. *Monthly Labor Review,* pp. 13–19.

Sichel, B. (1991). Virtue and character: Moral languages and moral education. *The Clearing House, 64*(4), 297–300

Simon, R. I., Dippo, D., & Schenke, A. (1991). *Learning Work: A Critical Pedagogy of Work Education.* New York: Bergin & Garvey.

Skinner, B. F. (1968). *The Technology of Teaching,* p. 856. New York: Appleton-Century-Crofts.

Stecher, B., & Hanser, L. (May, 1995). *Accountability in Workforce Training.* Institute on Education and Training, Rand Corporation.

Stephens, W. R. (1970). *Social Reform and the Origins of Vocational Guidance.* Washington, DC: National Vocational Guidance Association.

Stern, D., et al. (1994). *School-Based Enterprise: Productive Learning in American High Schools.* San Francisco: Jossey-Bass.

Stricht, T. G., & Mikulecky, L. (1984). *Job-Related Basic Skills: Cases and Conclusions.* Washington, DC: National Institute of Education.

Subich, L. M., & Taylor, K. M. (1994). Emerging directions of social learning theory. In M. L. Savickas & R. W. Lent (Eds.), *Convergence in Career Development Theories: Implications for Science and Practice* (pp. 167–175). Palo Alto, CA: CPP Books.

Super, D. E. (1951). Vocational adjustment: Implementing a self-concept. *Occupations, 30,* 88–92.

Super, D. E. (1957). *The Psychology of Careers.* New York: Harper & Row.

Super, D. E. (1969a). The natural history of a study of lives and vocations. *Perspectives on Education, 2,* 13–22.

Super, D. E. (1969b). Vocational development theory: Persons, positions, and processes. *The Counseling Psychologist, 1,* 2–9.

Super, D. E. (1976). *Career Education and the Meaning of Work.* Monographs on Career Education. Washington, DC: The Office of Career Education, U.S. Office of Education.

Super, D. E. (1977). Vocational maturity on mid-career. *Vocational Guidance Quarterly, 25*(4), 294–302.

Super, D. E. (1980). A life-span, life-space approach to career development. *Journal of Vocational Behavior, 16*(3), 282–298.

Super, D. E. (1981). Approaches to occupational choice and career development. In A. G. Watts, D. E. Super, & J. M. Kidd (Eds.), *Career Development in Britain*. Cambridge, England: Hobson Press.

Super, D. E. (1984a). Career and life development. In D. Brown & L. Brooks (Eds.), *Career Choice and Development: Applying Contemporary Approaches to Practice*. San Francisco: Jossey-Bass.

Super, D. E. (1984b). Perspectives on the meaning and value of work. In N. C. Gysbers (Ed.), *Designing Careers. Counseling to Enhance Education, Work and Leisure*. San Francisco: Jossey-Bass.

Super, D. E. (1985). *New dimensions in adult vocational and career counseling*. Occasional paper, No. 106. Columbus, OH: The National Center for Research in Vocational Education.

Super, D. E. (1990). A life-span, life-space, approach to career development. In D. Brown & L. Brooks (Eds.), *Career Choice and Development: Applying Contemporary Theories to Practice* (pp. 197–216). San Francisco: Jossey-Bass.

Super, D. E. (1994). A life span, life-space perspective on convergence. In M. L. Savickas & R. W. Lent (Eds.), *Convergence in Career Development Theories: Implications for Science and Practice* (pp. 63–74). Palo Alto, CA: CPP Books.

Super, D. E., & Bohn, M. J., Jr. (1970). *Occupational Psychology*. Pacific Grove, CA: Brooks/Cole.

Super, D. E., Sverko, B., & Super, C. E. (1995). *Life Roles, Values, and Careers. International Findings of the Work Importance Study*. San Francisco: Jossey-Bass.

Thomas, D, & Gray, K. (1992). An analysis of entry-level skills required for blue-collar technicians in electronics firms. *Journal of Vocational Education Research, 16*(3): 59–77.

Thurow, L. (1992). *Head to Head: The Coming Economic Battle Among Japan, Europe, and America*. New York: Morrow and Company.

Thurow, L. (Sept. 3, 1993). Companies merge: Families break up. *New York Times*.

Tilly, C. (Mar., 1991). Reasons for the continuing growth of part-time employment. *Monthly Labor Review*.

Tobin, D. (1996). *Transformational Learning: Renewing Your Company Through Knowledge and Skills*. New York: John Willey & Sons.

Toffler, A. (1990). *Powershift, Knowledge, Wealth and Violence at the Edge of the 21st Century*. New York: Bantam Books.

U.S. Bureau of Education. (1908). *Bulletin #1. Continuation Schools in the United States*. Washington, DC: U.S. Government Printing Office.

U.S. Congress. (1984). *Carl D. Perkins Vocational Education Act of 1984* (PL 98–254).

U.S. Congress. (1994). *The School-to-Work Opportunities Act of 1994* (PL 103–239).

U.S. Congress, Office of Technology Assessment. (1988). *Technology and the American Economic Transition: Choices for the Future*. Washington, DC: U.S. Government Printing Office.

U.S. Congress, Office of Technology Assessment. (Sept., 1995). *Learning to Work: Making the Transition from School to Work*. OTA–EHR–637. Washington, DC: U.S. Government Printing Office.

U.S. Department of Education/U.S. Department of Labor. (1988). *The Bottom Line: Basic Skills in the Workplace*. Washington, DC: U.S. Department of Labor.

U.S. Department of Education. (1991). *Combining School and Work: Options in High School and Two-Year Colleges*. Washington, DC: Author.

U.S. Department of Labor, Secretary's Commission on Achieving Necessary Skills (1991). *What Work Requires of Schools: A SCANS Report for America 2000*. Washington, DC: Author.

U.S. Department of Labor (1991–92). Apprenticeship. *Occupational Outlook Quarterly, 36*(1), 27–40.

Vanfossen, E., Jones, D., & Spade, J. S. (1987). Curriculum tracking and status maintenance. *Sociology of Education, 60*, 104–122.

Vocational Education Journal. (Sept., 1993). The state of certification, pp. 30–35. Arlington, VA: American Vocational Association.

Vocational Education Weekly. (Nov. 11, 1996). Players prepare for act two of Clinton–GOP drama, p. 27.

Vocational Training News. (May 9, 1995). *GAO: Job Training Participants Get Most After One Year*, p. 19.

Vocational Training News. (Nov. 9, 1995). *Training reforms bill back standards with penalties*, p. 45.

Vogler, D. (1995). *Performance Instruction*. Eden Prairie, MN: Instructional Performance Systems.

W. T. Grant Foundation, Commission on Work, Family, and Citizenship (Jan., 1988). *The Forgotten Half: Non-College Youth in America*. Washington, DC: Author.

Wagner, E. (Apr., 1993). Variables affecting distance educational program success. *Educational Technology*.

Walker, T., Adamsky, R., Brower, E., & Hart, K. (1992). *The reflective teacher: An outcome of program VITAL*. 29 (2), 23–35.

Wall Street Journal. (Feb. 9, 1990). *The Knowledge Gap: Smarter Jobs, Dumber Workers, Is That America's Future?*

Warnat, W. L. (1991). Preparing a world-class work force. *VOCED*, 66(5), 26–29.

Watts, A. G. (1986). *Work Shadowing*. Report prepared for the School Curriculum Industry Partnership. York, England: Longman.

West, P. (Apr. 3, 1995). Scholarships for voc.-ed. training go untapped. *Educational Week*, p. 3.

Wilson, B. (1997). Reflections on constructivism and instructional design. In *Instructional Development Paradigms*. Educational Technology Publications. Englewood Cliffs, NJ.

Winefield, A. H., & Tiggemann, M. (1989). Unemployment duration and affective well-being in the young. *Journal of Occupational Psychology*, 62, 327–336.

Wirth, A. G. (1993). Education and work: The choices we face. *Phi Delta Kappan*, 74(5), 360–366.

Wolfe, J. (1993). *The Pennsylvania Youth Apprenticeship Program Model*. Paper presented at the Governor's Conference on Workforce Development, Lancaster, PA, May 27–28.

Wood, S. (1990). Initiating career plans with freshmen. *The School Counselor*, 37, 233–239.

Zemke, R., & Zemke, S. (June, 1981). Thirty things we know for sure about adult learning. *Training/HRD*, pp. 45–52.

Zuboff, S. (1988). *In the Age of the Smart Machine: The Future of Work and Power*. New York: Basic Books.

NAME INDEX

SUBJECT INDEX

sticky wages, 58
   supply and demand analysis in, 59
strategic curriculum planning, 141
strategic preplanning in curriculum management,
      141–145
stress, 115
   in workplace, 102–103, 282–285
structural unemployment, 84
structured on-the-job training, 156
student assessment, legal issues, 168–169
student behavior, and grades, 169
student loan default rate, 271–272
students
   characteristics and curriculum design, 144
   development of career plans, 196
   reading level of, 182
   school expectations for, 196
supply, elasticity of, 61–62
supply curve, shifts in, 59–61
supply and demand analysis, 58–59
survival of the fittest capitalism, 11
Sweden, strategies for youth, 196–197
system, career development services as, 279

target group, for public policy, 241
task analysis, 150
   advisory committee methods, 175
   critical incident technique, 175
   to determine curriculum content, 172–174
   essential skills approach to, 176
   formal approaches to, 173–174
   to identify academic skills, 180
   introspective, 173
   limits of traditional methods, 175–176
   philosophical approach to, 172–173
   types of formal, 174–176
Task Approach Skills, 122
tax code, 244
tax credits, 266–267
Taylorism, 11–12, 13
"teachable" moments, 165
teachers
   credentials, 271
   liability for classroom injuries, 185–186
   negligence of, 186–187
   preparing for high school workforce education,
      261–262
   professional standards, 262
   for vocational education, 15
teaching
   essential academic skills, 181

occupational skills, 183
   supervision to improve, 166–167
   workplace literacy skills, 184–185
Tech-Prep, 197, 209, 211–212, 259–260, 265
technical education, 13
technical institutes, 278
technical occupations, 159
   associate degree for, 87
   education for, 85
   nonprofessional, 263–264
technical skills, importance of, 289–293
technologist philosophy, and competency-based
      education design model, 150
technologist view of curriculum design, 140
technology, 19
   and distribution of power and information,
      101–102
   and global economy, 97
   and worker displacement, 31–32
   and workplace stress, 102
technology adoption strategy, 187
technology transfer, 187
temporary workers, 97
terminal objective, 151
tests
   to assess individual characteristics, 118
   development of, 218
Texas Instruments, 70
theaters, in Super's Life–Career Rainbow, 134
time, as instructional design variable, 160–161
timeliness of training, 295
total employment, 83
total labor force, 83
total placement concept, 212–213
total unemployment, 83
TQM management approach, 184
trade and industrial education, 257
trainers, automated, 183
training
   academic skills and success in, 181–182
   changing content of, 288–289
   clinical, 208
   corporate size and, 16–17
   vs. education, 159–160
   flavor of the month, 294
   formal vs. on-the-job, 155–156
   goal of, 159
   and human resource development, 288–293
   moving target, 294–295
   national skills standards in, 255
   in small and large firms, 78